The Dostoevsky Effect

PROBLEM GAMBLING AND THE ORIGINS OF ADDICTION

Lorne Tepperman ◆ Patrizia Albanese
Sasha Stark ◆ Nadine Zahlan

OXFORD
UNIVERSITY PRESS

OXFORD
UNIVERSITY PRESS

Oxford University Press is a department of the University of Oxford.
It furthers the University's objective of excellence in research, scholarship,
and education by publishing worldwide. Oxford is a registered trade mark of
Oxford University Press in the UK and in certain other countries.

Published in Canada by
Oxford University Press
8 Sampson Mews, Suite 204,
Don Mills, Ontario M3C 0H5 Canada

www.oupcanada.com

Library and Archives Canada Cataloguing in Publication
The Dostoevsky effect : problem gambling and the origins of addiction
/ Lorne Tepperman ... [et al.].

Includes bibliographical references and index.
ISBN 978-0-19-544912-9

1. Compulsive gambling. 2. Compulsive gambling—Social aspects.
3. Compulsive gamblers—Psychology. 4. Compulsive gamblers—Interviews.
5. Compulsive gamblers—Biography. 6. Dostoyevsky, Fyodor, 1821–1881—
Psychology. 7. Dostoyevsky, Fyodor, 1821–1881. Igrok. English.
8. Dostoyevsky, Fyodor, 1821–1881—Influence. 9. Gambling in literature.
10. Psychology in literature. I. Tepperman, Lorne, 1943–

RC569.5.G35D68 2013   362.2'5   C2012-906871-3

Cover image: argus/Shutterstock.com

Oxford University Press is committed to our environment.
Wherever possible, our books are printed on paper which
comes from responsible sources.

Printed and bound in the United States of America

1 2 3 4 — 16 15 14 13

Contents

Acknowledgements

We are indebted to many hard-working individuals who were essential at the various stages that led to the final version of this book. We want to start by thanking the Ontario Problem Gambling Research Centre (OPGRC), which funded our work on this book as a piece of "knowledge translation." Over the years, OPGRC has funded much of the professional research in Ontario on which this book relies. Like many other professional gambling researchers, we could never have come as far as we have without their generous support and guidance. So, thank you, OPGRC—in particular, acting director Judith Glynn and grants officer Erika Veri Levett. We look forward to a continuing relationship with OPGRC under its new director, Gary O'Connor.

Next, we thank Carol Baker Lai and Rita Lam for postering downtown Toronto with our recruitment posters. We were fortunate to have many skilled interviewers help collect our interview data: Carol Baker Lai, Kristin Crandlemire, Hillary Killam, Rita Lam, Aimee Nygaard, Adrianna Robertson, Rajwant Sandhu, Alex Tepperman, Mark van der Maas, and Stacey Jean Wainwright.

Another large group of dedicated students transcribed these interviews: Carol Baker Lai, Kristin Crandlemire, Anita Feher, Jasmin Kortright, Michelle Kuan, Susan Kwan, Rita Lam, Richard Liu, Afsheen Merchant, Uriel Philosophe, Adrianna Robertson, Deirdre Ryan, Rajwant Sandhu, Brianna Sykes, Alex Tepperman, Laura Upenieks, Stacey Jean Wainwright, and Hoursa Yazdi. Nina Gheihman, Brianna Sykes, and Rebecca Young carried out the content analysis of memoirs and Internet postings. Qualitative analysis of the transcripts was a team effort on the parts of Pam Bautista, Olesia Bissett, Kristin Crandlemire, Cara Evans, Anita Feher, Oliver Lue, Laura Mercuriano, Deirdre Ryan, Jenna Valleriani, and Mark van der Maas. We thank Stephen Ham for assisting us with data management and Agata Falkowski-Ham for performing our quantitative data analysis.

Caitlin Hamblin was enormously helpful in researching the biographic material on Dostoevsky that makes up the first third of the book. Nikki

Meredith and Deirdre Ryan were helpful in turning our original research report—the other two-thirds of this book—into a readable first draft.

Finally, we thank all of those colleagues who provided critical feedback on an early version of this manuscript: Pat Erickson, Tara Hahmann, Kate Holland, Sytze F. Kingma, Richard Rosenthal, Garry Smith, Mark van der Maas, and Kristy Wanner. Particular thanks go to Alex Blaszczynski, internationally esteemed gambling researcher, for his advice and encouragement and Kenneth Lantz, internationally esteemed Dostoevsky expert, for his helpfully detailed critique of the biographical material.

At Oxford University Press Canada, we are grateful to President David Stover for encouraging our effort and providing dozens of wise suggestions for the improvement of this manuscript. As a seasoned editor, David could see important stylistic and organizational issues that we authors had lost in the minutiae, so thanks for everything, David. Likewise, we want to thank Heather Sangster at Strong Finish for her excellent line editing; it is always a pleasure to work with Heather, and as always, she improved the manuscript immeasurably.

Part I

Gambling in the Life of Dostoevsky

An Introduction to Dostoevsky's Life

Here's an easy question for book lovers: which of these two nineteenth-century novelists—Jane Austen or Fyodor Dostoevsky—had a serious problem with gambling? Easy answer: Fyodor Dostoevsky (1821–81).

To know anything at all about the books of these two novelists is to know a great deal about their lives, especially their childhoods. For biographical and psychological reasons, Austen could no more have written *The Brothers Karamazov* than Dostoevsky could have written *Pride and Prejudice*.

More particularly, consider their treatment of fathers. Jane Austen's fictional fathers—for example, Mr. Bennet in *Pride and Prejudice*—are kind, gentle, and supportive. There are no such fathers in Dostoevsky's fictional work, for reasons we will consider below. Indeed, Dostoevsky's fictional fathers—his men in general—tend to be unkind, ungentle, and unsupportive. Dostoevsky has a particular, scathing contempt for men like Stepan Trofimovich (in *The Devils*), who are pretentious, controlling, and lofty, a favourite word of contempt in Dostoevsky's vocabulary.

To know something about the early lives of Austen and Dostoevsky, and their vastly different (fictional) treatments of family life (and fathers in particular) is to know something important about their respective risks of serious addiction. That is the nub of what we will argue in this book, with particular attention to the addiction problems of Fyodor Dostoevsky.

Dostoevsky's gambling problem began in 1862 and ended in 1871, lasting nearly ten years—a large portion of his adult life. So famous is Dostoevsky's gambling problem that in 2005–6 his face was used on Russian lottery tickets, prompting his great-grandson Dmitry Dostoevsky to sue a national sports lottery. In an interview by NPR radio host Melissa Block, Dmitry remarks that he does not view this use of his ancestor's image as a tribute to the great writer. He remarked, through a translator, "I think that if someone wanted to pay homage to Fyodor Dostoevsky, the right thing to do is to create more libraries and name them after him and, also, maybe name some charitable venues after him. That would be appropriate, but not to put his image on lottery tickets."

Despite his personal shortcomings, Dostoevsky remains loved and revered by readers of serious writing, perhaps especially by Russian readers. Reviewing the Russian novel *Summer in Baden-Baden,* which has Dostoevsky as its central character, Eugene Goodheart (2004) writes that its author, Leonid Tsypkin, is "obsessed with Dostoevsky":

> The self-destructive emotions and actions of Dostoevsky's life determined the shape and energy of his art. . . . What would appear to be obstacles to Tsypkin's passion for Dostoevsky paradoxically, even perversely, stimulate it: the gambling, his poisonous anti-Semitism, his abusive relationships with his wife, in particular, and his friends. (301)

Along similar lines, Desmond O'Grady (1994) notes that, despite the passage of more than a century,

> in Saint Petersburg . . . there is proof that Dostoevsky lives on, and not only in libraries and bookshops but also in people who were led to Christianity by his writings during the Communist regime. . . . There is, of course, much more in Dostoevsky's novels that resonated with his countrymen a century after he died, and his life under the czars included scarifying experiences of a kind well known to the subjects of Stalin and his successors. (6)

Dostoevsky is widely read everywhere today, not for his religion or his politics, but for his literary style and his psychological and sociological insight. Yet, despite all that, the book you are reading now did not originate with an appreciation of Dostoevsky's literature. Rather, we fell into that topic while pursuing other goals. Our book began to germinate when we were studying the inheritance of problem gambling—also known as gambling addiction, compulsive gambling, or pathological gambling.

As researchers, we wanted to measure and explain the inheritance of problem gambling and to understand the mechanisms that pass the problem down from one generation to the next. Gradually, it became clear to us that inheritance is far from certain, but it is easy to understand. Inclinations toward problem gambling easily pass from parent to child through genetic inheritance (admittedly, a small factor), parental modelling and encouragement (a much larger factor), the creation of a family lifestyle that is gambling-friendly, and other ways we will discuss in this book.

No wonder, then, that the children of problem gamblers are far more likely than children of moderate gamblers (or non-gamblers) to develop a gambling problem themselves! Likewise, it is no wonder the children of non-gamblers are likely, as adults, to be non-gamblers or moderate gamblers.

More interesting, even puzzling, are the off-diagonal cases in our study: the children of problem gamblers who do *not* become problem gamblers themselves, and the children of non-gamblers who *do* become problem gamblers. How do we start to explain this last one: the people who develop a gambling problem seemingly "out of nowhere"? This question brought us, eventually, to an interest in Fyodor Dostoevsky. Because Dostoevsky, that famous—some would say leading—Russian novelist of the nineteenth century, perhaps even outdoing Tolstoy for this honour, not only wrote about problem gambling, he was a problem gambler himself, for a large portion of his adult life.

As our knowledge about off-diagonal cases increased, so did our interest in understanding the non-inherited factors that led Dostoevsky to become a problem gambler. To honour this famous novelist and problem gambler, in this book we call the combination of non-inherited factors "the Dostoevsky Effect." As we will show in later pages, we cannot understand Dostoevsky's gambling, nor perhaps even his work, unless we understand the childhood traumas, adult problems, and faulty coping efforts that marked his long and colourful life.

In reviewing our research files on local people with a gambling problem, we quickly realized that the so-called Dostoevsky Effect has a wide applicability. Problem gambling does not emerge out of nowhere—neither for Dostoevsky nor for present-day gamblers. Many of the present-day people we studied first-hand have the same combination of childhood and adult troubles as Dostoevsky. This likeness persuaded us that we might learn something useful about problem gambling by studying the life of Fyodor Dostoevsky. Equally, we thought we might learn something interesting about Dostoevsky by studying present-day problem gamblers.

To jump ahead a bit, one thing that is revealed by this comparison is the way an addict with artistic talent can glorify the banality of addiction. From our standpoint, between 1862 and 1870, Fyodor Dostoevsky is merely a gambling addict with the phenomenal ability to turn the dross of addiction into the gold of fiction and existential philosophizing. By comparison, present-day Toronto gambling addicts are—like Dostoevsky—abject slaves to their habit but lacking in Dostoevsky's flair for novelistic elaboration.

It is natural for addicts to want to sanitize, even glamourize, their addiction, and all addicts do so at one time or another, but few are able to succeed in this task like Dostoevsky did in his novel *The Gambler*. This insight may be of particular interest to present-day readers of *The Gambler*—also to therapists who listen to hour after hour of self-serving but inelegant rationalization.

As we reflected further on this connection, we realized that our approach was precisely what the great sociologist C. Wright Mills had called for in his classic mid-century work *The Sociological Imagination* (1959). For Mills, sociology consists precisely in making links between small events and large structures, between personal troubles and public problems, and (finally) between biography and history. After all, what is a society but the collective biography of all the people who live in it? Likewise, what is biography but the narration of one person's passage through life, under the constrained (or structured) conditions of a particular society at a particular historical time?

In short, good sociology means imaginatively using comparison and metaphor—as well as systematic data analysis—to understand how people, communities, and societies work. The test is, always, whether we can see and understand something this way that we didn't see and understand before.

So this book, brief though it is, links the gambling life of Dostoevsky to the gambling lives of people in present-day Toronto, through comparison and the exercise of sociological imagination. We think the book provides a richer understanding of both subjects: something of value both for people interested in Dostoevsky and for people interested in present-day gambling problems. However, in respect to both topics, this book is exploratory. It is neither a comprehensive contribution to Dostoevsky scholarship through the analysis of newly discovered nineteenth-century sources, nor the last word on why people gamble to excess—whether in nineteenth-century Russia or twenty-first-century Canada. We claim only that our analysis hints at new directions for gambling research and for Dostoevsky research.

Here are two caveats before we begin.

First caveat: the reader will encounter extensive discussions of Sigmund Freud's theory about Dostoevsky's gambling problem. These bits are perhaps longer than expected because Freudian analysis has largely fallen into disuse in the social sciences today. However, in this book, we give Freud his due for three important reasons. First, Freud paid a great deal of attention to the importance of childhood trauma in the development of adult behaviour problems such as addiction, and so do we. Second, Freud was the first researcher to develop a theory about the origins of problem gambling, and his theory continued to influence psychotherapists throughout the twentieth century. Third and finally, Fyodor Dostoevsky's gambling problem was so famous and so extreme that the father of psycho-analysis sought to explain it in one of his analytic essays, "Dostoevsky and Parricide," using his theory of infantile sexuality. Even today, it is impossible to discuss Dostoevsky's gambling without bumping up against Freud's classic essay on the topic. We do not agree fully with Freud's analysis, but it would be wilful ignorance to ignore it. The essay still holds a special place in twentieth-century intellectual history and the development of addiction therapy.

Second caveat: this is a book written for general readers as well as social science researchers. For this reason, we have ignored the conventional academic approach, which is to immediately and exhaustively introduce research literature on competing theories. The literature-first approach, though valuable (and valued) in professional journals, tends to alienate non-academic people—to distance them from the topic, rather than draw them in. So, to avoid reader alienation, we have organized this book as a story that (gradually and unrelentingly) becomes more complex. Then, finally, we have no recourse but to review the theoretical literature that, miracu-lously, simplifies the storyline. That is why abstract theoretical insights are not front-end loaded, but rather are introduced throughout the book.

With this in mind, let's start at the (narrative) beginning. Fyodor Dostoevsky was one of the leading novelists of the nineteenth century. He also remains the world's leading fiction writer about gambling, and the most famous problem gambler to contribute significantly to modern litera-ture. We aim to show that Dostoevsky's life experiences can help to explain his problem gambling. Beyond that, we will argue they clarify important problems surrounding modern-day problem gambling.

In important respects, our research shows the value of the import-ant Pathways Model of problem gambling, devised by Blaszczynski and Nower (2002). As in the Pathways Model, in our study we find that some individuals—the "behaviourally conditioned gamblers"—come to problem gambling largely through social learning; this is particularly true of those who "inherit" a gambling problem from problem-gambling parents. And like the Pathways Model, we find that other individuals—the emotionally vulnerable problem gamblers—are rendered susceptible by anxiety disorders, depression, traumatic family experiences, and substance use disorders. For these gamblers, like Dostoevsky, gambling is a form of escape and diversion from ongoing distress, when self-control is absent and coping skills are insufficient.

It seems doubtful that Dostoevsky fits into the Pathways Model's third, most serious category of problem gamblers—the "anti-social impulsivist problem gamblers"—who, in addition to vulnerability and opportunity, display significant anti-social tendencies and weak impulse control. In the biography that follows, we can see some indication of these traits in Dostoevsky—readers can fill in the dots for themselves if desired, but likely no one with significant problems of impulse control is able to spend an entire lifetime writing large, introspective novels about the human condition. Moreover, Dostoevsky's own spontaneous remission after ten years of gambling addiction suggests a slightly less deep-seated psychological pathology.

Where our approach differs from this and other psychological approaches to problem gambling is in its longitudinal focus and its emphasis on social context—the social, cultural, and historical setting in which people lead their lives and develop gambling problems. We will contend that there can be no valid theory of problem gambling that ignores the role of gambling in the society the gambler inhabits, or ignores the gambler's own history of earlier attempts to cope with distress. We cannot understand problem gambling through de-contextualized laboratory experiments or one-time, ahistorical surveys. A person's response to distress at any given moment, as we will see amply illustrated in the life of Dostoevsky, is a reflection of current needs and, also, past failures to deal with such distress.

As noted, in this book we try to answer two big questions. The first is, what can we learn about problem (or compulsive) gambling in present-day Canadian society by studying the life of Dostoevsky in nineteenth-century Russia? The second is, what can we learn about Dostoevsky's life by studying the problems of problem gamblers in Canada today?

In part thanks to Freud's (1976[1928]) essay, Dostoevsky's gambling problem became an important part of early writing about obsessive and neurotic behaviour. In this book, we take a contrasting approach to gambling—a sociological interpretation that we believe is more persuasive. Thus, another goal of this book is to contest the Freudian, or psychoanalytic, approach to problem gambling.

However, our analysis agrees in one important way with Freud's: both analyses view childhood trauma as an important factor in adult addiction. We believe—with Freud—that the developmental roots of problem gambling are long, deep, and slow to grow into full-blown addiction. What sets our interpretation apart from Freud's, however, is that we do not presume a sexual ingredient to the childhood trauma we will discuss. The analysis we offer here also challenges the dominant view in present-day psychology, which holds that problem gambling is mainly the result of a cognitive problem—or misperception—to be dealt with through cognitive therapy.

According to some, few lives illustrate and document trauma as thoroughly as Dostoevsky's life. As critic Alexander Burry (2010) notes in a recent article about Dostoevsky's novel *The Idiot*:

> Few writers have had more occasion than Dostoevsky to explore the phenomenon of trauma, an omnipresent element of his biography and art alike. Catastrophic experiences such as Siberian imprisonment, debilitating epileptic attacks, a decade-long gambling problem, and the death of two children continually shaped his fiction. Writing played a therapeutic role in his efforts to come to terms with such ordeals, and at the same time allowed him to arrive at considerable insights into traumatic processes. (255)

Others might find the word *trauma* a little too strong a description of Dostoevsky's life—especially his childhood. But even those people would say it was "troubled." Noted Dostoevsky expert Kenneth Lantz (2012) reports:

> I can't imagine his childhood was happy. The death of his mother must have been painful at least, [though] he was sixteen and not really a child. . . . Ditto for the death of his father. Actually, he rarely mentions his childhood, but the happiest times seem to have been the few summers he spent at the little estate in Darovoe. He writes about the delight of being able to roam freely through the woods and play games with his siblings and peasant kids, which suggests to me that his life in Moscow was rigidly structured

by his father and these summers were a welcome break. Growing up in a hospital—and a hospital for the poor—must have exposed him very early to human misery. Not trauma, perhaps, but hardly an idyllic childhood. (personal communication)

As mentioned, Dostoevsky developed a serious gambling problem, and Dostoevsky had his own theory about this topic, which he displayed imaginatively in a short novel, *The Gambler*. In this work, Dostoevsky implies that humans gamble to excess as a way of opposing fate, to protect their freedom, and preserve their free will. In other Dostoevsky novels, the characters do this by taking part in radical politics or committing murder or suicide. In *The Gambler*, they do so by betting against overwhelming odds. This challenging of fate allegedly makes the gamblers feel more alive than ever, as they await the result of each roll of the dice.

In this book, we do not endorse Dostoevsky's own theory of problem gambling. Specifically, we disagree with the idea that problem gamblers typically have a clear or developed inclination to challenge fate through their gambling. They may be risk takers, but it is doubtful they are deeply philosophical about their risky behaviour. Yet, Dostoevsky's theory is interesting, since it informs our understanding of his short novel on the topic and illustrates one way in which a problem gambler may rationalize his own addiction.

So, in this book, we have many agendas and many viewpoints to examine; while they all begin with Dostoevsky, none of them ends there. First, we will examine Dostoevsky's life to see if we can discover why he may have become a problem gambler, without much previous involvement with gambling. Second, we will delve into the lives of present-day problem gamblers to see how their stories, like Dostoevsky's, enrich our understanding of Dostoevsky's addiction and of problem gambling in general.

Third, we develop a new way of thinking about the origins of problem gambling, highlighting the so-called Dostoevsky Effect. At the centre of our analysis of this Dostoevsky Effect is an appetite for problem gambling that is fed by the forces of (1) childhood trauma, (2) adult stresses, (3) poor mental health, and (4) failed coping strategies. We will develop these ideas, and their relation to the existing literature, at greater length in the second half of this book.

In short, we argue that problem gambling emerges when people endure stresses in adulthood that reawaken their traumatic childhood experiences. This reawakening (or resurfacing) results in anxiety and depression, and a search for relief. Without positive, healthy alternatives, problem gambling offers a solution to the problem, a means for people to escape briefly from their troubles. Add to this a need for money and the availability of gambling venues, and problem gambling is a likely outcome.

As we will see in later chapters, many problem gamblers we interviewed led similar lives to Dostoevsky, in the sense that they were driven to gamble by similar factors. However, we will also learn about factors present in their lives that were not present in that of Dostoevsky. These include childhood gambling experience, having a gambling parent while growing up, or having increased opportunities to gamble because of easy access to gambling. We will also examine these non-Dostoevskian factors in our analysis of the influences that drive people to problem gambling.

Let us begin, then, with a skeletal overview of Dostoevsky's life. We will expand on it throughout the course of this book.

A Short Biography of Fyodor Dostoevsky

Dostoevsky's life has been meticulously described many times, leaving little disagreement or doubt about the bare facts. Where biographical accounts vary is in the importance they assign to different parts of this life story. Also, different biographies of Dostoevsky weigh the facts differently, in efforts to sketch a moral lesson or highlight some aspect of the author and his work. Naturally, in our present telling of his life story, we will highlight those facts that are relevant to understanding the Dostoevsky Effect and its influence on problem gambling.

The biographical information we rely on comes from three main sources. First is the celebrated five-volume biography of Dostoevsky by Joseph Frank, the first volume of which was published in 1979 and the fifth in 2002; a one-volume abridgement of the biography was published in 2010 by Princeton University Press as *Dostoevsky: A Writer in His Time*. A second source is a Russian biography of Dostoevsky by Konstantin Mochulsky, published originally in Russian in 1947, then translated and published in English in 1967. A third main source is the comprehensive *Dostoevsky Encyclopedia* by Kenneth Lantz, published in 2004.

The Joseph Frank biography excels in providing a literary and cultural context for Dostoevsky's life; Frank sees Dostoevsky's work as an expression of the cultural and intellectual turmoil of nineteenth-century Russia. The Mochulsky biography provides a psychological context and sees Dostoevsky's work largely as an expression of the author's own intellectual and psychological evolution. *The Dostoevsky Encyclopedia* provides hard-to-find details about the background characters and events in Dostoevsky's life, without putting an evident spin on the information. We have supplemented the information provided by these three main sources with details and opinions from other sources.

Born into a professional family, Dostoevsky grew up in several locales, including a rural estate. His father, a doctor, showed various signs of mental disturbance, including alcohol abuse, and he tyrannized young Fyodor and his siblings. In response, Dostoevsky showed signs of ambivalence toward his father throughout his life; by contrast, he felt unvarying love toward his gentle mother, who died when he was sixteen.

Inheritance—our original interest and one we will not discuss much in this book—plays a small but notable role in Dostoevsky's life crises. He inherited his father's irritable, "nervous" temperament and his epilepsy. As well, two of Fyodor's children—Fyodor Jr. and Lyubov—showed signs of debilitating nervousness and irritability. Fyodor's brother Nikolai, like his father, had a problem with alcohol, while his brother Andrei reportedly suffered from convulsions on occasion, although he had a placid and quite successful life as an engineer. There is no evidence that any of Fyodor's other siblings—brothers Mikhail or sisters Varvara and Vera—had nervous problems or abused alcohol, and none seems to have married someone with these problems. Likewise, neither of Fyodor's other children—Aleksei and stepson Pavel—are known to have had either nervous problems or problems with alcohol.

So far as we can tell, gambling did not run in the Dostoevsky family. None of Dostoevsky's forebears, siblings, or children is known to have had a gambling problem. That means we have to look elsewhere for an explanation of his gambling problem. That search is one purpose of this book. Note, however, that Dostoevsky's father did have a drinking problem and that early childhood experiences with an addictive parent (although not gambling-specific) may have played an important formative role in Dostoevsky's later gambling. Indeed, we argue later that alcohol and gambling may be alternative coping strategies for people who grapple with anxiety and depression.

On this, psychiatrist Richard Rosenthal (2012) has remarked that

> one could argue that there was a strong genetic component to his gambling. . . . At least five first-degree relatives, over a period of three generations, were alcoholics. The two disorders are genetically closely linked. [Note also] his impulsivity, emotional instability, and epilepsy, all strongly suggestive of a genetic, familial pre-disposition for his gambling. And [given] all the stresses in his life, you need to consider that some, indeed many, of the crises and dramatic situations were created by him, for psychological reasons. A number of pathological gamblers seem addicted to drama, or at least need it in their lives, and miss it when they stop gambling and get out of debt. (personal communication)

In his early youth, Dostoevsky rejected the career of engineer his father had chosen for him and got involved with artists, bohemians, and radicals. His engagement in radical politics soon landed him in a Siberian prison. After his release from prison and then forced service in the military, Dostoevsky married and tried to make a living from his writing. Through most of his life, he was poor and unable to cover all his expenses. Not many writers in that age got rich from their books, but Dostoevsky made a decent living and could have lived well had he been a better manager of his money. As well, throughout his life Dostoevsky had greedy relatives to support and a crushing debt load.

After the death of his first wife and a beloved brother, Dostoevsky found himself saddled with even greater financial difficulties. He now felt obliged to support his brother's family as well as his own. It was at this point—around 1862—that he began to gamble, mainly outside Russia in German resorts such as Wiesbaden and Baden-Baden. His book *The Gambler* was also written during this period, to meet a financial obligation to his publisher.

Here is a capsule description of Dostoevsky's brief but explosive gambling history, which we will unpack in the next few chapters. We find some slight disagreement about beginnings. Rosenshield (2011) reports that:

> Dostoevsky's gambling addiction, especially to roulette, lasted for about ten years, from 1862 to 1871. Saraskina (2003: 389–98) [however] shows

that Dostoevsky had gambled from his early years in Petersburg, losing large sums, including money from his inheritance. But when he arrived in Europe for the first time, roulette, a game of pure chance and no skill, turned a propensity into an addiction. (212)

On his first trip abroad in 1862, Dostoevsky gambled at the casino in Wiesbaden, winning 11,000 francs. Then, according to Lantz (2004),

The next summer, despite his eagerness to join his mistress [Apollinaria] Polina Suslova in Paris, he again stopped in Wiesbaden where he quickly won 10,400 francs. Unable to keep his resolve to leave the tables, he lost half his winnings. Part of the remainder he transferred to his wife and brother in St. Petersburg, but then returned after meeting Polina, lost everything, and had to ask his family to send him money from the winnings he had given them. (156)

In at least one commentator's view, Dostoevsky's goal in gambling now was "to assuage the pointed feelings of guilt that accompanied his desertion of his dying first wife to pursue an affair with the young writer and feminist Apollinaria Suslova" (Carter 2006, 186). This theme of guilt and gambling will recur throughout the book.

Dostoevsky's stormy, short-lived affair with the seductive "Polina" Suslova showed the wisdom of psychoanalyst Jacques Lacan's comment that "falling in love" means "giving something you don't have to someone you don't know." Often, such stormy affairs are a result of neediness and desperation, not the lucky meeting of two well-matched personalities. And it might be said, along similar lines, that by falling in love with gambling, Dostoevsky showed he was equally determined to give money he didn't have to a roulette wheel he didn't know.

However, Dostoevsky's gambling didn't stop with the end of the brief affair with Polina, or even with the death of his wife, Maria. Dostoevsky quickly remarried—this time his secretary, Anna—and the gambling continued intensely. In April 1867, Dostoevsky left Russia for central Europe, to escape his Russian debtors and to honeymoon with his new bride and stenographer, Anna Snitkina. Settling first in Berlin and then Dresden, gambling was never very far from his thoughts. He continued to imagine it might help him solve his financial problems, which had been only briefly alleviated by a loan from his publisher Stellovsky against future work. He travelled briefly to Bad Homburg; then shortly after, both he and Anna travelled to Baden-Baden where gambling could recommence in earnest.

This gambling expedition was a disaster that got worse the longer and further it went on: contrary to his hopes, life imitated art, and Dostoevsky was soon as hopelessly beset by the gambling demons as his fictional anti-hero, Aleksei, and with as little success. By the end of the summer, he had pawned many of his and Anna's belongings and systematically lost the gifts sent from Russia by friends to bail them out.

Of Dostoevsky's four-year period of recurrent gambling while living in Europe with Anna, critic Bruce Ward (1998) writes:

> Their time in Europe was marked by solitude and impoverishment, the latter at times rendered desperate by Dostoevsky's addiction to gambling and his lack of success at it. Ill health added to their woes: Dostoevsky discovered the European climate aggravated his epilepsy, and the couple had to endure the death of their first child at only a few months of age. Finally, they were plagued in the later stages by acute homesickness. (410)

The period 1865–71 was a time of remarkable creativity—what biographer Joseph Frank has called "the miraculous years." Critic Edward Wasiolek (1996), in reviewing Frank's book (1995) about the period, encapsulates the "miracles" Dostoevsky accomplished in this period of poverty and exile:

> These were the years of incredible creativity on Dostoevsky's part, the years in which he wrote *Crime and Punishment*, *The Idiot*, and *The Possessed*, as well as *The Gambler* and *The Eternal Husband*. Almost all of these were written abroad, where he went with his young wife to escape his creditors and his demanding relatives and where he remained for four years. They were difficult years. He suffered from poverty, ill-health, and obsessive gambling, and lived, barely, from advance to advance. One wonders how it was possible for him to write such magnificent works in such frightful conditions. He probably could not have were it not for the steadfast love and support of his new bride, Anna, and the unstinting subventions of his editor, Katkov. (387)

Moving around—from Dresden, to Geneva, to Milan, and to Florence, then back through Prague to Dresden again—Dostoevsky was displeased by much of what he saw. He complained about the "quiet boredom of Dresden, the excessive cold of Geneva, the excessive heat and noise of Florence, the outrageously high cost of living in Prague" (Ward 1998, 412). Most of all, he complained about the national character of the European people he met in his travels: "the French are simply 'nauseating'; the Swiss are dishonest, venal, and stupid; of course the boring, self-satisfied Germans are even worse, upsetting his nerves 'to the point of fury'—only the Italians are spared his ire, for the Italian peasant reminds him of the Russian peasant" (Ward 1998, 413). That said, Dostoevsky visited art galleries every chance he got, and throughout his life he admired European literature, philosophy, and painting.

From a distance of nearly two thousand kilometres—the distance between St. Petersburg and Dresden—Dostoevsky was able to think more clearly about the state of Russian society and culture. These were both tied up, in his mind, with religious and political issues, and they all received consideration in his novel *The Demons* (also known as *The Devils* and *The Possessed*), which he began to write in Dresden, shortly before returning to Russia for good.

This novel, begun at a distance in space from Russia, was also begun at a distance in time from his youthful experience in the Petrashevsky Circle.[1] Writing the book gave Dostoevsky a new opportunity to review and rethink his views on political radicalism and his own youthful experiences as a radical. The novel is a fictional representation of a contemporary political crime, the assassination of a student by the supporters of the anarchist terrorist Nechaev. "In *The Devils*, Dostoevsky focuses on the revolutionary left, and the novel has often been seen as a prophecy of the progression from revolution to Stalinism in his own country," writes Ward (1998, 414). However, Ward rightly points out that the novel is actually a critique of all political tyranny and all revolutionary doctrine, whether of the right or left. In that respect, it predicts Hitler's rise to power no less than it predicts Stalin's.

In this novel, as in several others, we see Dostoevsky's suspicion of programs that promise heaven on earth. In *The Devils*, as in *The Gambler* and other novels, Dostoevsky shows a yearning for freedom and justice on earth, and he evidently understood why many contemporaries could not believe these goals were attainable through subservience to a seemingly deaf and mute God. Yet Dostoevsky feared that, without subservience to God, there would be no subservience to moral limits on earth either.

Dostoevsky's new wife, Anna, provided a trustworthy anchor; she was a level-headed, prudent woman, wholly devoted to Dostoevsky. But she could do little to control, much less quell, his gambling problem. Dostoevsky was as tantalized by the gambling tables at Wiesbaden, Baden-Baden, and Hamburg as his fictional protagonist, Aleksei, was by the gambling tables at "Roulettenburg."

What was it about the casino at Wiesbaden that launched Dostoevsky on his explosive gambling career in 1862 and kept him coming back? For one thing, the casino welcomed travellers. As Eyres (2007) notes, the casino at Wiesbaden is housed in a magnificent 1820s neo-classical build-ing. Inside, the casino has "just the right degree of grandeur—chandeliers, wooden panels—without being pompous or intimidating" (22). Perhaps for this reason, people of all ages, races, and genders came here to absorb themselves in the chase for wins.

Dostoevsky began his gambling career by winning a great deal of money, so gambling at Wiesbaden was associated in his mind with suc-cess. This was unfortunate because initial wins increase the likelihood of gambling repeatedly, then gambling to excess, because of what behavioural psychologists call the power of *intermittent reinforcement.* The principle here is that unpredictable, infrequent rewards lock in behaviour patterns more securely than do predictable, regular rewards. As well, people who lose from the outset are less likely to return, therefore less likely to fall into problem gambling.

Worse still, as quoted in Breger (1989), Dostoevsky thought he had chanced on the secret to winning, which, in a letter to his wife's sister Varvara, he characterized as "terribly silly and simple and consists of keep-ing one's head the whole time, whatever the state of the game, and not getting excited" (77). For Dostoevsky, this first visit to Wiesbaden was a profound learning experience, not least because it convinced him that he could control his gambling and even control the chances of winning.

On his first two gambling occasions, Dostoevsky managed to hold on to at least some of his winnings, but he would not be able to do this in the future. Two years after the first casino win, he returned to lose all his money, writing to fellow Russian author Turgenev: "I have been five days in Wiesbaden and already I have lost everything, the whole lot, even my watch, and I owe my hotel bill."

For cognitive psychologists, it is this mistaken belief in the ability to control chance (or at least, avoid losses) that is central to the definition of problem gambling. However, for psychoanalytic theorists, it is guilt and punishment that are the key. They believe that gambling, for Dostoevsky, was always associated with guilt—not expectations of winning. So, for example, Carter (2006) claims that Dostoevsky gambled both to evoke and resolve "powerful sensations of guilt" (186) of that kind that were portrayed so vividly in the fiction he wrote at this time. The feelings of guilt derived, in large part, from his earlier hatred of his father.

Despite evidence that he lost more often and more extensively than he would ever win, Dostoevsky continued to gamble compulsively for nearly a decade. Then he quit. Kenneth Lantz (2004) notes that "Dostoevsky's final episode of gambling came during the last months of their stay in Europe . . . in the spring of 1871," (157) after a particularly humiliating loss. The gambling ended because Dostoevsky finally made it end—not because he was without access to European gambling opportunities. Lantz (2004) concludes:

> Whether it was due to his return to Russia and a more settled, stable life, or to his growing devotion and sense of responsibility to Anna and his two children, or simply the terror caused by the dream of his father [predicting a terrible calamity], he no longer visited the roulette tables. (158)

A decade after quitting gambling, Dostoevsky died, having enjoyed some fame and financial success from his *Writer's Diary* and his wife's publishing ventures, and having finally paid off all his debts.

Remember these facts in later chapters, as we explore the lives of present-day problem gamblers. Many of them also experienced hardships in their childhood and adult lives, hardships that were often similar to those Dostoevsky faced. In the closing chapters, we will link the experiences of present-day problem gamblers to Dostoevsky's own experiences. First, however, we will elaborate on Dostoevsky's life story—for the further we go into it, the more complicated becomes the link between childhood trauma, adult stresses, and the rise of a gambling problem.

Dostoevsky's Biography: A Thematic Version

As we will see in detail, throughout his life Fyodor Dostoevsky faced hardships that caused great distress: hardships ranging from physical and mental health problems, to financial and legal problems, to frequent exhaustion and frustration about his writing efforts. In efforts to cope with these distressing hardships or forget their causes, Dostoevsky eventually turned to gambling. The problems Dostoevsky struggled with arose at different times, making it necessary to analyze separately each part of his life—his childhood, youth, and adulthood—if we are to understand Dostoevsky's gambling problem. Let's start at the beginning, with his childhood experiences.

Family and Childhood

Fyodor Dostoevsky sometimes claimed to have enjoyed the years of childhood he spent in the countryside with his mother. Unlike his father, Dostoevsky's mother, Maria, was a mild, optimistic woman who bore her husband's moods and tirades stoically. She realized they were merely expressions of his nervous disorder. Despite unpleasant periods, the relationship between mother and father was good, and letters that passed between Maria and Dr. Dostoevsky suggest they had a loving relationship. Both Fyodor and his brother Andrei viewed their parents as being "close knit" (Lantz 2004, 106–7).

Despite his mother's gentle kindness, Dostoevsky's childhood was far from idyllic, and this had significant affects on his life and, of course, on his writing. Mochulsky (1967[1947]) writes that many contemporaries reacted to Dostoevsky's writings as "'ravings' and [their] despair as . . . the outgrowth of fanaticism and sickness. Dostoevsky was dubbed 'a sick, cruel talent' and quickly forgotten" (xvii). Repeatedly over the next hundred years, Dostoevsky's work was rediscovered and newly appreciated for its literary, religious, and philosophical qualities.

In this present book, we have no desire to dismiss Dostoevsky's work by calling attention to the author's troubled mind. Yet, since our goal is to understand his addiction to gambling, we can scarcely ignore the factors that troubled his mind. Lantz (2004) records that Stephan Yanovsky, Dostoevsky's close friend in the 1840s, remembered that:

[Dostoevsky] told me a great deal about the difficult and cheerless circumstances of his childhood, although he always spoke with reverence of his mother, sisters, and his brother Mikhail. He definitely did not like speaking of his father and asked me not to inquire about him. (109)

As we will see, Dostoevsky's father plays a central part in Freud's explanation of Dostoevsky's gambling. Freud seems to think that Dostoevsky signalled, in every way imaginable short of actual homicide, a desire to see his father dead. Who, then, was this demon that so occupied Fyodor's psyche?

Mikhail Andreevich Dostoevsky, Fyodor's father, was a doctor at the Mariinsky Hospital for the Poor. In 1828, he was promoted to the rank of collegiate assessor, the promotion making him a member of the minor nobility. This status promotion was in accordance with the Table of Ranks, a bureaucratic apparatus imposed on Russia in an attempt to create a modern bureaucratic system by Peter the Great at the end of the seventeenth century. However, this honour came without money. As a result, the Dostoevsky family led impoverished though genteel lives in a small apartment on the hospital grounds. The two older sons mainly relied on their own company and on reading for entertainment. Mochulsky (1967[1947], 9) notes that the Dostoevskys—both parents and children—were socially isolated and lacked much contact with the world outside their home. They had few friends or visitors and rarely went to outside entertainments.

To project an image of himself that matched his new social status, Dr. Dostoevsky often spent more money than he could afford to. He was not without virtues, despite his overspending. In *Dostoevsky: The Seeds of Revolt, 1821–1849*, the first volume of his five-volume biography of Dostoevsky, Joseph Frank (1979) notes the doctor was a serious, hardworking, and responsible father and husband. However, Dr. Dostoevsky was also stern—even harsh—and irritable. He suffered from an unnamed affliction (probably mild epilepsy) which often resulted in bouts of depression and nervous strain.

Often irritable, Fyodor's father was quick to anger, depressive, and suspicious (Frank 1979). On one occasion, he even accused his devoted wife, Maria Fyodorovna Dostoevsky (neé Nechaeva), of infidelity (Frank 1979, 19; Lantz 2004, 106–7).

Dr. Dostoevsky's nervous condition also strained the relationships with his children. His irritability and anger often created tension in the Dostoevsky household. Mochulsky, following Fyodor's daughter, Lyubov Fyodorovna, claims that the hated father in Dostoevsky's novel *The Brothers Karamazov* was modelled on Fyodor's own father. On the other hand, Kenneth Lantz (2012, personal communication) has suggested this may not have been the case. Fyodor Karamazov had many faults that Dostoevsky's father did not. He also had a real, though twisted, sense of humour that Dostoevsky's stern father apparently lacked. Moreover, though Dostoevsky and his father lacked a close, loving relationship, evidence suggests that Dostoevsky knew that his father made real sacrifices to help his children— sacrifices that the fictional Fyodor Karamazov never made.

Nonetheless, we can see elements of the real father–son relationship in the fictional relationship. Accordingly, Sigmund Freud (1976[1928]) felt that the murder of a despotic father in *The Brothers Karamazov* was Dostoevsky's way of sublimating hostile (or, at best, strongly ambivalent) feelings toward his own despotic father—the irritable doctor. Indeed, critic Anna Berman (2009) notes that the defective father figure is a recurring figure in Dostoevsky's fiction:

> In an often-quoted entry in his *Writer's Diary* from January 1876, Dostoevsky explained: "For a long time now I have had the goal of writing a novel about children in Russia today, and about their fathers too, of course, in their mutual relationship of today . . . I will take fathers and children from every level of Russian society I can find and follow the children from their earliest childhood." (263)

Kate Holland (2012, personal communication) notes that this is a clear reference to Turgenev's novel *Fathers and Sons* (also known as *Fathers and Children*) and to the extensive ideological debates the novel sparked in the 1860s. Thus, Dostoevsky, like Turgenev, is likely talking about the clash of generations—about symbolic fathers and sons, and not necessarily about his relationship with his own father. Berman (2009) continues, however, by stating that:

> Dostoevsky saw the breakdown of the family as connected to overall societal degeneration. Susanne Fusso posits that "Dostoevskii's last three novels are

devoted to exploring the ways in which the fathers of Russia have failed in their obligations to the sons, and therefore to the nation's future." William Leatherbarrow, too, writes that "the Karamazov family relationships are invested with a symbolism designed to imply a breakdown in the transmission of values and mutual responsibility between the generations." (263)

Biographer Konstantin Mochulsky (1967[1947]) asserts that Dostoevsky disliked and feared his father, causing him to develop a somewhat reticent and even devious way of dealing with him. The Dostoevsky children were united in this reaction, for their father comported himself like the lord of the manor. Of this, Mochulsky writes that:

> The children used to tremble before their father, fearing his angry outbursts. . . . During the summer, when the doctor would rest after lunch, one of the children used to shoo the flies away with a lime-tree branch. (4–5)

To handle his moody, demanding father, Dostoevsky developed a "saccharine exuberance" in his letters from school which some have mistaken for fondness. Mochulsky (1967[1947]) notes that "in order to move the harsh old man, the youth artfully played upon his more sensitive chords" (5). Listen to the tone of a letter that seventeen-year-old Dostoevsky wrote his father from school in 1838, asking for money. It opens as follows:

> My dear good father,
>
> Can you really think that your son is asking too much when he applies to you for an allowance. God be my witness that not for self-interest, nor even in actual extremest need, could ever wish to despoil you in any way. How bitter it is to have to ask my flesh and blood a favour which so heavily oppresses them. I have my own head, my own hands. Were I but free and independent, I should never have asked you for so much as a kopeck—I should have inured myself to the bitterest poverty. I should have been ashamed to write from my very deathbed, asking for support. As things are, I can only console you with promises for the future; however, that future is no longer a distant one, and time will convince you of its reality. (Dostoevsky 1914, 1)

This abject letter is written to request money for books and a trunk to hold Dostoevsky's meagre school possessions. Even allowing for differences of time and culture, the letter is humble to the point of near absurdity. Displaying such humility must have been difficult for a boy as imaginative and sensitive as Dostoevsky—qualities that are amply clear in the letters Dostoevsky wrote to his beloved brother Mikhail around the same time. We'll never know the true quality of relations between Dostoevsky and his father. Certainly, the relationship doesn't *sound* in letters as though it was as close as his relationship with his brother Mikhail or, later, with his wife, Anna.

In due course, Dostoevsky was disturbed to receive news of his father's death, initially ascribed to murder (i.e., suffocation) by fifteen local peasants. Though peasants likely hadn't killed his father, according to the thinking of current commentators, they apparently hated him enough that people believed they had done so. Yet Mochulsky (1967[1947]) notes, "In Dostoevsky's correspondence we do not find a single reference to the tragic death of his father. There is something frightening in this unyielding silence throughout the course of his entire life" (6).

How did Dostoevsky feel about his father? Regrettably, we have no unequivocal evidence on this matter. Likely, even Dostoevsky and his siblings recognized their father's severity and strictness reflected a concern for their well-being. True, the father often lost his temper and harshly reprimanded them for misbehaving or making errors in their schoolwork, but it was always for their own good. As well, Dr. Dostoevsky often reminded them that he was a "poor man" who would not always be able to provide for them financially. That is why he urged them, perhaps excessively, to prepare for well-paying professions whether they liked them or not. At best, we might view Dr. Dostoevsky as what we call a "tiger dad" today—pushing his children to excel and reprimanding them when they failed to live up to parental expectations.

So, while Fyodor Dostoevsky likely understood that his father was strict and harsh because he had (his own version of) the children's interests in mind, as a child Dostoevsky may not have received much affection or tenderness from his father. Additionally, Dostoevsky created a feeling of chaos and hypocrisy around him. Mochulsky (1967[1947]) writes, "The family of staff-physician Dostoevsky, the impoverished noble and petty landowner, completely conforms to the designation 'a haphazard household.'" Dr. Dostoevsky held up impossible standards for his children, but he was something of a pompous failure himself.

Dostoevsky's father may have been tyrannical and emotionally abusive, as Mochulsky (1967[1947]) suggests, but was he physically abusive? Despite his temper and irascibility, we have no uncontested information that Mikhail Dostoevsky beat Fyodor or his siblings, though some believe he did. Perhaps it is because corporal punishment was acceptable at the time that he removed his children from public schools and sent them to private schools instead; there, he could be sure they would *not* be beaten. However, it is equally likely that Dr. Dostoevsky moved the children to another school to increase their chances of educational and occupational success.

The move to a private school occurred when Dostoevsky was thirteen. Dr. Dostoevsky had already decided Fyodor and his older brother, Mikhail, should become military engineers. So, after their early studies were complete, he enrolled them in the prestigious Academy of Engineers. However, neither brother wanted to become an engineer. Both brothers were passionately in love with literature, and Dostoevsky was already interested in writing, not engineering. Soon, he began to resent his father for pushing him into a profession he didn't want.

Dostoevsky's mother provided brief respites from unwanted schooling and harsh fathering. Unlike the stern, sometimes harsh Dr. Dostoevsky, Fyodor's mother, Maria, was warm and loving. For four years, Fyodor and his brother Mikhail were able to spend four months each year with their mother at Darovoe, the small estate Dr. Dostoevsky had bought to display his noble status. These vacations in mother's company were among the most enjoyable times of Dostoevsky's childhood. Out from under the constant scrutiny of an impossible-to-please father, he could then enjoy his mother's tenderness and compassion to the fullest.

Sadly, Dostoevsky was deprived of his mother's love and care when he was sixteen. Maria was diagnosed with tuberculosis in the autumn of 1836 and died shortly afterwards, in February 1837. After Maria's death, Dr. Dostoevsky resigned his position at the hospital and moved permanently to Darovoe. The stress caused by losing his spouse at a young age (forty-six or forty-seven), as well as leaving the comfortably familiar routine of his job, aggravated Dr. Dostoevsky's nervous condition. His mental health started to decline rapidly after his wife's death.

According to Lantz (2004), Dr. Dostoevsky "began drinking heavily and quickly disintegrated emotionally and morally" (109), cutting all social ties and confining himself to the small, three-room house at Darovoe. Fyodor's brother Andrei later wrote that according to Alena Frolovna (the children's nanny), Dr. Dostoevsky started "talking to himself, supposing that he was speaking with his late wife, and answering her in his usual way! In such a state, while living in isolation, madness was not far off!" (109)

Dostoevsky may not have been fully aware of his father's declining health, since he had already begun his studies at the Academy of Engineers. He considered the years he spent there, 1838–42, to be some of the loneliest years of his life. He hated the strictness of daily life in close quarters, with barracks-like regimentation (Lantz 2004). Most students there were either German or Polish, not Russian. He did not share any of his colleagues' interests, so he spent most of his time alone, reading. Moreover, since most of the students there came from wealthy families, Dostoevsky quickly became aware of his low social standing, further increasing his alienation.

During these lonely years at engineering school, Dostoevsky's wish to become a writer continued to grow. Accordingly, the feelings of resentment toward his father intensified, since it was Father's wishes that kept him from pursuing his desire to write. Dutifully, Dostoevsky worked hard at the required courses, gaining high grades in even some subjects that bored him. However, Dr. Dostoevsky expressed frustration with his son's progress when, in his first year, Fyodor received a low grade in a course called "military drill" (Frank 1979).

Dostoevsky, as always, felt guilty about disappointing his father. On this, he wrote, "I would regret nothing if the tears of our poor father did not burn my soul" (Frank 1979, 83). However, even guilt couldn't keep him focused on the task at hand. Eventually, his lack of interest in the military academy led him to stray from the course his father had set for him.

Traumatic Childhood Experiences

Dostoevsky was still enrolled at the Academy of Engineers in 1839 when he received the news of his father's death. While at school, his only contact with his father had been through the letters they wrote to each other. His letters consisted largely of requests for extra money. Dostoevsky wanted to fit in with his school friends from wealthier families, and to do this he needed money to buy extra items beyond those he was regularly issued (Frank 1979).

That said, the relationship was not only about money. Kenneth Lantz (2012) remarks that it's true that Dostoevsky was

> often asking his father for funds, but the letters are also quite long and chatty, dealing with his studies, his friends, his readings. They're a bit flowery and formal, and he may have simply been developing his writing style. But they're not *only* about money. The letters don't necessarily show that there was a warm relationship between them; as I said, the style is a bit formal, but certainly respectful. (personal communication)

Despite the family's strained financial situation, Dr. Dostoevsky always sent his son the money he asked for. In his last known communication with Fyodor, Dr. Dostoevsky explained the terrible financial conditions at Darovoe and the dire problems the family was facing. Biographer Joseph Frank believes that this letter reached Dostoevsky around the same time he learned of his father's death.

Dostoevsky told everyone that the peasants had set upon Dr. Dostoevsky as he drove around his estate; in some versions of the story, they suffocated him by forcing vodka down his throat. Reportedly, there were three separate investigations before this story was finally laid to rest. Scholars today accept the medical finding that Dr. Dostoevsky actually died of an apoplectic stroke.

As Lantz (2004) remarks, "Much has been written about this incident and the effect it had on Dostoevsky, but the full truth simply cannot be known" (109). Some, basing their belief on a reportedly unreliable book by Fyodor Dostoevsky's daughter Lyubov, have claimed that this news had a shocking effect on Fyodor, causing him to have his first epileptic fit. Today, few believe this story either. However, it seems likely that his father's death affected Dostoevsky deeply.

Because he had been so demanding in the past, Dostoevsky probably felt guilty on hearing of his father's death. These feelings of guilt stemmed in part from his repeated requests for money: he had repeatedly asked for money even though he was aware of the family's money problems. Frank (1979) speculates that Dostoevsky must have doubted the peasants of Darovoe had murdered Dr. Dostoevsky without provocation. Perhaps Dostoevsky reasoned that, by putting extra pressure on his father, he may have encouraged his father to mistreat or overwork the peasants. In this way, he may have felt personally responsible for the alleged murder of his father.

Dostoevsky may have also felt guilty of failing to aim for success in the career his father had chosen for him. In a letter to his brother Mikhail in August 1839, Dostoevsky expressed grief over his father's death and concern for the welfare of his younger siblings. Yet, despite any feelings of guilt he may have had, he no longer felt obliged to fulfill his father's wishes. As he explained to Mikhail, he was now freed from these filial duties and could devote himself to becoming a writer (Lantz 2004). Thus, his father's death left Dostoevsky conflicted between feelings of grief and guilt, on the one hand, and feelings of freedom to pursue his own goals, on the other.

Dostoevsky's father—both alive and dead—contributed a great deal to the stressfulness of Fyodor's early life, but two other childhood experiences were also stressful. The first involved a childhood friend who, at the age of nine, was brutally raped by a drunken man. Dostoevsky had gone to get help from his father, but Dr. Dostoevsky did not arrive in time and his friend died (Lantz 2004). Dostoevsky later said that the memory of this traumatic event haunted him throughout the rest of his life.

A second traumatic event may have occurred when Dostoevsky was six. (There is some question about whether it actually occurred because Dostoevsky reports it only in his *Writer's Diary*, which is a semi-fictional work, not a diary in the conventional sense.) While playing in the woods near Darovoe, he began to have an auditory hallucination. He ran to a peasant named Marey for help and received comfort, leading Dostoevsky to see Marey's kindness as proof of the inherent goodness of Russian peasants. This frightening experience, and the peasant's benign role, may have helped to shape the nationalistic beliefs Dostoevsky developed in later life (a topic we will discuss shortly).

What then did Dostoevsky bring forward from childhood? Most clearly, as can be judged from a series of surviving letters, he brought a love of literature and a love for his brother Mikhail, with whom he discussed literature and various personal concerns throughout the rest of their lives. No wonder that Mikhail's death came as a terrible blow to Dostoevsky, because of their long, close relationship that was both emotional and intellectual. Less clearly, Dostoevsky brought certain attitudes to authority that resulted from relations with his authoritarian father. This we must infer from Dostoevsky's fictional writings, since he never discussed his father in surviving letters or conversations; nor, for that matter, did he discuss his mother or other siblings.

What will be become clear as we go forward is that Dostoevsky did *not* learn in childhood how to avoid problems, take care of his health, or deal with personal and financial adversity.

Adult Stresses

Throughout his adult life, Dostoevsky continued to suffer from difficulties that made his life abnormally stressful: they included problems with health, money, and personal relations. We will examine each of these in turn.

Physical and Mental Health

It is well known that Dostoevsky experienced severe epileptic seizures throughout his adult life. There is no clear evidence proving how old he was when he suffered his first seizure, however. Some sources say he was as young as six when it happened, but the only support for this is that he had had an auditory hallucination at this age. The first epileptic seizure of which we can be certain occurred in 1846, when he was aged twenty-five. From then onward, Dostoevsky had frequent seizures that gradually grew worse over time.

Other than epilepsy, Dostoevsky suffered from a large number of other health problems. His friend Aleksandr Rizenkampf, a medical student and Dostoevsky's roommate in 1843, notes that Dostoevsky had a sallow complexion and suffered from a chronic cough and hoarseness, nervousness, and frequent insomnia. Worst of all, Dostoevsky had an intense fear of falling into a deep sleep during which he would be mistaken for dead. Despite his many illnesses, however, Rizenkampf notes that Dostoevsky refused to take medication, was reluctant to seek medical help, and did not give up smoking though it aggravated his health.

A letter to his brother Mikhail also shows that Dostoevsky suffered greatly from anxiety. In it, he claims to have been so near death—his nervous system irritated and his heart congested—that leeches and bloodlettings were needed to "barely" ameliorate his condition (Lantz 2004, 199).

In another letter to his brother Mikhail, dated August 1849, he goes on further about his various afflictions, many of them connected to anxiety and exhaustion:

> Of my health, I can tell you nothing good. For a month I have been living almost exclusively on castor oil. My hemorrhoids have been unusually

tormenting; moreover I detect a pain in the breast that I have never had before. My nervous irritability has notably increased, especially in the evening hours; at night I have long, hideous dreams, and latterly I have often felt as if the ground were rocking under me so, that my room seems like the cabin of a steamer. From all this I conclude that my nerves are increasingly shattered. Whenever formerly I had such nervous disturbances, I could make use of them for writing; in such a state I could write much more and much better than usual; but now I refrain from work that I may not utterly destroy myself. I took a rest of three weeks, during which time I wrote not at all; now I have begun again. (Dostoevsky 1914, 47–48)

His nervous condition worsened whenever Dostoevsky came under pressure. The mockery he endured from members of the Belinsky Circle[2]—his supposed friends—made him anxious and worsened his condition, despite Dostoevsky's growing literary fame. Dostoevsky complained to Dr. Stephan Yanovsky of an irregular heartbeat, high blood pressure, and nervous irritability. Soon after this visit to Dr. Yanovsky, Dostoevsky began to complain of dizziness and fainting spells, which were often accompanied by hallucinations. Dr. Yanovsky suspected these spells were caused by epilepsy.

This suspicion was confirmed in 1847, when Dostoevsky suffered an acute seizure. However, he was not officially diagnosed as epileptic until 1857, and Dostoevsky accepted this belated diagnosis with some relief. For his part, he had feared he was slowly going mad, and this fear had been causing him much additional stress, making his nervous condition worse (Lantz 2004). For Dostoevsky, epilepsy was the lesser of two evils.

Dostoevsky's various health problems may have been brought on, or at least aggravated, by his lifestyle. He was a regular smoker, as mentioned above. Also, he often went without sleep so he could complete large writing projects. For example, while working as editor of the journal *Epoch* in 1865, Dostoevsky wrote to a friend: "I began publishing in three different printing shops at once, sparing neither my money nor my own health and energy. . . . I sat up until six in the morning and slept only five hours a day" (Lantz 2004, 126). While serving as editor of *Epoch*, Dostoevsky was also writing a journal, polemical articles, and a story titled "The Crocodile." This huge workload likely aggravated his nervous condition.

Gradually, other health problems came to torment Dostoevsky as well. As the frequency and intensity of his epileptic seizures lessened during the last five years of his life, he began to suffer from pulmonary problems and was eventually diagnosed with emphysema—the result of a lifelong smoking habit. Dostoevsky died from a pulmonary hemorrhage, after trying to move a heavy bookcase in his study. This hemorrhage may have been complicated by tuberculosis (Lantz 2004).

Alongside these various physical ailments, Dostoevsky also experienced significant mental health problems as an adult. According to his biographers, he was given to feelings of depression and often thought about suicide. These depressive and suicidal feelings typically followed public criticism of his writing. When his books were successful, he was happy and confident; but after the release of an unpopular work, he sank into depression for months.

Dostoevsky's numerous mental and physical health problems both reflected and increased the stressfulness of his life. However, poor mental and physical health was only one source of stress in Dostoevsky's adult life. Another was his trouble with the law.

Trouble with the Law

In 1849, the young Dostoevsky was arrested as a political conspirator because of his involvement in groups that gathered to discuss radical political ideas. A man named Nikolai Aleksandrovich Speshnev, another member of the Petrashevsky Circle, had persuaded Dostoevsky to participate in a more radical subgroup, with its own secret printing press (Lantz 2004). Dostoevsky described Speshnev's subgroup as "a special secret society with a printing press for publishing various books and even magazines." Apparently, the final goal of the group was to overthrow the existing regime (Lantz 2004, 409)—to take action and not merely debate all the time, as the Petrashevsky Circle tended to do.

Involvement in this conspiracy was nerve-racking for Dostoevsky, and it was also terribly dangerous. However, Dostoevsky could not extricate himself easily, even if he had wanted to. Always in debt, he had borrowed five hundred rubles from Speshnev, indebting himself to Speshnev financially—a problem that recurred throughout Dostoevsky's life. As well, Speshnev was a charismatic, almost demonic figure—likely a model for Dostoevsky's Nikolai Stavrogin in *The Demons*.

After a period of surveillance, an agent of the czar's secret police infiltrated the group in 1849 and arrests followed (Lantz 2004). Dostoevsky was charged with reading Vissarion Belinsky's subversive *Letter to Gogol*, which put forward an argument against noble despotism and serfdom. (The work takes the form of a letter berating Gogol for his defence of the autocratic regime of Nicholas I.) He was also charged with failing to report the existence of another rebellious work by a circle member (Lantz 2004, 312). Accordingly, Dostoevsky and other members of the group were sentenced to death. After being petitioned to reduce these harsh sentences, the czar finally gave in, but he didn't communicate his change of heart to members of the circle or even to the relevant authorities.

Dostoevsky's death sentence was announced only when he and the others had been brought to a square in St. Petersburg for execution, where a firing squad had been drawn up. He spent some very long minutes that he was certain would be his last watching the first three prisoners being prepared for execution. Suddenly, a messenger's arrival halted the execution ceremony at the last possible minute (Frank 1987).

On December 22, 1849, Dostoevsky was banished to Siberia for four years of penal servitude and an indefinite period of military service. As it turned out, the military service was terminated after five years on medical grounds (epilepsy). Part of the time in Siberia, he was in chains and was subject to frequent attacks of epilepsy. This stay in Siberia was his punishment for "criminal intentions to overthrow the existing state order in Russia" (Lantz 2004, 310). Dostoevsky was held in solitary confinement from April 24 to December 23 in the St. Peter and St. Paul Fortress—a secret prison built to house Russia's most dangerous criminals (Lantz 2004). During this time, he was allowed no outside visitors; only the head of the czar's secret police and the prison warden were allowed into his cell.

Other members of the circle who were arrested and housed in solitary confinement noted that their emotional energy was quickly drained by the lack of stimulation that left them alone with their thoughts. Dostoevsky himself left no detailed account of his confinement, but in three letters Dostoevsky wrote to Mikhail and Andrei during this time, he complained of stomach problems, hemorrhoids, upset nerves, and tormented dreams.

Following this brief imprisonment, Dostoevsky was sentenced to exile in Siberia. He arrived at Omsk Prison in January 1850, where he lived the next four years in the overcrowded, freezing barracks, forced to carry loads of bricks, unload trucks, and pound alabaster stone. During this time, he was banned from reading or writing as he wished; the only book allowed within the walls of the prison was the New Testament. However, the prison doctor, I.I. Trotsky, provided Dostoevsky with books and writing materials and offered to hide his journal. In this way, Trotsky broke the prison rules to allow Dostoevsky to continue working and saved him from being punished for doing so.

The stress of this interlude in radical politics—especially the secrecy and danger of conspiracy, the wait for death by execution, and the privation and degradation of prison life—no doubt worsened Dostoevsky's mental and physical health. In this way, it may have led to the development of addiction problems in his later life. And though we have no record of this, it is likely Dostoevsky was exposed to gambling in prison, just as he would later be exposed to gambling in the military.

Strained Relationships

Even his personal life provided no respite for Dostoevsky. Bear in mind that, as a child, he had extremely limited social relationships and little opportunity to develop an independent personal life. Both his father and mother were, in different ways, reclusive. His main relationship in life, until his marriage to Anna Snitkina, was his link to his brother Mikhail.

Dostoevsky married twice, the first time to Maria Dmitrievna Dostoevskaya (née Constant); however, this was a far from happy marriage. Dostoevsky's friend Baron Wrangel wrote that Maria didn't hold Dostoevsky or his writing in high esteem; moreover, she didn't seem to be in love with him (Lantz 2004). Dostoevsky confirmed in a letter written to Wrangel a year after Maria's death that the two had not lived happily together (Lantz 2004).

Dostoevsky had met Maria while in exile in Semipalatinsk (Siberia). Married at the time, Maria tormented Dostoevsky in the letters she wrote, telling him she loved him but intended to stay with her husband in the Siberian town of Kuznetsk, five hundred kilometres away (Lantz 2004). Maria even wrote him about her other suitors and expressed delight over being desired by so many men (Lantz 2004). Even after her husband died, Maria was slow to decide between Dostoevsky and another suitor.

Finally married to Maria, Dostoevsky found himself disappointed with—even tormented by—married life. Maria taunted him about his age and his epilepsy, for example; this worsened his health, causing him to suffer epileptic seizures more often than in the past. Of this relationship, Kenneth Lantz (2012) reports:

> She was a very high-strung, difficult woman who enjoyed making him jealous when they were courting. Their life together when they returned to St. Petersburg was also very troubled: his family disliked her, she disliked D.'s friends, and the damp climate was bad for her advanced tuberculosis (which made her even more irritable than normal). They separated after a few years, but to his credit D. did arrange for medical care for her and spent the last months of her life by her bedside. (personal communication)

In an effort to cope with the stress his marriage was causing him, Dostoevsky began an affair with Apollinaria (Polina) Suslova. Dostoevsky took Polina as his mistress between 1862–64, when his marriage to Maria had essentially broken down. Polina was a young idealist, a feminist, and a radical. Dostoevsky may have believed that having an affair with her could help him escape from his many worries: his journal was doing poorly and eventually went under, he was chronically short of money, and his wife was dying. However, Dostoevsky's affair with Polina failed to provide such an escape. Instead, he was overwhelmed by feelings of guilt over abandoning Maria while she was ill.

It was around this time that gambling appeared in Dostoevsky's life. He and Polina had planned to travel around Europe together, and occasionally, he stopped to gamble. First, Dostocvsky spent several days at the roulette table in Wiesbaden, where he won 10,000 francs, before joining Polina in Paris, where she was awaiting his arrival. By the time he arrived, Polina had fallen in love with another man. Within a week, however, Polina's new relationship had broken off and Dostoevsky agreed to be "like a brother" to her. By this time, Dostoevsky had lost all he had won at the roulette tables in Wiesbaden and was forced to have funds sent from Russia. Shortly after, he returned to Russia to be with his dying wife, but he continued to write to Polina, who remained in Paris.

It is important to know that Dostoevsky wrote his novel *The Gambler*— of which we will say more later—while he was trying to rekindle his romance with Polina. In fact, their troubled relationship is mirrored in that novel, whose narrator Aleksei is tormented by his own "Polina" (Lantz

2004). Suffice it to say at this point that Dostoevsky's relationships were often troubled, were often mirrored in his novels, and were (in this period of his life) increasingly often related to gambling.

Polina was not to remain in Dostoevsky's life for long, however. Soon, he had hired a secretary, Anna Grigoryevna Snitkina, to whom he became increasingly attached. Her dedication helped Dostoevsky to produce a massive body of publishable writing and to enjoy a domestic life too. However, his gambling placed a heavy strain on this relationship and burdened her with debt. Moreover, it forced her to put large amounts of time and energy into caring for him, since the excitement of gambling caused his epilepsy to worsen (Frank 1995).

Dostoevsky consistently returned to Anna from the roulette tables begging forgiveness and harshly reprimanding himself for his losses. This emotionalism caused Anna to worry that he would suffer other epileptic seizures. Because she had witnessed so many of these during their time together, Anna recognized how traumatic they could be for her husband and for herself.

Thus, Anna wanted to avoid further gambling episodes and their aftermath: having to constantly soothe her irritable, nervous, and bad-tempered husband when he returned from the casino empty-handed. In his review of Frank's volume of biography, *The Miraculous Years, 1865–1871*, critic Stanislaw Baranczak (1995) lists all the difficulties Anna had to face from her much older husband:

> The epilepsy and the gambling were only the first of her husband's troubles that she had to bear. He was also highly irritable and unpredictable in his reactions; it was entirely possible for him to start a quarrel about nothing (about, say, the size of the guard of the King of Saxony) and to continue it with petty-minded obstinacy until the first of Anna's tears reduced him to begging for forgiveness. His concentration on his work made him not just a hard companion to live with but also a hard companion to see at all: he worked mostly at night, slept until noon and spent a large part of the afternoon devouring Russian newspapers in a library or café. (36)

Anna, however, never expressed contempt for her husband's weakness. Instead, she was understanding and compliant, providing comfort instead of chastisement even when he lost the largest bets. This gentle reaction to her husband's addiction was common and even approved of at the time, as we will see later in a discussion of the nineteenth-century gambling context.

Deaths in the Family

Dostoevsky had married Anna Grigoryevna Dostoevskaya (née Snitkina) in mid-February 1866, shortly after the death of his first wife, Maria. Despite Anna's gentle support, family life again caused a great deal of stress for Dostoevsky, in this case largely because of the deaths of two children. The first child Anna bore, Sonia, died at just two months of age. Both Anna and Fyodor were overcome with grief; Anna worried about her husband, as his despair was so unbearably intense (Lantz 2004, 99).

Fyodor and Anna had three other children: Lyubov, Fyodor, and Aleksei. In yet another tragedy that caused Dostoevsky great sadness, Aleksei died at the age of three, after suffering violent convulsions. Anna notes that again, Dostoevsky was affected by the child's death because he had loved Aleksei "with an almost morbid love, just as if he had sensed that he would not have the child with him for long" (Lantz 2004, 101). He felt particularly guilty because it was from him that his son had inherited the condition of epilepsy that killed him. Thus, the deaths of an eldest daughter and youngest son endangered Dostoevsky's always-fragile nervous condition.

Aside from the death of these children, in 1864, Dostoevsky faced both the death of his first wife and (more important) the death of his brother and confidant Mikhail. As noted earlier, besides the suffering it caused, Mikhail's death also put Dostoevsky in dire financial straits. Mikhail's death was particularly shattering because Dostoevsky was closer to his brother than to anyone else except Anna. The two were soulmates, as his letters to Mikhail reveal. As well, the two were business partners in publishing. With Mikhail's death, Dostoevsky's always-fragile financial condition worsened decisively, for he vowed to pay off his brother's debts and help support his family.

Financial Troubles

Dostoevsky experienced financial problems for most his life, starting when he was a young pupil at the academy. As we noted earlier, Dostoevsky was always writing to his father for more money. It is likely that Dostoevsky was acutely aware of his own (relatively low) social standing and wanted to give the appearance of wealth to fit in with his peers.

However, financial conditions were far worse when Dostoevsky was an adult, trying to support himself and his family. Gambling had made Dostoevsky's financial situation worse, but taking on the debts of his deceased brother Mikhail placed an even heavier load on Dostoevsky during the last fifteen years of his life.

Because he did not want his brother's reputation to be tarnished, Dostoevsky took on all twenty-five thousand rubles of Mikhail's debt (Lantz 2004). Though it's almost impossible to translate nineteenth-century rubles into current dollars, the purchasing power of such a sum would likely be worth about six or seven times a reasonably good annual salary at the time—perhaps Can$600,000 to Can$700,000 in today's money.

Besides assuming responsibility for the debts of his brother and the living expenses of his brother's family, Dostoevsky continued to support a large number of other people. Aleksandr Rizenkampf, Dostoevsky's friend during the 1830s, notes that "Fyodor Mikhailovich [Dostoevsky] was one of those people whose whole entourage lived well while he himself was continuously in need" (Lantz 2004, 260). Members of this "entourage" now included Mikhail's widow, Emiliya Fyodorovna, and her four children, as well as Mikhail's mistress and her son. Dostoevsky also supported Pavel, a stepson from his previous marriage to Maria.

Further, even when Dostoevsky was hard up for money, he regularly sent money to his younger brother Nikolai, who had become poor because of his alcohol addiction. Finally, Dostoevsky also financially supported Martha Brown, a young vagabond whom he pitied. Because he was so intent on helping all of these people through their own monetary struggles, Dostoevsky had next to nothing left to provide for his own needs.

Dostoevsky's wife, Anna, notes that these people took advantage of Dostoevsky's kindness. The moment he "got hold of any money, all his relatives—his brother, sister-in-law and nephews—instantly put forward their sudden but urgent requests." (Lantz 2004, 261). To make matters even worse, Dostoevsky's maid was stealing from him. Everyone took advantage of Dostoevsky's good nature, and he was unwilling to investigate, much less prosecute the servants, friends, and acquaintances who took advantage of him (Lantz 2004, 260).

To survive financially, Dostoevsky was forced to pawn his and Anna's possessions and take loans from moneylenders. He was also forced to agree to the terms of grossly unfair writing contracts. For example, he gave

Fyodor Timofoevich Stellovsky the right to publish an edition of his collected works in exchange for the advance of a mere three thousand rubles. Along with this, Dostoevsky promised to provide Stellovsky with a new 160-page novel (*The Gambler*, mentioned earlier) by November 1, 1866. The contract stated that if he failed to meet these terms, Stellovsky could claim the right to publish all of Dostoevsky's works for the next nine years without having to pay royalties (Lantz 2004, 412).

Dostoevsky felt that working under this pressure hindered his writing, and he was likely right to think so. He complained to Mikhail that "out of poverty I am *compelled* to write hastily and to write for money; so it follows that my writing *suffers*" (Lantz 2004, 261). To his friend Aleksandr Wrangel he wrote, "Working out of need has crushed and corroded me" (Lantz 2004, 261).

Financial strain forced Dostoevsky to work under this continuing pressure, as he would be unable to provide for his dependents if he did not meet all his deadlines and fulfill his contracts. Money problems thus caused Dostoevsky to feel he wasn't able to produce his best work—yet another source of stress.

Ironically, some of Dostoevsky's greatest masterpieces were produced under these harsh conditions. *The Gambler, Crime and Punishment, The Idiot,* and *The Devils* were all written when Dostoevsky was hardest-pressed for money, mainly because of his gambling and family obligations. Of all Dostoevsky's major works, only *The Brothers Karamazov* was completed during a time of financial stability. These results may be impressive—may even seem like an endorsement of pain and deprivation. However, Dostoevsky's mental and physical health suffered to produce these works under such conditions. Moreover, working out of desperation for money caused Dostoevsky to feel anxious and unsatisfied with his work.

In short, a near-permanent combination of stress, anxiety, and financial need set the stage for Dostoevsky's gambling problem. Dostoevsky himself claims that he gambled in order to win money quickly and easily, money he could then use to pay his debts and support his many dependents. Some might conclude, therefore, that need was the main factor driving Dostoevsky to gamble. Supporting this view, we have quotations from Dostoevsky explaining that he always gambled in hopes of winning money and had developed a system or strategy that he felt guaranteed consistent winning.

Yet, if we adopt this simple explanation of Dostoevsky's gambling, we are stuck with important unanswered questions. First, why do the majority

of impoverished people—in nineteenth-century Russia and elsewhere—
not become gamblers, much less problem gamblers? Second, why do so
many people—in nineteenth-century Russia and elsewhere—gamble
beyond their means even if they are *not* impoverished? Third and finally,
why did Dostoevsky continue to gamble long after it became apparent—
was apparent to anyone—that he was *not* solving but worsening his financial problems by gambling?

So, the perpetual shortage of money is an important part of Dostoevsky's
gambling problem—as cognitive psychologists might call it, a "trigger" for
gambling—but not the entire explanation. We must also remember that
Dostoevsky had already tried a variety of other strategies for dealing with
his life stresses. In the end, we will see that gambling was just another in a
long line of strategies he tried. But first, we will consider the alternatives.

Strategies Dostoevsky Used to Cope

In previous sections, we have described various problems that caused
Dostoevsky a great deal of stress and anxiety. They have included physical
ailments, epilepsy, and anxiety attacks; imprisonment and exile; strained
relations with a wife and a mistress; the deaths of two children, a wife, and
beloved brother; and an endless shortage of money.

Against this backdrop of severe and continuing adversity, we can see
Dostoevsky's involvement with religion and nationalism as responses to,
or supports against, the stress and emotional damage of everyday life. Of
course, Dostoevsky and many other young people—nourished by forbidden revolutionary writings from Europe—had good reason to rebel against
the repressive czarist regime of his day, so Dostoevsky's political response
was not purely personal. Still, we cannot doubt a personal element in his
political actions, since the vast majority of young Russians did *not* become
active revolutionaries, nor ardent nationalists.

So, in this section, we will give a brief outline of the religious and
nationalistic values Dostoevsky held, and the way in which they may have
distracted him from his problems, however briefly.

Religious and Nationalistic Beliefs

Religious orthodoxy was nothing new to the adult Dostoevsky. He had
been born into a family of devout Orthodox Christians. Dostoevsky
claimed that his religious education began in his childhood, with his

mother's use of a book called *One Hundred and Four Sacred Stories from the Old and New Testaments* in teaching him and his siblings how to read. Thus, Dostoevsky and his siblings "knew the Gospel almost from the cradle" (Frank 2009, 24). Following these lessons from their mother, the Dostoevsky children received a more formal education from a church deacon (Frank 2009). Beginning in 1831, Dostoevsky's mother took her older children on annual pilgrimages to the Trinity-St. Sergei monastery, some one hundred kilometres east of Moscow. Andrei later described these journeys influencing the children's lives.

In adulthood, Dostoevsky's religious views were deeply connected with his nationalistic, Slavophile beliefs. Slavophilism was a Russian intellectual movement that emerged in the 1830s and contained religious Orthodoxy at its core (Lantz 2004). It was rooted in the idea of a free and harmonious Slavic collective united under a single, common faith. Members of a Slavophilic commune were expected to renounce their egoism and their individuality, to speak in a single voice. Doing so was viewed as a noble, Christian act (Lantz 2004). In short, the Slavophiles argued that Russians were able to live in a genuine community precisely because their Orthodox faith meant a renunciation of egoism.

Some have claimed to find evidence of "unconscious Slavophilism" in Dostoevsky's work, though Dostoevsky never fully identified himself as a Slavophile (Lantz 2004, 399).

Dostoevsky's friend Aleksandr Miliukov claims that Dostoevsky felt the aims of socialism were noble, yet viewed the socialists as "estimable dreamers." Dostoevsky, like the Slavophiles, looked to Russian rather than to Western ideologies for guidance—a theme that is evident in his writings, including *The Gambler*, as we will see.

Dostoevsky's dispute with socialism was not only that it sought answers outside Russia, but also that it was fundamentally atheistic and materialistic. Along these lines, Dostoevsky argued, "the socialists go no further than the belly" and deny the spiritual essence of human nature (Lantz 2004, 404).

The only socialism Dostoevsky viewed positively was that of the 1840s, a socialism that was heavily influenced by the novelist George Sand and that emphasized spiritual concerns. Dostoevsky favoured "Russian socialism." However, this "tribal socialism"—this union of people by blood—had little to do with real socialism, since it failed to address a theme central to socialism, namely, the struggle between people in different classes who shared the same blood.

No doubt, Dostoevsky was a nationalist more than a socialist— even an ardent nationalist from an early age. He was convinced that a significant difference existed between Russians and Europeans, even before having studied Slavophilism in depth. Dostoevsky noted that he "grew up on Karamzin" (Lantz 2004, 212). Karamzin's (2004) *History of the Russian State,* from which Dr. Dostoevsky read to his children, proclaimed that Russia needed a strong central power to defend itself from its enemies. Perhaps because of this upbringing drenched in nationalistic ideas, Dostoevsky deeply believed that Russians needed to create a distinctive nationhood grounded patriotically in traditional Russian values.

During his four-year stay in Europe (1867–71), Dostoevsky's Russian nationalism increased, giving rise to beliefs similar to those of the Slavophile thinkers. For example, Dostoevsky came to accept the Slavophile belief that Orthodoxy lay at the core of Russian culture. Thus in the 1860s, Dostoevsky began to believe that "Russia's salvation lay in a return to . . . Orthodoxy and the monarchy" (Lantz 2004, 269). The character Shatov in Dostoevsky's political novel, *The Demons,* offers the most forceful expression of this nationalism. For Shatov, a character who mouths the views of the pan-Slavist thinker Nikolai Danilevski, the essence of a nation lies in its religion, and the force that moves a nation to develop is the nation's search for God. Shatov is a caricature of nationalist ideology, but in this respect only an exaggeration of Dostoevsky's own views.

So, it is evident that Dostoevsky's religious views were deeply connected to his nationalistic beliefs, and both helped him cope with adversity, since both provide a sense of meaning and potency in difficult times.

After the death of two of his children, for example, Dostoevsky sought religious counsel in his efforts to relieve feelings of guilt and grief. Dostoevsky also tried to cope with his health problems by convincing himself that sickness improved his religious practices, for he believed that he couldn't be truly spiritual while completely healthy. Rather, he saw suffering and hardship as the only road to salvation. Likewise, Dostoevsky turned to his nationalistic and religious beliefs when faced with prison and exile, using these beliefs to cope with the physical and emotional hardships.

Encounters with the cosmopolitan, secular ideas of the 1840s had led Dostoevsky to question his nationalistic upbringing. However, his imprisonment in Siberia gradually strengthened his traditional Russian beliefs. Nationalism made imprisonment and exile in Siberia somewhat easier for Dostoevsky. The exile also brought him into close contact with people who were largely untouched by Western ideas, and who were hesitant to socialize with non-Russians as a result. While in exile, Dostoevsky wrote the following to the Russian poet Apollon Maikov:

> They were the Russian people, my brothers in misfortune, and I had the happiness more than once to find generosity even in the soul of a robber, precisely because I was able to understand him; for I myself was Russian. (Lantz 2004, 268)

Thus, Dostoevsky was able to feel comfortable with his fellow inmates mainly because of his nationalistic values. These values helped Dostoevsky cope with his dire circumstances while imprisoned and exiled. Dostoevsky turned once again to his strong nationalistic beliefs during the four years he spent in Europe fleeing his Russian creditors. He noted that feeling isolated and excluded from Russian intellectual life strengthened his nationalistic sentiments. By appealing to nationalism with Orthodox Christianity at its core, Dostoevsky was able to overcome his feelings of alienation while abroad.

Though not devised for the purpose, these nationalistic and religious beliefs were mechanisms through which Dostoevsky tried to cope with his various health, financial, and relationship problems. Additionally, Dostoevsky's commitment to these beliefs provides a sign of what the researchers Theodor W. Adorno et al. (1950) called the "authoritarian personality." Nationalism, ethnocentrism, religiosity, and anti-Semitism—which Dostoevsky displayed to varying degrees at different times—are all correlates (or indicators) of a personality constellation with other interesting and biographically relevant correlates.

Nowhere is this authoritarian tendency more evident than in articles Dostoevsky wrote in March 1877 on "the Jewish Question" and on the accusations of anti-Semitism that had already been levelled at him (Dostoevsky 2009[1877], 349–74). Here, Dostoevsky blames "The Jew" for exploiting the Russian people, endlessly demanding pity for the hatred he's suffered, and keeping himself apart from the Christian population. Obviously, this document reads differently with the Holocaust as a backdrop, but even in its time, no one could have mistaken Dostoevsky's impatience with "the Jewish Question."

As Adorno et al. (1950) show in their hallmark study of authoritarians (or proto-fascists), the kinds of ethnocentric views Dostoevsky embraced are also correlated with excessive conformity, submissiveness to authority, intolerance, insecurity, and rigid thought patterns, and particularly with anti-intraception, superstition and stereotyping, and projectivity. Some might say the whole of Dostoevsky's literary corpus can be viewed as an effort to sublimate and project outward deeply troubling emotions and beliefs about good and evil.

True, Dostoevsky was not submissive and conformist in all of his behaviour, as one might expect from an authoritarian. In fact, he struggled throughout his life with the themes of freedom and constraint. But the fact of his continued struggle with these themes—highlighted in works like *Crime and Punishment, Notes from the Underground, The Demons,* and *The Gambler*—hints at an authoritarian background from which Dostoevsky was struggling to emerge.

Further, if this analysis is correct, Adorno's theory supports our understanding of Dostoevsky's development as a person and an artist. In their research, Adorno et al. (1950) found that authoritarians tend to grow up under the authority of cold or harsh parents who brook no criticism and disobedience. In effect, these children learn authoritarianism from authoritarian parents. Also, as Freud might have proposed, they react to this harsh parenting by building fantasy worlds full of evil, danger, and sexual misdoings. Driven by a sense of chaos and immorality lurking outside the walls of orderly submission, they impose harsh rules on themselves and others. They seek conformity and submission at any price; otherwise, guilt and fantasy prevail.

This is *not* to argue that the whole of Dostoevsky's work might be explained by his authoritarian tendencies; it is to assert that there are more than a few authoritarian tendencies in his thinking, and these tendencies are—in our view and Adorno's—traceable back to childhood. Thus, in understanding his work, one can no more ignore Dostoevsky's authoritarian upbringing than one can ignore the social and cultural context in which he was writing.

As is well known, Dostoevsky was particularly critical of what he considered European—especially, Jewish European—utilitarian morality, which he considered a form of "merchant culture" in which anything could be bought and sold. This presumed moral laxity fuelled his anti-Semitism, which grew apace with his nationalism and religiosity.[3]

So, his nationalistic and religious dedication are important as much for what they signify about Dostoevsky's personality as they are for helping him to cope with everyday adversities. But in the end, even nationalism and religion failed Dostoevsky, and he needed other coping strategies. In much the same way as he used his nationalistic and religious beliefs, Dostoevsky used gambling to feel confident, soothe his nerves, and forget (and hope to alleviate) his problems—in short, to cope with the harsh stresses of living.

Gambling

Dostoevsky didn't begin gambling heavily until his travels abroad in the early 1860s; however, he had been exposed to gambling for much of his life. Kenneth Lantz (2012) reports that:

> The earliest reference I can find to D.'s own gambling comes from his brother Andrei's memoirs. He says: "I don't know how it was in later life, but during his early days as an officer my brother was very keen on playing cards. Games of whist or preference were only the beginning; the evening always ended in gambling at *shtoss* or faro." Andrei doesn't give a date for this, but it would have been during D.'s one-year military career after finishing the Engineering Academy, from mid-1843 to mid-1844. He also lost part of his inheritance playing billiards in 1844. And while serving in the ranks in Siberia he would watch in fascination as other soldiers gambled, though he had no money to participate himself. (personal communication)

To repeat, Dostoevsky's fascination with gambling began in 1844, when he lost 1,000 francs in a pool game. He was reintroduced to gambling during his Siberian exile, when he watched the soldiers gamble. But Dostoevsky didn't participate then; though infected by the gamblers' excitement, he lacked the money needed to play. He later told an acquaintance in Semipalatinsk: "A devilish game like that is like quicksand. I see and understand how vile this monstrous passion is . . . and yet it draws me as if it's sucking me in" (Lantz 2004, 156).

On his first trip abroad in 1862, Dostoevsky visited a casino in Wiesbaden, where he quickly won 11,000 francs. The next summer, although he had planned to meet Polina in Paris, Dostoevsky went again to Wiesbaden, where he won again, this time 10,400 francs. However, because he could not keep his resolve and walk away from the table, he ended up losing half of his winnings. After meeting Polina in Paris, Dostoevsky returned to the casino again. This time he lost everything and was forced to ask his family for money to fund his return trip home (Lantz 2004).

In 1863, Dostoevsky described these early instances of gambling to his brother Mikhail as follows:

> In Wiesbaden I devised a system of playing . . . and immediately won ten thousand francs. The next morning I strayed from the system . . . and immediately lost all my money. . . . In the evening I returned to the same system in all strictness and I soon won three thousand francs. . . . People win tens of thousands here without even trying. (Lantz 2004, 157)

His desperate need for money to support himself and his dependents encouraged Dostoevsky to continue gambling, but like most gamblers, he lost more than he won, worsening his already dire financial situation.

What's also obvious from this letter is Dostoevsky's belief that he could build a "system" that would allow him to win consistently at his favourite game, roulette. In 1859, Dostoevsky read an article called *From the Notes of a Gambler*, from which he devised his supposed "system." He determined not to succumb to greed or passion while at the roulette table, planning to walk away from the table each day with a small sum of winnings. But, like all problem gamblers, he broke his own rule repeatedly. After losing all his money, he rightly blamed the loss on his inability to follow his own rule and stop playing once he had won.

Dostoevsky's gambling resurfaced while he and Anna were living in Europe. During the summer of 1867, while in Baden-Baden, Dostoevsky repeatedly pawned and reclaimed Anna's jewellery and various articles of clothing to fund his gambling at the roulette tables. Eventually, he used up all of their money and had to request funds from Anna's mother to reclaim the items he had pawned. With the money in hand, Dostoevsky went to reclaim Anna's jewellery, only to return that evening in tears, having once again lost everything at the roulette table. Anna was finally forced to go with him to recover their possessions (Lantz 2004).

In various respects, Anna did not hold the same views as her husband about Dostoevsky's gambling.[4] In her memoirs, Anna wrote that she found it unusual that a man who had endured so many hardships with fortitude could not resist gambling away the money they needed to survive. According to Lantz (2004), her patient attitude changed:

> Soon [she] realized this was no simple "weakness of will" but an all-consuming passion, an elemental force against which even a strong character could not struggle. One had to come to terms with it, to look at his gambling passion as an illness for which there was no cure. (157)

Despite many letters to Anna promising he would never gamble again, Dostoevsky gambled one more time during the last few months of their stay in Europe. In the spring of 1871, Dostoevsky felt depressed about the progress he was making with his new novel, *The Devils*. Anna decided to let him risk half of their savings at the roulette table. She knew from experience that Dostoevsky's creative forces could be rejuvenated if his "itch to gamble" was satisfied (Lantz 2004, 157). As expected, Dostoevsky lost everything, including the money Anna had sent him for his fare home.

There may be no better, and certainly no earlier, description of life with a gambling addict than what Anna Snitkina has provided in *Dostoevsky Portrayed by His Wife: The Diary and Reminiscences of Mme. Dostoevsky* (Dostoevsky 1926). The portion of this diary concerned with the period 1867–71 (pages 51–137) is peppered with references to Dostoevsky's gambling preoccupation and gambling losses. Repeatedly, Anna presents herself as a bystander watching a tragedy unfold. For example, she writes:

> We had now fifty Louis and could go on quite securely. I asked Fedya to do me the favour of not going to the tables today; for I had observed that if one won, one ought not to go back the same day, otherwise, one would lose. And why, indeed, not be satisfied. But Fedya asked me for five Louis just to try his luck; perhaps today was his lucky day and he would win more. Not to

give him the money was impossible; so I gave it him and was sure he would lose it. (Dostoevsky 1926, 73)

Was Anna an "enabler," who unintentionally encouraged Dostoevsky's gambling addiction? What was going through her mind when she gave him the gambling money he wanted? Here is what she thought, in her own words:

To relieve his anxiety and disperse his gloomy thoughts, which prevented him from concentrating on his work, I had recourse to the device which had always helped to distract and amuse him. As we possessed then about three hundred thalers, I said that it would be worthwhile to try once more our luck at roulette. I pointed out that as he had occasionally happened to win, there was no reason why we should not hope that our luck would turn this time. I certainly did not entertain any hope of his winning at roulette, and I was very sorry to part with the hundred thalers, which it was necessary to sacrifice; but I knew by experience of his former visits to the tables that, after those exciting emotions, after satisfying his craving for risk, his passion for gambling, Fiodor would return home calmed, and that then, realizing the futility of his hopes of winning at the tables, he would sit down with renewed strength to his novel, and in a couple of weeks would make good his losses. (Dostoevsky 1926, 135)

Dostoevsky, pleased with this offer, set out with 120 thalers, stipulating that if he were to lose these, Anna should send him his return fare. He stayed at Wiesbaden for a week and, as expected, lost all his money—or, as Anna says, "his playing ended in disaster."

According to Helfant (2003), Anna comes to terms with her husband's gambling in two ways:

First, she places it in the context of the political persecution and personal tragedies that he had endured, thereby both . . . implying that his need to gamble may have reflected these earlier traumas. Second, she identifies his addiction as a poetic weakness, rather than simply a result of lack of willpower. (241)

Yet, finally Dostoevsky's addiction came to an end. In a letter to Anna dated 1871 in which he asked for more money, Dostoevsky swore that he would never gamble again. He told her that he had a terrifying dream of his father, "looking so dreadful, such as I had only dreamt of him twice before in my life, predicting a terrible calamity, and both times the dream came true." He continued:

> Anya, I lie at your feet, I kiss them, and I know that you have every right to despise me and so to think, "he'll gamble again." . . . But, my angel, you must understand: I know full well that you would die if I gambled again! . . . [N]ow my hands have been untied; they have been bound by gambling, but now I will think about my work and not dream for whole nights at a time about gambling, as I used to. (Lantz 2004, 158)

After this final humiliation, Dostoevsky stayed true to his word. The episode in 1871 was, as promised, his last encounter with gambling. Anna reports that:

> I, of course, could not all at once believe in such great happiness as Fiodor's indifference to roulette. He had promised me not to play so many times before and never found the strength to keep his word. But this time the happiness was realized. Later on, during his travels abroad (in 1874, 1875, 1876, 1879) Fiodor never once went to a casino. . . . He was no longer drawn to it. It was as though Fiodor's "fancy" of winning at roulette was a sort of diabolical suggestion or disease of which he suddenly and forever cured himself. He returned from Wiesbaden cheerful and calm, and immediately sat down to the continuation of his novel, *The Devils.* . . . All my husband's thoughts were turned to the new period opening before us [back home in Russia], and he speculated on how he would find his old friends and relations, who, he thought might have changed considerably in the last four year. In himself, he was conscious of certain definite changes in his views and convictions. (Dostoevsky 1926, 136–37)

Problem gamblers today still express the agonized, self-abasing sentiments Dostoevsky wrote after his last loss, and that's a good thing. Such self-abasement is usually the beginning of recovery from addiction, as it was in Dostoevsky's case.[5]

But what of the ten-year gambling urge that seems to have disappeared into thin air after 1871? Where did Dostoevsky put his wild imagination, his desire for risks, his need for provocation and moody self-expression, now that the roulette wheel was off-bounds? Here, psychiatrist Richard Rosenthal (2005) may have suggested a useful clue:

> Alcoholics Anonymous refers to the alcoholic who has stopped drinking, but who still demonstrates alcoholic attitudes and behaviors, as a "dry drunk." Such individuals are said to have abstinence but not sobriety. They are considered at risk for relapse. Although the concept of the dry drunk has been adopted by other self-help programs, "staying in action" is an equivalent and arguably more meaningful expression to use for the understanding and treatment of many pathological gamblers. The author discusses covert gambling, mind bets, switching and fusing of addictions, procrastination, risk-taking, and power games: a repertoire of ways in which the individual can remain in a gambling mind-set while technically abstinent.

Perhaps, we can view Dostoevsky's last major work—*A Writer's Diary*, written in pieces between 1873 and 1881—as a way of "staying in action." Not a true diary so much as a series of mind games—indeed, power games—with the reader, perhaps this last work was Dostoevsky's last attempt to thumb his nose at fate and the various "lofty" personages in his world, in this way releasing his now pent-up need to "stay in action." Perhaps this was Dostoevsky's final way of gambling, now that he had given up the roulette wheel.

Gambling in Nineteenth-Century Russia

It is easy to view Dostoevsky's gambling problem as nothing more than a psychological aberration: a flawed, foolish way of coping with continued stress, hardship, and failure. But Dostoevsky turned to gambling nonetheless: he "chose" this coping mechanism (or neurotic symptom of depression)—not suicide, homicide, drugs, or anorexia, for example. Nor did he choose another way of gaining needed money—not burglary, bank robbery, or embezzlement, for example.

To understand why Dostoevsky chose gambling, we need to understand the role of gambling in nineteenth-century Russian society. So, we will briefly explore the cultural norms and values associated with gambling at that time. These were the norms and values that pushed and pulled Dostoevsky toward gambling in his times of trouble. Here, the key work on the topic is Ian Helfant's 1997 dissertation, *The High Stakes of Identity: Gambling in the Life and Literature of Nineteenth-Century Russia*, published as a book in 2002. It should be noted that this is a book of literary criticism grounded in history, not a book of history illustrated by literature, yet the two topics and approaches intermingle, and sometimes get confused, because they are so closely related. Indeed, where Dostoevsky scholarship is concerned, it is almost impossible to separate sociology from history and literary criticism.[1]

Why Russians Gambled

Helfant (2002) tells us that, by the beginning of the nineteenth century, gambling was well established as both a form of entertainment and a business, all across Europe. Moreover, gambling was already popular in Russia, where members of almost every social class took part in it. Gambling was particularly popular with the nobility, and, as result, many Russians associated gambling with status, courage, and bravado. They believed they could gain respect from others by emulating the aristocracy and displaying noble qualities while they gambled.

Many people used gambling to bolster their reputation by making themselves into "pleasant players." As Helfant (1999) notes in his article "Pushkin's Ironic Performances as a Gambler," Prince P.A. Viazemskii, an observer of aristocratic life in nineteenth-century Russia, even claimed that gambling style could influence the way other people thought of a person:

> In Russia the card game often serves as a touchstone and standard of a person's moral stature. "He's a pleasant player" is sufficient praise to establish a person favourably in society. (Helfant 1999, 375)

"Pleasant" meant being good-natured about the game and paying off one's debts promptly: doing so led people to see you as honest, well mannered, and well brought up. Possessing these characteristics helped you develop a reputation as a respectable, honourable individual, all because you were a "pleasant" person to gamble with.

The specific attitudes and emotions gamblers were supposed to display were even laid out in a manual on gambling. According to this manual, an admirable gambler showed composure, dignity, calmness, and confidence. This same admirable gambler continued to play and place bets after winning a lot of money, to give other players a chance to win the money back. Another stipulation was that debts should be repaid within twenty-four hours. In short, well-mannered gamblers in nineteenth-century Russia were supposed to obey a strict behavioural code; if they did so, they could develop and maintain a good reputation.

Russians of all social classes gambled, but wealthy aristocrats gambled the most often. This is likely because they had time and money to spare for leisure activities; as a result, gambling allowed them to signal their prestige, wealth, and high social status (Helfant 2002)—the privilege of having leisure time.

Another such aristocratic activity was duelling. It involved risking your life for the sake of saving your reputation in society. Both of these behaviours—gambling and duelling—made nineteenth-century Russian noblemen feel they were defending their honour and reputation. A challenge to duel is paralleled in gambling by a challenge to match a large bet. Failure to accept either challenge marked you as a coward, threatening your sense of honour and tarnishing your reputation. Further, any dispute over a game (such as an accusation of cheating, for example) could result in a duel, with the men involved fighting to defend their honour. Just as duelling was seen as an integral part of the Russian aristocratic identity, so, too, was gambling seen as a way for gentlemen to distinguish themselves as honourable and worthy.

Gambling and duelling were particularly common among those in the army, but they were even popular among noblemen who were unable to fight in wars. Men who were unable to participate in battle often felt they could display heroism and bravery by gambling or accepting challenges to duel (Helfant 2002). Like war, duelling demands physical combat and can often lead to death. Gambling seems at first to be very different, unrelated to war. However, many Russians viewed gambling as a "war-like arena" for asserting dominance. Both activities supplied an opportunity for heroism and bravery. By doing so, they gave Russian men an opportunity to build reputations as noble, respectable, and honourable.

Both gambling and duelling also let nobles show off their refinement and status. In both activities, the participants are put under great pressure. Their ability to show "grace under pressure"—to remain calm, confident, and composed—marked them as having an aristocratic character. The highest stakes—a challenge to fight to the death, or to match a hefty bet— were the hardest to face with calm and composure. So, men who could calmly handle the highest stakes gained a reputation for being pleasant, refined, classy, and (therefore) honourable. On the other hand, a show of uneasiness or anxiety when faced with these high stakes led to disrepute for cowardice, therefore shame.

Because gambling gave people an opportunity to display their admirable characteristics, even gambling losses had social value. Such losses were tests of character, just like battle. After incurring a heavy debt, the loser could enhance his reputation by paying the winner graciously and in a timely manner. For this reason, many men even paid their debts to winners whom they knew had cheated. This was because, as Helfant writes, "one's honour could be imperilled by refusing to pay even an opponent who appeared to have been cheating—if he portrayed the event differently" (Helfant 2002, 15).

What makes this even more impressive is that gambling debts were not recognized, nor payments enforced, by the Russian government at this time. Nonetheless, Russian gentlemen felt bound by a "debt of honour" after losses at gambling. This was not unique to Russia; indeed, it was characteristic of the European aristocracy as a whole. Thomas Kavanagh, in his 1993 book, *Enlightenment and the Shadows of Chance*, about gambling in the court of Versailles under Louis XV, asserts that gambling—like duelling—was meant to show bravery and a disdain for risk and loss. Of this French aristocratic outlook, so like the Russian one, Helfant (2002) writes:

> Kavanagh (1993, 42) argues that the notion of the debt of honour marked gambling as an aristocratic pursuit. Gambling debts had no legal status; therefore, an aristocrat who chose to pay a gambling debt was demonstrating his freedom of choice, rather than submitting to a legal code imposed upon him by the state. (7)

In short, upholding a respectable reputation was far more important to these aristocratic gamblers than making or losing money. In fact, showing no concern for the money they could (and often did) lose may have been the real reason these aristocrats did gamble. This carefree attitude about money marked them as members of the upper class. By gambling extensively and placing large bets, they were asserting they could afford to lead a risky, glamorous lifestyle. Not all of the Russian nobility were wealthy—what they had in common was a history (and ethic) of service to the state. Although they were not a landed aristocracy, as in Britain, for example, many of them did possess land and considerable money.

No wonder, then, that their behaviour recalls the "conspicuous consumption" discussed in Thorstein Veblen's (1912) famous commentary on the American leisure class at the end of the nineteenth century, and its equally inane and honorific practices of conspicuous consumption (sometimes also called "conspicuous waste"). Veblen's book *Theory of the Leisure Class* is a critique of "barbarism" in early twentieth-century Western society, especially a critique of the "conspicuous consumption" of the upper-class bourgeoisie, whom Veblen described as living a life of ease and leisure as though every day were a holiday. Veblen argued that the symbolic nature of social prestige—with its emphasis on fads and fashions, for example—encouraged a wasteful, even barbaric consumption of time and goods. This manner of living he contrasted (unfavourably) with Germany, and its fascination with science, technology, industry, and industriousness.

Nevertheless, Veblen (1912) shows that even this conspicuously wasteful consumption serves a purpose: it reaffirms the status and power of people who can afford to live that way. It is through such costly waste that the upper classes distinguish themselves from people less wealthy than themselves. For example, the practice of topiary requires great skill, time, and money, so through topiary people with elaborate gardens can prove they have access to plenty of money and labour power. Along similar lines, they will give lavish costume parties, in which guests are expected to wear expensive one-occasion costumes, coming as Cardinal Richelieu or Marie Antoinette. Even guest celebrities may be hired to attend at great cost to the host, so that this party will be the party of the year.

For Veblen (1912), nothing is more conspicuously wasteful, therefore honorific, than activities that require a great deal of skill yet have no intrinsic value. Take the learning of new, complicated dances: these dances hold no value except as entertainment, yet because of their complexity, only rich people can afford the time to learn and practise them (and afford the teachers to teach them). As a result, familiarity with these new, complicated dances is a clear marker of people's social standing, via their conspicuous waste.

In nineteenth-century Russia, similar activities were used to define and identify high social status. Additionally, gambling played this role as a "status marker." Helfant (1999) writes that "treating a serious gambling loss with nonchalance signified a nobleman's independence from material cares" (376). Dostoevsky was obviously aware of this outlook, since his protagonist in *The Gambler*, Aleksei Ivanovic, described gambling in the following way:

> There are two sorts of gambling: one the gentlemanly sort: the other the plebeian, mercenary sort, the game played by all sorts of riff-raff. . . . A gentleman . . . must on no account display an interest in winning. . . . In fact, he must look on all gambling, roulette, *trente et quarante,* as nothing else than a pastime got up entirely for his amusement. (Dostoevsky 2003[1867], 184–85)

In another passage from *The Gambler*, Dostoevsky writes that "[a] true gentleman should not show excitement even if he loses his whole fortune. Money ought to be so much below his gentlemanly dignity as to be scarcely worth worrying about" (Dostoevsky 2003[1867], 186).

Of course, not every gambler could *afford* to bet lavishly in this way. So, precisely because gambling was a sign of wealth and high social status, some ambitious men (but rarely women) gambled to create a noble image for themselves. (Aristocratic women might participate in card games out of sociability, but women generally were expected to behave moderately and exercise a moderating influence on their husbands in relation to drinking, carousing, and, of course, gambling.) Their aristocratic opponents could easily handle huge losses and debts, but often these lesser men could not. So, when the young men had incurred large debts they were unable to pay, they often resorted to suicide rather than suffer dishonour. Suicide was a way to erase the stain of irresponsible, embarrassing behaviour that had tarnished their reputations; in this way, suicide restored their honour and reputation, posthumously (Reyfman 1999, 16).

In this respect, gambling and duelling were similar. Both were matters of honour, therefore matters of life and death. The way men conducted themselves while gambling or duelling could gain them a reputation for being calm and confident, thus reinforcing their noble status. Conversely, the refusal to accept a challenge to duel, or to match an outrageously large bet, showed cowardice and tarnished one's reputation. And, just as dying in a fight to the death was better than surviving with a reputation for cowardice, committing suicide was more honourable than living but being unable to pay one's debts. In battle and gambling, death was favoured over dishonour.

Both gambling and duelling were also seen as forms of rebellion against the autocratic nineteenth-century Russian government. Because the government had banned duelling, men who took part were sometimes seen as rebels against the czarist regime. Similarly, because gambling had been strictly outlawed for a long time, men who gambled were sometimes also thought to be opposed to the czarist government. Gambling was thus viewed as a way to rebel or protest against a government whose primary injustice was to ban gambling—an activity that aristocrats relied on to display their wealth, status, and cultivation.

However, as Helfant (1999) points out, this was an autocratic age, and aristocrats could get away with behaviour that gentry, workers, and peasants could not. He writes:

> Gambling symbolized an age in which autocratic whim prevailed over the
> rules of law, in which social and economic privilege depended as much

upon arbitrary factors as upon one's skills. In this context, card play, which had been imported from western Europe in the seventeenth century and was endemic among the Russian nobility by the early nineteenth century, formed both a central preoccupation and a multivalent area of significan[ce] in Pushkin's milieu. (374)

Both card games of calculation (or skill) and games of chance were popular. The aristocracy mainly favoured games of calculation over games of chance, because games of calculation require skill, hence the leisure time to develop this skill. Today, a common and thoroughly Russian game of calculation is Durak, which allegedly every Russian and Eastern European adult knows how to play. Its goal is to avoid being "the fool" left holding unwanted cards.[2] In the nineteenth century, popular games of calculation included Whistle, Rakombol, and Three and Three. They were won by accumulating cards of the same value or suit, or in sequences, and often they were played in teams, or with partners. Thus, they required shared strategies of bidding and betting, and careful attention to the flow of cards on the table.

To engage successfully in a complex game of calculation, you needed prior knowledge, practice, and skill (Helfant 2002). For this reason, people tended to view games of calculation as more challenging and respectable than games of chance: they were brainy as well as courageous. Most important, they were—in Veblen's (1912) terms—a form of conspicuous waste: elaborate entertainments that few people could bother to learn and practise, while lacking intrinsic value except as a status marker.

So, games of calculation were often played by older, more experienced, and wealthier members of the gentry and aristocratic classes. By playing these games "pleasantly," they showed themselves to be people of substance. They displayed their skills and expertise, as well as their ability to pay their debts quickly and easily. And they we able to show they had the money, hence leisure, to perfect the skills needed for these games.

Playing games of calculation also showed you had been born into the aristocracy. You were less likely to know these kinds of games and play them well if you hadn't been born and raised by a noble family. As well, these games of chance had the highest stakes, so they offered the best opportunities to display confidence and calmness under the worst circumstances. Thus people who played games of calculation were readily recognized as noble by birth, while those who engaged in games of chance could, at best, be seen as trying to improve their social status by showing they possessed noble qualities. And since these games of calculation were allowed by the czarist regime, playing them did not constitute rebellion against the government.

Unlike games of calculation, games of chance (like roulette or dice) were entirely based on luck and didn't require any previous practice or skill. Most often, young men, especially military men, played these kinds of games. Playing these kinds of games bestowed no honour or respectability in the way that games of calculation did, since neither skill nor experience was needed to play. Because Russian law had forbidden certain (lower class) games of chance—for example, roulette and other games of pure chance—many gamblers, including Dostoevsky, travelled abroad to gamble.

Why (Non-Aristocratic) People Like Dostoevsky Gambled

Because (almost) everyone—at least, all males—gambled in nineteenth-century Russia, there were many conflicting ideas at the time about what kind of person "a gambler" was. Obviously, not every gambler was "noble" or "honourable," nor was every "noble" or "honourable" person a gambler. Some people were regarded as aristocratic for placing huge bets carelessly and showing no concern for the money they might lose. Other people who bet this way were regarded as fools. Helfant (2002) notes that impoverished people like Dostoevsky were viewed as irrational and wasteful when they gambled away their hard-earned money. Though aristocrats could use gambling to buttress their image as wealthy, high-class people, people like Dostoevsky could not do the same; they could not even use gambling to improve their social standing.

It is doubtful that anyone took Dostoevsky for a carefree aristocrat when he gambled. He had huge debts and was financially responsible for his deceased brother's family, as well as for his own. Gambling seemed to him a good way to gain the money he needed to improve his finances. He probably wasn't able to remain calm and confident when he lost large sums of money, or even interested in trying to do so. Instead, he would have been anguished by the huge problems each gambling loss created for him financially. Yet he seemingly could not stop.

Because he was concerned with winning money, Dostoevsky tried to come up with a "system" for winning. By observing other gamblers while on his frequent gambling trips, he came to believe that he had discovered the secret to winning at roulette. In a letter written to Mrs. W.D. Konstaninoff in September 1863, Dostoevsky claimed:

> For the last four days I have been examining the gamblers. Many hundreds of people take part in it, but only two really understand how to play—a French woman, and an English lord. They understand how to play and lose nothing; they even almost broke the bank. . . . I know their secret, and it is amazingly simple and stupid: at every moment one must compose oneself, and at no phase of the game can one get overheated. That is all. . . . It is only a question of whether the man who knows this secret also has the strength and the capability to use it properly. (Carter 2006, 186)

Dostoevsky genuinely believed that by controlling his emotional reaction to the outcome of his bets, he could behave rationally. This would allow him to act in a cool, calculating way, which he believed was the key to winning at roulette (Carter 2006).

For, if he could control his betting (and his losses) by controlling his emotions—by walking away from the table with winnings as soon as he started to lose—Dostoevsky could reduce the risk of loss from games of chance. And if he could reduce the risk by following the rules of his "system," he wasn't gambling at all—just earning money. Yet, paradoxically, Dostoevsky also loved risk. In *The Gambler*, Dostoevsky writes, "I was overcome by a terrible thirst for risk. Maybe having gone through so many sensations, my soul was not sated but only exacerbated by them and demanded more sensations ever stronger and stronger to the point of utter exhaustion" (Dostoevsky 2003[1867], 296). This does not sound like a prudent, rational, and systematic approach to gambling at all.

Where was his long-suffering second wife when Dostoevsky was losing all the family funds? Like most Russian women, she tolerated the gambling of her husband. In failing to show her disapproval for his roulette habit, Anna Dostoevsky was following the present-day cultural rules. Instead of trying to stop Dostoevsky from gambling entirely, Anna merely tried to limit his gambling. For example, as trustee of the household funds, she was able to limit the money she dispensed for each of her husband's trips to the casino (Helfant 2002). In this way, she tried to minimize his losses without alienating him, as she might have if she had forbidden him to gamble at all.

However, by giving Dostoevsky the semblance of support for his gambling, Anna enabled it and, in this way, perpetuated it. So, Anna's co-operation kept Dostoevsky's affection, but it did not improve their financial situation. The huge responsibility Dostoevsky had taken on, to provide for both his brother's family and his own, put great financial pressure on him. The gambling had also gotten him further into debt, intensifying the financial pressure.

Yet Dostoevsky continued to gamble recklessly, even with money he got by pawning their possessions. "Several times, they were reduced nearly to penury, having already pawned Anna's jewellery and fur-lined coat, as well as both their wedding rings, and were granted a reprieve only with the arrival of money sent by Anna's mother in Petersburg" (Helfant 2003, 237). Dostoevsky became accustomed to having Anna—and, at times, her mother—bail him out of trouble.

As noted by Helfant (2003), like other addicts, past and present, Dostoevsky kept his wife in line with a combination of lies, tears, kisses, and violence:

> Dostoevsky manipulated his wife and encouraged her acquiescence to his gambling with expressions of adoration for her meekness, on the one hand, and with emotional outbursts ranging from accusations of coldness, to threats to jump out of the window, shoot himself, or go out of his mind, on the other. (237)

Helfant (2003) also notes that, in her memoir, Anna remembers an occasion when Dostoevsky came home after having lost all the money he had taken from her:

> He asked me to give him some things to pawn immediately . . . Fedia said that he felt sick and guilty looking at me, that he was taking from me the things I valued, but what could be done. . . . He knelt before me and kissed my breast, kissed my hands, said that I was kind and good . . . and that there was no one better than me in the world. (238)

Dostoevsky's ability to manipulate Anna ensured that he faced little opposition to his gambling. This manipulation of women and their property was common in nineteenth-century Russia. Women nominally began to control their own property in the middle of the nineteenth century, when Russian noblewomen came to enjoy legal protection of their assets. During marriage, they were entitled to retain possession of both their dowry and any property they inherited, and they were to keep this property in the event of a divorce (Helfant 2003). However, these rights were rarely enforced as written. On this, William Wagner (quoted by Helfant [2003]) writes:

> Legal norms were accorded little intrinsic value by either state officials or society generally and in any case appear often to have been poorly known, unevenly enforced, and often subordinated to considerations of state policy. (231)

This meant that men, in practice, remained in charge of women's property and could do whatever they liked with it. Because of this lax enforcement of the law, and his wife's gentle nature, Dostoevsky could manipulate his wife to get the money with which to gamble. As a result, Anna—like other Russian women—was subordinate to and financially dependent on her husband, a condition only worsened by her husband's gambling problem.

Why People Travelled Long Distances to Gamble

Many men were so intent on gambling that they were willing to travel long distances to satisfy the urge. Because certain gambling practices— for example, roulette and other games of pure chance—were banned in Russia, many gamblers, including Dostoevsky travelled abroad to gamble. In Germany, where Dostoevsky liked to gamble, French investors had set up luxurious resorts in the previously obscure spa towns of Wiesbaden, Baden-Baden, and Bad Homburg (Carter 2006).

In the early nineteenth century, Wiesbaden developed into a leading casino-spa destination, attracting a wide variety of visitors from Europe and elsewhere. With the arrival of railroads after 1840, the casinos in Germany became a lot more accessible (Carter 2006), just as air travel made Las Vegas accessible to all North Americans. So, Russians like Dostoevsky who weren't legally allowed to play games of chance in Russia often visited these popular venues in Germany to gamble.

The introduction of these casinos in Germany was significant for Dostoevsky, since he did not gamble in private, informal venues, only in casinos (Carter 2006). A trip to Germany, for Dostoevsky, was like a child's visit to the candy store. Helfant (2003) writes that, three months after their marriage:

> Dostoevsky left his wife at their hotel in Dresden and went to Homburg, the site of one of Europe's major casinos, to gamble. . . . Two weeks after his return, they departed to Baden-Baden, where he played roulette for up to ten hours at a time while she, experiencing bouts of nausea caused by her first pregnancy, languished in their hotel room or went for long walks in the city. (235)

Dostoevsky thus "entered in contact with the roulette in Germany and became a slave to it with his body and soul" (Meyer and Hayer 2009, 85).

Shortly after the first of these jaunts abroad, Dostoevsky began experiencing the kinds of troubles that come with problem gambling.

The Gambling Excesses of Artists

Dostoevsky was not the only Russian author who gambled a lot, then wrote about it. Several earlier authors, including Pushkin, had written about gambling and the problems it brought. For many, writing served an almost therapeutic purpose, allowing them to openly admit their gambling-related troubles. Along these lines, in the book *Suicide as Cultural Institution in Dostoevsky's Russia,* Irina Paperno (1997) writes, "In nineteenth century Russia, literature promised solutions to problems that could not be solved by religious, social, and scientific authorities" (4). The literature of the nineteenth century highlighted the troubles of authors who (like Dostoevsky) gambled.

Critic Andrei Anikin (1993) notes that nineteenth-century writers also recognized the need for unusual steps to gain quick, easy wealth. He writes that in Pushkin's short story "The Queen of Spades" (1834):

> The story's protagonist is a young army officer so obsessed with the idea of getting rich quick that he ends by committing a murder (although an involuntary one). . . . The situation described by Pushkin also anticipates many aspects of Dostoevsky's novels. Indeed there are direct references

to both "The Queen of Spades" and "The Covetous Night" in several of Dostoevsky's works. (103)

Like Dostoevsky, other nineteenth-century Russian authors used profits from the sale of their writings to fund their gambling problem. Pushkin— the Russian equivalent to Balzac or Dickens in fame and popularity—put the money he earned from his books into gambling. In the paper "Pushkin's Ironic Performances as a Gambler," Helfant (1999) writes that Pushkin sold manuscripts of some of his early poems to his friend N.V. Vsevolozhkii to settle a gambling debt of five hundred rubles. He eventually bought these poems back, only to sell them again many times, to many other people. In effect, he pawned his poems the same way Dostoevsky pawned his wife's jewellery to pay gambling debts. Thus, classic works of nineteenth-century Russian literature financed the gambling problems of several famous writers. Even the wealthy young Count Tolstoy had to sell part of his family home to pay his gambling debts.

How Russian Gamblers Wanted to Be Viewed

To summarize, in nineteenth-century Russia, gambling could bolster a person's reputation as honourable and respectable, and could signify wealth, prestige, and high social standing. Gambling also let ordinary people (especially those who couldn't engage in battles or duels) show off their bravery, thereby gaining an honourable reputation. But this wasn't Dostoevsky's goal. Even in nineteenth-century Russia, gambling had different outcomes (and meanings) for people of different social classes, and these different people were motivated to gamble by very different reasons.

That said, understanding the Russian cultural background is important in our present study. Even for poor people like Dostoevsky, aristocratic practices gave gambling an aura of normality and nobility that helped to justify what might otherwise have been viewed as merely wasteful and deranged behaviour. The Russian cultural milieu made it easier, therefore more likely, for a gambling problem to flourish. Even though it didn't provide easy opportunities for gambling to people like Dostoevsky, who sought games of chance, it made gambling mania seem noble, artistic, or at least unexceptional. As well, the patriarchal culture of wifely compliance meant that men were free to pawn and lose the family jewels—or poems— many times over.

Gambling in nineteenth-century Russia may have meant a trip abroad, but the trip itself promised the gambler an extraordinary experience in Wiesbaden, Baden-Baden, or Homburg, just as a gambling jaunt today promises an extraordinary experience in Las Vegas, Reno, or Atlantic City. Even in those days, gamblers may have felt that "What happens in Wiesbaden stays in Wiesbaden."

But of course, we are speculating about Dostoevsky's views, beliefs, and motivations when we assume he shared the norms and values that were common in nineteenth-century Russia. Fortunately, we can learn more about Dostoevsky's own views directly from his own writing, especially from his novel *The Gambler*. However, as we shall see in the next chapter, the examination of his writing for this purpose poses new challenges, even as it offers new rewards.

3

What Do Dostoevsky's Novels Tell Us?

There are three primary sources for analyzing Dostoevsky's gambling problem: his novel about gambling, his letters, and his wife's diary. In this chapter, we pay particular attention to his novel *The Gambler*. But what importance and meaning should we attach to the presentations of gambling (and family life) in Dostoevsky's novels as evidence for our theory about the Dostoevsky Effect? Naturally, this kind of question arises whenever people analyze biographic sources in connection with fictional characters, and vice versa.

Specifically, how should we interpret Dostoevsky's writing in relation to his own personal experiences with and motivations for gambling? How much of the writing by Dostoevsky directly reflects his personal views and personal problems?

Some might deny there is solid evidence that Dostoevsky infused fictional protagonists with his own personal thoughts on, or experiences with, gambling. So, we need to tread carefully when drawing biographic conclusions from Dostoevsky's own writing and recognize that there's no certainty behind the conclusions one might draw.

That said, the patterns we see seem to make a lot of sense. For example, the tradition of Dostoevsky scholarship epitomized in the five-volume literary biography by Joseph Frank shows that many scholars see a strong link between Dostoevsky's characters and his own life experiences. So, in treating Dostoevsky's characters almost as though they were real people, we are following in a long tradition of Dostoevsky scholarship. (Although, as Kate Holland [2012] notes, all professional scholars of literature are aware that, even "if literature is a mirror of life, it is a distorting mirror subject to its own laws and principles" [personal communication].)

As a gambler, Dostoevsky developed strong views about gambling, based on many first-hand experiences. As a result, he has left the best-written insider descriptions of gambling problems one can find in world literature.

His short novel, *The Gambler*, focused on gambling and its potentially devastating consequences. As mentioned earlier, Dostoevsky wrote this novel to fulfill a financial obligation, in a remarkable twenty-six days. However, the novel is more than merely an insider account of problem gambling: it is also a pre-sociological analysis, as we will see. For it tells us a lot about the social and cultural context in which people gambled to excess during this period: for example, a great deal about the dominant "codes of behaviour" around gambling at this time.[1]

Is Dostoevsky's Work Autobiographical?

Scholars differ on how we should interpret this work, with some emphasizing certain features and others emphasizing other ones. The novel, though short and with relatively few incidents comprising its plot, is hard to interpret. In part, this is because the narrator is intentionally unreliable. We have trouble settling on a single interpretation of this novel, though we know it will provide clues into Dostoevsky's thinking about the topic of gambling. On this, Peter Rabinowitz (2001) writes:

> *The Gambler* [though confusing] is not primarily . . . "about" the difficulties of the act of reading. More immediately, it's about gambling, about the entanglements of sex and money, about the fate of Russians transplanted to Europe (Frank 170–83), about the "Woman Question" (for a good feminist analysis, see Straus 37–52), about the paradoxes of humiliation and self-destruction as means to freedom. (207)

Whatever interpretation we come to prefer, we will not doubt the autobiographic significance of this work. Dostoevsky's eminent biographer Joseph Frank (1993) notes that Dostoevsky's own comments in a letter written around this time strongly suggest the biographical nature of his work. Consider some examples:

> In 1863 Dostoevsky was travelling in Europe with his erstwhile mistress Apollinaria Suslova, who was refusing him her sexual favors; . . . Dostoevsky was gambling uninterruptedly during this trip; and it is not difficult to see *The Gambler* as a version of these events. The two main characters are Aleksey Ivanovich, who becomes a confirmed gambler, and his capricious

ladylove Polina, who both confides in him at one moment and repulses him the next. (303)

On these grounds, Frank says the resemblance of the two leading figures—Aleksey and Polina—to Fyodor and Polina could not be "more self-evident." Yet, Frank (1993) warns against imagining that this short novel is *merely* a thinly veiled autobiographical account. There are other aspects to the novel that lead readers to see somewhat different elements in it—something that would be impossible if it were merely an autobiographical account with the names changed. Consider the views of eight scholars who have introduced different editions of *The Gambler* over the years: Amoia (1993), Andreyev (1962), Coulson (1962), Jones (2008), Mann (1945), Meyers (2001), Pevear (2007), and Wasiolek (1972). They are in general agreement that the book is heavily autobiographical and thus, for our purposes, a window into Dostoevsky's own thoughts about gambling and the gambling experience.

All agree that both Polina Suslova's diary and Dostoevsky's letters written during their time in Europe reflect much of what happens in the novel (for example, Wasiolek 1972). Nikolay Andreyev (1962) goes so far as to say that *The Gambler* is "almost an abstract from Dostoevsky's own life" (ix). Dostoevsky himself states he intended the novel to truthfully depict the game of roulette, saying in a letter "I endeavour to make this description of a kind of hell . . . into a real picture" (Andreyev 1962, ix).

Commentators often cite the characters, particularly Polina, as evidence that the novel is autobiographical. Alba Amoia (1993) claims that the character Polina is *directly* modelled on Polina Suslova, and most commentators agree with this statement.

On this matter, Edward Wasiolek (1972) disagrees somewhat, saying it would be a mistake to assume that the fictional character of Polina is directly modelled on Suslova, or to assume that Suslova alone served as the model for all the demanding women in Dostoevsky's writing. Wasiolek notes first that demanding, hysterical women appeared in other of Dostoevsky's works before he met Suslova. Second, Polina Suslova was reportedly much less complicated and intelligent than the enigmatic Polina Dostoevsky supposedly modelled after her. Suslova's diary and short novel *The Stranger and Her Lover*, depicting her relationship with Dostoevsky, reveals a dull and self-interested woman lacking the depth and intelligence of Polina. Indeed, Wasiolek claims that Maria—Dostoevsky's first wife, who in many ways tormented him as much as Suslova—may have also been used as inspiration. However, we cannot assume the fictional Polina is directly modelled on Maria either.

Suffice to say that Dostoevsky appeared to run to type in selecting difficult women for his passionate relationships, and the fictional Polina is an ideal amalgam of this type.

Other characters in the novel are commonly thought to reflect Dostoevsky's philosophy, if not actual people. For example, some illustrate the desirable qualities of Russianness. Dostoevsky's own xenophobia is seen in Aleksei's descriptions of other characters in the novel. Aleksei, the protagonist, indulges in the stereotypes Dostoevsky himself held concerning the Germans, the French, and the Polish (Meyers 2001). The General, another fictional character, aligns with Dostoevsky's ideas about the Russian abroad, who, being cut-off from all things Russian, has become rootless (Wasiolek 1972).

The next most frequently cited similarity is the seemingly irrational manner in which both Dostoevsky and the fictional protagonist Aleksei deal with money. Although both continuously think about money and work tirelessly to win it, as soon as they get it they give it away. This way of interacting with money reflects Dostoevsky's deepest urge to revolt against reason (Wasiolek 1972). Dostoevsky's two passions, gambling and Polina, serve in real life and in the book to satisfy this irrational urge. Not surprisingly, Dostoevsky's favourite game, roulette, is a game of pure chance—completely irrational—where the gambler must abandon any hopes of calculating the odds. Dostoevsky's relationship with Polina Suslova was also irrational, in that she would provoke him only to reject him for no apparent reason.

Dostoevsky's wife, Anna, in her diary, notes his seeming need for the irrationality provided both by roulette and by his relationship with Polina. It was such a strong need that, even after he had given up both roulette and Polina and settled into a calm life with Anna, he would attempt to recreate these dramas. The calm and rational Anna however refused to satisfy Dostoevsky's desire for irrationality (Wasiolek 1972).

The fictional Aleksei likewise revolts against reason in the way he deals with his two passions. Aleksei loves the *quest* for Polina—its frustration, rejection, and uncertainty. However, once Polina gives herself to him, Aleksei turns his full attention back to roulette as a substitute for the (now suspended) irrationalities of her character. This action is mirrored in Dostoevsky's own life: remember, he rushed to the casino in Baden-Baden rather than going straight to his lover Polina (Suslova) who awaited him in Paris.

Still, despite these similarities, no novel is a direct transcription of experience. It was from his imagination as well as his experiences in Wiesbaden that Dostoevsky gained the material he fashioned into *The Gambler*, which he characterized simply as "a very detailed first-hand account of the game of roulette." In quoting from the novel below, we reference the edition translated by Richard Pevear and Larissa Volokhonsky (New York: Vintage Classics, 2007). The novel was written rapidly, dictated by Dostoevsky and transcribed by his new secretary, Anna Snitkina, almost without prior planning. Yet the novel shows a complex structure and deep understanding of problem gambling.

The Novel Described

The Gambler is the story of an intelligent, unstable young man, Aleksei (or Alexei, and sometimes given in English as Alexis), working as the tutor for a Russian family abroad in the spa and resort town of Roulettenburg (a place much like Wiesbaden, we conclude).

Anna offers us an amusing vignette about Dostoevsky's creative process when she recalls the origin of this fictional town's name. Anna had just been interviewed for the job of secretary—indeed, had just met Dostoevsky. It was getting late and she wanted to get home, as she had promised her mother. At the same time, she wanted to get going in her new job, so "to my great pleasure, he himself said he was going to begin dictating."

> He started pacing the room with long strides, from the fireplace to the door, and every time he reached the fireplace, he invariably knocked twice on it. He was smoking cigarettes all the while, taking a fresh one and throwing the unfinished one in the ash tray on the desk. After he had dictated to me for some time, he asked me to read to him what I had written, and at the very first sentences he stopped me. "From Roulettenburg? Did I say Roulettenburg?" he asked. "You dictated that name," I answered. "Impossible!" "But is there a city of that name in your novel?" I asked. "The action takes place in a city where there is a casino, which I must have called

Roulettenburg," he replied. "If there is such a place you must have dictated its name, otherwise how could I have known it? This geographical term is perfectly new to me," I said. "You are quite right," Dostoevsky admitted. . . . I was glad the misunderstanding was cleared up. Dostoevsky was evidently absorbed in thought and troubled, or perhaps he was too tired. (Dostoevsky 1926, 16–17)

Aleksei comes to Roulettenburg without any knowledge of gambling but is eventually drawn to the roulette tables. In particular, he is determined to win money for Polina, the woman he loves, whom he hopes to keep from having to become the mistress of a cynical French pseudo-aristocrat.

Soon, an aged relative of Aleksei's employer arrives, immediately launching herself into an orgy of gambling. Immensely rich, she first wins 12,000 florins, and then loses everything. Now, Dostoevsky reveals his true theme: to depict the excitement and other-worldliness of a gambling problem. Gambling for Dostoevsky, we see in this telling, is a passionate, surrender to the ministrations of Pure Chance. The gambler lives by staking everything on the throw of the dice, putting himself outside the grubbiness of prudence and human calculation. Dostoevsky's ideal gambler goes against all the odds, fully giving himself over to fate.

Of course, we cannot be certain that, in this novel, Dostoevsky was expressing his own opinions about gambling through the words, thoughts, and actions of Aleksei and the other characters. However, Dostoevsky and Aleksei have a lot in common. Consider a few parallels between Dostoevsky and Aleksei, and their respective gambling patterns. We might begin with the simple observation that Aleksei's beloved in *The Gambler* has the same name, Polina, as Dostoevsky's beloved mistress shortly before the novel was written.

Also evident in *The Gambler* is Dostoevsky's knowledge and understanding of the norms and values that Russians held in the nineteenth century with regards to gambling. In fact, many of the codes of behaviour we discussed in the previous chapter are discussed in *The Gambler*. There, for example, Dostoevsky attacks the notion of gambling as merely a way of displaying money, noting that other people consider it a way of making money.

Another specific similarity between Dostoevsky and Aleksei is their use of gambling as a means of escaping reality. In the novel as in Dostoevsky's real life, the gambler uses gambling to escape from his prison-like everyday experience, which he feels inhibits his personal will. In real life, Dostoevsky is being smothered by the responsibility to provide financially for his dependents, to meet his obligations to the publisher Stellovsky by writing speedy novels, and so on.

In the fantasy world of the casino, Dostoevsky is free, subject only to the whims of chance and luck. Neither wives nor partners or dependents can dictate the outcome of chance, giving Dostoevsky the sense that he is acting on decisions he has made freely and independently. In his review of the book *Gambling, Game, and Psyche* by Bettina Knapp (2000), renowned gambling expert Alex Blaszczynski (2002) remarks that in the novel *The Gambler*:

> Without doubt, Fyodor Dostoevsky's gambler uniquely captures the pervasive driving force and exquisite pleasure associated with risk. Here, we have the quintessential description of how base urges can overwhelm an intellect and lead into a state of complete moral debasement. (1109)

Both Dostoevsky and Aleksei lose themselves in their games of roulette: this loss of self is another kind of freedom, and it is exciting. Here's how Aleksei speaks of his own passion for gambling in *The Gambler*: "What am I now? *Zero.* What may I be tomorrow? Tomorrow I may rise from the dead and begin to live anew! I may find the man in me before he's lost" (Dostoevsky 2003[1867], 320). Dostoevsky, like Aleksei, may have believed he could gain momentary freedom and autonomy by gambling, but he also recognized the dangerous possibility of losing himself to the game forever.

As well, both Dostoevsky and Aleksei share a belief that they have discovered the secret to winning. As discussed in the previous section, Dostoevsky thought that he had stumbled on a system that enabled him to win his games of roulette consistently. It simply required discipline and control, to avoid what gambling researchers call "chasing losses"—trying desperately (and irrationally) to win back money you have already lost.

Dostoevsky's superstitious belief in his "system" is similar to Aleksei's belief that he would only win if he played for himself. Aleksei states that, "I'm perfectly convinced that when I start playing for myself . . . I'll win" (Dostoevsky 2003[1867], 201). Earlier he had said that, "the reason [he] could not play for others was not that [he] did not want to, but because [he] was sure to lose":

> The thought that I was setting out to play for someone else somehow threw me off. It was an unpleasant sensation, and I wanted to be done with it quickly. I kept fancying that by starting out for Polina I was undermining my own luck. (Dostoevsky 2003[1867], 187)

Both Aleksei and Dostoevsky, thus, gambled in accordance with superstitious "systems" they believed guaranteed that they would win at games of chance.

Dostoevsky and Aleksei also share a desire for money, and this desire motivates them both to gamble. Aleksei takes up gambling because he wants to win money to impress and protect the woman he loves, Polina. He thinks of gambling as a sort of career, just another way of making money. He makes this clear by asking, "Why is gambling worse than any other way of making money—trade, for instance?" (Dostoevsky 2003[1867], 183–84).

Similarly, Dostoevsky considered gambling to be a quick, easy way to make the money he needed, as we can see in a letter he wrote to his brother Mikhail: "I needed money, for myself, for you, for my wife, for writing my novel. . . . I came here to save you all and to rescue myself from disaster." Dostoevsky responded to all of these demands for money by gambling because, as De Jonge (1975) says, Dostoevsky "seems seriously to have been able to believe that roulette would make him rich. He looked to gambling for a solution to his financial difficulties" (81). In their desperate need for money, both Aleksei and Dostoevsky turned to gambling.

Finally, with financial need motivating their gambling, both Dostoevsky and Aleksei oppose those aristocrats who gamble merely to show off their wealth and status, and to create reputations as honourable, respectable men. By making Aleksei a gambler who isn't interested in raising his social standing, Dostoevsky challenges the gambling norms that dominated nineteenth-century Russian society.

This devaluation of aristocratic codes of behaviour can be seen in the passage below, describing Aleksei's first entrance into a casino. Here, the author states that:

> There is no magnificence in these rooms, and as for the gold, not only are there no heaps on the tables, but there's scarcely even the slightest trace. Of course, now and then during the season some odd duck suddenly shows up, an Englishman, or some Asiatic, or a Turk, as happened this summer,

and suddenly loses or wins a great deal; the rest all play for small change, and on the average there's very little money lying on the table. (Dostoevsky 2003[1867], 183)

In these words, Dostoevsky challenges the image of gambling as a purely aristocratic activity. The casino atmosphere in which he sets his novel is far from glamorous, and the people who frequent it are not all wealthy, elegant aristocrats. Many are sordid or unattractive or, like Aleksei, out to make money. Further, no one in this casino makes outrageous bets that could be interpreted as displays of wealth. Dostoevsky thus questions the prevailing view of gambling as a recreation for men who are so wealthy, they do not care if they win or lose.

This theme is evident in a well-known passage from *The Gambler*, in which Aleksei makes the following distinction:

There are two sorts of gambling—one gentlemanly, the other plebeian, mercenary, a gambling for all kinds of riff-raff. Here they are strictly distinguished and in essence, how mean that distinction is! A gentleman, for instance, may stake . . . for the game itself, only for amusement, only to watch the process of winning or losing; but by no means should he be interested in the actual winning. (Dostoevsky 2003[1867], 184–85)

In this passage Aleksei notes there are people who do not care for winning but also those who do. Shortly after he describes these two different types of gamblers, he aligns himself with the "plebeians," claiming that, "I sincerely and conscientiously classed [myself] among all this riff-raff" (Dostoevsky 2003[1867], 186). He plainly states that he sees "decidedly nothing filthy in the desire to win sooner and more." Moreover, he thinks it is this desire that distinguishes him from the "gentlemen" who aren't interested in whether they win or lose (Dostoevsky 2003[1867], 184). Thus, Dostoevsky drew a clear distinction between people who gambled to win the money they needed to survive and those who gambled for reputation's sake.

Despite an intense desire to win money by gambling, both Aleksei and Dostoevsky get rid of their winnings almost as quickly as they acquire them. Aleksei seems most at peace with himself during the weeks he spends with Mme Blanche, a woman whose attention he attracts only after he had gained his gambling fortune. He seems not the least bit bothered by her outrageous demands and the fact that she is spending all the money he won gambling. When Mme Blanche asks Aleksei if he resents her spending the money so quickly, he replies, "Who cares, the quicker the better!" (Dostoevsky 2003[1867], 311). As Wasiolek (1972) notes:

> Dostoevsky, like Aleksei, was unable to hold on to his money for long. . . .
> The recklessness with which he divested himself of whatever money he made suggests that he enjoyed being without money more than having it. He often expressed contempt for money, especially for money amassed in a systematic way, a practice he identified especially with the German outlook. At the roulette table . . . he would play until he lost everything he had. He seemed at peace with himself only when there was nothing left and no possibility of getting more. (xiv)

Similarly, another commentator, Carol Apollonio (2009), notes that:

> Throughout his life, Dostoevsky was never able to accumulate and keep money, even when he earned a respectable income. His acquaintances report the writer would give away any cash that came his way, almost immediately, to those more needy than himself. (52)

This need to get rid of money as quickly as possible may seem ironic, considering Dostoevsky's desperate efforts to win it. However, the contradiction makes perfect sense if we examine how Dostoevsky viewed money and the kinds of things he associated with it. Specifically, he associated money and the rational and systematic acquisition of money with the civilized Western world. By contrast, he associated beloved Russia with a lack of materialism and qualities such as spontaneity and a love of life. On this, Apollonio (2009) writes: "In Dostoevsky's universe, money serves as a symbolic representation of the means by which a deadening rational, quantifying worldview is applied to living human interactions, reducing them" (48).

The World-View of This Novel

Dostoevsky opposed this Western reductive view of the world based on rationalistic calculation. This opposition is clear in *The Gambler* when Aleksei says to the Frenchman De Grieux:

The ability to acquire capital has entered the catechism of virtues and merits of the civilized Western man historically and almost as the main point. While a Russian is not only incapable of acquiring capital, but even wastes it futilely and outrageously. (Dostoevsky 2003[1867], 196)

And just to clarify that he still thinks better of the Russian mentality, Aleksei goes on to say, "It really is not clear yet which is more vile: Russian outrageousness or the German way to accumulate through honest work" (Dostoevsky 2003[1867], 197).

On this matter, critic Alex de Jonge (1975) asserts, "Dostoevsky cannot help admiring the Russian's reckless capacity to abandon all caution in the pursuit of intensity. He associates it with a love of life and excitement which represents much that is finest in the Russian character" (168).

If all this were true, Dostoevsky would have viewed some of Aleksei's gambling as a rejection of Russian values, particularly when Aleksei played systematically, in cold-blooded pursuit of money. When Aleksei chooses money, rationality, and calculation over love, Polina, and spontaneity, he seems to choose Western values over Russian ones. This echoes a theme in Pushkin's wonderful short story "The Queen of Spades," in which the hero is half-German and half-Russian. Part of him wants to follow the German pattern of success through hard work and calculation, while part of him—the Russian part—wants to risk everything on the turn of a card.

In *The Gambler*, this theme is most obvious in the scene where Polina, with whom he is in love, waits in his hotel room to tell him she loves him too. Aleksei knows she has taken a great risk in coming into his room alone. Yet, instead of accepting the love she offers, he flees to the casino and returns with an offer of money in exchange for her love. What does this mean? Interpreting this scene, Apollonio (2009) notes that:

By turning away from love and plunging into the world of gambling, Aleksei rejects what for Dostoevsky are the quintessentially Russian values: love, community, and spirit. His home now becomes the hotel, a transitional space maximally distanced from the Russian soil. (61)

Polina in the novel thus represents the traditional Russian values of love and spontaneity. Gambling and the casino, on the other hand, symbolize Western values of money, rationality, and logic. Thus Aleksei's departure for the casino, this Westernized space, signals his rejection of Russian principles.

Yet, later in the novel, Aleksei's gambling conforms to Russian qualities of spontaneity and irrationality. Aleksei claims to be gambling to win money to impress Polina, yet he quickly forgets about his love for her. He says that, "I do not remember whether I even once thought about Polina during all this. . . . I barely remembered what she had told me earlier and why I had gone, and all those recent sensations which had been there an hour and a half ago now seemed to me long past, corrected, out-dated" (Dostoevsky 2003[1867], 279).

Aleksei can't even remember what had originally motivated him to go to the casino. The moment he begins winning, his love for Polina retreats into the background and his obsession with gambling comes to the forefront. When he tosses the money he won supposedly for Polina on the table, he says, "the enormous pile of banknotes and rolls of gold covered the whole table, and I couldn't take my eyes off it; at moments, I completely forgot about Polina" (Dostoevsky 2003[1867], 298). And when Polina finally leaves him, he shows no need to understand why or to bring her back. He may have been prompted initially to go to the casino because of his love for her, but Aleksei soon develops a passion for gambling that is even greater than his love for Polina.

In a recent commentary on the novel, Rosenshield (2011) argues that *The Gambler* is best understood as a response to Pushkin's classic work, "The Queen of Spades," and a reinterpretation of the role of romance in relation to gambling. Here, Rosenshield (2011) challenges many of the interpretations we have discussed:

Aleksey's narrative lends itself easily to a maximalist interpretation. The hero is destroyed by passion, by gambling, or some combination of both. I have argued the case for passion. But whether intentionally or not, the novel includes the possibilities of still other ambiguities affecting the ending. Aleksey makes arguments about the Russian national character that seem to strengthen the case for Russians as the archetypical gamblers who, once infected with the passion of gambling, are doomed. This association of Russianness and gambling is a commonplace of criticism on the novel (Lotman, 488). But as Aleksey confesses, he sometimes exaggerates to either emphasize a position or simply to shock. (225)

Alternative Interpretations

For Rosenshield (2011), *The Gambler* is mainly a story of doomed love and secondarily a story about gambling, nationality, or otherwise. From this standpoint, it can be viewed as a resolution of Dostoevsky's failed romance with the "real Polina" or an artistic pastiche—a tip of the hat to Pushkin. In any event, it may not be a deep insight into the nature of gambling:

> In *The Queen of Spades* Pushkin had largely decoupled the almost mandatory Sentimental or Romantic love story associated with stories of gambling. In *The Gambler*, Dostoevsky redoes Pushkin's *Queen of Spades* by injecting passion back into the life of a gambler, thereby transforming the notions of accumulation, risk, fortune, and daring. He turns a tragedy of gambling into a tragedy of love—albeit with loopholes. (Rosenshield 2011, 226)

In the novel, besides his seeming loss of interest in love and Polina, Aleksei loses his interest in money too, showing no resistance when Mme Blanche drains him financially. By now, he's no longer gambling to win money or to impress Polina. He has developed a full-blown addiction where gambling is an end in itself, with no acquisitive motivation behind it. Love, social importance, and even money are no longer of any value to Aleksei. He loses all sense of past loyalties and future goals. Instead, he is absorbed by the need to gamble. This view of problem gambling is the view that Freud held, as did Anna, Dostoevsky's wife. Now, Aleksei no longer gambles for any rational purpose, choosing instead to revel in the irrationality and chance of the game:

> Dostoevsky knew and said many times that the deepest urge in human beings is to revolt against definition and the fixities of life; the violation of reason, which sanctified definition and fixity, had, as he was well aware, its destructive side and it may be that side that he was celebrating in the portrait of Aleksei. (Wasiolek 1972, xv)

Critic Edward Wasiolek (1972) says that gambling, for Aleksei, is mainly a way to experience the thrill of pure chance. Aleksei has no interest in a position for himself in the upper classes of society, or in defending his honour and reputation. Gambling has become an end in itself—the sole source of pleasure in an otherwise flat and meaningless world. Aleksei initially gambled in an effort to change or control his fate, but in the end, he gambles to revel in the irrationalities of fate. Pure gambling, by now, is a celebration of pure chance, completely free of human influence and human control. Nothing can show more bravery or self-confidence, or promise more freedom, than that!

We can read the same ending a different way, however. Robert Jackson (1981) says in his book *The Art of Dostoevsky: Deliriums and Nocturnes* that in Dostoevsky's novel *The Gambler*, "the very act of gambling becomes a conscious or unconscious affirmation of the meaninglessness of the universe, the emptiness of all human choice" (210). Along similar lines, but more graphically, critic W.J. Leatherbarrow (2005) notes that:

> In the great novels of his maturity, [demonic] signs assume a significant structural role, as well as helping to define the ideological landscape on which those novels are played out. In particular, they serve to elucidate and demonize the motifs of intellectual alienation, spiritual rebellion and loss of faith in the Russian Christ. (599)

If so, it may not be outlandish to view the casino, or even the whole fictional town of Roulettenburg, as a demonic representation of Dostoevsky's own alienation, rebellion, and even loss of faith. A few decades later, in a brief note, the Norwegian painter Edvard Munch (1891) referred to the casino he visited as "an enchanted castle—where the devil is throwing a party—the gambling hell of Monaco" (quoted in Stang 1977, 86).

Later in the novel, Aleksei shows a desire to conquer fate when he hopes that Polina, "would see that I was above all these absurd jolts of fate" (Dostoevsky 2003[1867], 321). He explains that he could not leave the casino because "some strange sensation was born in [him], some defiance of fate, some desire to give it a flick, to stick my tongue at it" (Dostoevsky 2003[1867], 195). By the end of the novel, however, Aleksei no longer sees gambling as a way to challenge fate. Instead, he begins to accept the irrationalities of fate that make gambling random and unpredictable. He notices that:

> Calculation meant rather little in itself and had none of the importance many gamblers give it. They sit there with their ruled sheets of paper, note down the stakes, calculate, deduce the chances, reckon up, finally placing their bet,

and—lose, in exactly the same way as we simple mortals, who play without any calculations. (Dostoevsky 2003[1867], 194)

By the end, Aleksei realizes that the human need to understand, control, and predict chance is irrational in itself. Instead, the only way to gamble is to accept its irrational, random nature. By his suggestion that trying to calculate and predict chance is ridiculous and paradoxical, Dostoevsky challenges the popular notion that "gamblers" who play games of calculation have a remarkable skill. If gambling is bested by skill, it is no gamble. If winning comes down to luck and chance, no amount of skill will let you win.

The Novel as a Carnival

Because *The Gambler* disrupts so many social conventions, norms, and popular beliefs, some believe it can be read as a carnivalesque novel. Carnivalesque literature subverts hierarchical social relations through humour and disorder. Malcolm Jones, in his introduction to a 2008 edition of *The Gambler*, says that:

The medieval carnival . . . was an institutionalized occasion when all the normal hierarchical relations in society were temporarily reversed. Kings became paupers and paupers kings, normally impermissible *mésalliances* were allowed, and the rules of social decorum could be breached with impunity—provided everything reverted to normal when the carnival was over. [Mikhail] Bakhtin sees *The Gambler* as a striking example of carnivalization within Dostoevsky's fictional world, because the gambling table is the means by which all these social relations can be, if only temporarily, reversed. The rich become poor, the poor rich, the suppliant becomes master, and the master suppliant. (xviii)

In this novel, gambling is carnivalesque in that it allows one character, Aleksei, to become rich while it causes another wealthy character, "Grandmother," to lose all of her money. Another carnivalesque scene in the novel involves Aleksei's sojourn with Mme Blanche. She barely even noticed Aleksei before he won his fortune. Aleksei accepts this turn of events willingly, almost indifferently. Thus, Dostoevsky's characters move freely between social classes as their fortunes rise and fall by chance.

Repeatedly, social order is disrupted at random, making *The Gambler* a carnivalesque novel.

Dostoevsky displays his views of gambling in other novels as well. In *Notes from the Dead House,* for example, a book based on his own experiences in prison, Dostoevsky pictures the accumulation of money as a way of expressing freedom. He describes how the imprisoned characters slowly and painfully amassed small sums of money that they often then squandered in brief sprees of gambling and drunkenness. It was not a desire for money itself that motivated the convicts to slowly gather funds, but rather the brief moment of freedom that money can buy. Spending their money in any way they chose gave these prisoners a fleeting sense of autonomy inside a system designed to stifle and inhibit them (Lantz 2004, 146).

Did Dostoevsky himself believe that money had the potential to provide a sense of liberty? Or did he see all financial matters as burdensome and merely trivial, fleeting matters of chance? As a metaphorical prisoner to his publisher Stellovsky and to his financial dependents, Dostoevsky likely felt he could set himself free from these financial debts only by winning the money he needed.

Dostoevsky and his fictional character Aleksei were different in some—perhaps many—respects. But in the end, it was the appeal of freedom, provided through the magic of chance, that drew Dostoevsky and his protagonist Aleksei back to gambling time and again, despite the inevitable, painful losses. Gambling researchers would say that Dostoevsky and Aleksei were repeatedly, compulsively chasing their losses. But Dostoevsky and Aleksei might have said that they, like other Russians before and since, were questing for the impossible dream: freedom.

On the other hand, a case can be made that this novel offers the antithesis of freedom through gambling: rather, it provides a picture of slavery through gambling, by eliminating any sense of progress or improvement. On this matter, critic Jeff Love (2004) writes persuasively:

> This affirmation and denial of temporality as linear, purposive movement is the appropriate narrative emblem of the peculiar world of Roulettenburg and its inhabitants, a world where beginning and end continually risk equivalence and where the parameters of structure have therefore begun to dissolve. What emerges is an acceptance of inevitable boredom, of permanent failure to resolve conflict, that is both constricting and liberating. (361)

According to Martin, Sadlo, and Stew (2006), Dostoevsky—like many key writers of the nineteenth century—was deeply interested in the topic of boredom, which Love (2004) properly equates to stasis and lack of resolution—entrapment in an uncontrolled universe. Perhaps that was the theme of *The Gambler*.

In short, this seemingly simple novella allows multiple explanations and multiple theories about the motives behind problem gambling. That means the novel cannot speak for itself as an explanation of problem gambling, so we will need to consider some scientific (as well as humanistic) theories on the topic.

4

Explanations of Dostoevsky's Gambling

How have other commentators understood Dostoevsky's gambling? Let's jump ahead fifty years, to the beginnings of a scientific study of compulsions and addictions, and of problem gambling in particular. Dostoevsky's gambling problem cannot be explained by family inheritance, since (allegedly) neither of his parents gambled. True, as we have noted, that Dostoevsky's father had a drinking problem and one can argue that Dostoevsky inherited this tendency to addiction, if not the tendency to excessive drinking. Yet the problem remains: why gambling? Why not drinking?

So, we will now look at some alternative approaches to explaining Dostoevsky's problem gambling, focusing only on theorists—especially, researchers and therapists—who have specifically mentioned Dostoevsky.

The first approach grows out of a psychological interpretation put forward by Sigmund Freud, the father of psychoanalysis. As we will see, most of the subsequent analyses of Dostoevsky's gambling are familiar with Freud's analysis, agree with it at least in part, and build on it.

Freud's Psychological Explanation

Freud lays out his theory of problem gambling, and particularly his theory of Dostoevsky's problem gambling, in an essay titled "Dostoevsky and Parricide," published in 1928. As always, Freud has several agendas in his writing, and understanding Dostoevsky is only one of them. Indeed, another topic is evident in the essay's title: parricide (or father-killing). Of this topic, Freud (1976[1928]) says:[1]

> It can scarcely be owing to chance that three of the masterpieces of the literature of all time—the *Oedipus Rex* of Sophocles, Shakespeare's *Hamlet*, and Dostoevsky's *The Brothers Karamazov*—should all deal with the same

subject, parricide. In all three, moreover, the motive for the deed, sexual rivalry for a woman, is laid bare. (188)

In this essay, Freud (1976[1928]) begins as follows:

Four facets may be distinguished in the rich personality of Dostoevsky: the creative artist, the neurotic, the moralist, and the sinner. . . . The creative artist is the least doubtful: Dostoevsky's place is not far behind Shakespeare. . . . The moralist in Dostoevsky is the most readily assailable. . . . To consider Dostoevsky as a sinner or a criminal rouses violent opposition. . . . [But consider] three factors from Dostoevsky's complex personality: . . . the extraordinary intensity of his emotional life, his perverse instinctual disposition, which inevitably marked him out to be a sado-masochist or a criminal, and his unanalysable artistic gift. (179, 190–94)

The essay argues that Dostoevsky's epilepsy and his gambling problem were both ways in which the writer punished himself to assuage feelings of guilt. Early in the essay, Freud (1976[1928]) makes clear that he does not believe Dostoevsky was a true epileptic. Instead, he thinks the seizures Dostoevsky reportedly experienced were forms of self-induced punishment for having wanted to kill his father (the "parricide" named in the title of Freud's article). Likewise, Freud claims, Dostoevsky punished himself by incurring huge financial losses through gambling. Dostoevsky's goal in gambling was not to win money—for if that were his actual goal, he failed miserably. In fact, says Freud, his goal was to lose money, and here he enjoyed considerable success. This self-inflicted punishment, according to Freud, momentarily freed Dostoevsky from his feelings of guilt over wanting to kill his father.

To jump ahead a bit, we will propose that Dostoevsky's epilepsy was real and grew more severe throughout his life; moreover, it contributed to Dostoevsky's urge to gamble. By gambling, Dostoevsky likely hoped to escape from or forget about his poor health and other troubles. He believed that he could achieve this, however briefly, by losing himself in gambling. Second, we will propose that Dostoevsky never intended to lose all of his money or to "punish" himself by doing so. Other factors encouraged him to gamble, including a desire to pay his debts by winning money quickly and easily. Dostoevsky may have wrongly believed he had devised the perfect system for winning.

However, Freud, for the most part believed that human behaviour of all kinds—including even errors, accidents, forgetting, slips of the tongue, and ordinary mistakes—were a result of conscious or unconscious motives. Nothing human was random or unchosen at some conscious or unconscious level in his view.

Thus, for Freud, even the most painful fears and neuroses were "chosen" to serve an existential purpose: to promote action or inaction, bring reward or punishment, re-enact shameful circumstances or blot them out, and so on. In Freud's mind the goal of problem gambling was, precisely, to lose money and thereby to suffer, not to win money and avoid suffering. The therapeutic question for Freudians then becomes, why does the problem gambler want to suffer? What is his "backstory" which, more often than not, is to be sought in the depths of infancy and childhood.

Freud begins this essay on "parricide" by discussing the key ingredients of Dostoevsky's personality, one of which Freud describes as his "neurotic" aspect. This neurotic aspect, Freud believes, is expressed through Dostoevsky's frequent seizures. Dostoevsky himself believed these seizures to be symptoms of epilepsy, but Freud asserts that they were displays of neurosis or hysteria. According to Freud, when Dostoevsky believed he was having an epileptic seizure, he was trying to rid himself of neurotic excitement his body was unable to handle. Dostoevsky's epileptic seizures were merely symptoms of his hysteria—an escape valve for pressures caused by a deeper, unconscious mental problem.

Freud also offers an explanation for the increasing severity of Dostoevsky's seizures over time. The first few attacks Dostoevsky experienced as a young boy were brought on by a "fear of death," he says (Freud 1976[1928], 228). In these early days, rather than convulsing violently as he did later in life, Dostoevsky merely became sleepy, sluggish, and depressed. This lethargy washed over him, leaving him in "a state exactly similar to real death" (Freud 1976[1928], 228). Freud claims that these early seizures symbolize death and express a death wish. In Freud's view, such invocations of death serve to memorialize someone who has died, or a living person the seizure victim wishes to see dead.

Dostoevsky's supposed Oedipal hatred for his father comes into play at this point in the explanation. It rests on Freud's famous theory of infantile sexuality, first stated in 1897 and widely reviled in turn-of-the-century Europe because it seemed to deprive even infants of innocence. Unlike

Freud, most nineteenth-century Europeans loved to view children as morally and spiritually innocent of any bad thoughts, much less bad actions. Freud, however, harboured no such illusions; in his world, no human was innocent of bad thoughts. The whole point of a psychoanalytic cure was to find and expose these thoughts to daylight. People were born into this state of something like original sin, and psychoanalysis could absolve them through confession.

To simplify, in this theory of infantile sexuality, Freud asserts that even the youngest boys have sexual desires that lead them to want their fathers dead so they can replace them as Mother's lover. Because of power dynamics in the family, boys also identify with the "father figure." That is, they want to take their father's place because they "admire him and want to be like him" (Freud 1976[1928], 229). So, for both reasons, they want Father out of the picture. But if Father were to get wind of this, he would retaliate by castrating his envious son as punishment. This fear of castration gives little boys something big to fret about.

So, to protect their budding masculinity, little boys repress their desire to kill Father and sleep with Mother. They drive this sexual desire underground, into their unconscious. Here, it continues to work on their minds in unseen ways.

Whenever the desire briefly resurfaces, it brings feelings of envy and hatred, then feelings of guilt and shame. Guilt, for this reason, is an inevitable part of growing up in a family—even an inevitable part of all social life and of civilization itself, says Freud. There can be no civilization, including no family life, without repression and guilt, so all social life is repressed and guilt-ridden. And with repression and guilt come neurosis, fantasy, and sublimation—the highest form of which is the creation of great art. This last translation of libidinal energy—from repressed desire to great art—means that Freud will always look to great artists like Dostoevsky for tests of his theory of repression.

To repeat, according to Freud (1976[1928]), Dostoevsky's feelings of guilt made him want to be punished for wanting to kill his father. His death-like epileptic seizures were just Dostoevsky's way of punishing himself for wanting his father dead, according to Freud. Perhaps Freud was put in mind of this possibility by Marmeladov's statement in *Crime and Punishment* (Dostoevsky 1917[1866], 18): "That's why I drink too. I try to find sympathy and feeling in drink. . . . I drink so that I may suffer twice as much!" Perhaps Dostoevsky, like some of his fictional characters, was driven by guilt and a need to suffer.

Moreover, Dostoevsky's Oedipal crisis was complicated by what Freud considered his bisexuality. Freud (1976[1928]) claims that Dostoevsky displayed his latent homosexuality "in the important part played by male friendships in his life, in his strangely tender attitude toward his rivals in love, and in his remarkable understanding of situations which are only explicable by repressed homosexuality, as many examples from his novels show" (230).

Freud, it seems, is drawn to the hypothesis of latent homosexuality by an assumption that Dostoevsky's seizures represented the hysterical display of a guilty wish for punishment. In European medicine of the time, doctors imagined hysteria to be a uniquely female (or feminine) malady. So the chain of reasoning is as follows: the epileptic seizures were deemed hysterical; hysteria was deemed feminine; therefore Dostoevsky was deemed partly feminine; and therefore he was deemed bisexual.

Freud uses Dostoevsky's novel *The Brothers Karamazov* as evidence that Dostoevsky wanted his father dead. According to Freud, the wished-for fate of Dostoevsky's own father is mimicked in the murder of the father in *The Brothers Karamazov*. Freud claims that Dostoevsky used his writing to reveal his subconscious parricidal wishes in a socially acceptable manner. *The Brothers Karamazov,* according to Freud, is thus Dostoevsky's admission of guilt for having wanted to murder his father.

According to Freud, a child's identification with his father, or the desire to kill Father to make room in Mother's bed, eventually takes up a permanent position in the child's mind as the superego. Since Dostoevsky's father was, according to Freud (1976[1928]), "hard, violent and cruel," Dostoevsky's superego took on those traits too (231). These became desirable traits, at least in Dostoevsky's unconscious. But in response to this supposedly "sadistic" superego, Dostoevsky's ego—the seat of cool reasoning—became passive and feminine. Thus, Dostoevsky's unconscious was to be permanently at war, between the supposedly sadistic, masculine superego and the masochistic, feminine ego. This permanent antagonism between his ego and superego caused Dostoevsky continued mental irritation and distress, says Freud.

Freud claims that Dostoevsky's hysterical (epileptic) seizures can be traced back to his identification with his father. This identification caused the ego to feel guilty, passive, and masochistic for wishing his father's death and caused the superego to punish the ego for wishing it. Over time, Dostoevsky's "death-like" seizures gradually worsened, increasingly resembling true epileptic seizures. Dostoevsky's neurosis reportedly did not take a true epileptic form until he was eighteen, when he received the shocking news that his father had been murdered (Freud 1976[1928], 226–27).[2] This horrifying experience caused Dostoevsky's worst seizure yet.

Freud claims this happened because Dostoevsky had continued to unconsciously hate his father and wish he were dead, despite having repressed those urges throughout childhood. Consequently, when his death wish for his father came true, Dostoevsky still identified with his father, or wished he could take his father's place. He therefore suffered a death-like experience, mirroring the death of his father in the form of a violent seizure.

Freud also claims that the victims of such seizures feel "supreme bliss" for an instant during the seizure (1976[1928], 233). Perhaps, hearing the news of a father's long wished-for death makes the seizure victim rejoice, however unconsciously. This instant of pleasure, however, is followed by even more severe punishment, for not only was the father's death desired, it was also celebrated.

If this theory were correct, Dostoevsky would have had fewer epileptic fits when imprisoned or exiled in Siberia, since others were then punishing him and he didn't need to punish himself as vigorously. However, Dostoevsky's seizures reportedly did not stop or become less severe when he was imprisoned or in exile. Dostoevsky reported that his seizures got worse, reaching their greatest intensity when he was in Siberia. Unwilling to accept disconfirming evidence on this matter, Freud (1976[1928]) attacks Dostoevsky's own claims about his health, writing: "Unfortunately there is reason to distrust the autobiographical statements of neurotics . . . their memories introduce falsifications" (228).

This lengthy discussion of Freud's approach to Dostoevsky's epilepsy is justified for several reasons. First, it illustrates the general style of a Freudian explanation or explanatory narrative. Second, it shows how Freudian explanations resist disconfirming evidence, making them more suggestive than conclusive. Third, it notes the important link between epilepsy and gambling in Freud's theory, since both are seen to reveal guilt and a desire for punishment. And just as Freud (1976[1928]) dismissed

Dostoevsky's own explanations of his seizures (i.e., as caused by epilepsy), he dismissed Dostoevsky's explanations of his gambling problem as mere excuses or "pretexts" (238).

What's more, some influential readers of *The Gambler* have sided with Freud on this. For example, the great German novelist Thomas Mann (1945), in his introduction to *The Gambler*, provides a thoroughly Freudian reading of the novel. Mann's interpretation of Aleksei's gambling addiction reflects the ambivalence Freud finds in Dostoevsky's epilepsy. Mann sees sickness and suffering as a key aspect to Dostoevsky's writing. He makes a connection between the thinking of Dostoevsky and Nietzsche—noting especially the importance of sickness and suffering for both (Mann 1945).

This similarity is understandable, as Nietzsche was heavily influenced by Dostoevsky's ideas and called him "The Great Teacher." Dostoevsky, as we have seen, did attach great importance to sickness throughout his life, describing his epilepsy as something almost sacred: a source of over-whelming pleasure, followed by crippling guilt (Mann 1945). Dostoevsky likely received the same "sacred" feeling from gambling: the anticipation of winning, the despair of losing (Mann 1945).

According to Freud, Dostoevsky didn't gamble to excess because he wanted to return to Russia and pay his debts there. Instead, he gambled to punish himself for wanting to see his father dead. As we know, Dostoevsky never left the roulette table until he had lost everything. Freud claims that Dostoevsky even found pleasure in reducing his family to a state of poverty, for it increased his guilt. This guilt about the state of his family was another kind of suffering he felt he deserved for having wished his father dead. By burdening his conscious mind with loathsome behaviours, Dostoevsky could unburden his unconscious mind of loathsome memories.

So, for example, another self-punishment Dostoevsky could inflict was to abase himself to his wife after confessing his gambling losses. Routinely, like other problem gamblers, he berated himself for being so irresponsible and reckless, and for losing so much money. In this way, he was able to "unburden his conscious" and momentarily relieve himself of the intense guilt he suffered because of an unresolved Oedipal complex. But Freud assures us that as soon as he obtained relief in this way, he started to feel the need to punish himself again, through a return to gambling.

Freud turns to statements by Dostoevsky's wife for support of his arguments. Anna reports, for example, that Dostoevsky was able to write much more easily after he had gambled away all of their money and possessions. This may have showed that Dostoevsky now had to pay the bills through his writing. To Freud, this showed that Dostoevsky could relieve his feelings of guilt only by gambling and losing. Only after gambling and losing could Dostoevsky write freely without interference from feelings of guilt. But eventually his feelings of guilt resurfaced, driving Dostoevsky back to the roulette table in hopes of once again unburdening his conscious through suffering.

But why does Dostoevsky choose gambling as the route to suffering—why not some other route? In answering, Freud (1976[1928]) brings the argument back to infantile sexuality and the matter of sexual repression. He argues that a strong desire to gamble signals a "repetition of the compulsion to masturbate" (241). Stated otherwise, an intense desire to gamble in adulthood reflects (and remembers) the intense desire to masturbate during puberty.

Gambling and masturbation have a few things in common, says Freud (1976[1928]). For example, both provide pleasure and excitement and both involve the hands. Freud writes that the "passionate activity of the hands" displayed by gamblers while playing cards is like the passionate activity of the hands during masturbation. Further, "playing" is a euphemism for masturbation, since it was "the actual word used in the nursery to describe the activity of the hands upon the genitals" (241).

Thus, problem gambling for Freud not only signals a desire for self-punishment through losing, but also a desire for self-gratification through masturbation, free of adult controls. By this reckoning, Dostoevsky's adult neurosis, expressed in gambling, is the result of a desire for masturbation frustrated by the hated father. Dostoevsky's gambling makes complete sense, says Freud, if we accept that an adult compulsion to gamble reflects and relieves an adolescent compulsion to masturbate.

As with the infantile urge to possess Mother, the adolescent urge to enjoy masturbation (to "abuse" him- or herself, as doctors used to describe it) is thwarted at every turn by an all-powerful, hated Father. Of this, Freud writes, "the relation between efforts to suppress it [the urge to masturbate] and fear of the father are too well-known to need more than a mention" (Freud 1976[1928], 242). Boys fear that father will castrate them if they masturbate, so they try to control this urge and store it away, fuelling a repressed urge to kill their father. And this leads Freud to speculate that Dostoevsky's seizures, previously interpreted as self-punishment for wanting his father dead, may have also been a form of self-punishment for Dostoevsky's thwarted (and guilty) desire to masturbate.

Flaws in Freud's Theory

There are obvious defects in Freud's theory. First, Freud's theory has a tendency to stereotype all instances of father–son conflict and all forms of sublimation. However, as psychoanalyst Louis Breger argues in *Dostoevsky: The Author as Psychoanalyst* (1989), Dostoevsky's work is more than a mere sublimation of Oedipal fantasies. Dostoevsky imaginatively transformed painful life events into world-inspiring literary creations. Moreover, Dostoevsky's anger against his father was caused by more than stereotypical reasons. Breger details the particular reasons for this son's rage at this father, without giving in to the Freudian urge to stereotype Dostoevsky's anger as just another Oedipal drama.

Finally, Breger views Dostoevsky as, himself, possessing deep psychoanalytical insights—hence, the title of his book. We should no more distort or undervalue Dostoevsky's ideas on the grounds of Oedipal rage than we should distort or undervalue Freud's ideas on these grounds.

Second, Freud's theory is deficient because it fails to explain the lack of sibling rivalry in Dostoevsky's work. In keeping with the Freudian Oedipal theory, we expect to see sibling rivalry in Dostoevsky's life. For Freud, the sibling relation—especially, the relationship between brothers—was based on rivalry and competition. Yet, as critic Anna Berman (2009) reminds us, in Dostoevsky's fiction,

> as the vertical relations between fathers and sons fail, lateral, nonhierarchical sibling bonds offer an alternative model of love, support, and understanding. With their focus on the hierarchical relations, critics have tended to overlook this second, horizontal layer in Dostoevsky's scheme, but in fact from the title to the last lines of the book, siblings are present in *The Brothers Karamazov*, offering a positive alternative to the failure of fathers. (263)

Third, it is doubtful that people gamble in order to lose, or, more generally, that people want to experience punishments: that they gain satisfaction—even pleasure—from punishing themselves. In Freud's view, Dostoevsky chose to gamble and wanted to lose huge sums of money, to make himself suffer. This contradicts our modern understanding of addiction, which argues that Dostoevsky could not—for a time—choose to gamble or not gamble. He was robbed of choice by his addiction, a compulsion he could understand only imperfectly.

Fourth, Dostoevsky is far from the only European writer to discuss parricide, yet we would be ill-advised to suppose all of this literary tradition grows out of infantile sexual frustration. Literary traditions don't work this way: they have their own artistic logic. Thus, *The Brothers Karamazov* is only one member of a distinguished literary set that begins two thousand years earlier with the Greek drama *Oedipus Rex*. Indeed, parricide has been one of the most common literary tropes since the age of Greek tragedy. As Lacoursiere (2003) notes, parricidal fantasies continue to emerge today in fiction, psychotherapy, and real-life crime investigation. So, Freud was on to something when he focused his laser-like intelligence on this topic, but we have to wonder if he came to the right conclusions.

Fifth, where we are able to assess Freud's theory with the tools of modern science, the theory falls flat. In particular, present-day experts disagree with Freud's assessment of the causes of Dostoevsky's epilepsy. This issue was examined by a trio of Swiss neurologists (Baumann et al., 2005) in a journal article titled "Did Fyodor Mikhailovich Dostoevsky Suffer from Mesial Temporal Lobe Epilepsy?" The neurologists concluded, "The exact classification of Dostoevsky's epilepsy remains elusive. We believe, however, that many signs indicate that this famous writer might have suffered from medial temporal lobe epilepsy" (330). That is because, both in his novels and his letters, Dostoevsky reports familiarity with, and experience of, symptoms linked precisely to this form of epilepsy.

Along similar lines, American neurologist John R. Hughes (2005) concludes:

> A review of recent data on the risks to offspring of epileptic fathers confirms that the etiology of Dostoevsky's epilepsy was probably inherited and that he probably had an idiopathic generalized epilepsy with minor involvement of the temporal lobe. A relationship is seen between his severe obsession with gambling and his epilepsy. Finally, Fyodor Dostoevsky is an excellent example of the "temporal lobe personality." (531)

These findings undermine Freud's assertion that Dostoevksy's epilepsy was a result of guilt and without any organic basis. What's more, the findings undermine Freud's claim that epilepsy was a punishment for Dostoevsky wishing his father dead. Far from being a punishment, the epilepsy was a mixed blessing and may even have contributed to Dostoevsky's creative productivity as a novelist.

Drawing on evidence from functional imaging, drug studies, and lesion analysis, neurologist Alice Flaherty (2005) notes that:

> Temporal lobe changes, as in hypergraphia, often increase idea generation, sometimes at the expense of quality. Frontal lobe deficits may decrease idea generation, in part because of rigid judgments about an idea's worth. . . . The appropriate balance between frontal and temporal activity is mediated by mutually inhibitory corticocortical interactions. Mesolimbic dopamine influences novelty seeking and creative drive. . . . Creative drive is not identical to skill—the latter depends more on neocortical association areas. However, drive correlates better with successful creative output than skill does. (147)

Flaherty is not alleging that epilepsy made Dostoevsky a great writer; but she does argue (2005) that his epilepsy was a benefit to his writing:

> Hypergraphia reflects a drive to write, not always writing skill. Although a few great writers such as Dostoevsky were thought to have epileptic hypergraphia, many hypergraphic writers merely write interminable office memos, or make lists of their favorite songs. Nonetheless, creative drive can secondarily improve creative skill. One way is a practice effect: the more subjects write or paint, the better they get at doing so. (148)

Most important for our present purposes, Baumann et al. (2005) conclude, "The theory that Dostoevsky did not suffer from interictal neuropsychological deficits cannot be maintained" (329). In short, Freud was wrong, at least on this point.

For Dostoevsky, epilepsy was not a guilt-induced neurotic symptom without any organic origin. Moreover, the epilepsy may have been inherited from his father. In a recent biography of Dostoevsky, Richard Freeborn (2003) notes that the death of Dostoevsky's father was not due to murder by peasants, as Freud had believed, but a natural death from epilepsy. This assertion raises the possibility that Dostoevsky's epilepsy was inherited—as perhaps was his nervous irritability.

Dostoevsky's Gambling: Fiction and Reality

What can we reasonably infer about Dostoevsky's gambling from his novels? Here, literary scholars are likely to be more rigorous and demanding of the evidence than Freud was. For example, returning to the example of Marmeladov—the character from *Crime and Punishment* mentioned earlier—Kenneth Lantz (2012) remarks:

> On the subject of gambling and alcohol and their links, I've always been struck by the story of the Marmeladov family in *Crime and Punishment*. The scene of the drunken Marmeladov pouring out his soul to Raskolnikov and abasing himself so emotionally puts me in mind of D.'s own letters to Anna after losing his shirt at roulette. Marmeladov, who seems to have got back on his feet again with a secure job and, apparently, has given up the bottle, blows it all on an epic spree. "I drink to multiply my sufferings," he says. I don't share Freud's view that D. was punishing himself through gambling (and like you, I think he really wanted to win), but he certainly understood the self-punishing addict. I also think that Marmeladov can't stand the prospect of spending the rest of his life in the "prison" of a nine-to-five job, dutifully handing over his pay cheque to his wife each week. Drink, not gambling, is his path to freedom. (personal communication)

However, despite these flaws, there may be a nub of truth to Freud's theory, nonetheless. First, we can have no doubt that Dostoevsky had a strong dislike for his father and a strong sense of victimization dating back to his childhood. Returning to the presentation of family life in *The Brothers Karamazov*, Laurie Langbauer (2008) argues convincingly that Dostoevsky was much obsessed with "suffering children." She notes that:

> The Grand Inquisitor passage [in *The Brothers Karamazov*] is actually a translation of, an explanation for, a gloss on everything Ivan has been telling Alyosha before it. Sick in his soul at the world around him, he unrelentingly forces his gentle child-brother to listen submissively to detail after detail of stories of child murder, child torture, child abuse of every sort, details shocking in the "refinements of cruelty" to children they exhibit—all the worse because these are stories Dostoevsky took from contemporary newspapers, stories of the here and now, stories of what we understand as

the real. "It is a peculiar characteristic of many people," Ivan says, "this love of torturing children, and children only. . . . It's just their defenselessness that tempts the tormentor, just the angelic confidence of the child who has no refuge and no appeal, that sets his vile blood on fire." (96–97)

One finds equally convincing proof of Dostoevsky's preoccupation with child abuse in his essay titled "The Case of the Dzhunkovsky Parents and their Children," published in *A Writer's Diary* in July and August 1877 (Dostoevsky 2009[1877], 415–19). Here Dostoevsky reports on a court case that receives testimony about the savage beating of the young Dzhunkovsky children. What is surprising, says Dostoevsky, is not that this occurred: it occurs in nine out of ten households, he says. Nor that the parents were acquitted. What is surprising to Dostoevsky is that the case even came to trial, given the widespread tolerance of child abuse in Russian society. In short, he viewed abuse as a normal part of Russian childhood.

Second, Dostoevsky may not have been seeking punishment, but he endured it nonetheless, because of his gambling. Problem gambling does cause people severe problems that include heavy debts and interpersonal conflicts. As we have already noted, Dostoevsky's gambling problem caused him to increase his already-large debts and strain his marriage. Not only did he repeatedly pawn his wife's belongings to finance the gambling, he also tormented her with self-abuse and requests for forgiveness. Further, his wife was obliged to invest extra time and care in calming him after a visit to the roulette tables, since the excitement caused by gambling often led Dostoevsky to have seizures.

There is good reason to see Dostoevsky's gambling as self-destructive, and, in this respect, he was operating within the cultural climate of the time. Indeed, this was a time when suicide became a recognized act of social rebellion. Of this, Morrissey (2004) has written:

It would fall to Russia's first well-known radical and most famous suicide of this era, Aleksandr Radishchev, to develop a philosophical justification for political suicide. . . . Arguing that the world particularly in Russia had fallen into abject slavery, a condition which contradicted the nature of man, he posited that the task of the enlightened philosopher was not just to proclaim the truths of freedom and citizenship but to translate them into life. To effect the transition from slavery to freedom it was necessary to awake the people to their enslavement and their ability to grasp man's inherent liberty. (277)

Third, as Freud says, gambling is connected to freeing the libido from normal restraints, often in connection with drinking, noise, sex, and other celebratory activities. One need only go to Las Vegas to see this in full flow. Gambling—even gambling to excess—is somehow connected to a need for freedom from day-to-day repression. Freud is right in supposing that daily routine requires that we repress our impulses. And gambling is associated with breaks in repressive daily routine.

Fourth, for this reason, we can suppose that people who want to gamble a lot have a stronger-than-usual desire to avoid or break from routine. Whether motivated by guilt, depression, or anxiety, this desire to escape the everyday world may result, ultimately, from an unhappy childhood and inadequate socialization into the adult world. One point that Freud emphasizes in his analysis is the apparent correlation between gambling and creative productivity in Dostoevsky's life: specifically, that Dostoevsky always was most productive (during the 1860s) after he had been gambling and losing money. From this, Freud concludes that losing money relieved Dostoevsky of feeling that he needed to punish himself, so he could get back to work again.

Joseph Frank, Dostoevsky's most thorough biographer, hints that this alternating pattern of work and gambling may have been a part of Dostoevsky's bifurcated character—an alternation between his attraction to Russian manners (creative, passionate, and honest) and European manners (mercenary, elegant, and worldly). Of this, Frank (1993) writes:

Each time he lost, he returned to his work with renewed vigor and determination; it was as if, having proven to himself that he was too Russian to win at roulette, he decided to put into practice his belief that Russians must learn to discipline themselves through work. (321–22)

Pisak (1997), comparing several nineteenth-century novels about money and speculation, reaches a similar conclusion, that gambling, for Dostoevsky, was tied up with Russianness and freedom:

In *The Gambler* the rational calculation of speculation is contrasted with the irrational, spontaneous, and non-materialistic pursuit of freedom and authenticity in gambling. This structure is reflected in the gambler Alexei's sense of self as a non-finalized, and therefore free subjectivity. . . . However, the freedom generated by the activity of gambling, just as the sense of self experienced as a multiplicity of options, proves to be illusory when gambling becomes addictive. (5)

Kenneth Lantz (2012) offers a slightly different explanation, based on a reading of all Dostoevsky's works:

I don't have any theory about D.'s gambling, but I have some (unanswered) questions about it. Why did it all (as far as I know) take place in Europe? That's where the roulette tables were, of course, and that was his game. But if he was truly an addict, wouldn't he have sought out some back room games in Russia? Then again, maybe these were too seedy (and illegal). Was there some feeling of liberation in Europe—Russian standards no longer applied? But he was never happy living in Europe. The closest thing I have to a theory is that gambling was a way of getting his creative juices flowing again. His most frequent episodes came while he was working on *The Idiot*, a novel he had huge trouble with. The excitement of the roulette tables might take his mind off his literary problems for a time, and even losing—sinking right to the bottom—was a way forcing him back to his pen and paper. (personal communication)

Many commentators are inclined to view Dostoevsky's gambling as a failed but noble attempt to declare freedom or find diversion, not an ignoble grubbing after winnings. If so, Freud is wrong that Dostoevsky gambled in order to lose his money and punish himself.

So, there are pluses and minuses to the Freudian theory, a continued flow of oppositions and contradictions. In part, that is because of the complexity of the life story and the multi-pronged causation of any addiction or mental health problem. Kingma (2010) argues that the psychological and sociological analyses of Freud and Dostoevsky (respectively) focus on different, opposed, and contradictory aspects of the problem. In effect, Kingma (2010) says the contradictory interpretations of Dostoevsky and Freud anticipate two different branches of theorizing gambling addiction.

From the psychoanalytic approach to gambling excess evolved a clinical brand of theorizing, mostly based on accounts by gamblers under treatment. This approach has gradually been extended to a broader disease model which in its turn was extended by the psychological control model of "problem gambling." . . . Within this perspective, gambling is considered to be an accepted leisure form, of which excessive use and destructive consequences should be confronted. (17)

If we take a sociological or subcultural approach, we understand that gambling brings its own rules and expectations. It is not wholly normless and pathological.

Was Dostoevsky "in it for the money," as he sometimes said? Was he addicted, and therefore out of control and powerless? Or did his gambling have a meaning and structure? Gerda Reith (2007) thinks it did have meaning, for him and other problem gamblers:

Although representing the supreme measure of value in the world outside, for problem gamblers, money is simply the medium of play, the price of a good time, or alternately, the cost of an escape from a bad one. Either way, it is dissociated from material consumption and prized not as an end in itself but for its ability to allow continued consumption in repeated play. The inveterate gambler Fyodor Dostoevsky, who would by today's standards be considered pathological, articulated this indifference toward money when he stated that "the main thing is the play itself: I swear that greed for money has nothing to do with it" (Dostoevsky 1914, p. 119). (42)

Oldman (1978), writing on "compulsive gamblers," argues similarly that we do best to understand gambling—even excessive gambling—if we understand it as a social (and socially meaningful) occasion. Here, he recalls Erving Goffman's classic statement that gamblers are people who want to be "where the action is":

Goffman's argument is that the element of uncertainty in games allows a person to demonstrate . . . the strength of his character. . . . The trouble with this analysis is that it ignores the "work" element which is characteristic of . . . the involvement of the habitual gambler and it also ignores the social organisation of gambling scenes. For Goffman, play at a casino is characterised simply as a player, an uncertain outcome and an audience. Play, however, is very much more than this, particularly in a setting . . . in which the "regulars" are of long standing and both staff and punters have detailed knowledge about each other. (364)

Gambling, by this standard, is an organized, social confrontation with chance. Along similar lines, Malaby (2007) writes about the dice players he watched and interviewed in Greece as showing a similar orientation to their gambling:

> Like Max Weber's puritans, the dice gamblers of Greece see in the tumbling dice and their fickle outcomes ephemeral signs of their place in the world, that is, whether they, for at least a moment, are in a state of grace. At stake, then, over a dicing table in Greece is something utterly removed from questions of "fun," "leisure," or "entertainment." For many players, it is an existential engagement with the game, quite similar to that characterizing the protagonist of Dostoevsky's *The Gambler*; indeed, I was often directed to the story by Greek dice gamblers as the only way I could understand their relationship to the game. (99)

Thus, what may seem like addiction from the outside may be viewed as devotion, dedication, or deep engagement from the inside. If so, the very idea of "addiction" is a social construct—an imaginary state of lost control—perpetrated by the experts who medicalize social behaviour, as noted by Kingma (2010):

> Almost all cultural pursuits are considered to be susceptible to (being labelled as) addiction. No gambler is regarded as an addict until the gambler is in fact labelled as such. The degree of commitment to the game and the social legitimacy of gambling are held significant. Herman (1976, 103), an advocate of this subcultural perspective on gambling addiction, even claims straightforwardly: "no useful purpose is served by describing a category of compulsive gamblers." (17)

In the present book, we argue there is something usefully viewed as "addiction," though it is a far from simple concept. At the same time, we agree with Kingma that gambling—also problem gambling—must be viewed within a subcultural and historical context.

Later Explanations of Dostoevsky's Gambling

Freud's approach to problem gambling continued to dominate the psychoanalytic community well into the twentieth century. In a review of the research literature on problem gamblers in 1968—forty years after Freud's seminal paper—Bolen and Boyd gave lengthy prominence to Freud's theory of gambling and parricide. They also gave attention to the writings of Edmund Bergler, a mid-century psychotherapist of the Freudian school, who upheld Freud's view that problem gambling was aimed at losing, to expiate guilt.

In a review of the psychodynamic approach to gambling addiction, Rosenthal and Rugle (1994b) rightly point to the important place of both Freud and Bergler in this field:

> The conceptualization of compulsive gambling as a disease began around the turn of the century with the writing of the psychoanalysis. Furthermore, the contributions of Edmund Bergler to the newspaper and popular magazines of the 1950s were extremely valuable in raising public awareness of the disorder, and may have been an impetus for the founding of Gamblers Anonymous. The work of these early psychoanalysts . . . is largely ignored today . . . [and] often dismissed by reductive one-liners, i.e., Freud equated gambling with masturbation, Bergler believed all gamblers wished to lose. (22)

Bergler, like Freud, focused on the causes of self-destructive behaviour—specifically, on guilt and neurosis, often a result of the conflict that arises during childhood out of the gap between social norms (the superego) and anti-social (or non-social) impulses. Bergler's lengthy study of problem gamblers and their behaviour gave rise to the first systematic model of behaviour traits associated with problem gambling. He concluded that the six basic traits of compulsive gamblers were:

1. The gambler habitually takes chances.
2. The game precludes all other interests.
3. The gambler is full of optimism and never learns from defeat.
4. The gambler never stops when winning.

5. Despite initial caution, the gambler eventually risks relatively too large sums.
6. Thrill is experienced between the time of betting and the outcome of the game. (Rosecrance 1985, 276)

All six points aptly describe Dostoevsky's behaviour, though they are based on the findings of twentieth-century clinical studies. According to Bergler (1957), the pleasure and thrill associated with uncertainty makes gambling exciting, perhaps even overshadowing the desire (or need) to win. From this lack of interest in winning, Bergler concludes the problem gambler subconsciously wants to lose. Whether motivated by feelings of guilt, masochism, or a death wish, problem gamblers do not want to stop until they are ruined and have no more money.

But as with Freud's theory, there is no way to test Bergler's view that the problem gambler is driven mainly by an unconscious, self-destructive desire to lose. Thus, Bergler provides little more than interesting speculation: an elaborate footnote to Freud. Moreover, like other Freudian theorists, he proceeds from the assumption that unconscious forces drive all behaviour. (Here, remember Freud's theory about the role of the unconscious in parapraxes—mistakes and accidents that reveal unconscious wishes—as well as jokes and double entendres.)

By the time of Bolen and Boyd's literature review, a decade or two after Bergler's work, much more psychiatric evidence had been amassed. Most important, these authors brought methodological awareness to the table in examining the evidence on problem gamblers. As the authors report, typically the treatment of problem gamblers—and the case studies that resulted—came at the request of legal authorities or distressed friends and relatives. Problem gamblers rarely sought treatment of their own accord. This means that a particular (even, peculiar) subset of problem gamblers was likely to receive treatment and documentation. Freudian theories were all based on this particular subset.

Bolen and Boyd (1968) note that when the problem gambler seeks out psychiatric treatment independently, his gambling is just one of many complex symptoms. Often:

He presents with other complaints such as depersonalization, impotence, marital difficulties, suicide attempts or ideation, etc. . . . The arduous course of therapy with the patients' frequent relapses and secondary complications . . . often causes interruption or discontinuation of treatment. (628)

That said, the review by Bolen and Boyd contains three comments that remain intriguing today. First is the claim that "extensive psychoanalysis has been held to be the only effective treatment. Psychoanalysis, or variants of it, is the most often used treatment reported in the literature, and the success rate is reportedly quite high" (1968, 628). This is a claim rarely if ever heard today among gambling researchers and therapists, for whom cognitive therapy is the preferred treatment.

Second, Bolen and Boyd (1968) observe that case studies since Freud's time have noted the importance of family dysfunction as a cause of problem gambling:

> The parents are portrayed as similar to Dostoevsky's with the father described as a cold, rigid, moralistic, and critical authoritarian, and the mother characterized as weak, submissive, devoted to the father, and stimulatory of overdependence in the son and eventual gambler. (628)

We have found a great deal of support for this view in our own research, as will become evident in the next part of the book.

Finally, Bolen and Boyd (1968) note that "in nearly all of our patient-gamblers, at least one of the parents and many of the siblings have been social or pathological gamblers" (629). This observation does not seem to hold true of Dostoevsky but correctly characterizes many of the present-day gamblers we studied.

Through the twentieth century, writers who talked therapeutically about Dostoevsky tended to cover the same ground. Refreshingly, a review of the psychiatric literature on gambling by Richard Geha (1970) begins with Ernst Simmel, for whom gambling represents foreplay; winning, orgasm; and losing, ejaculation, defecation, and castration. It swiftly moves on to the customary discussion of Freud's essay on Dostoevsky and parricide, then to less familiar material by other eminent psychoanalysts, including Theodor Reik, Otto Fenichel, and Edmund Bergler. They all agree that Dostoevsky's gambling problem conforms to Freudian or neo-Freudian psychoanalytic interpretations of problem gambling, and that Dostoevsky's book *The Gambler* also conforms, largely by conforming to Dostoevsky's life.

Summarizing, Geha concludes that certain biographical patterns are common in the psychoanalytic assessments of both Dostoevsky and other problem gamblers. First, there is the love and loss of a warm, gentle, and unselfish mother, which not only creates a permanent sense of loss and defeat but also sets the ground for troubled relations with women generally.

In particular, Geha (1970) reports, the problem gambler feels a need to rescue women. Second, and for convoluted reasons that are unclear at this remove, there is an "Oedipal search for knowledge; the giving and getting of secrets as an act of love, the equation of the secret with the genitals; and finally, the need to physically incorporate the secret" (296). Rescue fantasies involve "paying a debt to mother, but also defiantly clearing accounts with father as well" (299).

Geha's essay ends by reaffirming the traditional Freudian (i.e., psychoanalytic) conviction that gambling is ultimately about punishment—punishing (or wanting to punish) the castrating father and receiving punishment in return for doing so. Geha (1970) quotes Marcel Proust's insightful comment that "*Crime and Punishment* could be the title of all Dostoevsky's novels. . . . There certainly was a crime in his life, and a punishment . . . but he has preferred to allot them severally, to attribute in case of need the impression of punishment to himself . . . and the crime to others" (300).

Geha (1970) ends his analysis by asserting that:

> even though the gambler does finally lose, it need not follow that he wishes to lose. That he wishes through punishment to assuage his guilt seems probable. But his hopes, his dreams we mean, are first and foremost to win the mother's body . . . that childhood cornucopia. (288)

Not all of the literature that mentioned Dostoevsky's gambling problem is psychoanalytic in method or outlook, however. An ethnographic study of gamblers by Cotte (1997) confirms evidence in the literature that people bring many motives to gambling: some are instrumental, aimed at making money, while others are expressive (or "autotelic"). As well, some gamblers are focused on objects (the game, the winnings), while others are focused on themselves or other people in the environment. Cotte notes, in the table reproduced below, that all of these motives have been discussed at one time or another by gambling researchers.

Table 1   Prior Research on Gambling and Leisure Motives

Motive Base	Motive
Economic	Money makes gambling more important and involving
	Money has lost market value but still acts as an incentive
	Simple economic gain
Symbolic	Risk-taking to symbolically add risk or "action" to a mundane existence
	Symbolic sense of control for those in society (lower and working classes) who lack control of their own situation
Hedonic	Partial, intermittent reinforcement
	Pleasure induction to enhance self-esteem, self-image
	Pure entertainment; diversion; play

Source: Cotte (1997)

Many of the problem gamblers we have studied, including Dostoevsky, imagine their motive for gambling is mainly instrumental—to make money or even take risks—but in fact their motive is emotional or expressive—to experience the rush associated with taking the risk. As Cotte (1997) says of some purely recreational gamblers, "the motive here is to experience emotional highs and lows—to generate a 'rush' of reactions" (394), or as some gamblers describe it, to put themselves wholly "in the moment" (394), outside any extraneous concerns and worries.

The attractiveness of Cotte's analysis is that it takes note of work by gambling researchers who think outside the psychoanalytic framework, and outside the framework of "gambling pathology." And partly for this reason, it takes note of research that includes "normal" gamblers in "normal settings," not merely problem gamblers in therapists' offices.

Repeating and extending a theme we encountered earlier, Sallaz (2008) reaffirms that gambling is typically a social behaviour, carried on in the company of other people in organized social settings. Therefore, we are obliged to interpret it in a specific social context. To illustrate this, and following anthropologist Clifford Geertz's (1973) anthropological insights, he compares gambling in a South African casino and an Indonesia cockfight, highlighting the differences even among avid gamblers:

Three differences are delineated regarding the position of gambling as an institutionalized practice within the larger social matrix; the organization of the individual games; and the subjectivities produced through participation in the contests. . . . Social and political dimensions of gambling are here subsumed within an economic framework of action and understanding. (5)

Psychoanalyst Peter Shabad (2000) offers another insight on Dostoevsky that may help make sense of his problem gambling. In a paper titled "Giving the Devil His Due," Shabad (2000) argues that spiteful behaviour— sometimes characterized as "cutting off your nose to spite your face"—is a form of "reactive passivity" growing out of a child's initial "sense of shame, powerlessness, and resulting fatalism" (690). Instead of directly confronting the oppressor through self-assertion, or hiding a sense of hurt and failure, the spiteful person struggles "to recapture one's individual dignity through an opposition to power" (690). Under the best circumstances, this spiteful self-destruction may succeed in "arousing and punishing the conscience of the powerful, exploiting other" (690).

It can scarcely be argued that roulette wheels or casinos suffer a bad conscience from the spiteful actions of a problem gambler who makes one losing bet after another, until all the money is gone. Nonetheless, the "spiteful" gambler is at least following Dostoevsky's view, expressed in *Notes from Underground*, that "the whole meaning of human life can be summed up in the one statement that man only exists for the purpose of proving to himself every minute that he is a man and not an organ stop!" (Dostoevsky 2011[1864], 289). Along similar lines, Dostoevsky declares, "All men want is an absolutely free choice, however dear that freedom may cost him and wherever it may lead to" (Dostoevsky 2011[1864], 284).

From this standpoint, even problem gambling—to the extent that it is a choice and not a compulsion—is a declaration of freedom, hence a declaration of humanity, in spite of cruel and seemingly invincible chance.

A Sociological Interpretation of Dostoevsky's Gambling

In this book, we propose an alternative interpretation of Dostoevsky's gambling—a sociological or social-psychological interpretation. We have validated this interpretation (or theoretical model) in three different ways, as we make evident in an academic report, "The Intergenerational Transmission of Problem Gambling" (2010, available at the Ontario

Problem Gambling Research Centre website), written about this material. First, this interpretation is congruent with the published research literature on problem gambling. Second, this interpretation is congruent with the deeply detailed qualitative interview data we collected. Third, this interpretation is supported by a statistical analysis of the overall model, using a variety of multiple regression analyses. By common statistical standards, the model receives strong support from this quantitative assessment.

Our theoretical model focuses specifically on the sociological factors that are involved in the transmission of problem gambling from parent to child. In this way, we bracket the role of personality—impulsivity, sensation seeking, and arousal—and genetic factors. We acknowledge that genetics and personality are important for understanding problem gambling and its inheritance, though the genetic heritability may be quite low (Walters 2001). However, we argue that these factors interact with social conditions—social and environmental factors predispose or activate the genetic and personality potential for problem gambling by bringing gambling tendencies to the surface.

The importance of personality and genetics can still be seen in our results. It is likely that the stories that do not fit our model involve a peculiar interaction between social conditions and genetics or personality. For example, personality and genetic factors can influence perception. An individual's perception of an event as stressful or not stressful has important repercussions for their risk of becoming a problem gambler. Also, perception about oneself, such as self-esteem, can influence an individual's vulnerability to developing a gambling problem (which we refer to as emotional vulnerability below).

Prior to our research, the understanding of the sociological mechanisms involved in the transmission of problem gambling from parent to child was underdeveloped. Other sociologists have previously identified several factors that play a role in the inheritance of problem gambling. However, the literature is unclear on which factor or group of factors more strongly predicts the transmission of problem gambling. Accordingly, our model considers all of these factors simultaneously to clarify their roles in the process of inheritance.

Our model begins with parental problem gambling. Because of their parent's or parents' gambling problem, the children experience social learning of gambling. This includes learning gambling behaviours and beliefs, being exposed to positive attitudes toward gambling in the household, and an increased level of gambling opportunities within the family. Parental problem gambling also results in a stressful childhood, which includes parentification, abuse, and neglect. Parentification, or children parenting parents, has rarely been considered as a factor in the development of problem gambling, so we include it here to address this deficiency. Suffering emotionally during their development years predisposes the children of problem gamblers to mental illnesses, including depression and anxiety.

Adulthood stressors later contribute to the poor mental health of these individuals. In order to relieve stress and cope with mental health issues, children of problem gamblers often employ poor coping strategies learned in childhood, such as gambling as a means of escape. Because of the emotional vulnerability created by high stress and mental illness, and low levels of positive coping, the children of problem gamblers are highly likely to become problem gamblers themselves. Based on this theoretical model, we hypothesized that problem gambling inheritance occurs when the vulnerabilities of childhood distress and the social modelling of gambling are triggered by adulthood stress.

Our model of the developmental process of problem gambling inheritance fits well with the predominant conceptual model of problem gambling development—Blaszczynski and Nower's Integrated Pathways Model (2002). According to this model, all pathways to problem gambling begin with the availability and acceptance of gambling, and the learning of

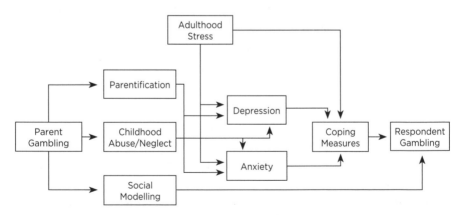

Theoretical Model of Problem Gambling Inheritance

irrational beliefs. From there, the pathway splits into three, where each successive pathway contains additional risk factors. The first group— behaviourally conditioned problem gamblers—is at risk of problem gambling due to irrational beliefs about the odds of winning at gambling. The second group—emotionally vulnerable problem gamblers—is at biological risk and emotional risk from childhood stress and mental illness. The last group—anti-social impulsivist problem gamblers—is at biological and emotional risk, but is also characterized by impulsivity, anti-social personality disorder, and attention deficit.

Our own model fits best into Blaszczynski's second pathway— emotionally vulnerable problem gamblers—because it, too, focuses on the social learning of gambling (availability and acceptance) in addition to the emotional vulnerability created by a stressful childhood. However, our model is best understood as an interaction between all three pathways. Though our focus is on the role played by pathway 1 (social learning) and pathway 2 (emotional vulnerability) in understanding problem gambling inheritance, we acknowledge the role played by pathway 3 (personality factors) and biological risk factors. So our model is similar to the integrated Pathways Model in terms of the factors we feel are important for understanding problem gambling. Where we diverge is in viewing these factors not as separate pathways but as conditions that interact with each other.

The results from our study of present-day gamblers provide general support for our developmental model of problem gambling inheritance. Our analysis suggests that the factors of childhood learning, childhood distress, and adulthood stressors can account for intergenerational and non-generational transmission: we found that nearly all problem gamblers in our content analysis (an astounding 97 percent) experienced one or more of these three factors, while 87 percent of the problem gamblers we interviewed experienced at least two of these three social factors.

Quantitative analysis of the answers to our questionnaire finds that our model explains 42.3 percent of problem gambling inheritance. The remaining percentage is likely accounted for by unmeasured genetics and personality variables, and the additional variables we identified through our analysis of the interviews (such as social learning of gambling outside of the household and during adulthood, and proximity to gambling). Our quantitative analysis also shows that, as predicted, most of the factors in our model contribute indirectly to problem gambling—they are steps in a longer process.

However, some of the steps included in our model are not found among our participants. Namely, parentification, neglect, and abuse do not necessarily lead to mental health issues. Also, stressful adulthood events do not lead to poor coping behaviours, only poor mental health does. Finally, child problem gambling is not explained by the social modelling of gambling, likely because the learning can be positive or negative (as we will discuss in a later chapter). Based on these findings, we offer a revised model of the developmental process below.

We recognize that childhood trauma (for example, childhood neglect or abuse) may play a large part in the motivation of a problem gambler, just as Freud and the Freudians have said. But the theory is incomplete if it stops there, because as sociologists we hold that people express their motivations in the context of social constraints and opportunities. This means that a theory needs to say something about the post-childhood factors—adult constraints and opportunities—that make some abused children into problem gamblers, other abused children into over-eaters (for example), and still other abused children into perfectly normal members of the community.

In our revised model of problem gambling, childhood trauma is the starting point. However, it only becomes important in the context of adult stresses (which inflame the childhood-induced vulnerability) and factors that may mitigate these stresses: strategies for coping with stress, on the one hand, and social support networks, on the other. Competing with these are incentives and opportunities to express neurotic impulses: opportunities

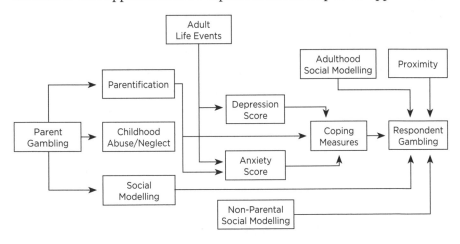

Theoretical Model of Problem Gambling Inheritance: Revised

for gambling to excess, for example. Often, we talk about the variables in our model as "risk factors" for problem gambling.

According to current research, many factors put people at a higher-than-average risk of developing a gambling problem. These include experiencing emotional problems, having a problem gambling family member, and experiencing a big win early in one's gambling career. Having easy access or being exposed to gambling also makes a difference. Lacking interests or hobbies and not having friends or family to provide emotional support also increase the risk that a person will become a problem gambler.

As we know, Fyodor Dostoevsky displayed many of these risk factors. Yet, fully blind to any pathology in his behaviour, Dostoevsky claimed that he gambled mainly to pull himself out of poverty, repay his debts, and support his dependents. Gambling seemed attractive because Dostoevsky believed he could win the large amounts of money he needed quickly and with little effort. His first experiences with gambling encouraged this outlook, since he won a large amount of money the first time he gambled.

As we have noted, Dostoevsky's wife, Anna, found it impossible to keep Dostoevsky from gambling. Living in Europe, far from the Russia he loved, Dostoevsky lacked a network of social controls and also lacked a network of social supports. Because he was far from his home when the gambling problem was at its worst, Dostoevsky may not have realized just how important this lack of friends and family may have been in contributing to his gambling problem. The deaths of both his first wife and favourite brother further reduced his already inadequate support network.

Dostoevsky's gambling problem caused many of his other problems, but he may have also gambled to cope with his problems. His feelings of depression, for example, may have been both a cause and effect of his gambling problem. The various stressors he faced—including strained finances, the deaths of his wife and brother, his failed journals, and being forced to write under heavy contractual pressure—likely deepened his depression. In turn, Dostoevsky may have gambled to escape from these problems, or at least distract himself from thinking about them. But huge losses, putting him further in debt, probably worsened the depression. Dostoevsky thus created a downward spiral in which depression drove him to gamble and the gambling intensified factors (like poverty) that caused his depression.

Further, Dostoevsky tended to gamble excessively after long, intense periods of writing, when he was mentally exhausted. As we saw earlier,

Anna quickly learned that a session at the roulette table restored her husband's emotional balance and creative vigour (Lantz 2004). Playing roulette helped Dostoevsky relax after working hard for an extended period. In particular, it helped him relieve the stress that resulted from being under intense pressure by contractual partners like Stellovsky.

In the end, despite an inclination to gamble recklessly, Dostoevsky finally followed through on his promise to Anna to stop playing roulette. Kenneth Lantz (2012) remarks that:

> The fact that he and Anna now *could* go back to Russia (his most pressing debts had been paid off, and he wasn't faced with being thrown into debtor's prison, which was why they hadn't returned earlier) was a huge factor. He was looking ahead to a more stable life in Russia, away from the lure of the roulette tables. And, perhaps, he really had hit bottom at last. (personal communication)

Contrary to Freud's belief that guilt caused Dostoevsky to gamble, guilt may have helped Dostoevsky to stop gambling. For one thing, Dostoevsky started to worry about Anna's health. He was worried that she became frustrated with him, and that his unreliability and huge losses at the roulette table took a toll on her well-being. In a letter to her, Dostoevsky expressed this concern: "I know that you will die if I were to lose again!" (Frank 1995, 426).

The terrible dreams that plagued Dostoevsky throughout this part of his life reveal that he worried that his gambling problem might cause Anna's death. Dostoevsky also described a dream in which Anna "turned gray" or died because of the stress she underwent because of his addiction (Frank 1995, 427). Dostoevsky felt so guilty about the suffering he was causing Anna that even his dreams tormented him. Given the importance of guilt in Dostoevsky's life, it is likely that this intense guilt about Anna drove him to take control of his habit.

However, guilt was only a small part of the sociological story. Far more important was the support and control that Anna provided. By the early 1870s, his financial situation and family life had stabilized, giving Dostoevsky less need to "lose himself" or escape from his troubles.

Largely, this was due to the close relationship Dostoevsky had developed with his prudent and affectionate second wife, Anna. Her unvarying love provided the support Dostoevsky had previously lacked. He and Anna grew closer while living together under trying circumstances in Europe. Because Dostoevsky's heavy losses prevented them from returning home when they had planned, he and Anna sought comfort in each other whenever they felt "homesick for their native land" (Frank 1995, 427). This close-knit relationship provided the support Dostoevsky needed finally to overcome his gambling problem.

As critic Galya Diment (1997) has noted:

> In order to save her husband and herself from the abyss of misery and poverty, from which many of her husband's literary creations were incapable of escaping, Anna Dostoevskaia soon transformed herself into a fairy godmother who for the rest of Dostoevskii's life tried to steer him away from disaster. . . . She was quick to realize that if she wanted to preserve her sanity in the world as it existed around her, she could no longer afford the luxury of playing the role of a mythical Cinderella. (444)

Anna's supportive behaviour was ideal, from one standpoint. Despite the financial and emotional strain Dostoevsky repeatedly put on their relationship, Anna provided a fixed point in Dostoevsky's life around which routine, regularity, and productivity could flourish. Rewards would follow, with no further need for gambling. As Alexandra Popoff (2012) has written recently about her study of the wives of six Russian authors:

> Dostoevsky's achievement was . . . impossible without Anna, whom he called his guardian angel, collaborator, and a rock on which he could lean. . . . Anna nursed Dostoevsky through his gambling addiction and epileptic attacks. Being a stenographer, she also helped Dostoevsky produce his novels, remarking that the hours he dictated to her were the happiest. . . . [M]uch like Sophia Tolstoy, she loved her husband's literature while still in her girlhood. . . . Dostoevsky never failed to acknowledge Anna's contributions; he called her his idol and his only friend. . . . After decades of publishing Dostoevsky and establishing his museums, Anna remarked, "I did it out of gratitude for . . . the hours of highly artistic enjoyment I experienced reading his works." (n.p.)

Part II

The Dostoevsky Process Today

5

Childhood Distress

In Part II, we report on the findings of a study of present-day problem gamblers in the Greater Toronto Area in Canada. The theoretical framework that informed our methods is described in Appendix 1. The three methods we used to collect our data are described in Appendix 2. From a sample of Torontonians, we collected and analyzed questionnaire data, which permitted a powerful statistical analysis of our results. Face-to-face interview data permitted a deeper exploration of people's thoughts. Finally, data from published memoirs and blogs were used, along with the transcribed interview data, to furnish illustrative quotes throughout the book.

All three types of data pointed consistently, and powerfully, in the same direction. In the beginning pages of this book, we introduced what we've termed the Dostoevsky Effect—a developmental model of gambling that applied to both Dostoevsky's life and to the lives of present-day gamblers we encountered in our study.

The Dostoevsky Effect begins in childhood, with traumatic experiences that create anxiety and other mental health disturbances, and stunt coping skills. In adulthood, a new variety of life stresses raise anxiety and call for the coping strategies acquired in childhood. Where the coping strategies are stunted and maladaptive, the result may be an increase in anxiety and depression—even a cycle of new troubles and failed efforts to deal with them.

In the following three chapters in Part II, we will discuss each of the three forces—childhood distress, adult stresses, and maladaptive coping strategies, respectively—that contribute to the development of problem gambling, showing precisely how they interact to produce problem gambling. A fourth chapter will explore the devastating effects of a gambling problem for the daily lives of gamblers, as well those of their friends and families. We will see how the experiences of present-day problem gamblers are similar to the experiences of Dostoevsky, discussed in the preceding part, and in a closing chapter, we will draw attention to specific similarities between the experiences of Dostoevsky and present-day gamblers.

In the early 2000s, the US Centers for Disease Control and Kaiser Permanente, a well-known managed care consortium, combined forces to embark on a large-scale, landmark investigation into the role played by adverse childhood experiences in addiction. Following the study of more than 170,000 middle-class Americans, the Adverse Childhood Experiences (ACE) study's chief investigator, Dr. Vincent Felitti, concluded, "The basic cause of addiction is predominantly experience-dependent during child-hood" (Felitti 2003).

We will see that stressful childhood experiences play two key roles in predisposing people to problem gambling. First, they do long-term psychological damage, predisposing the person to lifelong anxiety, depression, or both. Second, they hinder the development of positive, effective coping strategies. We will see that, in childhood, adult problem gamblers were likely to have suffered such traumatic experiences as physical abuse, neglect, abject poverty, parental divorce, and the death of a loved one. The psychological damage is evident in their behaviour and in the anger, regret, and loss they expressed to our interviewers. In childhood, they were thrown into situations for which they were not developmentally prepared. This hindered their ability to gradually develop mature coping skills—and, for most, mature coping skills failed to develop at all. As a result, for these problem gamblers, negative emotions continue to intrude on their daily lives, creating new sources of anxiety and depression.

It is important to understand that in this study, we approach stress as a subjective experience. Lazarus and Folkman's (1984) model of stress and coping, which defines stress as a unique interaction between the individual, his or her environment, and an external stressor, is the predominant model in the field of sociology. If the individual experiences this interaction as harmful to his or her well-being and challenging his or her resources and ability to cope, the individual will experience stress. This model is useful to us because it creates a place for idiosyncratic interpretations of per-ceived stress and trauma and allows us to propose how two individuals who experience similar circumstances are differently affected—and in the case of this book, how one may go on to become a problem gambler, and another avoids gambling's grasp.

Throughout our study, we identified a wide range of stressful events and situations that pushed the people in our study toward problem gambling. In this book, we focus on the most common kinds of stressful events and situations for our study participants. In addition to stressful (or traumatic, singular) events, we identify several stressful situations that continued throughout the childhoods of many participants. They include recurring instances of physical, emotional, or sexual abuse; chronic neglect; and parentification (itself a form of neglect in which children are forced to take on adult roles and responsibilities) in a variety of forms, including homelessness and financial stress. In the pages that follow, we will discuss and illustrate all of these childhood traumas in greater detail.

Most of the distressing incidents experienced by gamblers in our study took place in their family settings, with only 2 percent of traumatic events occurring outside the family. This reminds us that families can be danger zones—places of profound victimization—for many children in our own society, and in Dostoevsky's. Problem gamblers tend to come from what are often referred to as "dysfunctional" families—families who, often despite best efforts, are frequently caught in self-perpetuating cycles of poor relationships, maladaptive habits, and circumstances of social disadvantage. For those individuals raised in such an environment, it is not surprising that the distress they endured in childhood can be linked to their family relations. In order to cope with the memories and consequences of these experiences, many people turned to gambling. In this section, we will explore the reasons why gambling, of all possible outcomes, was the outlet for these individuals.

One factor that contributed to childhood distress in some cases was the presence of a problem gambling parent. In fact, as we will see, having a problem gambling parent in the home increases the likelihood of childhood stressors and family dysfunction. Not surprisingly, children who are raised by problem gamblers experience more stresses and develop poorer coping skills than children who do not have problem gambling parents, putting them at a greater risk of becoming problem gamblers themselves.

However, in our study we will be introduced to many problem gamblers who did not have a problem gambling parent. In this respect, they are like Dostoevsky: they suffered from childhood trauma and developed a gambling problem only after reaching adulthood.

Consider the example of Marilyn, a study participant whose parents were not gamblers but were addicted to alcohol. Marilyn told us that her

parents' addictions harmed her as a child and that she thinks their alcoholism contributed to the development of her gambling problem in adulthood. "My parents both had drinking problems so if addictive, compulsive
behaviour is hereditary, then I believe my poor coping skills came from my
parents," she said. Growing up in a household with two alcoholics guaranteed distressing experiences for Marilyn, for reasons that will become
apparent in the course of this part. In short, her parents' addiction exposed
Marilyn to stress and anxiety; her parents' poor coping skills, as illustrated
by their reliance on alcohol, taught Marilyn the wrong ways to cope with
stress and anxiety.

Up next, we'll turn to some particular occurrences of childhood distress that surfaced in the course of our interviews to examine how these
instances helped set the stage for a future of problem gambling. First, we
will hear the stories of people who suffered a traumatic event during their
childhoods. Keep in mind that the distress they suffered as children or
teenagers continued to resonate into their adult years, contributing to the
development of problem gambling tendencies.

Trauma

What makes a particular event or situation a "traumatic" one? As we
discussed with the concept of stress, trauma is defined by the subjective
experience. "Traumatic occurrences" are specific, singular events that leave
lasting feelings of stress and despair in the children who experience them.
They are frequently sudden and unexpected, a characteristic that mini-
mizes the ability to mentally or physically prepare yourself to cope with the
situation, and because you are unable to adequately react, you are left feeling overwhelmed, challenged, distressed, and disarmed. In this way, and
because both are characterized by subjective interpretation, trauma may be
understood as a response to extreme stress. Often, the horrific memory of
a traumatic experience remains with individuals for the rest of their lives,
and they carry it with them into adulthood.

There is ample evidence suggesting that problem gamblers in particular experience several stressful situations in their childhoods, which
could cause them to employ poor coping strategies, like gambling, later
in their own lives. Taber, McCormick, and Ramirez (1987) found that
23 percent of problem gamblers in treatment reported severe trauma,

which included sexual or physical trauma. These same respondents were also more depressed and anxious, which we know is correlated with gambling severity. Additionally, Petry and Steinberg (2005) found that problem gamblers are more likely to have experienced physical neglect, emotional abuse, and sexual abuse, and that the severity of the abuse was associated with a younger age of problem gambling onset and more severe gambling problems. Kausch, Rugle, and Rowland (2006) found a similar pattern, reporting that 64 percent of in-treatment pathological gamblers experienced emotional trauma, 40.5 percent experienced physical trauma, and 24.3 percent experienced sexual trauma, all of which occurred mostly during childhood.

Wolkowitz, Roy, and Doran (1985) proposed that problem gambling often follows a major life stress, such as the illness, injury, or death of a parent. Regardless of the type of trauma, these instances affect the individual mentally and physically for years to come. Research consistently shows that early life adversity increases the risk of psychopathology later in life, both via physiological alterations in neurobiological systems responsible for stress response and via psychological changes that leave individuals ill-equipped to cope with future stress.

One of the traumas participants reported to us was the death of a loved one.

Death and/or Loss

Nemeroff (2004) found that children who are exposed to the death of a parent are at higher risk of depressive and anxiety disorders later in life, both of which our survey data found to be strongly associated with the severity of our participants' problem gambling. Not surprisingly, several problem gamblers who participated in our study experienced the trauma of losing a loved one. This loss forced them, at a young age, to experience profound feelings of abandonment and loneliness, and affected their future psychological development. Denise, for example, experienced this trauma at the age of fourteen, when her mother died:

> When I was fourteen, everything changed. My mother died of complications from a routine surgery for stomach ulcers. Diane [her sister] had finished high school and moved out. Within two years, my father remarried and we moved in with my stepmother in Flint, about an hour's drive north

of Detroit. Losing my mother, my sister, and the rest of my family made me angry and rebellious.

Seemingly out of nowhere, Denise's world was turned upside down. The sudden and unexpected loss of her mother is undoubtedly considered to be traumatic, and the additional change in household structure (i.e., her sister leaving and the arrival of her stepmother) left her without the familiar faces and environment that might have helped her cope with the loss of her mother. The anger, resentment, and rebelliousness Denise felt in response to the situation led her toward ineffective coping behaviours, one of which was gambling.

Bill is originally from Melbourne, Australia, and talked with us about how he also experienced the death of a family member. Bill's father passed away when he was just a child, and the difficulties associated with his father's death stayed with him for many years: "When my father passed away I was only . . . six. It really influenced my life. . . . I was always very, very negative, I was always relatively depressed, I always felt very, very lonely because I'd been abandoned basically." The trauma of his father's death set the stage for how he would interpret events and his environment from then on. A negative disposition and the self-debasement that comes alongside a depressed mood put him in a vulnerable position in terms of his ability to positively and adequately cope with stress. Bill turned to gambling in an effort to generate some positive emotions—the adrenalin rush that comes with a potential win and the excitement in the atmosphere— but the end result was a self-perpetuating cycle of stress and defeat when gambling caused problems that further gambling couldn't solve.

Like Bill, many other participants felt it was difficult to overcome the pain they felt over the death of a parent. Several said that they still felt upset about the event, even as adults. Nancy, for example, had lost both of her parents to diabetes when she was a teenager, yet this traumatic experience continued to affect her in adulthood: "To this day I'm still stressed out [by their deaths] and I wish I would have spoken to someone and they've been gone for over ten years now." The loss of such important figures in one's life, particularly in the formative years of youth, means triggers for such painful memories are ubiquitous and the stress associated with those memories is easily brought upon Denise, Bill, and Nancy. When faced with those moments of stress, they turned to gambling as a means to cope.

Tim was also shaken emotionally when his father disappeared from his life. Only ten years old when his father left home and twelve when he committed suicide, Tim was too young to handle these situations emotionally. He felt as though his father had abandoned him twice: first, by walking out on him and his family, leaving Tim to feel he wasn't good enough for his father, then two years later, when his father's suicide meant Tim had to give up the hope of seeing his father again. Tim remembers, "He did it in a car. Closed the windows up and got carbon monoxide poisoning. He just never got rid of his alcoholism and he'd also been in the war. I think it was post-traumatic stress disorder."

Discussing the suicide in retrospect, Tim is able to understand some of the reasons for his father's behaviour. Yet, he struggles to understand and remains unconvinced by his father's reasoning, and as such, has been unable to achieve emotional closure on this event. In an effort to deal with the stress, Tim sought relief in gambling. The prospect of winning and the entertainment associated with gambling allowed him temporary relief and distraction from the pain and frustration associated with his loss.

Related to the death of a parent was a parent's absence from their child's life. Liam, for his part, had to cope with his mother's long-term institutionalization while still a child. More troubling to Liam was the thought that this may have been brought on by a suicide attempt. His mother's absence also threw Liam's household into turmoil, depriving Liam of the stability and structure that might have helped him to cope with his mother's absence. He described the event as follows:

> I don't know if my mother tried to commit suicide, or if she was just really sick. I was around nine or ten years old, or actually thirteen or fourteen. So it was a stressful event, you didn't know what was going to happen. And Father had to sorta take over responsibilities, which he didn't; he tended to isolate himself.

In his mother's absence, the family environment became unstable. Isolated by his father's response, Liam was frightened and lonely, and with his father unable to take on his wife's parental duties, family life disintegrated and Liam was left to find his own way.

Losing or almost losing a loved one is something our study participants never erased from their memory; in fact, it continued to haunt them well into adulthood. In losing a parent they lost one of their main supports at a vulnerable age. Their lives became unstable and unpredictable, therefore increasingly stressful. Many never learned how to cope with this pain in positive ways, so as adults, they turned to gambling, often in addition to secondary addictions, such as nicotine and alcohol, in efforts to escape from these troubles.

Death or loss is a common occurrence among problem gamblers and has repeatedly been reported as a risk factor for problem gambling development. For example, a study done by Hewitt (1994) in Alberta found that 75 percent of Aboriginal problem gamblers had experienced the death of a friend or family member, while almost half had experienced some other form of substantial loss. It is reasonable to accept the notion that the grief, anger, and frustration associated with the loss of a loved one provides a strong, intrinsic motivation to escape those feelings, which our participants have chosen to do by means of gambling. Considering the distraction of the often flashy gambling environments and by the activity itself, the social connectivity, and also the adrenalin rush and thrill that comes with even the prospect of winning, it is reasonably understood why our participants were drawn to gambling and eventually succumbed to its allure.

Moving and Immigration

Another trauma for some was the experience of moving, and particularly immigration, as a child.

Sociologists have been studying the disruption and upheaval associated with migration for the last ninety years or more, starting with Thomas and Znaniecki's *The Polish Peasant in Europe and America* (1958 [1918–20]), a now classic and seminal study on the migration of Polish peasants to America. Subsequent research has also shown that young people found migration experiences particularly upsetting, with many suffering from identity crises and mental health problems after immigration.

In keeping with the Polish peasant study, the authors revealed that when foreign families immigrated to France, their family relationships changed drastically. This was because the father figure had a lower job status than he had held previously. Not only did this harm the fathers' self-esteem and changed his relations with his spouse and children, but the families were also forced to enjoy fewer material comforts. This deprivation caused great strain in the households affected.

Many members of these families also found it difficult to adapt to a new cultural environment, and they held unrealistic expectations for how quickly they should begin to feel comfortable again. Further, immigrating often meant that these people lost the close ties and proximity to extended family, integral sources of support for most families. This loss made them feel isolated and dejected.

Lena, a study participant, suffered many such changes to her family composition when her place of residence changed:

> We left home during the war back in Vietnam. We lost everything. The communists came and they took everything away—everything run by/owned by the state. We left and my family moved out. My brother and sister—I have them, but it's not like having them because they live in other countries and my mom lives in another country. I came here with my father and stepmom and my sister.

She "lost everything" at once. Family members separated, resulting in a deep sense of loss: "it's like not having them." At the same time, the family's possessions were taken away and they were forced to move overseas. Lena's sense of stability was shaken, and the comforts of home and family were taken away.

A few of the gamblers we interviewed had experienced long-distance moves as children, often between countries and continents, as described by Breanne: "I liked living in Ethiopia, and when I moved, I lost a lot of friends. I always wanted my childhood based on the experience of living in my home country. [But] I left, and that was stressful." The loss of friends meant that Breanne associated loneliness and isolation with life in her new "home." She felt uprooted, which made her new country feel strange and foreign, not home.

Wan also felt the stress associated with immigration when he moved to Canada as a young adult. "I didn't understand anything: couldn't read, couldn't write," he told us. Immigration was an isolating and destabilizing experience for Wan, as it was for others. The hardship of leaving home behind was further complicated by a period of confusion, when he strained to learn a new language and culture.

Other participants, who did not have to learn a different language and culture, still found moving to a different Canadian city difficult. Some of their stressful experiences were like those of children who had emigrated from another country. Some participants even reported moving constantly from one place to another, and with each move, they had to say goodbye to their home, neighbourhood, and friends, to establish new friendships and adjust to new school and neighbourhood relations. Each of these moves created instability and prevented them from establishing a stable, secure, and protective sense of "home" that would otherwise temper feelings of stress and provide a sense of comfort in times of hardship.

For those people who moved multiple times, adjustment became increasingly difficult. They were never in one place long enough to feel comfortable, and they suffered a great deal of distress as a result. This is evident in Taylor's interview, where she described the frustration with her family's frequent moves into new homes:

> My dad also liked to buy places—and I don't mean dumps or anything—but I mean nice homes and then just take all the wallpaper down, and change the wallpaper. It seemed to me that as soon as he bought a home and all the work was done "Oh! Time to move again!"

The frequent changes in housing caused Taylor to feel unstable. She felt she could never settle anywhere with the certainty that she would stay, nor live in any one place long enough to acquire meaningful friendships and feel "at home." The instability of these moves led to much uncertainty and stress in Taylor's life.

To reiterate its importance in the development of problem gambling, frequent moves and international immigration led many people to experience changes in their family's status and organization, and this, too, contributed to a great deal of anxiety they were ill-equipped to handle. This was especially true in the absence of strong support systems— of extended family and friends—which children often lost in a family move. Moreover, their parents were unable to provide enough structure and support for the child, as they, too, were struggling to cope with stress and anxiety related to the move. Lena, Wan, and Taylor are thus prime examples of problem gamblers who were displaced throughout their childhoods and lacked the support systems and opportunity to learn to effectively cope with the associated stress. Eventually, this helped lead them to gamble.

Dysfunctional Family Dynamics and Divorce

Just as changes to children's physical environments were stressful, so were changes to family structure among the gamblers in our study, who often referred to their family environments as sources of stress in their childhood. Those who witnessed unstable family relationships as children were at greater risk of forming their own unstable relationships as adults, and our survey results showed poor relationships to be correlated with problematic gambling. Instances of divorce and otherwise dysfunctional family dynamics are harmful to a child's psychological development and contribute to future struggles with mental health. These situations are particularly common among children whose parents were also problem gamblers, and who make up a large proportion of our participants. For example, Hogan (1997) finds that children of problem gamblers experience inconsistent parenting, lack of parental involvement, parental emotional unavailability, increased family tension and discord, parental separation, parental irritability, and varying levels of physical and verbal harshness. Children whose parents' relationship is rocky often don't receive the attention they require, as their parents are often absorbed in their own stress. Compatible with this suggestion, Vachon et al. (2004) found that low levels of parental monitoring and inadequate discipline were related to youth gambling problems. In contrast, and consistent with previous findings, adolescents with engaged and monitoring parents gamble less and are less likely to be classified as problem gamblers (Magoon and Ingersoll 2006). Inadequate discipline and limited monitoring can be seen not only as sources of stress themselves, but also as the inverse of social modelling, as the parental figures are absent and parental modelling is severely limited.

Among our participants, family dysfunction was a common complaint. The stress and instability created by changing family structures is evident in Melissa's account:

> My older sister did have a problem and left home early at age sixteen. . . . We had a divorce in the family . . . so we had a stepmother . . . when I was about five years old. . . . But my three older siblings had difficulty adjusting to that! [laughs] . . . I always accepted her as my mother, but the three older children, they had problems between the three of them, because they were teenagers, particularly my older sister, who left home when she was sixteen. So to some extent I didn't really grow up with her . . . and my two older

brothers, my memories of them . . . when I was very young and when they grew older they left home as well. So, they were brothers but, they left . . . and so I grew up as an only child, until a younger sister who was eleven years my junior came along!

As is evident, Melissa "accepted [her stepmother] as my mother," but the changes caused tension in the family, especially among the older siblings. The drastic changes to her family composition introduced an element of instability into her life that was stressful and confusing for her as a child and, as we would later learn, caused problems for her in adulthood, one of which was gambling.

Often, divorce was the cause of changes in family life in our study. Parental divorce often causes logistical difficulties for children: for example, being shuffled between homes or enduring custody arguments. As well, many study participants grew up at a time when divorce was less common. Thus, the parental separation and divorce was somewhat taboo and often caused them to feel they were different from other children they knew. So in addition to feeling as though their family was falling apart, these children felt isolated from their peers. Asked if she thought her family was the same or similar to other families she knew, Stacey said, "No, because of the different family structure that I had . . . and how things changed after the divorce." Besides struggling to understand and cope with her parents' divorce, Stacey felt as though she couldn't relate to her peers. Unable to rely on friends for support, she had to deal on her own with stressful feelings associated with both the divorce and with being "different."

Besides the trauma of divorce, many participants suffered from their parents' fighting prior to their separation—inevitably a source of confusion and anxiety. Most disturbing were the instances when children felt they were to blame for their parents' breakup. As well, some divorces were preceded by abuse in the family, and those experiences of abuse additionally left the children emotionally and physically scarred. Apart from the detrimental consequences of stress itself, and the lack of family cohesion and support needed to model appropriate behaviours and coping skills, the extreme stress caused by such dysfunctional and disruptive family environments can cause or exacerbate particular mood disorders in children, and the occurrence of these psychological problems makes them more vulnerable to becoming problem gamblers (Darbyshire, Oster, and Carrig 2001).

Childhood Maltreatment

John Briere (1992), a seminal figure in maltreatment research, suggests that childhood maltreatment significantly influences later behaviour and adaptive psychological functioning. However, the impact is likely mediated by the severity and type of maltreatment, by additional stressors, as well as by the child's level of development. The most common forms of childhood maltreatment include abuse (physical, sexual, and emotional) and neglect (physical and emotional). The literature surrounding childhood maltreatment and gambling disorders is certainly evidenced. Hodgins and Schopflocher (2010) surveyed 1,145 adults in Alberta and found that childhood maltreatment was associated with a higher frequency of gambling and a greater likelihood of gambling problems, even after accounting for individual and social factors such as age, gender, substance use, and other psychopathology, suggesting that childhood maltreatment is independently associated with problem gambling. Similarly, Felsher, Derevensky, and Gupta (2010) found a strong linear relationship between maltreatment and problem gambling among 1,324 young adults aged seventeen to twenty-two; the fewest instances of maltreatment occurred among non-gamblers and the most among gamblers. This relationship held for all forms of abuse and neglect. Among those young adults identified as at-risk or problem gamblers, 14.8 percent admitted that the occurrence of childhood maltreatment continued to negatively affect their current daily life, suggesting that it is both the experience itself and the long-lasting memories that trigger stress and affect their daily behaviour. This finding is in line with those of others, such as Jacobs (1986), Blaszczynski and Nower (2002), and Derevensky and Gupta (2004), who suggest that problem gamblers gamble to relieve stress by escaping thoughts and modulating negative mood states. In any case, it is clear that instances of childhood maltreatment bring about long-lasting and impactful consequences that cause severe psychological vulnerability and increased reactivity to later stress. Among our participants, these adversities led them to seek relief and escape in gambling.

Abuse

Abuse was common among study participants, showing itself in many different forms and to varying degrees. However, its results remained the same: abuse always led to feelings of distress, despair, and worthlessness in the people who experienced it. Regardless of the type of abuse experienced—whether physical, sexual, or emotional—the experience left children feeling degraded, betrayed, and unloved. Often, the abused children also had to tread lightly around their abuser and could not express their true selves for fear of punishment. Consequently, their confidence plummeted and they were unable to develop and become comfortable with their own personal identity, as they'd been shamed and intimidated into silence.

Moreover, our analysis of the (quantitative) survey data revealed that the likelihood of experiencing neglect or abuse was nearly five times greater for children with a parent who was a problem gambler. The effects of abuse persisted into adulthood, as we see repeatedly in this study. Participants who suffered childhood abuse were considerably more likely than non-abused counterparts to adopt abusive or maladaptive coping practices in their adult lives, including problem gambling and, often, co-occurring substance abuse (i.e., alcohol or drug abuse).

The people we interviewed were typically exposed to two forms of physical abuse as children: they witnessed spousal abuse (often, the abuse of their mother by their father), and they suffered abuse first-hand. When one parent abused the other, the child was often not directly involved; however, children who witnessed this abuse remembered it as traumatizing for the rest of their lives. Participants who witnessed such abuse had many different reactions to these situations when they were children. Most often, they reported feeling a sense of powerlessness, tension, and fear while watching one parent harm the other.

Rhonda, for example, watched her father physically harm her mother but was too afraid to intervene:

> I didn't run . . . if he [dad] was hitting on my mom. I would scream but I wouldn't go close. Because I didn't want to get hit. I was quick to run for the police. I would . . . get the policeman but I wouldn't go [back into the home].

As a young girl, Rhonda knew it was wrong for her father to hit her mother, so she sought help from the police because she was afraid to stand up to her dad herself. One can imagine the feelings of guilt and regret she carried with her into her adult years for not helping her mother and feeling powerless against her father. These feelings of helplessness, fear, and distress continued to affect Rhonda well into adulthood. Feeling they had no control in the face of harm and danger was common among abused children in our sample and often caused them to remember their childhood as traumatic.

Stephen also remembered a distressing, frightening childhood. He had felt helpless because of the emotional turmoil between his mother and father. What made matters worse was that, at times, his parents were civil toward each other and even seemed in love. Then, often abruptly, a fight erupted between them:

> My family growing up was [like] Jekyll and Hyde. Mother and father would be like World War 7, fighting, screaming, [and] yelling. The next morning my father would be "Oh yes, can I have a bacon and eggs?" and I would be like, "What is this?"

The most frightening aspect for Stephen was his family's unpredictability; the emotional tone between his parents could change at any time. Stephen was constantly on edge because he could never predict when the next outburst would occur. This constant uncertainty and instability followed Stephen into adult life, contributing to a lack of confidence in his own decision-making and poor judgment, particularly with regard to gambling.

Witnessing domestic abuse also created tension between children and their parents. The tense parent–child relations caused great stress for participants and undermined trust in their parents and other adults who might have provided support and stability during times of need. For example, the conflict between Jonathan's parents led to tension between Jonathan and his father:

> My parents were never happy together or comfortable. He'd [my father] be unhappy and take it out on me sometimes. There was always tension between me and him. And I think sometimes my father would take out his . . . they call it displaced aggression. Like you get mad at somebody, so you'd kick the dog or basically he'd be unhappy so he'd take it out on me sometimes.

The anger that his father directed toward Jonathan led him to feel he was incapable of solving problems—that there was nothing he could do to better his situation or that of his family.

Some problem gamblers in our study were the victims of direct physical abuse by their parents. As children, they lived in fear of the abuse they received from people who were supposed to protect them. This robbed them of their sense of security and self-worth. Like those who witnessed the abuse of another family member, children who were abused themselves felt isolated and powerless to change their lives.

As a result, their adult lives were often coloured by the same feelings of distress, isolation, and helplessness. Rachel describes a particular instance:

> She hit me; it was a big fight between me and my mom, and then she threatened to cut off my arm [with] a butcher knife. She had a cutting board in another arm and then she kept hitting me with that and then I was just on the floor.

Rachel was completely bewildered by the experience, which we know makes it that much more traumatic and stressful, since she was unable to mentally or physically prepare for the incident. She explains, "It was pretty stressful, I guess, 'cause I was really young and didn't understand what I did." As we discussed, it was the unpredictability of the violence that made it particularly "stressful" for her. To Rachel, it seemed like anything could set off her mother's fury and result in a vicious beating; the sheer randomness of it contributed to her fear and anxiety. As a child (and even looking back as an adult), Rachel simply could not understand why she was subjected to such violence.

Chris reported that his parents abused him whenever he let his parents down or failed to live up to a standard: "Report card days were very stressful, every single report card day was stressful, usually my dad would yell at me if I got bad report cards, [and] when I was younger he would actually beat me if I got bad report cards."

Robbie, too, was physically abused when failed to excel academically. "If I came home and had an A+ on my report card, it wasn't good enough. Punishment, I had to redo my homework all over again. He was just downright mean. Nowadays he would have been charged. He'd bounce me off [a wall] a couple of times, [though] very rarely."

Some participants were under extreme stress to meet their parents' high expectations. However, for Ryan and others, in time, the shame of failure changed to anger and resentment for the deliberate pressure and intimidation his parents placed on him, rather than a more productive way of encouraging success. Ryan describes this process of moving beyond shame as he matured, toward anger:

> When I was younger, I either felt really bad or really scared: bad because I was like I wish things were going better, and scared 'cause I'm like, "Shit, I'm going to get beat again." When I was older, I wasn't as scared because they wouldn't beat me as much, I would fight back. For a period of time, I thought it was my fault; but when I got older, I was like, "Well, that's your problem because you lost your temper, you didn't have to lose your temper."

Abuse taught Ryan to fight back, but in remembering these childhood episodes, he continues to feel angry today. Like Ryan, the majority of our participants who experienced abuse in their youth still carry feelings of anger, confusion, and resentment with them. However, many of our participants were not as active in absolving themselves of blame and instead continued to house the guilt and shame into their adulthoods. Constant feelings of inadequacy that had been ingrained since childhood put self-defeating mechanisms into motion and tinted their worldview, causing them to be more likely to experience and interpret events as stressful even as adults. Our participants were lured into gambling as a way to escape these negative feelings.

Sexual abuse was less common than physical abuse among the problem gamblers we interviewed, but some participants did experience it as children. In one participant's particularly devastating story, Debbie and her sister were both sexually abused by their stepfather. Debbie revealed that her stepfather took advantage of her emotionally as well as sexually because she was too young to realize what he was doing to her. Debbie's mother was both an alcoholic and a problem gambler; ultimately, her preoccupation with her own addictions and its consequences left her unable to care for and protect her daughters. By her early twenties, Debbie had been twice impregnated by her abusive stepfather, and the children now serve as constant reminders of her victimization:

> It was okay until my stepfather had sex with me. . . . First it was my sister and then it was me. . . . He just told me he loved me and all this stuff and I believed it 'cause I didn't have a boyfriend. I didn't know anything

about sex and then I fell in love with him. I never knew it was abuse until someone told me later on. It only lasted three years though. Then my sister moved out with him. . . . I left home when I was in my twenties and I got pregnant—I had two kids with him. My sister had three by him. So [it was] a bit of a triangle.

Undoubtedly, this is a traumatic experience that will stay with Debbie for life as she struggles to reconcile her past experience and memories with what she now understands was an unfathomably abusive experience; the enduring psychological damage and confusion puts her at risk for serious psychopathology. Debbie deals with the painful memories through gambling, as it gives her an opportunity to focus her attention elsewhere.

All of these abuse incidents left the victims emotionally scarred. In fact, physical and sexual abuse usually went hand-in-hand with emotional abuse. For example, Adam was left feeling embarrassed and ashamed by the physical beating his father gave him, leaving him with a low sense of self-esteem. He remembered:

One specific memory is me taking two maraschino cherries out of the fridge and my dad gave me my worst beating ever. I couldn't take my shorts, my pants off for gym because I was too embarrassed to show my legs, because they were all black and blue. That was a traumatic event for me as a child.

What Adam remembers most is not the physical pain his father's beating caused him, but the embarrassment of the bruises. It was "the worst beating ever" because it left visible marks for others to see—marks that reminded him of his supposed failure in his father's eyes. The actual experience has long since passed, but the memory lingers and reinvents itself over time, as most memories do, such that Adam can find little relief. Gambling allowed him to distract himself from the pain and embarrassment he continues to feel over the abusive incident.

Emotional abuse did not only occur in the context of physical or sexual abuse. In fact, it was the most common form of abuse participants reported and often resulted in the child feeling rejected, degraded, fearful, isolated, and exploited. The damaging psychological consequences of emotional abuse were particularly common among children who went on to become problem gamblers.

As in Adam's case, the childhood emotional abuse experienced by the people we interviewed often left them feeling incompetent. They felt they could never be good enough for their parents; feelings of shame about their inadequacy caused their self-esteem to plunge. As adults, their low self-esteem made them more vulnerable to maladaptive coping strategies like gambling.

Some participants described being called names, manipulated, being put down, or humiliated. Amrit, for example, described one of the many traumatic events of childhood that involved her mother, who was a problem gambler and an alcoholic.

> I had a . . . little bowl with a fish in it and I didn't clean it, so she flipped the light on and I woke up to having the water tossed on me and then my fish died and she got really abusive. She said, "I told you to clean the fucking tank." She dumped it right on my head at three in the morning. She said, "Now you don't have to clean it." She was really drunk. [The next morning], my fish is dead and I had to go to school and be woke up by her.

Amrit's mother often used harsh words against her, such as, "'you should have been born a boy," and "you bastard child" whenever Amrit came to her with a problem. Even though she understood, in theory, that her mother's drunkenness may have led her to shout insults she did not mean or would never have said while sober, still her words left emotional scars.

Other participants also said they were victims of verbal abuse by their parents, including Sophie, whose father emotionally abused her. "He used to yell at me, [saying] things like I'm stupid, I'm shy, I'm fat. . . . I got that all the time. . . . I'm insecure, I'm not trying hard enough, [I should] be better, stronger, shake it off . . . just words!"

Remember Debbie, who was sexually abused by her stepfather? As we mentioned earlier, our participants tended to experience more than one type of abuse, and in Debbie's case, the second type was emotional abuse by multiple family members. "They told me every day that I was stupid. Every day I heard it. I was always put down. I was always the target, not my brothers, and not my sister either." The only one of her siblings to be degraded in this way, Debbie blamed herself for this abuse, thinking there must was something wrong with her that made her deserve this treatment. She felt confused, but also ashamed of herself, believing her family saw her as a failure. Debbie now struggles with a severe gambling problem. In addition to the escape and relief functions gambling serves, inundated with self-shame and feelings of failure, perhaps it is the prospect of winning big, being a "success," that drives Debbie to continue gambling.

Many participants grew up with certain insecurities that resulted from the emotional abuse they experienced in childhood. Take Megan, who was told that she was a mistake and an unwanted burden on her mother:

> I've known I was a mistake my whole life. As long as I could remember, maybe as young as seven. . . . She [mother] didn't want to get married to him [father], but she did because of me. . . . I sort of felt alone because I didn't know anybody else that was a mistake. Most of my friends seemed like they were planned, or even if they weren't, they seemed to have stable families so it seemed like it went well. Yah, so knowing I was a mistake was difficult.

Megan was reminded of this fact continually by her mother. It caused her to feel a sense of detachment and displacement from her parents but also from her peers, since she did not know any other children who had been unwanted. Unconditional love and acceptance is something that every child needs to thrive, to learn to trust others, and to develop emotionally. Megan was deprived of that as a child, and her emotional growth was hindered knowing she was an unwanted mistake. Her choice to cope via gambling reflects her stunted emotional development.

These physically, sexually, and emotionally abused children were deprived of the physical and emotional security that people need to feel around their parents. Instead, the abuse made them feel a sea of negativity— worthlessness, shame, guilt, failure, inadequacy, incompetency, anger, resentment. They felt they were not good enough for their parents or anyone else and undeserving of love. Such feelings in victims of abuse do not disappear or even weaken as they grow older; often, the feelings are carried forward into adult life, making it hard for victims to form healthy relationships. This is particularly problematic in terms of gambling development, since healthy relationships, as we discuss, are protective factors against the risk of becoming a problem gambler.

Without positive and compassionate relationships to help guide and support them in times of stress, our participants were particularly vulnerable to maladaptive behaviours like problem gambling. Their feelings of powerlessness over the abuse they had endured as children translated into feelings of powerlessness over the appeal of addictive activities and substances. The transcribed interview data, as well as the statistical analysis of our survey data, consistently reflect these experiences.

Neglect

Being a child in a dysfunctional household proved to be very difficult, and experiences of neglect were common among study participants. These children were often deprived of the parental attention they needed, and their parents often spent long periods away from home. These stories were especially common among our participants who had a parent with an addiction, whether to gambling, alcohol, or something else. This finding in our own interview data replicates findings reported in the gambling literature as well. For example, in a retrospective study, Grant and Won Kim (2002) determined that adult problem gamblers reported lower rates of care and protection as children and higher rates of neglectful parenting. Similarly, Hardoon, Derevensky, and Gupta (2002) find that "youth who report having family problems and perceive their families to be unsupportive appear to be at an increased risk for the development of gambling problems" (61).

In the first years of life, most parents form significant and stable emotional connections with their children that are critical to the child's emotional development. The forging of this connection or bond is known as "attachment." According to social control theory, increased levels of parental attachment, commitment, involvement, and belief are linked with a decreased risk for gambling (Kalischuk et al. 2006). From a social development perspective, the family is a core system that is a source of both risk and protection for deviant behaviours, such as gambling (Kalischuk et al. 2006). In this model, items such as parental attachment would be considered protective factors. However, parents need to be present and actively involved in their children's lives for attachment, bonding, and positive modelling to occur, and this was unfortunately not the case for a large portion of our participants. For the children of problem gamblers, for example, the lack of these parental resources can manifest itself as a form of stress, which increases the child's likelihood of becoming a problem gambler as an adult. As we mentioned earlier, low levels of parental monitoring and inadequate discipline are statistically related to youth gambling problems (Vachon et al. 2004).

Sometimes, parental absence was work-related. Other times, addiction itself was the reason these parents were preoccupied or absent. Often, it was a combination of the two reasons; one parent gambled away the family finances, while the other worked extra hours to make up for the financial shortfall his or her partner was creating and tried otherwise to deal with her or his own distress. As a result, both parents were occupied or absent for extended periods, unable to provide their children with an attentive environment that is necessary for healthy psychological and emotional development.

In the cases where our participant had a problem gambling parent, the gambling parent was rarely physically present in the home because he or she followed a schedule that revolved around working and gambling. Darbyshire, Oster, and Carrig (2001) describe the "pervasive loss" felt by the children of problem gamblers, that is, "the loss of the gambling parent, in both a physical and an existential sense; the loss of the child's relationship with extended family; the loss of security and trust, as well as more tangible financial losses, such as the loss of savings and even the family home" (32). This preoccupation with gambling not only left these parents with no time for their family, it also normalized a set of problematic behaviours (i.e., gambling, neglect, selfishness) for their children to internalize as adults.

Neglect, for those who experienced it, often made the children feel they were unimportant, unwanted, and undeserving of love. Neglect therefore affected children in much the same way that abuse did, both falling under the umbrella of childhood maltreatment, of which neglect is the most common form (Hooper 2007). Just like the abused children, the neglected children felt devalued—low in importance compared with their parents' gambling or other addictive habits. The feelings of unworthiness and inadequacy they developed as a result not only affected the relationships with their parents, but also made it hard for them to form stable relationships as adults.

Also as a result of their gambling parent's absenteeism, they came to feel lonely and burdened with stress. One participant, John, remembered: "That is probably a downfall in my upbringing, that I don't remember having active family time." In adulthood, to distract themselves from feelings of isolation and anxiety, some of them turned to the same behaviours—excessive drinking and gambling—their parents had enjoyed (and neglected them for) when they were children.

Surprisingly, often these victimized children believed at the time that they were receiving normal treatment from their parents. They became accustomed to parental absences, and many said that they knew no other way when they were growing up. Noel, for example, was unaware of the negative impact his father's absence would have on him as an adult. In the interview, he explained:

> [My father was] a supervisor for a construction site, and then after [work] he would go to the track or to the trailer park and go drinking and gambling and you'd never see him, maybe on the weekend or on Saturday morning. I never knew what time he would get home, maybe one or two in the morning and then he'd wake up at six and be off for work. So I didn't see much of him; but that's life, that's the way it goes.

Evidently, Noel learned not to question his father's absence and it soon became normalized. If Noel had children of his own, it is possible that he would repeat the cycle of neglect in favour of his gambling habit without so much as realizing that such a degree of absence from a child's life is detrimental to the child's well-being.

Jackson reported a similar experience of neglect. His father was also a problem gambler and spent more time feeding his addiction than he spent at home with his children. When asked about his father, Jackson said:

> He would come late at night, four or five o'clock, and he would sleep and wake up the next afternoon. Then he would go gambling again. Sometimes he would go for work, maybe my mother pushed too much. But if he doesn't have any work, he goes to his friend's house, and goes to other friend's house, and then of course goes gambling.

Evan discussed his father's frequent absences as though they were entirely ordinary: "When I used to live with him he . . . used to leave the house around six, . . . finished work around six, but then he goes to the underground gambling from like seven till ten then comes home around eleven just to sleep." Both Jackson and Evan had a father on paper, but the extent of their fathers' involvement in their sons' lives ended there.

Sometimes, and frequently among our Asian participants, parents left their young children unattended—a practice that was accepted in their own culture, though not under Canadian law. For example, some participants from China said leaving a young child alone at home was not frowned upon where they came from. After moving to Canada, some parents continued to practise these behaviours without considering whether they were legal (or culturally accepted) in Canada. Once the children learned that this practice was not acceptable here, they began to feel confused and different from the other children they went to school with. The resulting feelings of neglect, isolation, and loneliness plagued these individuals throughout their childhood and into adulthood. These participants often turned to gambling in an effort to fill the void created by these feelings.

As noted, as adults, some of the people who had been neglected as children took up the same practices their parents had engaged in instead of spending time at home. Of the people who participated in our study, over half of those with children of their own reported that they had neglected them because of their gambling. Elaine, for example, admitted she neglected her children, saying that her addiction made her less concerned about the well-being of her children. "Gambling made me nervous, selfish, and neglectful toward my children. My head was constantly in a fog." Her problem gambling made her lose sight of her parental responsibilities.

Physical absenteeism was only one form of neglect that participants experienced. Other parents failed to provide their children with basic necessities, or with appropriate supervision or discipline. In other families, children came to feel their parents barely cared about their personal well-being.

This kind of emotional neglect is illustrated by Craig's childhood experiences. Craig fought constantly with his father over everything from video games to "the kinds of friends I had, and me drinking" but the most significant argument was over schoolwork:

> My dad thought I was just wasting my time that summer, and he's like you're going to have to study for four hours a day or I'm going to kick you out, and I said that's ridiculous, it's summertime, I have nothing to study, and he was like, "Well I'll find you something to study," and I'm like, "That's absurd."

Seeking to understand this conflict over academics, Craig said:

> I think my family cared a lot more about my academics versus my personal life. I thought other families cared equally about personal life, because my

parents rarely asked me "How's your girlfriend?" or "Are you happy with the school you're in?" stuff like that, or "What hobbies are you interested in?" or "Can we sponsor you on a sports team?" They were just like "Are you getting 90s in math?" "Are you getting 90s in science?" "Are you passing all your courses?"

Schoolwork became a source of conflict because Craig felt that his parents were neglecting his other needs. Though they valued his grades, they did not value other parts of his life and, as such, did not value him as a person. Without the meaningful interaction Craig craved from his parents, he became absorbed in video games—a solitary activity. The stimulation, competition, and engagement of video games was a natural precursor to gambling, in which he soon also became absorbed.

Ted had a similar experience as a child. His parents enrolled him in a school for gifted children, where he was lonely and unhappy. The fact that his parents kept him enrolled in the school despite his negative feelings about it made him think that his parents did not care about his happiness: "I was getting a better education supposedly and I was with the top 5 percent of the city. So it's like, 'Okay, that's what is important . . . it doesn't matter what he feels like or thinks or whatever.'"

Other participants said they had been unhappy and felt neglected because their parents became obsessed with them excelling in sports. Take Max, who remembers feeling a great pressure to win because his father had led him to feel that he was the "one person responsible for making or breaking" the situation. Attaching consequences (no dinner) only served to heighten the pressure Max felt to focus on winning above all else:

One time, my father, when we were doing swimming, he told me if you didn't win you were really in bad trouble with him. And swimming meets are not like hockey meets, where you have one person responsible for making or breaking; but the family would get very pressured. I remember everybody was [supposed to go] to this Gentleman Jim [restaurant] and he says, "We're not going for dinner," and we didn't eat because we didn't win.

Many said that, as children, they were expected to fulfill unrealistic parental expectations. They felt emotionally distanced from their parents because of a gap between their parents' expectations and their own goals, abilities, and needs. This, for some, resulted in an inability to form positive, stable relationships in adulthood. Further, it predisposed some participants to gambling, which they saw as a way to combat their loneliness and boredom. The pressure to do well in childhood, and the amount of time these parents forced their children to spend on competitive schoolwork or sports, made these children feel like they were losing their youth.

In this way, they came to feel like the children who had to care for their parents or take on adult responsibilities, much like our participants who experienced parentification.

Parentification

When we picture a healthy, stable family, we imagine a loving partnership between two parental figures committed to loving, caring for, and supporting their children. Parents who abuse or neglect their children have obviously failed to fulfill these duties; in fact, they have done the opposite by inflicting physical and emotional pain on them. And other parents inflict pain on their children through frequent or prolonged absence.

A third kind of maltreatment is known as parentification—the circumstance where children are called on to fill the void produced by an absent, neglectful, or abusive parent. In a well-known book, *Families of the Slums*, Minuchin and colleagues (1967) coin the term *parental child* for those who assume parental responsibility in the home due to a myriad of economic and social conditions. Shortly thereafter, Broszormenyi-Nagy and Spark (1973) expanded on the notion of a parental child and described an active process of "parentification," defined by the operation in which a parental figure expects a child to fulfill parental roles within the family system. Parentified children frequently engage in managing or contributing to household income, preparing meals, and raising younger siblings.

Role reversal is another term used to describe parentification; it describes the child who acts as a parent to his or her parent(s) and/or siblings. The child-as-mate role is also considered a form of parentification, in which the child acts as confidant, friend, or decision maker for the parent (Earley and Cushway 2002). Parentified children often find themselves in key caretaking roles that include the care of younger siblings. They may also be called on to provide comfort, advice, and support to other family members, even including their parent(s). In these situations, the parent–child roles are reversed: teenaged (and younger) children must care for their parents, in effect, parenting themselves and other family members around them. For example, they may even have to mediate marital conflicts between parents, or serve as a confidant to one or both parents.

Some literature distinguishes between two types of parentification—instrumental and emotional. Tasks such as meal preparation, extensive household chores, and handling family finances are instances of instrumental parentification, and these fall more in line with the child-as-parent role reversal than with the child-as-mate. This is distinguished from emotional parentification, in which children respond to the emotional needs of their parents and/or siblings, including addressing issues of low self-esteem, for example. Other times, children are forced to act as the peacemaker or mediator in the family in times of conflict (a particularly common occurrence among our participants).

A key point that defines parentification is the fact that these children are not developmentally or emotionally ready to assume the adult roles that have been assigned to them. In this way, parentification has been described as a pathology that leads to emotional, physical, and psychological deprivation for the child of the parental caregiving, guidance, and secure attachment that is essential for child development (Jurkovic 1997). The parentified child then becomes one who sacrifices his or her own needs for attention, comfort, and guidance such that he or she can tend to the instrumental and emotional needs of parents and/or siblings.

Erik Erikson's stage theory of psychosocial ego development (1950), perhaps one of psychology's best known theories, is extremely relevant to the ill effects parentification can have on a child's well-being. Erikson's theory proposes that when inappropriate demands are placed on a child that naturally cannot be met, the child will come to view him- or herself as inadequate, guilty and inferior. Further, because the parent is unresponsive to the child's needs for comfort, support, and guidance, the child is robbed of the ability to safely express and contain those emotions. This would undoubtedly affect the child's future ability to cope with stress and would hinder the development of appropriate and mature coping strategies. Thus, it is not surprising that parentification has been linked to serious adverse psychological outcomes later in life. Parentification adversely affects interrelational development and has been linked to co-dependency (excessive physical or psychological dependence on either the needs of or control of another person, depending on which side of the relationship you fall) and proneness to experience shame, which may be rooted in the child's perceived inability to meet his or her parents' unrealistic and inappropriate expectations. Taking on adult roles as a child has also been significantly and positively correlated with emotional distress (Earley and Cushway 2002).

Barnett and Parker (1998) identify circumstances in which parentification is likely to occur. These include divorce, substance misuse, and sexual abuse. In our study, given the presence of all three of the aforementioned circumstances, it should thus not come as a surprise that many of our participants reported instances of parentification. Barnett and Parker (1998) also noted that the impact of parentification can only be determined toward the end of an individual's developmental lifespan, which makes our retrospective interviews particularly suitable for discussing this unique factor that contributes to the development of problem gambling.

We found that our participants with a problem gambling parent were more than twice as likely to experience parentification as participants whose parents were not problem gamblers. This is in line with research on the adult children of alcoholics, who also report more parentification, instrumental caregiving, emotional caregiving, and past unfairness (Kelley et al. 2007). Parents who misuse substances such as alcohol or drugs, or those who gamble, tend to create an environment that promotes parentification by being generally unavailable, incapacitated, or preoccupied. Energy and effort they are able to muster tends to be put toward their habit rather than their family.

Children who experience parentification are forced to grow up too quickly, by experiencing situations they are not developmentally prepared to handle, and by taking on responsibilities that should not be expected of them. As a result, they suffer emotionally, often feeling anxiety and failure. Not having had the opportunity to learn sociability with their peers, they often have less developed social skills than do children who never experienced parentification. Alternatively, they come to depend too heavily on peer support, rather than addressing some typical developmental issues within the family unit.

Parentification and neglect often go hand in hand, although the former could be considered a type of the latter in that parents who parentify their children neglect their children's needs for affection, attachment, and emotional guidance and support. Children in our study who experienced parentification also had to take care of themselves or their siblings, assuming a lot more household responsibility than was appropriate for their age. Some children took on the extra work because the parent had a gambling problem and was continuously absent. Others took on extra work to help the other parent get all the household work done, feeling that if they did not help out, the household would fall apart. Many did not consider this parentification abnormal, since this was the only way of life they had known. Yet, even they suffered from it; being overburdened with adult duties as a child caused them great stress and hindered their ability to learn healthy ways of coping with this stress. So, children subjected to parentification were more vulnerable to maladaptive coping and, consequently, at greater risk of problem gambling as adults.

Barbara was one of our participants who kept her experience of abuse a secret from everyone, including her alcoholic parents. Reflecting on this, she said she felt as though she had lost her childhood because, in addition to the abuse she suffered, she had to take on adult responsibilities at an early age. Both of her parents were alcoholics and they were unable (or unwilling) to take care of her and her siblings. As a result, Barbara had to raise her brothers and sisters. Looking back on this, she felt she had missed the opportunity to develop close friendships with other children her age. When asked if she had many friends growing up, she responded, "Not really, because I would just basically go to school then come home and take care of my brother and sisters."

In Barbara's story, the effect on her interrelational development is clear. The isolation—virtual house arrest—stunted Barbara socially, and she became unable to form and maintain positive relationships. For her and other participants with similar experiences, gambling came to offer an opportunity for social engagement (of a kind) and thrills they could not find in their personal relationships. Moreover, she lacked the positive and supportive relationships that might have steered her away from gambling in the first place, or at least helped her recognize when it started to become problematic.

Also recall Stacey, whose parents divorced when she was a child, at a time where divorce was still uncommon. The divorce left her vulnerable and feeling like she didn't fit in with her peers. Consequently, she had no support to deal with the feelings of confusion, depression, and anxiety that came with her parents' divorce. Instead, she provided a shoulder for her mother to lean on. Worse still, the divorce brought extra household responsibilities for Stacey. This made her feel unresolved, different, and alone during her childhood.

Naveed also experienced parentification. His parents often left him at home to take care of his baby brother while they went gambling. Being only eight years old at the time, Naveed was just a child himself and should not have had to look after an infant.

> Definitely it was hard . . . a lot of the time I didn't know what to do. [The baby] would cry, but it was okay because if he cried he wanted food or he pooed. But sometimes he would just not stop crying, and I wouldn't know what to do.

Naveed's experience of parentification was a direct product of his parents' gambling problem and the absences this occasioned.

Grace, too, took on extra responsibilities as a child, but they were not directly connected to the problem gambling of her grandmother and mother. Gambling aside, her mother and grandmother put exceptionally high demands on Grace around the household. So, she was forced to take on more household chores than most children her age:

> Dusting, cleaning the bathroom, washing the stove, vacuuming, getting the supper ready, and then what was it? My mother mentioned she would do a commercial with the white glove test and she'd come home, make sure I did under the bed, make sure I did this, make sure I did that. You know, it wasn't good enough. My friends used to come, my one friend Janet after school, in high school, and she'd sit there at the counter watching me do it, you know? "Did you do all the housework right?" Every Friday without fail and then Sundays was laundry and ironing day. That was my job too.

Children whose parents were *not* problem gamblers sometimes also experienced parentification. For example, they took on extra responsibilities if one of their parents was chronically ill. These children took on the responsibility of caring for this parent and often became almost entirely self-sufficient, taking care of themselves too because they couldn't rely on anyone else to do it. Hannah exemplifies the latter kind of parentification. Her mother was depressed and often incapable of caring for herself, let alone her daughter. Hannah became an emotional caregiver for her mother and learned to take care of herself while she was still very young.

> It's almost like she's disabled basically. She's able [to care for herself] some-times, but at other times she's totally unable. It's tough, especially growing up with an absent stepfather and a totally absent biological father. At times I'd have to take care of her. It was tough, but it helped me grow up faster, I think. . . . It was more taking care of myself, I think, than taking care of my mother—doing the things for myself that a mother would normally do. Like getting ready for school in the morning, [and] getting to school with-out talking to her about how I'm going to do it, even at a young age.

Her father and stepfather were physically absent, unable and unwilling to offer Hannah any kind of support, and her mother was emotionally unable to do so. Being forced to care for a parent and deal with the stress of par-ental mental illness meant Hannah's childhood was filled with stresses that most other children would never encounter. Without care, guidance, or positive role models at home, Hannah had no one to teach her productive coping skills as she was growing up.

Daria's childhood was similar to Hannah's: she, too, had to take on the responsibility of caring for her mother because her father was often absent. Daria's mother had been diagnosed with multiple sclerosis, which meant that she needed help in such everyday tasks as walking. Daria provided this assistance, but she was too young to fully understand her mother's condi-tion, so she often felt fearful and confused. She explained her caretaking experiences as follows:

> Sometimes she would have troubles going downstairs and walking to the car so I would have to help her do those things. . . . One day she couldn't move at all, she was lying on the floor. I didn't know what was going on, but I guess I realize now, yeah, she has to take these drugs and stuff.

Many of these children accepted their responsibilities as normal, but some realized they were losing their youth and felt uneasy about the daily tasks they had to carry out. Paulo initially felt he was having a normal childhood, having become accustomed to his caregiving duties around the home. His mother suffered from severe asthma that incapacitated her for a few days at a time every month. During these episodes, Paulo had to take over her household duties:

> It [doing housework when his mother was ill] . . . just ended up being so normal that it didn't really feel any different. I think if you don't have any [duties], and if you get it [assigned duties] once or twice, it may be a shock to the system and you feel awkward if you don't do it. But if you did it all the time, then it becomes a habit: you don't see the difference, you think it's normal.

In contrast to Paulo, Charlene never felt comfortable in her role as a caregiver to her aging grandfather. She said:

> I used to help out around the house 'cause my grandfather was in his early seventies and both my parents were working, so I had to feed him and cook for him, and I was only twelve years old. I didn't even cook for myself and I had to cook for him.

The resentment in her voice was clear: she felt her grandfather was a burden. She felt that it was unfair that she had to take care of him when other children her age were out playing.

Both Paulo and Charlene experienced the loss of their childhood through the illness of a family member. Despite the distress this caused them, they never blamed those they had to care for. In contrast, some participants in our study did blame their parents for forcing them to grow up too quickly. In many of these cases, the father was a problem gambler whose addiction left the mother overburdened with financial strain and household work. The children then became responsible for taking on tasks their mother could not handle. Sometimes, these children wrongly laid the blame on their mother because these responsibilities were "supposed" to be hers.

Perhaps this tendency to blame the non-gambling parent helps to explain why these people became problem gamblers themselves, despite the devastating effects gambling had on their family. They associated their family problems not with their father's problem gambling but with their mother's inability to cope with it without involving the children. This tendency to blame the mother—typically, the non-gambling mother—was most common in traditional nuclear families, where wives were supposed to do all the work and endure their husband's peccadilloes. Consequently, the children in these families felt they had been saddled with extra tasks because their mother was unable to get all the assigned work done as expected.

Rhonda illustrated this viewpoint when she described her upbringing. She remembered that, because her mother was out working for pay, she herself had to take on extra chores:

> We had to cook and do all the housework while my mom was supposed to do that but because she is selling in the market at 4 a.m. we had to do what she was suppose to be doing. . . . That's her role—we are doing her work because now I am fifty-five looking back at that time that was supposed to be my mother's work. My mother's job!

It was her father's gambling problem that forced her mother to get a second job selling food in the market every morning. Yet Rhonda did not blame her father for the extra household chores she and her siblings had to take on. At the time, she was too young to make the connection; as an adult, she still hadn't revised her views, much to her own detriment. Perhaps she might have avoided problem gambling herself if she had blamed parentification on her father's problem gambling.

Mikhail, too, was saddled with duties that normally would have been performed by a parent. His father's gambling problem, combined with a bad temper, led to arguments between his mother and father. In turn, this made Mikhail feel like he had to take on adult domestic chores to quell the fighting, even though he was only a child. He remembered his experiences as follows:

> I'd have to make my own food. I felt like I had to clean, keep everything tidy. 'Cause my dad would leave the house if he felt really angry, and my mom would go to her room. So nothing would get done, they just didn't seem to care, that's what my opinion was. I mean, I'm sure she cared; she just had to do her own thing.

Other participants were forced to take on adult responsibilities because their mother was a problem gambler. In these cases, the effects of parentification were intensified because typically mothers carried heavier chore-loads than fathers. Worse still, mothers with a gambling problem tended to put off doing their chores, since their gambling kept them away from the house. Eventually, they were swamped by the burden of managing both the household and the demands of their addiction.

For example, one woman we spoke to had nine children and an abusive husband, and made three meals a day, besides gambling. Another had six children and gambled her nights away after the housework was done. Both sets of children noticed their mother's high stress levels and became distressed themselves as a result. The hectic household environment made them uneasy, especially when their mother complained to them, revealing details about her personal anxieties.

Mae's mother, a problem gambler, had subjected her to a constant stream of complaints during her childhood. Mae's mother often felt stressed by the demands placed on her, and she vented about this to Mae. Mae became the emotional caregiver for her mother.

> My mom always complained that she had too much to do. . . . She was always stressed; the littlest chore would be a big deal for her. She would remind us how much chores she had, [and] remind us about how ill she was. I think my mom was the type to overexaggerate; I was very unsympathetic toward her—less than other people in my family. They are really sympathetic toward her illness.

Like Rhonda, Mae resented her mother, yet she carried the negativity she learned from her mother into her adult life. Even though gambling was part of the reason she had such a stressful childhood, Mae learned that gambling was a way to forget about her negative world, however briefly.

The people in our study most often affected by this type of parentification came from Asian backgrounds. Chris, for example, had a lot of stress growing up; his Chinese parents held out high expectations for his performance both in school and at home. Speaking about his childhood, he said:

> They expect you to do the housework, do good in school, [and] help out your siblings. . . . My parents are Chinese, and 'cause I was born in Canada they wanted us to make sure we had some of our own culture, so they sent us to Chinese school. That was even more difficult than English school because they had homework every single night—three hours' worth. But then you're expected to do well in English [too], pass as well. And you just, it's too much homework and studying and stress and doing housework and

there's no way you can do well in both subjects. . . . Basically it was full time. . . . Chinese school's even worse 'cause you had to go to school six days a week. It was Monday to Saturday, so the only day off was really Sunday. And then you're doing chores and housework and housework's a chore you need to do. You wouldn't even have a day off. . . . seven days a week. I figure we had to do studying and homework as well, right? It was very stressful. And if you didn't do well in a subject, then you got in trouble.

For this reason, Chris felt he did not get a proper childhood, with friends, games, and family time. Instead, his youth was filled up with school, homework, and home responsibilities. By his account, his parents were unsympathetic and focused more attention on his academic success than on his happiness. The stress that filled his childhood may have contributed to adult gambling problems. Chris found gambling to be exciting and fun—sensations in short supply during his childhood.

In many families, children were also obliged to serve as peacekeepers, a form of parentification discussed earlier in this section. Jonathan, often a victim of his father's aggression, also had to play the peacekeeping role in his household, stepping into the middle of arguments between his parents: "I remember, one time standing between the two of them and saying 'stop this.' I don't know how old I was but I was pretty young. I just told them to stop fighting."

Similarly, Luca had to stop a physical fight between his mother and father:

When I was eleven years old . . . all hell broke loose. They were going to break up [and] my mother attacked my father with a pair of scissors. . . . I was twelve around that time. I ended up being peacemaker, had to sit them both down. It was really inappropriate, now that I think back on it.

This kind of parentification puts children in roles they are not mature enough to handle. Often they do not even understand why the argument is happening; all they know is that it is wrong and they want to end it.

Our quantitative analysis confirmed the hunches we drew from our open-ended interviews: namely, parentification of all kinds is highly harmful to children's development. Experiencing parentification—having to regularly care for distressed parents or serve as their confidant, for example—increases the chance of becoming a problem gambler almost five-fold. The stressful experiences associated with parentification stay with people for the rest of their lives, hindering their ability to function normally and form healthy relationships as adults.

Homelessness

Homelessness has been associated with numerous mental health risks, including low self-esteem, loneliness, feeling trapped, and suicidal ideation. Guilt and self-blame are also felt among homeless youth and have a considerably strong impact on an individual's mental health (Kidd 2007). Being homeless in childhood is certainly traumatic, and to some, it is a form of parentification, since it forces children to care for themselves. Youth who take to the streets encounter many dangerous situations and sources of stress in an effort to support themselves and survive. They may struggle to find work; resort to panhandling, drug dealing, or prostitution; and face the possibility of victimization without shelter and protection. Addiction is a significant problem among homeless youth, and there is a strikingly high incidence of mental illness, including depression, post-traumatic stress disorder (PTSD), and suicidality (Greene and Ringwalt 1996; Kidd 2004). Sadly, death rates among this population are up to forty times higher than in the general population (Shaw and Dorling 1998). In addition to all the negative factors homeless youth are exposed to, they also often miss out on positive experiences that could help preserve them, such as school and recreational activities. However, pervasive social stigma combined with extremely low self-esteem generally steers homeless youth away from protective institutions (Kidd 2007). Consider the example of one participant we interviewed.

Blake left home at sixteen because of the continuing conflict with his parents and spent a month living in shelters and on the streets. He remembered, "That homeless period, the first few days were very stressful, I was like, 'Where am I going to get food?'" When he could no longer handle this stress, he returned home, only to continue witnessing his parents' constant and violent arguments. "It just went back to the same; but by then I had already threatened to be homeless, and I already had been, so there was no point in doing it again." Blake was trapped. If he went back to the streets, he would have to struggle to find food and shelter, which few children of sixteen are equipped to do; if he stayed home, he would have no control over his parents' arguing and would continually be exposed to and involved in this abusive environment. He would just have to live with it or at best try to ignore it.

Others we interviewed described similar situations to Blake's: their parents were always fighting, so they left home to seek peace. Mark found his home environment too violent to endure any longer. "I basically left home when I was sixteen so that I could finish high school. I couldn't work under those circumstances and it got worse monthly almost. There was a three-month threshold, where it got worse and worse."

Sooner or later, they all realized that life on the street was no better than their destructive home life, so eventually they all returned home, where at least they had food and shelter. One might imagine that a stay on the streets would have helped these youth develop better-than-average coping skills—after all, they had weathered the harshest challenges imaginable, going out on their own in this way and in a dangerous environment. In fact, however, those who experienced homelessness often developed poor coping skills. When they got back home, things only got worse. They had proven they couldn't make it without their warring parents. Shame, embarrassment, and low self-esteem took over, and they felt doomed, like losers. This in combination with their tendency to feel trapped is a deadly combination. Feeling trapped, a construct that involves feelings of helplessness and hopelessness, is a driving force in suicidality among youth who have experienced homelessness (Kidd 2004).

For these youth who have already struggled with such a wide range of stressors and challenges, these stints on the street and the shame associated with both being homeless and then having to return to an abusive home only serve to further compromise their mental health. As adults, many turned to gambling as a way of (unsuccessfully) escaping their problems that, as we have seen, are carried with them into adulthood.

Financial Strain

From a young age, many study participants were exposed to the family's financial troubles, and these troubles continued to affect them throughout childhood. Sometimes the lack of money itself was stressful; more often, the parental conflicts over money were the main cause of childhood distress.

Being hard-pressed for money often meant that parents could not afford suitable housing, and this sometimes meant that relatively large families were forced to live in small apartments. Given that the family lives of our participants were characterized by unhealthy relationships and behaviours, abuse, and neglect, living in cramped quarters with little money led to more than just bickering. With family members crowded into small spaces and pressed by a shortage of money, conflicts were frequent and wholly inescapable. When the fighting began, this lack of space meant there was nowhere to hide from the fighting. Debbie experienced this situation. Her parents were both alcoholics and, in addition, her mother was a problem gambler. Her family's financial situation meant she had little room to breathe as a child. "It was stressful. It was a two-bedroom apartment and there were so many people in it. We had a house at one point, but it didn't work out."

Debbie felt like she didn't have any space to herself, physically or emotionally. With no room of her own to seek solace in, and no quiet amidst the yelling to simply hear her own thoughts, Debbie was overwhelmed. In addition, with two alcoholic parents and a mother who gambled to excess, there was no shortage of conflict while she was growing up. Debbie felt imposed upon, confined, and unable to escape.

Often, study participants had problem gambling fathers whose habits caused serious financial problems for their families. These fathers gambled away the family's money, leaving their partner and children stressed out with worry. Arguing over family finances was a common theme among our participants. More often than not, their mothers accused their fathers of being unable to keep their spending in check and sacrificing the family's well-being just for "one more bet." Responses were typically forms of verbal assault and spiteful attempts at vindication.

Dustin had a father who illustrated this behaviour. His father often gambled and lost everything, then argued with Dustin's mother when she needed money to handle basic household expenses. We asked Dustin what caused most of the conflicts between his parents, and unsurprisingly, he answered:

Money, money, money. He asked her for money, I guess he went broke, and then the next morning he would need this and we would need that, and so they'd argue back and forth.

Listening to their mother and father argue about money all the time turned these children into adults who were completely preoccupied with money. Mikhail's family discussed property ownership and mortgage rates every day, making Mikhail very concerned about finances. He also felt "poor" as a child because he could not afford the same leisure activities his friends enjoyed, like skiing. As well, Mikhail noted the subtler social differences between himself and his wealthier friends, such as table etiquette and manner of speech. Money, class, and social position can become very salient when you don't have enough to live on. We also know the harmful effects that "feeling different" can have on self-esteem, which in turn compromises mental health.

Arguments about money taught the children who witnessed them that money was very important. Perhaps for this reason, many problem gamblers we spoke to continued to gamble because they hoped to make "big money," though they mainly lost money. The lesson they learned in childhood—that acquiring money is more important than good health or good relationships—contributed to their decision to try to support themselves financially through gambling.

What was even more stressful to children than just listening to their parents argue about money was their forced involvement in the family's finances. Often, this meant helping to pay the family's bills, usually through a part-time job. This should sound reminiscent of our discussion of parentification—being expected to hold a job in order to contribute to and help manage family finances definitely qualifies as a form of instrumental parentification.

Dustin's mother expected Dustin to learn how to pay the bills when he was very young: "At the age of twelve to thirteen, I learned how to pay the bills. . . . My mom would sit me down and be like, 'Okay, I have to pay this bill,' and she had online banking." The financial tasks Dustin took on were inappropriate for his level of psychological and emotional development. In learning to pay the bills, he acquired a duty that his mother should have taken care of, thus burdening him with an adult stress at an early age. Particularly when Dustin struggled with financial tasks that were beyond his capability, he was made to feel inadequate and his confidence was unjustly compromised.

Max lost much of his childhood working at his family's business. "It wasn't fun, it was work," he said. All of his time away from school was consumed by hours worked at the family business, leaving Max with no time for friends or recreation. Max was like other problem gamblers we spoke to: he reported financial strain as a source of childhood distress and highlighted the (potential) financial gains of gambling when he reached adulthood. He was fascinated by strategies to maximize his winnings, going so far as to attend seminar courses at the racetrack, to learn how to place good bets. Max's emphasis on financial gain reminded us that gamblers gamble for different reasons. While most seek an escape from their problems, others are focused wholly on the financial gain, hoping to win their way out of poverty and to forget the deprivation they endured growing up. Indirectly, then, this is also a form of escape.

Not everyone responded to childhood financial deprivation by becoming a problem gambler; some rebelled against their parents' pattern. Evelyn, for example, described her own financial attitudes as being opposite to her parents':

> They're all into working and making money—not enjoying as much— whereas I'm the opposite. I try to enjoy a lot and not care about money. . . . I don't see the point in working all your life, and not using the money you saved up.

Because Evelyn hadn't been able to spend money freely as a child, she developed reckless spending habits as an adult. These habits were directly opposite to those she had been forced to practise while growing up. In rebellion against her parent's money-conscious (and penny-pinching) attitudes, Evelyn came to feel that placing large bets at the casino was a fun and exciting way to spend her money. Either extreme, whether it is a frivolous attitude toward money or an overly conscious hoarding of funds, is an unhealthy approach and focus point for attention.

As we've seen, children who grew into problem gambling adults often experienced financial problems during their childhoods. Whether the financial strain was caused by a parent's problem gambling mattered less than the constant stress and worry about money, whatever the cause. Listening to their parents argue about money, or taking on financial responsibilities at a young age put them at a higher risk of developing gambling problems in adulthood. Perhaps the environment in which they grew up emphasized money so heavily that they came to believe that money was an all-important priority in life. Perhaps they came to believe that, through gambling, the quick, easy "big win" could solve all of their financial (and other) problems. Unfortunately, for the vast majority, this was not the case.

Interactions of Childhood Stressors

None of the events we have discussed in this chapter occurred in isolation: they tended to come in clumps. This interaction of stressors is particularly typical of mental illness and addiction, and forces us to reject the medical model of addiction due to biological error as a complete explanation for why people become addicts. The process, as we continue to exemplify throughout this book, is complicated and highly variable, yet nonetheless is typified by an interaction of stressors and situations throughout the course of one's life. Abuse and parentification often went hand-in-hand, for example, as did neglect and financial problems.

Robbie is one problem gambler we spoke to who had experienced almost every form of childhood trauma that we have identified. He was subjected to emotional and sexual abuse, parentification, and a number of other stressors. He recounts instances of parentification, when he was forced to shoulder the responsibility of worries that should not have concerned him:

> I was the oldest of four siblings and I continuously heard that I should be "responsible." Many things occurred in my childhood that I thought I was responsible for. At age four I had to give up my closest friend, my dog, Teddy. I thought I was responsible for giving my best friend away. During my early childhood, I incurred several severe injuries and illnesses. I felt responsible for my parents' medical debts.

Robbie went on to describe the fear that had been instilled in him lest he be "irresponsible," leaving him vulnerable and carrying shame and guilt whenever he behaved as a child might:

> My parents forced me to attend a church where God was portrayed as a vengeful god. God would have "bad" things happen to me because of my bad behaviour; therefore, I was responsible for the outcomes. At age eleven, my fourth grade male teacher molested me. He was allowed to continue teaching even though he admitted it. It must have been something about me. At age

twelve, I was molested by a man with the carnival troupe that was in town. At age sixteen, I got caught stealing twenty dollars from a clothing store I worked at. This was the first time that I felt so embarrassed and shameful that I considered suicide. I had let everyone down. . . . I felt like I was responsible for everyone else's feelings and that I was an embarrassment to them.

"It must have been something about me"—Robbie was right. He was taught to believe that he was responsible for the outcomes of his behaviour, which made him an easy target for victimization, both by his teacher and by the man from the carnival troupe. Particularly because he was unable to understand that he was simply the victim of an unjustifiable crime, he was unable to absolve himself of the embarrassment, shame, and guilt that resulted from those incidents and, instead, carried them with him until he couldn't any longer, suicidality being the ultimate means of escape.

Unfortunately for Robbie, it didn't end there:

Also, at age sixteen, I found out that I had been adopted. [This] re-affirmed to me that I indeed was different. Had it not been for a girlfriend at the time, I probably would have ended my life. She became pregnant the next year and we got married out of state. I was age seventeen.

While this story may not be typical of the people we spoke to, there's no denying Robbie had been emotionally damaged by his experiences in childhood. Robbie blamed and held himself accountable for all the terrible things that had happened to him, and consequently he lost all sense of self-worth and felt continuous shame. Bogged down with such an extreme sense of worthlessness and inadequacy, he was simply unable to cope with the stressors that continued to come his way, including the news of his adoption. This combination of traumatic events in childhood paved the way for his problem gambling as an adult; the themes of gambling as an emotional anaesthetic, as a means to relieve and escape stress, and as a counter to feelings of inadequacy certainly apply to Robbie's narrative.

Another participant, Caylee, also experienced multiple types of trauma throughout her childhood. For example, she continually witnessed her parents' physical fights. The anxiety this caused her to experience led her to develop serious health problems that, in turn, made her do poorly in school, for which she was then physically abused at home.

My mother and father got into violent fights. I was up all night refereeing. It affected my childhood. I had stomach ulcers as a kid. I was hospitalized a whole bunch of times because of it. . . . I wanted to keep my mother from murdering my father. I didn't want to end up in the papers. . . . Literally, she would smash a bottle over his head, and he would be all cut up and bleeding. It was horrible, horrible. When I would go back to bed, I couldn't sleep because I was so stressed. So I would be falling asleep all day in school. I'd get in trouble. Teachers would be yelling at me, and they would phone home and say your kid is falling asleep in school. So I would get whipped for that.

Caylee's childhood experiences show that multiple forms of trauma combine in intricate and devastating ways, often producing unforeseeable results. In the next two chapters, we will talk about these results.

In this chapter, we've explored some of the various traumas and challenges our participants faced in their childhood. These make up the first component of the Dostoevsky Effect, which you'll recall begins in childhood, with traumatic experiences that create a platform for anxiety and other mental health disturbances, and stunt coping skills that are carried through to adulthood. We saw how the situations that our participants encountered instilled a sense of worthlessness and inadequacy in many of them, draining them of their self-esteem and, in extreme cases, driving them into depression and suicidal ideation. Many anxiously awaited the next stressor they knew would inevitably come, as we saw that one stress tends to beget another. The psychological damage is more than evident in their behaviour and in the resentment, regret, and sense of loss they expressed in their one-on-one interviews. According to our model, in adulthood, a new variety of life stresses raises anxiety and calls for the coping strategies acquired in childhood. When the coping strategies are stunted and maladaptive, the result may be an increase in anxiety and depression, particularly when it has already been conditioned, or perhaps a cycle of new troubles and failed efforts to deal with them.

We cannot possibly understand problem gambling without understanding what benefit it offers the gambler, or what relief he or she is seeking by pulling the slot handle, laying a bet on a horse, or buying a lottery ticket. As we've discussed, rather than being about an intent to gain money, problem gambling is more often than not an attempt to escape distress. An important take-home theme in this chapter is that a gambling addiction, like other addictions, whether it be drug or alcohol use, overeating, or shopping, almost always finds its origin in pain, be it physical or emotional. Our participants' stories are marked by endless pain: neglect, fear, humiliation, physical beatings, and ruthless character assassination. Growing up, they witnessed their parents' unhealthy and often violent relationships, addictive behaviours, maladaptive life patterns, and poor coping behaviours. In their parents' absence, actual or symbolic, they cared for themselves, their siblings, and sometimes their parents as well, taking on responsibility and stress no child should have to face.

Although our participants often remembered being unhappy during their childhood because of financial strain and the fights between their parents, many could not connect the causes of their problems—often, a parent's gambling or otherwise maladaptive patterns of behaviours—with their own negative experiences. This inability to recognize the causes of their unhappiness may have kept them from avoiding problems in adulthood that would cause even worse unhappiness. Yet, many participants believed that this was normal, just "the way things were." This means they were likely to reproduce these situations with their own adult families, continuing the tradition of what they came to believe "normal life" looks like. In effect, all they had learned from childhood was how not to be healthy adults, and yet these patterns and behaviours came to be understood as "normal" to them. Then, what they believed was normal, about themselves and about the world, continued to manifest in their adult lives through their learned actions and both the conscious and unconscious beliefs they had been conditioned to hold. They then became trapped in a continuous pattern of stress and negative behaviour to relieve that stress. When they find themselves facing serious stresses in adulthood, they have trouble bouncing back precisely because there can be no bouncing back if they are trapped in cyclic behaviour—only temporary relief. The only solution is to break the cycle, which victims, their friends and family, and professionals will tell you, is not as easy as it sounds.

6

Adult Stresses

The childhood problems that participants experienced were largely responsible for making them into troubled adults; we continue to stand behind the opinion that problem gamblers are made, not born. However, a childhood laden with hardships and traumas did not guarantee problem gambling later in life. Nor did childhood hardships and traumas inoculate people against problem gambling. The "school of hard knocks" was neither a guarantee of resilience in adulthood, nor did it ensure doom.

For many participants, childhood hardships and traumas produced poor coping skills, which they brought into adulthood and used unsuccessfully. But the number and severity of their hardships in adulthood were also important, and a clear additive effect emerged. The quantitative analysis of our survey data strongly supports this, showing that the chance of a participant becoming a problem gambler increases almost threefold with every additional stressful event encountered in adulthood. It is generally accepted that a correlation exists between the amount and degree of stress one experiences, and health problems. However, this doesn't necessarily mean that stress is a direct cause of illness. Many people experience numerous stressful events and hardships throughout their lives, and emerge relatively happy and healthy on the flipside. The relationship between stress and illness is instead mediated and moderated by individual and socio-environmental factors (Lazarus and Folkman 1984).

In adulthood, participants often found undesirable, unexpected, uncommon, or uncontrollable events to be particularly stressful. However, what was considered stressful was highly subjective and varied widely from one person to another; what one person found intensely stressful, another brushed away as if it were a mere annoyance. There is a plethora of factors influencing how people react to stress, including but certainly not limited to the precipitating event, personality traits, coping skills, social support, and the overall amount of stress happening in one's life at the time.

Additionally, stress isn't always a bad thing. Planning a wedding, starting a family, and changing jobs or careers are all undoubtedly stressful, but many people understand these as positive and exciting experiences, despite the stress inherently involved. Stress can also at times be adaptive when the pressure encourages us to perform our best, as in the case of starting a new job, for example. So, it is crucial that we enter this discussion of adult stress and anxiety experienced in adulthood with recognition of the subjective nature of stress, and that we appreciate the fact that the same stress may lead some people to problem gambling but not others.

As we will see, stressors that caused mental health problems in childhood continued to plague participants in their adult lives. For some, this in turn triggered problem gambling. As well, other common stressors drove many participants to gamble in excess; these included problems with employment, financial hardship, relationship troubles, and the stress of caregiving duties. While these stresses may seem trivial and ubiquitous, when they occur to an extensive degree in combination with the childhood stress and trauma our participants often carried with them, the result was an additive burden that was simply too much to cope with in a healthy way. For many participants, gambling became a way of coping that they believed could help them deal with these daily stressors.

Poor Mental Health

In general, our participants who emerged from a childhood filled with stress, lacking the ability to cope well, went on to experience a great deal of stress and hardship as adults. As suggested by our theoretical model and confirmed by our quantitative analysis, childhood stress, trauma, and parentification predicted stressful life events in adulthood, such as illness and unemployment. These, in turn, were closely connected to anxiety and depression in adulthood. Anxiety and depression, as we will see, is strongly correlated with problem gambling.

An extensive literature base exists linking poor mental health with problem gambling. For example, problem gamblers are more anxious, both in specific situations and in general disposition (Ste-Marie, Gupta, and Derevensky 2006). This tendency to experience anxiety ensures they will be more likely than the average person to seek some tangible relief from the anxiety that plagues them—and that plagues them that much more often and in response to things that might seem trivial to others. When they are equipped to deal with this anxiety only with the immature and ineffective coping strategies that they developed in response to stress and trauma as children, the outcome is far from hopeful.

Research also finds higher levels of depression and poorer motivation among problem gamblers (Clarke 2004), as well as a higher incident of obsessive compulsive disorder and personality disorders, and more frequent and extreme childhood attention deficit disorders (Johansson et al. 2009; Carlton et al. 1987). These findings remain true even after taking into account other potentially explanatory behaviours such as substance abuse.

Mental illnesses are damaging to well-being, in part because of the social stigma attached to these illnesses. Much of the work in the social sciences surrounding social stigma can be attributed to offshoots and refinements of Erving Goffman's 1963 book, *Stigma: Notes on the Management of Spoiled Identity*. According to Goffman, a stigma is a socially discredited attribute, behaviour, or reputation that causes the afflicted person to be judged by others as undesirable and unacceptable. Mentally ill people are often seen as unstable and are shunned or ridiculed instead of being treated. Nowadays, addictions, including gambling problems, are understood to be forms of mental illness—indeed, in our study, many participants met the criteria for a diagnosable pathological gambling problem. Many, however, don't accept this definition and attribute blame to the individual's ill will to control his or her behaviours.

Goffman separates addiction from mental illness and distinguishes between three types of stigma: defects of the body, defects of character (such as mental illness), and extremist beliefs or addiction. With this distinction in mind, it becomes clear that problem gamblers who also suffer poor mental health experience the dual burden of being stigmatized both for their mental health concerns and for their gambling behaviours.

Stigmatization has widespread negative consequences that directly and indirectly contribute to further ill health. Stigmatized individuals carry with them a negative label that causes others to discriminate against them, seeing them as incompetent and untrustworthy, thereby limiting their opportunities for employment, social interaction, housing, and access to medical care (Link and Phelan 2006). Further, constant negative evaluation by society undoubtedly results in low self-esteem and more symptoms of depression. The behaviour associated with low self-esteem and depression, such as avolition (a lack of motivation) and apathy, only serves to further limit their quality of life. For example, these consequences might make problem gamblers less likely to seek treatment, for both their gambling behaviours and their mental health concerns. Stigmas always imply negative evaluations and consequences; thus people who are stigmatized are forced to develop coping strategies to protect themselves. Again, because they are ill-equipped as far as coping strategies go, by turning to gambling or other maladaptive behaviours, problem gamblers often end up reinforcing the stereotypes and negative consequences that contributed to their gambling in the first place. It is yet another vicious cycle at play.

Given this preamble, it should not be surprising to you to hear that many of the problem gamblers we studied did indeed struggle with mental health issues ranging in severity from depressive symptoms to diagnosable conditions, including post-traumatic stress disorder (PTSD), major depressive disorder, and bipolar disorder. It was often the case that these illnesses and their consequences could be traced back to childhood experiences that went on to influence their adult lives, including their decision to gamble. Problem gamblers in our study exhibited a strong trend shown in the addiction literature (Sher et al. 2005) in using gambling as a "self-medicating" response to depression or anxiety. Recall that this depression and anxiety can result from its own etiological pathway and be reinforced via stigma and the negative consequences of their gambling behaviour.

One of our participants, Luca, illuminates the struggle with stigma faced by people with mental illness. He experienced mental health problems when he worked as a paramedic. As a child facing extreme stress and trauma, Luca never learned how to cope effectively with his feelings. Later, as a paramedic, he was regularly exposed to traumatic events. It is not surprising that, in this professional role, he went on to suffer from post-traumatic stress disorder; he regularly had nightmares and flashbacks about the cases he had handled. This illness disabled him; additionally, the attitudes of his co-workers and supervisors toward this mental illness made Luca feel inadequate, as if he didn't have what it took to do his job well. Recall how we mentioned that stigma can also lead to perceived incompetence.

When asked to elaborate on his experiences with PTSD, Luca said:

I finally went to my family doctor, and was like, ". . . I've been having terrible dreams." So he sent me to a psychiatrist, and we worked it out. I would say regarding the variety of PTSD for an urban paramedic, some stuff you just really can't handle. We were debriefed at the time, but certainly that order has to be maintained, and you were seen as weak if you weren't handling it right.

Because he feared that others would think his nightmares were foolish and he was "weak" for letting them affect him, Luca went a long time before seeking the medical help he needed. This reluctance to seek help due to stigma only served to worsen his illness.

For Luca, ineffective coping skills magnified the problem of PTSD but also made him feel ashamed and embarrassed about his distress. In turn, this made it more difficult for him to acknowledge his illness and seek help. In addition to the nightmares, Luca exhibited other symptoms, including flashbacks that interfered with his ability to function in his daily life; finally, he was forced to choose another, less stressful career. But until his new career got moving, his anxiety disorder combined with the stress of unemployment made Luca's life intolerably stressful. The stress of the situation (and, in light of unemployment, the possibility of winning money) led Luca to gamble.

Many other participants reported experiencing depression in adulthood. Their depression amplified feelings of worthlessness, isolation, and boredom that were born from their childhood experiences of abuse and neglect. To quell these feelings, our participants chose gambling and other self-destructive behaviours. Jonathan was diagnosed with depression in high school and continues to be affected by depression in his adult life. In our interview with Jonathan, he explained:

There's something wrong around my life—something very, very wrong. Anything good I've ever had in my life has never lasted. Be it a job, a relationship . . . it's almost like . . . it's just unbelievable. If I was a weaker man, I would have committed suicide years ago. I'm serious. There's something wrong. And anti-depressants aren't going to help me. I would never take them. I've read horror stories about them.

Jonathan experienced job and relationship troubles in adulthood; at the root of these problems was depression, which itself was rooted in a stressful, abusive childhood. As a victim of abuse as a child, Jonathan was made to feel unworthy and unlovable, and as he grew up, such limiting beliefs and self-loathing continuously manifested themselves in his life, affecting his ability to maintain employment and meaningful, positive relationships. Moreover, Jonathan had not had the opportunity in childhood to develop the coping skills needed to handle negative feelings. As a young child, he was not at an appropriate developmental level to understand his experiences of abuse and neglect as victimization. Rather, he felt he was to blame and instead internalized those feelings of unworthiness and self-loathing, which continued to persist into adulthood. Eventually, Jonathan spiralled into a major depression.

As an adult, Jonathan's depression led him to view everything in a negative light, making him feel his life was barely worth living. Furthermore, he suffered from the misconceptions and social stigma attached to mental illness in our society. For this and other reasons, Jonathan refuses to take medications to treat his condition. As with Luca, stigma magnified and compounded the problem. By failing to seek treatment, Jonathan was forced to live with his illness and allow it to persist, profoundly dissatisfied with his daily existence.

Angela also fought an ongoing battle with mental illness. In our interview, she admitted that she tried to internalize her stress, relying on her psychiatrist for support and help with her problems: "I don't share it [stress] with anyone except therapists. . . . My children don't even know half of what's been going on and it's been going on since my second child was born and I've been fighting it since it came." Angela believes it would be selfish to drag her family into her mental health problems. However, her secrecy has only compounded her troubles. Like Luca, Angela feels isolated by her struggle with illness and seeks solace in gambling.

Gambling to excess is often a way of self-medicating for people like Luca, Angela, and Jonathan. It gives them, and other people who suffer from mental disorders, a thrill or a jolt of excitement they can't find elsewhere. Depression fuels their gambling problem because they can feel something other than numbness when they gamble. It is this feeling that kept them coming back for more, despite frequent losses and damaging effects on their lives.

Several participants in our study suffered from bipolar disorder, which causes people to alternate intermittently between manic and depressed feelings. They, too, often used gambling to coax them out of depression and also to channel their excessive energy during manic episodes. Peter, for example, said that he gambled to cope with the depressive phases, much as Angela and Jonathan did. Like other people who struggle with depression, people with bipolar disorder turn to gambling to provide the thrill and excitement that briefly counter feelings of depression.

In short, for people living with mental illness, gambling helped them deal with the stress of their day-to-day lives and escape from the mental health problems—especially, the depression and numbness—that often overwhelmed them. Although it was often deficits in mental health that drove our participants to gamble, keep in mind that such internal struggles, as we have seen, are frequently traceable to the social environment that surrounded our participants.

Poor Physical Health

Many other participants in our study struggled with physical health conditions, which added stress to their daily lives and pushed them to begin or continue to gamble, often via negative effects on mental health. For example, Rodin and Voshart (1986) found that depressive disorders are present in up to one-third of medical inpatients. Besides the biological effects of physical illness, which could elicit depression, physical illnesses impose functional and psychological limitations that often kept our participants from developing healthy social lives and rendered them incapable of filling a variety of social and occupational roles. With physical illnesses, particularly those that are chronic and/or serious, individuals experience a sense of loss, damaged body image, poor self-esteem, a conflicted sense of identity, and an impaired capacity (mentally and/or physically) to work and maintain relationships (MacHale 2002).

A particular challenge for some of our participants who suffered from physical illness was their inability to participate in the same leisure and recreation as their healthy peers. Doreen was one of our participants who sees a therapist for drug and alcohol addiction while struggling to make ends meet for herself and her two cats. In addition, she also has chronic obstructive pulmonary disease (COPD), which limits the activities available to her: "I can't do the things [that I enjoy] because I have COPD . . . it's emphysema from the smoking. I get tired really easily."

Because of her activity limitation, Doreen became bored and restless; gambling gave her a leisure activity that was thrilling but not physically taxing. Many other people we spoke to also suffered from physical limitations and, like Doreen, felt restless and bored as a result. Many also experienced compound mental health problems from having to deal continuously with their physical health problems.

Odelia, for example, was limited by the physical pain of fibromyalgia and arthritis. At the same time, she felt pressure to overcome this limitation so she could be a strong member of her family and help her husband with household responsibilities. She said, "If I feel up to it, I will try and help him do certain things, you know. I wish I could [do more], I [would] rather be well than sickly all the time." Besides wanting to help her husband, Odelia wanted to be healthy for her children and grandchildren: "When they [her children] do come, I try not to be sick. I try to be up and really not let them see me at my worst." Like Angela, who didn't want to burden her family with her mental illness, Odelia struggled to hide her physical pain from her family. She tried to keep her worries to herself and so had no one to share her pain with, no one to sympathize with her, and no one to offer social support. Further, Odelia didn't like taking pain medication because it made her feel numb. However, she gave in and took it whenever her family was going to visit, so that she could better hide her symptoms:

> Lots of times, I won't take anything for pain, I'll just handle it. I don't like taking medication anyway because it's just masking the feelings. [But], if I know they're coming, well then I gotta take my medication, so that I'm not limping around. Especially with the little ones. I don't want them to see me sick.

Odelia felt her responsibilities—as a wife, mother, and grandmother to help with household tasks and to appear well for her family's sake—trumped her responsibility to herself. Unfortunately, by hiding her physical and emotional pain, she came to feel isolated and alone, even with her family around her. She was living a lie. No one understood what she was going through, and she could not tell anyone what she was feeling, because she did not want to upset them. She dealt with her burden alone, which only made it a harder burden to carry. To deal with feelings of isolation, Odelia gambled in social arenas. Here, she was able to engage with others in an activity that was physically undemanding and emotionally stimulating.

Employment-Related Stress

It is not a far cry to suggest that money is important for everyone. People have mouths to feed and bills to pay, which most do by way of paid employment. So, it is fair to conclude that paid employment is also important for almost everyone. But not everyone is lucky enough to have stable employment and a secure income. In fact, many of the participants in our study— like Dostoevsky—did not have a secure or sufficient income to guarantee them enough money for basic necessities. Understandably, this caused them a great deal of stress. Many had trouble finding a job, experienced problems at work, or had been laid off. In these cases, unemployment and money shortage became a source of great stress for a number of our participants. Many gambled specifically in hopes of reducing that stress. But those who gambled tended to compound the severity of the issue because gambling requires, and more often than not gobbles up, large sums of money.

Other participants had jobs that provided them with enough money to live comfortably, but these jobs caused them tension and stress. In explaining, they spoke about daily workplace tensions, having to work under someone else, or feeling unsatisfied with their career.

Chase, for example, said his boss put him under extreme pressure, causing him to feel exceptionally anxious at work. "I get really stressed out if co-workers or the boss is down my neck. I get really tense and angry. I can't handle this. I get really tense and angry." When asked to describe specific situations that made him feel this way, he elaborated, "If I'm packaging or doing something, putting stuff on the shelves and one of the co-workers ask me to do too many tasks, I'll just say, 'buzz right off!'" Chase found the pressure of unreasonable expectations especially upsetting. Some might have found these completely reasonable and not stressful, but for Chase, the perceived pressure at work and his inability to find common ground on workplace expectations caused him significant stress, for which he sought comfort in gambling.

Some people felt stressed by the amount of work they had to do. For example, Kieran mentioned how he quickly became overwhelmed by the sheer amount of work he had to do at school, as well as in the multiple jobs he held to pay for his schooling:

> I'm at school right now; the time when work piles up and deadlines pile up, that's probably the biggest [stress]: just juggling a lot of things. Right now, [I'm] trying to juggle three different jobs and schoolwork. I get stressed by the big picture of it all—with seeing that everything gets done.

For Kieran, trying to balance his paid work and schoolwork was physically and mentally taxing. Gambling gave him a break from it all—a chance to relax and enjoy himself and forget about the stress of juggling so many things at once. And, in the event of a win, perhaps Kieran wouldn't have to juggle three jobs.

Unstable employment created another kind of work-related stress that often caused financial and emotional difficulties. Vedran, for example, experienced financial stress because of his decision to leave a steady job and pursue an independent career path. "I had a full-time job. I left that job in January and now I'm trying to start up a business on my own. So my biggest stress is financial independence—just making money on my own."

The choice to leave his steady job distinguished Vedran from most other people in our study, who described their inability to find a steady job as a source of emotional strain. Most people we spoke to had fallen into financial insecurity unwillingly and often abruptly.

Margaret experienced employment stress because of her inability to hold down a job. She continually changed jobs, trying her luck in a wide range of job categories, but failing to settle down anywhere. "I worked in a hotel . . . as a concierge. Sales warehouse. Graphic design was my trade . . . Film production . . . and then graphic design. Collating, stitching, folding was part of the company, graphics, IT." Despite the employment instability that resulted from numerous career moves, Margaret expressed pride in her ability to find work, especially jobs that provided her with enough money; getting a steady job, even a well-paying job, posed no problem. "I've had steady jobs. It wasn't like a day or two, but I had steady work and steady jobs for a year or two."

Jonathan was less fortunate: he was only able to find part-time work. Without full-time work, he received no company benefits and knew he could be fired or replaced at any time. Jonathan looked for full-time work, but was unsure what kind of steady work would suit him best. He mainly focused on making money. "I'm looking for something full-time. I don't know exactly what I am going to do yet. I'm exploring different options—obviously something profitable for the future. Money is always important."

One participant, Harold, had lived on the cusp of financial insecurity his entire life and had been unable to save up enough money for his retirement. Now retired, he lived on his disability cheques, which were barely enough to cover minimal expenses:

> They put me on . . . ODSP [Ontario Disability Support Program]. Seriously, that's what I'm on right now to live on. I'm at a seniors' building . . . because that's all they give you a month. Five hundred and seventy-eight dollars. That's what you get, so you have to buy your TTC [Toronto Transit Commission] tickets, your food, whatever, for yourself.

Doreen also worried that her income did not suffice. She was unemployed and often worried that she did not have enough money to care for her pets and herself: "Six hundred doesn't go very far, plus I have two cats and I have to take care of them. I have to get them food, litter, and water." She echoed Harold's frustration with his current living quarters, listing among her places of residence "a bedbug-infested crack house." Harold and Doreen remind us, if we need reminding, that financial troubles can lead to poor housing and nutrition and can result in other (secondary) stressful conditions.

The people we spoke with who were currently unemployed or had experienced unemployment at some time in their adult lives blamed their joblessness for creating a sense of stress and uncertainty in their lives. Being without a job meant they had trouble financing even their most basic needs. Unfortunately for many, one of these basic needs was the need to gamble, and frequent lateness or absence from work due to gambling would certainly precipitate job loss or an inability to gain employment. Again, we see a cycle at play. Not knowing how they were going to pay for their next meal or monthly rent bill was unnerving, and our participants eased their nerves by gambling, to relieve both the emotional stress associated with unemployment and the instrumental stress of minimized income via the possibility of winning money.

Status-Related Stress

Everyone yearns for respect, and today, most people see an opportunity to gain respect from the job they hold and/or the income they earn. A person's profession and income influence how the rest of society looks at that person—how it ranks that person within the social hierarchy. And because many study participants were unemployed or held low-status, low-income jobs, they discovered first-hand how disrespect and stigma affected their self-esteem. For many, the experience of low social status resulted in low morale and constant worry. These feelings were particularly common among participants who had never gone to college or university, or who were in a line of work they disliked.

Remember Jonathan, who was employed part-time and had been undecided about the type of career that suited him best? These challenges caused him a great deal of stress and also made him feel he was low on the social totem pole. "Right now, my worst thing is my self-esteem, because my self-esteem is not very good right now. I'm not happy with myself. I'm not happy with my position in life." Jonathan was unhappy at least in part because he realized that many people ascribe a low social status to part-time and unskilled workers. Without the respect of others, Jonathan found it difficult to muster respect for himself.

For some participants, social status was significantly more important than financial stability to their sense of accomplishment and happiness. Stephen, for example, became dissatisfied with his life when he lost his high-ranking, high-paying executive job and wanted nothing more than to recover his prestigious status. Gambling appealed to him because it served as a social marker, identifying him as someone wealthy enough to put his money at risk. He explained:

> When I had that management job, I was making about $110,000 a year. I had no worries about money, about anything. I'm single, so I could fly to Vegas three or four times a year with my friend Mike, take down like two, three thousand, and gamble. Since I got downsized, life is much more tedious at the bottom of the food chain.

Stephen was much more frustrated by his new (lower) social standing than he was with the loss of money that resulted from his fall to a lower position.

Jonathan and Stephen both put pressure on themselves to attain a higher social standing and bolster their self-esteem. Others experienced pressure to do so from family or friends. For example, Bill, whom you'll recall moved to Canada from Australia many years ago, said he experienced this kind of pressure from his wife. Not only did he suffer a blow to his sense of self-worth when he lost status, worse still, he feared that his wife's love for him would diminish if he could not give her the lifestyle she desired.

> Sometimes my wife has to "keep up with the Joneses." Sometimes she sees other people, especially my friends; they are millionaires and have a lot of money. We used to be very close friends, we worked together and did business together, and they made a fortune, and we didn't. In Canada, I just do ordinary work; so . . . when she mentions those people and I'm doing an ordinary job, I feel unhappy about that.

Bill lived in fear of losing his job. "[When] about ten people were laid off . . . another colleague came to me and hugged me and I felt very stressed, I felt that I was laid off, and she hugged me and said goodbye, [but] she was laid off, not me." In the end, he was spared this dreaded disaster. However, the anxiety Bill felt over his social status was compounded by his belief that he might lose not only his job, but also his family in the process—especially, his relationship with his wife. Bill's dissatisfaction with his current status was aggravated by his wife's comments on how ordinary Bill was, compared with their friends.

For many, relationships were, indeed, the key problem in their lives; though they did not always realize this was so.

Relationships

Having positive, stable, and supportive relationships in adulthood is a strong defence against addictive behaviours. However, considering the childhood trauma that many participants experienced, it is not surprising that, in adulthood, many formed poor relationships. Some of their adult relationships were strained and problematic and, as such, additional sources of stress and unhappiness. These troubled relationships directly influenced people's gambling, especially for people who had friends or partners who gambled compulsively. Others found that the stress caused by a strained relationship pushed them to gamble compulsively.

Consider the strained relations that Valerie had with her children. They left her feeling like an inadequate parent.

> I often wonder, if I'd had a different upbringing, would I have learned to parent. I've had three children. My son's dead. My twenty-six-year-old, who's in law school, blames me for everything. And my twenty-year-old, she hates my new husband. . . . I've failed as a parent. My kids were all very successful as human beings, certainly in their own areas, but [not] in their relationship to me. I had a good relationship with my [deceased] son, iron-ically. But with my daughters right now . . . since I left their father, it's been not so good.

Despite her children's disapproval of some of her decisions and actions, Valerie has managed to maintain contact with them. That was not possible for all study participants, however. In some cases, their children cut off communication out of resentment about their upbringing. In other cases, their children had been taken away because of their lifestyle and living conditions. This is Susan's story:

> I was a single parent with my kids until about 1998, and then I had drinking problems like my father. . . . I turned into an alcoholic so I put my kids in Children's Aid. Then I lost custody of them and then I didn't see them for a long time. I went on a drinking binge for three months and then my friends would take the kids and take care of them. They suggested that I do some-thing [about the drinking], so I went into detox and phoned Children's Aid and they took the children [again]. I went to court and they said that I wasn't capable of handling them. I've been sober since.

Susan has managed to turn her life around, but she has to live the rest of her life feeling like she failed her children. To handle this stress, instead of drinking, Susan has turned to gambling at the casino.

Poor relations with their children were a particularly difficult, and com-mon, subject of worry for parents who participated in our study. Losing contact with their children tended to worsen people's gambling problems because they felt deprived of the only positive thing in their lives. Further, they felt they had no one to be a role model for and therefore no reason to stop their destructive gambling habits.

Besides troubled relations with their children, many participants had troubled relations with their romantic partner, causing further stress. Some had grown up witnessing their parents' marital conflict and thinking that dysfunctional family relations were normal and inevitable. Thus, they carried dysfunctional behaviours into their own adult relations. In general, they found it hard to trust and co-operate with others. As a result, nearly half the people in our study had divorced at least once or had never married. Even the non-gambling people we spoke with said they were, or had been, in strained, stressful personal relationships that strongly resembled the parental relationship they had witnessed in childhood.

For example, it's no coincidence that Louisa's father had a serious gambling problem, and Louisa ended up in a relationship with a man who also had gambling problems and behaviours that strongly resembled those of her father:

> I actually had a partner who had gambling problems. He didn't realize he had gambling problems. I'm no doctor or anything, but I felt like he had a gambling problem. Maybe I overanalyzed the situation; because of my past I have stronger senses toward gambling.

Louisa "cut if off" whenever a partner showed signs of problem gambling, but she kept forming these relationships. Indeed, the tendency to form relationships with people who struggle with problem gambling was common among study participants. Sometimes they realized their adult relationships were just as dysfunctional as the relationships they had witnessed between their parents, and dysfunctional in similar ways; most of the time however, these relationship patterns were normalized early in life and not understood as problematic when they found themselves in similar situations as adults.

Anne-Marie exemplified this pattern. Married and divorced twice, she admitted that both of her former husbands resembled her father in their domineering manner—they were typical, aggressive "alpha males." She said:

> My second husband, even though we had a very nice life, he was quite an aggressive arguer. He was argumentative and a little domineering. So I had

stress with him. He wasn't as bad as my dad, but I had some problems with him. It was difficult . . . By some definitions, he was verbally abusive, but not all the time. Not constantly, and not just with me. He was very argumentative. If he didn't agree, he'd be like, "What the hell is wrong with you?"

Throughout this marriage, Anne-Marie experienced constant insult and negativity, forcing her to continually second-guess herself and watch her step. What should have been a loving, supportive relationship was a source of stress that threatened her emotional well-being. Like Anne-Marie's mother and father, who were in constant conflict when she was young, Anne-Marie found herself in unhealthy relationships as an adult.

Every relationship has a backstory. As a child, Anne-Marie often heard her father verbally abuse her mother, even threatening to kill her if she tried to leave. As an adult and free to choose among a variety of mates, Anne-Marie ended up with men who verbally abused her in the same way her father had abused her mother. Her parents' relationship taught her to think that those kinds of behaviour were normal and acceptable, or perhaps that she didn't deserve a healthier relationship. Still, she found her marriages stressful and she managed her stress inappropriately, through gambling and casual sex. She had "lots of flings in the years I lived with the woman roommate. Okay, I'll give you an example. I went to Club Med with the woman I worked with, and I slept with six different guys that week." The unhealthy relationship she had witnessed between her parents combined with her own abusive marriages made Anne-Marie mistrust others and fear commitment. She lost the desire to marry again after having been mistreated by both husbands. Her childhood experiences and unhealthy adult relationships combined to destroy her sense of self-worth and limit her exposure to positive, protective, and supportive interpersonal relationships.

Divorce triggered the onset of problem gambling for a number of study participants (while the opposite was true for others). Kevin watched his marriage disintegrate after his wife's brother and sister died in an accident. He notes that the first fifteen years of his marriage, when his children were growing up, were happy years. "I think my wife and I did a great job raising our kids." After his divorce, however, Kevin turned to gambling. Gambling became particularly problematic when he used it as a crutch, to cope with the stress of his divorce:

Before [the divorce], it was just a form of entertainment and then things started to happen in my life that just "steamrollered." . . . Basically the start [of his problematic gambling] was when I got divorced. I had to deal with everything. I had my own debts, loads that she didn't know. I made big investments in stocks that went belly up, so that killed it all.

Similarly, another participant, Frank, noted: "I wasn't a big gambler . . . when I was married. It was after the marriage broke up and I was on my own that I had more time to gamble." Gambling helped Frank pass the time and forget about the pain of his breakup.

The loss of a family member during their adult years—be it a parent, sibling, or spouse lost to illness or death—was also very stressful for participants, just as it was when it happened during their childhood years. Recall the confusion and devastation our participants discussed over the trauma of losing a loved one in Chapter 5. Similarly, Janice was overcome with sorrow over her mother's death and still struggles to cope with her loss:

It was harder for me when my mom died. Don't get me wrong, I say I love both of them, but up till now I still can't get over it, my mom dying. . . . I still can't cope with it, doesn't matter. . . . I just can't get over it. That's it, that's the bottom line.

Similar testimonies came from people who had lost a beloved spouse, child, or sibling. These unexpected deaths were extremely hard to deal with, and many of the people affected by them suffered deeply. Often, gambling provided an outlet for this suffering—a temporary respite from the thoughts and sorrows they had to endure.

Caregiving

Having to take on caregiving duties beyond those of parenthood caused a great deal of stress for many people we spoke to. These duties might include tending to ill spouses, siblings, parents, and/or grown children. Participants agreed that this kind of caregiving was time-consuming and physically demanding. Worse still, they were emotionally draining, as the participants had to witness the pain of a loved one and force themselves to be positive, despite feeling exhausted and stressed. In effect, this source of stress parallels the detrimental impact parentification has on children by burdening already emotionally disadvantaged individuals with further unexpected stress and responsibility that they are ill-equipped to handle.

Carol discussed these feelings in relation to her own caregiving duties. She revealed that her husband had severe arthritis, which limited the work he could do around the house. Although she was sympathetic toward her husband's pain, Carol resented the amount of housework she was forced to take on because of his illness: "On a daily basis, I would say he doesn't do that much. I do the bulk of things in the apartment and whatever." She also said, "My husband probably agrees with the situation," when she talked about the way the chores within their household were unfairly distributed.

Deep down, Carol felt that she had taken on a lot of extra work that should have been her husband's responsibility. This made her feel that his physical illness was not only holding him back but was also limiting what she was able to do. Gambling relieved those feelings of stress and resentment for Carol. When she was at the casino, she felt free from these perceived restrictions: "I think it's more freeing being there with the [slot] machine. There is no one else there to affect your decision. It's your decision, what you are doing." While she was at home, Carol always had to make decisions with her husband in mind. Gambling gave her a sense of liberation and independence that she could not find in her confining home life.

People, like Carol, who were forced to provide near-constant care for their spouse often considered their situation to be unfair. Providing this kind of care is never part of anyone's life-plan; it is always unexpected and undesired, which makes it all the more stressful. Parents with children affected by debilitating diseases often had a similar experience. When people plan to become parents, they expect to dedicate a certain amount of time and care to raising their children. But if their child becomes ill, these expectations no longer apply; the caregiving responsibilities intensify and parents are left with little time for themselves.

For example, Doreen had to provide extra care for her two young children with type 1 diabetes. Their illness made the daily routine stressful:

> They've had diabetes almost since they were born. . . . We have to check their blood sugar levels three to four times a day. That is a stressful part of life. . . . We would have had a different kind of life if it hadn't happened.

Checking her children's blood sugar levels eventually became routine for Doreen. Still, these extra caregiving duties affected her lifestyle dramatically. Her life could have been "different" and undoubtedly less stressful if her children did not suffer from diabetes.

Gambling became a way for Doreen to relieve the stress of her children's illness. Eventually, she involved her whole family in the activity:

> Lately, the casino has been so super kind to me, they keep on framing it as, "Come over here, we'll give you a free week of the hotel there. Stay on us—free food and everything." I end up taking my whole family there. They go for their swim while I'm in the casino gambling. . . . I try to tell them, "We're having a good time here, so you're in this luxury five-star hotel . . . good food and all that stuff."

The giveaways encouraged Doreen's gambling problem by letting her pass off her gambling trips as treats for the family. Doreen seemed vaguely aware that bringing her children to a casino was inappropriate, but she convinced herself (and them) that it was all for the sake of a "good time."

We have examined several adulthood stressors, which vary in cause and severity: unemployment, underemployment, low or insecure wages, poor mental or physical health, poor relationships, and overbearing caregiving duties, among others. All of these are stressful to varying degrees depending on the way each individual perceives and interprets the stressor within the context of her or his own unique life situation, and each of these sent study participants looking for ways to cope with this stress. Some invariably coped better than others.

All of the problem gamblers in our study found their lives particularly stressful and lived with constant worries, or in a state of uncertainty. Some felt the constant burden of financial problems, while others struggled constantly with illnesses or relationship problems. They seemed more sensitive than other people to the stressfulness of adversities they encountered, in large part because they are, in fact, more susceptible. As we've discussed, our participants experienced serious early adversities, which affect the brain in ways that make it more sensitive to future stress. In effect, early stressors lower our physiological stress system's set point such that it requires a lesser degree of stress to set it off and throw our participants into a stressful state. Regardless of the source of their stress, they were naturally and compulsively driven to seek relief. The commonality among the individuals presented in our book is that they all chose to use gambling to escape from or otherwise cope with their everyday stresses.

This "escapism" was especially marked among people who held the role of caregiver, as caregiving typically meant extra, unwanted responsibilities that continued to make them stressed and anxious. But stressors like role restriction, social comparison, and illness led other participants to also use gambling in an attempt to escape from the stress and anxiety they were suffering.

Some of the participants in our study felt incapable of fulfilling their duties as spouses, parents, friends, or children, or felt limited in their ability to perform these roles adequately. Others felt inadequate in many respects when they compared themselves to other people. Gambling allowed them to feel optimistic about their lives and gave them an opportunity to temporarily forget about their problems.

Some of the people we spoke to were motivated to gamble by the belief it could give them a chance for social interaction. This was especially appealing for people who struggled with loneliness or strained personal relationships. Spending time at the casino allowed people to interact with others who shared similar interests—other gamblers—or provided an atmosphere in which they could be alone in a crowd, with others who were like them.

The problems some participants had with employment and money added allure to the financial payoff they thought gambling could offer. Many saw gambling as an attractive "career"—one that required little effort and offered the chance of quick, easy money. For people distressed and frustrated with their jobs (or lack thereof), gambling let them believe their lives could get better overnight. Gambling offered the possibility of winnings large enough to change their lives, by means of nothing more than luck and persistence.

People with smaller incomes felt that more conventional types of recreation were off-limits to them because they were too expensive. For them, gambling offered an exciting, "affordable" leisure activity, as they could choose to bet more or less money, and thus control the amount they spent—or so they thought.

However, the choice of gambling turned out—for most of our participants—to be a bad choice, a bad coping strategy. Why, then, hadn't they chosen a better coping strategy, and what would such a strategy have looked like? These are questions we explore in the next chapter.

7

Maladaptive Coping

As we've mentioned throughout the previous two chapters, gambling played a significant role in our participants' coping strategies, which were called upon to relieve the negative effects, such as anxiety and depression, that were a result of and plagued their childhood and persisted into adulthood. That gambling helped them escape, forget about, or solve their daily problems was a consistently common sentiment, whether these problems were caused by their job, their financial situation, their health, their relationships, or a combination of these factors. But given all the possible coping mechanisms, both healthy and risky, we asked ourselves, "Why gambling?"

The Role of Childhood Stress and Coping: Setting the Stage

The Dostoevsky Effect model holds that stressful childhood experiences predispose people to problem gambling in two main ways. First, traumatic experiences in childhood cause psychological damage that often persists into adulthood, as was clear from the anger, regret, and loss that study participants expressed with us when discussing their childhood. These negative emotions have continued to intrude on their daily lives, giving participants a constant source of stress to struggle with as adults. Often, these emotions—fear, loss, loneliness, worthlessness, inadequacy—are reawakened by adult stresses of the kind we discussed in the previous chapter.

Second, there is a unique interaction at play between experiencing such traumas and stresses at a young age, on the one hand, and a lack of opportunity for positive, healthy, growth-fostering experiences, on the other hand. Such factors as physical and emotional neglect, lack of parental support and encouragement, and parentification strip children of the ability to develop self-esteem and a sense of personal efficacy that would foster positive, effective coping strategies when needed, as in the case of traumas and stress. Instead, these children were deprived of the opportunity to grow into self-confident, healthy individuals. As if that wasn't bad enough, they were then faced with the terrors of physical and emotional abuse, and family conflict, among other stressors, with which they felt completely overwhelmed and unable to cope with effectively (and which they should never have had to in the first place).

Childhood should be a time when people learn and accumulate positive experiences and a personal belief in self-efficacy that can be called upon both in everyday tasks and in more serious events of adulthood adversity. Children with traumatic histories are robbed of positive experiences, positive role models, and opportunities to develop effective approaches to problem solving for the future; instead, they are constantly in survival mode. Because these individuals are deprived of sufficient opportunity to acquire developmentally appropriate coping skills in childhood, mature coping skills fail to develop at all. This leaves participants, now adults, at the mercy of a wide range of adult stressors, with no effective or mature way to cope.

Often, these poor or insufficient coping mechanisms produce new problems in response to existing ones. This is exactly what happens to people who use gambling (or alcohol, drugs, or violence, for that matter) to deal with anxiety and depression: their problems only get worse. Nonetheless, many who lack another means to relieve stress turn to gambling for relief.

Coping in Childhood

To begin, we will examine the ways participants handled their stress and problems as children, since, as we've explained, the coping mechanisms they learned and used in childhood were often the ones they carried with them through adulthood.

Escape and Avoidance

Hiding or running away from their problems was among the most common strategies that the gamblers in our study used throughout their childhood. Often, they had learned these unhealthy strategies from their parents. Addictions were a prime example, since there is strong evidence that addictions are transmitted socially and psychologically. One woman we have already discussed, Marilyn, told us: "My parents both had drinking problems so if addictive, compulsive behaviour is hereditary, then I believe my poor coping skills came from my parents."

Many other people who participated in our study dealt with their childhood stress in similar ways. Most often, their coping strategies were ineffective. Avoidance was very common among these people, meaning that they ignored or tried to escape from whatever problem was troubling them. Typically, they did so by going up to their room to be alone or by leaving their house. Some children even ran away and became homeless for a time to avoid the turmoil of their home life.

James was someone who used this kind of ineffective coping strategy as a child. Whenever his parents got into a heated argument, James said he had "to be by myself, go outside. [I didn't] want to be around that."

Liam used a comparable approach to deal with conflict in his family: "Thinking back, I don't think they [his parents] ever addressed things, just let it blow over. . . . We [his brother and he] hid in our rooms and waited for the storm to pass." Liam's strategy of hiding out and avoiding his parents until they stopped fighting is a version of the way his parents dealt with their problems. He learned to avoid and hide from their fighting; they refused to "address things," and "just let it blow over." So Liam, like many participants, learned his poor problem solving skills from his parents.

Many other participants experienced similarly conflicted family lives during childhood, and, like Liam, they learned to flee the fighting and just "let things blow over." Liam's childhood was like that of many other people we studied: "I was never home . . . because I didn't like being at home. My parents were in constant arguments."

Yarina used the same coping technique, often hiding from her alcoholic mother to avoid abuse when her mother got out of control. She described her childhood as follows:

> I spent a lot of time just trying to find ways to get around my mother. I had hiding spots. I would go out into the woods or out on the farm and pretend there was nobody there. I would just get away to avoid getting confronted by anybody. . . . I read a lot. Again I would just go off on my own and escape. Whenever I could find time to get away to just go back into the woods and not think, I would.

Avoiding or escaping from the situation helped participants temporarily ease the distress in their childhood home. While their avoidance techniques often included removing themselves physically from a situation, they also incorporated mental aspects. These "psychological avoidance" or escape methods included finding ways to avoid discussing or even thinking about the topic that was causing the individual distress.

Disengagement and Denial

Other children reacted in quite a different way. Instead of vigorously rebelling, they just gave up and became completely apathetic (note that apathy itself is a symptom of depression). Unable to find the energy to care about anything, they bottled up their negative emotions, claiming they didn't have a care in the world. Noel used this kind of coping strategy and dropped out of school at the age of sixteen:

> Not too much bothered me back then. I mean, some people go ballistic over the small stuff, but most things just kind of rolled off my back. . . . Just Mom and Dad arguing used to stress me out, so I would just take off. But other than that, that was pretty much it. . . . I would just leave, go play ball hockey or baseball with a few of my buddies, and then gamble once I got older.

Besides avoiding his parents when they were arguing, Noel also used a more mental technique to cope with stressful situations. That technique was denial. He refused to acknowledge how much his parents' fighting, or anything else, bothered him. But this approach backfired, leading to worse adaptations. Noel admits that his efforts to escape from his parents and their arguing led him to gamble, because he gambled with friends to avoid his home life. So, not only was this denial and escape strategy ineffective for him as a teenager, it contributed to the development of Noel's gambling problem, making problems for him as an adult as well.

However, not all forms of maladaptive coping were as passive as these strategies of physical and psychological avoidance. Some participants also acted out as children, as a way of dealing with their distress. This acting out sometimes included drinking excessively at a young age or engaging in other risky behaviours, such as drugs or sexual promiscuity.

Rebellion

Andrew exhibited this pattern because he was angry at his parents' unrealistic expectations and the pressure they put on him. So, he became a rebellious teenager trying (through rebellion) to regain a sense of control. It was during this rebellious stage that Andrew began gambling. In response to his disobedient rebellious acts, Andrew's parents became neglectful and Andrew was now free to do as he pleased:

> When I would go out and do whatever the hell I wanted, gamble and stay away from my house, I felt like, to a certain extent, I didn't have my parents in my mind when I was doing these things. I was out of the house [and] they would rarely monitor me.

Samuel, too, showed this kind of rebellious behaviour, doing as he wished as a teenager. He went to school at nine o'clock in the morning and did not return home until well after midnight, staying out of his home except to sleep. How did he fill his time?

> My friends and I, we played [poker] quite often because we were bored. . . . We didn't, like, have that much to do; all we did was, like, go to the park, drink, or smoke weed. That gets boring after a while, so we would go to someone's house after a while and just play cards.

Samuel engaged in these activities to avoid his home life. He didn't want to go home and have to deal with the "unrealistic expectations" his parents had of him, always constantly pushing him to improve his school grades. For Samuel, playing poker with friends was a relaxing way to fill his spare time that allowed him to avoid his parents and the pressures they put on him.

In trying to handle various childhood stresses, some participants turned to behaviours that gave them a sense of control when they felt otherwise helpless. One such behaviour became an eating disorder, and Tina employed this particular coping strategy. In an effort to deal with the stress of an overly critical mother and constant exposure to her parents' conflict-ridden marriage, Tina became anorexic and bulimic:

> I was never diagnosed, but all the symptoms were there: I was probably anorexic for a couple of months and then I was bulimic for two and a half years after that. My parents were going through some rough times in their marriage and my father would talk to me, occasionally suggesting to me that he might even split up with my mom.

Tina said these eating practices gave her a sense of control she craved because her family life was so chaotic and painful. However, as Tina grew up, these maladaptive coping mechanisms translated into problem gambling, as she continued to employ the same types of strategies she had used in her childhood to cope with her adult problems. Like disordered eating, problem gambling gave Tina a sense she was wholly in control of some part of her life. Problem eating showed she had control over her body. Problem gambling showed she had control over her money and her risk taking.

Now we'll discuss how participants dealt with stresses in adulthood, seeing how they translated patterns learned in childhood into adult coping strategies.

Coping in Adulthood

In previous chapters, we have characterized gambling as a kind of escape—an activity that provides temporary relief from anxiety or fills the void created by loneliness and depression via an artificial high of sorts, whether it be the thrill of the game, the adrenalin rush of winning or from the prospect of winning, a sense of competence from the false belief that one is "good" at gambling, or the social interaction that comes with gambling in social arenas. Clear and recurrent themes emerged from our interviews: gambling to relieve stress; gambling as an emotional anaesthetic; gambling to counteract boredom, fatigue, or alienation; gambling to soothe a conviction of personal inadequacy; and gambling to combat loneliness. In this section, we bring all of these ideas together. We argue that all the problem gamblers we studied were unable to deal with their stresses in direct, healthy ways, both as children and as adults. Problem gambling became, for them, a crutch on which they relied for support.

Avoidance, Internalization, and Denial

In response to the problems they faced in adulthood, problem gamblers first called on the ineffective coping strategies they had learned in childhood. They had all learned—especially those experiencing traumatic incidents as children—that running away from problems could provide immediate, though momentary, relief. In adulthood, they resorted to gambling for the same reason and to compensate for their lack of effective coping skills. Those who had experienced parentification in childhood were the most likely of all to use escapist or avoidant coping strategies, that is, strategies that encourage retreat into activities, behaviours, or mental states (whether it's substance use, risk-taking, or withdrawal) that don't require them to directly address the stressor. Avoidant coping strategies are contrasted with active coping strategies, which are responses that encourage the individual to either address the nature of the stressor itself or change how one relates to or thinks about it.

In our quantitative analysis, among other specific relationships, we set out to determine the relationship between coping skills and mental health under the presumption that our participants' childhood experiences had taught them maladaptive coping techniques and also negatively affected their mental health, making them less able and less likely to take up positive, mature coping techniques. To measure the relationship between these two factors, we used the Ways of Coping Questionnaire (WCQ; Folkman and Lazarus 1988) (a widely used measure of how people cope with stress) and industry-standard measures of mental health, including the Center for Epidemiologic Studies Depression Scale (CES-D) and the Beck Anxiety Inventory (BAI). The CES-D measures depressive symptomatology among the general population (Radloff 1977), and the BAI assesses the severity of anxiety (Beck and Steer 1993). Our results revealed that those of our participants who suffered from depression were 2.6 times more likely than others to use escapist or avoidant techniques; participants who suffered from anxiety were 5 times more likely.

Many of the people we spoke with said they used gambling to relieve their stress. They also talked about other maladaptive coping mechanisms they used, including the avoidance of troubling problems (as they had done as children) and the abuse of substances such as alcohol and drugs. We also know from recent research that depression is directly related to gambling severity, with increasing severity of depressive symptoms leading to an increased urge to gamble and to gamble longer than the non-depressed individual (Romer et al. 2009).

Some people we interviewed had developed a tendency in childhood to internalize their pain and continued doing this in adulthood. Lawrence, for example, revealed that when he was upset, he preferred to be alone. "I just like to be by myself. That's how it affects me. I just don't want to be bothered. I just want to be by myself."

Oscar did everything he could to avoid direct confrontation, especially confrontation with his wife. He had the same poor problem solving skills as many other participants, a shortcoming he discussed during his interview:

> I don't know how to address the problem, so I do nothing. She [my wife] also doesn't know or doesn't care about that. So we can't fix the problem because we don't know how to handle the problem, and sometimes I think we need assistance from a counsellor or hospital. But it didn't give me any great force to do that. . . . I don't want to do anything.

Incapable of addressing his marital problems, he gave up trying to do anything about them, completely avoiding them instead.

Often, these techniques of avoidance and internalization had been learned in childhood to avoid dealing with family conflict. They became habits, learned coping mechanisms, which were unconscious and hard to overcome, even when people became aware of them. Viktor, for example, came to realize that he was handling his problems unsatisfactorily and wished his family had been more open when he was growing up. When asked if there was anything he wished he could have changed about his relationship with his family, he said, "I guess I would talk to them more about things, like about troubles that I have." But he said he had never felt comfortable discussing problems with his family, because they never talked about those sorts of things when he was growing up.

As a result, Viktor had a "Why start now?" mentality. Because everyone in his family avoided dealing with their problems directly, Viktor learned to deal with his problems in the same way. If he had learned a better way to manage problems while he was growing up, his gambling might not have gotten out of control in adulthood.

This tendency to withdraw and avoid problems was not always the product of an emotionally distant childhood. Evelyn, for example, became an avoidant adult even though she grew up in a very open family. Though other family members discussed their problems with one another, she couldn't bring herself to do so. "I guess if it's related to my stress, I don't like to discuss it. But if there has been a time when my dad has been stressed, or my brother, they're more open to each other, so they'll work it out." When asked why she chose to avoid discussing her problems, she said, "I wouldn't like it if someone judged it [the problem she had], and parents kind of have that tendency [to judge], so that's why." Afraid of being "judged" negatively by her parents, or seeming weak for being unable to handle her own problems, Evelyn kept her problems to herself.

Likewise, Brent chose to internalize his stress and hide his problems because he did not want others thinking of him as a negative person. He kept his worries to himself and tried to avoid thinking about them at all in fear of bringing down the mood of others around him. This was the way he coped with the stress his job was causing him:

> I found out that I wasn't going to be getting a promotion at work. That was very stressful because I definitely feel like I deserved it. How I deal with it, I try not to think about it. If I think about it at work, it will appear in my workplace demeanour, and people will think that I'm negative. So I deal with it by trying to internalize it.

Though this happened in his past and he said it wasn't a big deal anymore, he still seemed flustered when talking about it. Brent's efforts to internalize his feelings didn't keep him from worrying and feeling upset about what had happened. Moreover, his feelings of hurt and frustration were still evident years later, suggesting his efforts to hide these emotions under a smile had failed.

Whether because of the way they were raised or because they wanted to avoid a negative judgment by others, many participants used avoidance and internalizing mechanisms to cope with their various problems. As part of this, they sought distractions to avoid thinking about their problems, and they found that gambling was a very effective form of distraction.

Just as they had done as children, as adults many participants avoided and ignored situations that caused them stress. To cope with the stress of being unemployed, for example, Lawrence shut himself off from the world. Oscar, who was terrified of creating conflict with his wife, used a similar approach to deal with his relationship problems. Rather than using active coping strategies to address relationship problems and try to solve them, he chose to avoid the problems, feeling this was easier than confronting his partner. Even when participants talked about their current conflicts with particular family members, many said they tried their best to avoid the conflicts entirely. Some said they didn't want to confront the other individual, or that they would wait for the other person to take the first step.

Some problem gamblers we spoke to said that they had tried to use positive, functional supports like professional counselling or organized religion in their efforts to cope with stress. However, most found that these methods lacked the appeal of gambling, or did not provide the same amount of relief as gambling did. Despite their best efforts, they found the appeal of gambling to be too intense and they continued to use it as a (dysfunctional) coping strategy.

Denial

Some people we interviewed described their gambling as an avoidance technique, while others admitted they used drugs or alcohol to deal with their stress. Though they may not have handled their problems in the healthiest ways, they at least realized and admitted that they had problems. Moreover, they were usually aware that the ways in which they were trying to cope with their problems were not the best approaches possible.

On the other hand, some participants acted as though their problems were trivial—even as though they didn't have problems at all. These instances of denial were often used when people didn't want to admit to, let alone talk about, their problems with gambling. Take Doreen. She sees a therapist for her drug and alcohol addictions, and when we asked if she had ever considered getting therapy for her gambling problems, she replied, "Not yet. I don't think it's there yet. I mean I've hit rock bottom with the drugs and the alcohol, so I know what that feels like and I'm nowhere near that with the gambling." Despite its interference with her daily life, she still felt her gambling was less troubling than her depression and substance addictions, and as a result, she refused to seek the help she needed to treat and overcome it. Yet, even though she didn't consider her gambling as troubling as her other addictions, Doreen said her gambling sometimes made her feel "terrible," "'cause [she] should [have been] buying groceries."

Like Doreen, Evan also saw a therapist for a mental disorder, but he didn't want therapy for his gambling problem. He said he was afraid he would be criticized for his gambling problem, explaining, "I have always seen a doctor for all my mental health problems, [but] I rarely discuss gambling because I always felt that I would be prejudged even more so." Evan considered problem gambling to be even more taboo (or humiliating) than mental illness:

There is a sense of shame when you talk to other people because it's not like I got cancer and people are like helping you. If you say, "I have a gambling problem and these are the things that have happened because of my gambling problem," they are like, "It's your fault." Even I would think that, in all honesty to somebody.

If you'll recall our discussion on stigma in Chapter 6, you'll see its pervasive impact in full effect in the above statement. We noted that a social stigma is a negative attitude that implies there is something morally wrong in the stigmatized individual that causes them to be rejected from society. We also discussed how and why addiction and mental illness are both, unfortunately, highly stigmatized in our society (although it is worthwhile to note that the effects of recent efforts to destigmatize mental illness and addiction are currently becoming more widespread). In any case, individuals who experience stigma perceive and often internalize a sense of self-blame, which causes them to experience their behaviours as shameful. The resultant low self-esteem, depression, apathy, amotivation, and so forth decreases the likelihood that they will be forthcoming with their problems and actively seek out treatment. Thus, stigma becomes a major barrier for our participants to getting the help they require, leaving them stuck in the self-perpetuating cycle of gambling to relieve stress.

There are different forms of avoidance and also different types of denial. In the face of pervasive social stigma, denial is a mechanism to neutralize the negativity of gambling, both in terms of how it's perceived by the gambler and how it's perceived by others. Mac's comments provide a good example of this mechanism. Her gambling was hurting her family, but she tried to downplay the problems she was causing, saying casually, "I've fallen behind paying some of my bills. A couple of times the money I had to send my daughter to school the next day, I gambled some of it. But that's basically it." Probed by our interviewers, she instead shrugged off the fact that she had spent money her daughter needed for school expenses, as if her child's concerns were not a big deal.

Mae also denied that she was personally responsible when there had been no money to send to school with her daughter. Whether this was a serious problem or not, it simply wasn't her responsibility as far as she was concerned. By positioning the consequences of her actions as neither significant nor her fault, Mae was attempting to downplay the serious-ness of her problem both to herself and to others who might judge her for her actions. Many other participants also denied responsibility for the effects of their gambling. Like Mae, they often used this technique when they felt they had lost control over their gambling, saying they couldn't be blamed for the completely unpredictable outcomes of their bets. That's life, after all.

Another form of denial is seen in the way some problem gamblers criti-cize the people who disapprove of their gambling. The act is one of deflec-tion. These gamblers claim that others make their gambling problems seem worse than they actually are, or fail to understand their gambling entirely. For example, Greg condemned his girlfriend for criticizing his gambling. He blamed her for the tensions that had arisen between them, though these conflicts were the result of his gambling. Of this, he said, "My girlfriend is really cheap. She hates that I am gambling too because I am losing money [at it] and sometimes she doesn't want to go to a movie because it costs too much money, even though I am the one paying for her." Greg did not think she was justified in criticizing his habit because he was still able to pay the bill when he took her out. To Greg, however, precisely because he was still paying the bill and asserting his financial independence, he was able to nonchalantly justify his continued gambling.

People like Mae (who deny responsibility for their problems) or Greg (who condemn their condemners) may be unaware of the severity of their gambling problem. They may have suppressed their feelings of guilt and shame generally, or may have downplayed their guilt when they talked to us. Regardless, denial is an impediment to dealing with an addiction, as it is a widely accepted precedent that the first step toward overcoming an addiction is admitting that a problem exists. So, gamblers who deny the extent of their gambling severity will first have to recognize that their behaviour troubles them and those around them if they hope to recover from their addiction.

Alcohol and Drugs

Many of the problem gamblers in this study also used and abused drugs or alcohol—yet another way to distract themselves from their stress, boredom, relationship problems, and other troubles. In fact, about half of problem gamblers are also alcoholics, and upwards of 60 percent have a nicotine addiction; to boot, research has shown that the more severe the gambling, the more serious one's concomitant addictions to alcohol and cigarettes are (Potenza 2001). These additional substance addictions were like the gambling addiction: they served as coping mechanisms that worked briefly and imperfectly by dulling the pain.

Liam was one of the people who struggled with a comorbid addiction to alcohol. He experienced feelings of depression and a recurring desire to commit suicide, both of which (he eventually realized) were made worse by his alcoholism:

> I was pretty suicidal back then. . . . I would drink, and after I drank, I would feel compelled to take a bullet to my head, so I'd try to sleep. But it was weird because that feeling was almost biological. I would sleep, but I would be like, "Okay, I can't sleep because I am thinking of blowing my head off."

Liam drank to try to dull the feelings of depression that were at least in part due to the negative consequences of his gambling problem, but the alcohol made him feel even more depressed. It was an unhealthy, unsuccessful way of dealing with his mental disorder.

Daria had a drinking problem too. She admitted drinking a 350 ml bottle of liquor almost every day of the week since she was seventeen or eighteen years old. When asked why she drank, she said the alcohol took the edge off her problems and helped her feel good about her life, if only for a while. She also went drinking with her friends to avoid having to deal with her gambling mother: "I would drink a lot I guess. I would always drink until I threw up in high school, because that's what I thought people did, like all my friends would throw up."

Since getting married and divorced, Daria has cut back a bit on the alcohol. "I hate vodka now [that] we're divorced; I just drink beer." It is interesting to note how Daria equates her drinking with her personal relationship with her ex-husband. With the divorce came her dissociation from vodka, suggesting that perhaps vodka was (not surprisingly) tied to the negative factors in her relationship. Hopefully it is the case that, now she is outside the grips of an unhealthy relationship, she no longer feels the need to seek solace in vodka.

Linda's drinking habit also went well beyond being purely social. She drank herself into drunkenness every day, risking alcohol poisoning on a near daily basis. Like many other people who tried to cope with their stress by drinking, Linda's "self-medication" was dangerous and caused as much stress as it was supposed to relieve.

The harmful effects of binge drinking and alcoholism have been widely publicized in the media—unlike the harmful effects of binge gambling. However, even knowing the effects of alcohol on them failed to make it any easier for the participants who suffered from alcoholism to avoid drinking. Vedran, for example, said he tried to avoid using alcohol to cope but often found himself unable to resist, "because when I drink it makes me forget about all my stresses." Unlike Liam, who realized his problems worsened when he drank and was thus able to eventually give up the habit, Vedran felt sure he could gain temporary relief through alcohol and continues to drink excessively today.

We propose that alcohol and drug addictions can be seen as extensions of avoidant coping strategies; people who drank or got high often did so in an effort to forget something that caused them pain. Noel's heavy involvement with drugs, alcohol, and gambling illustrates this kind of avoidant coping, as he used his addictions to deal with his stressful divorce. In our interview, he acknowledged this fact: "We got divorced. That was stressful. That's when I started to get into the drugs and booze bad."

Not everyone we spoke to saw their addictions as a way to actively deal with problems; some people had simply become habituated. They desperately craved the high it gave them, even though they were aware of the damage substance abuse was causing them. However, while they may now be physically dependent, this dependency most certainly evolved from an initial coping behaviour. Adam, for example, started to use substances to deal with employment and relationship stresses. Eventually, after a continual influx of stressors and the need to cope with them, he became physically dependent. Adam continued to abuse both drugs and alcohol simply because he saw no reason to stop; he did not think his life could get any worse (or better). He said:

> I turned to alcohol and drugs, just about everything in the book. It's hurt my relationships in the past, it's hurt my jobs in the past, it's hurt just about

everything, as well as myself. I have hit rock bottom a few times [and] I came to the conclusion that I can't hit rock bottom anymore.

Even though his substance abuse had destroyed almost every aspect of his life, Adam couldn't break his habit and continued to feed it.

Some alcohol- and drug-abusing participants liked to engage in their addiction with other people, but others liked to drink and/or use drugs alone. Megan demonstrated the latter preference, using drugs and alcohol to calm herself down and tune out the world, rather than as a buffer for social interaction:

I don't drink or do drugs with people. Sometimes I would just go to the LCBO [Liquor Control Board of Ontario] because you can get less or more, and I'll come home and just lock myself up in the room and drink and drink until I go to bed, then get up and just do it again!

However, many of the people we interviewed loved the combined thrill of gambling and a drug or alcohol high. Nick, for example, told us "there were very few times when we weren't drinking when we were gambling." Many participants found the greatest thrill engaging in both of their addictions simultaneously. Patty was one of those who linked her drinking to her gambling. She went out gambling and drinking "almost every weekend, you know, I'd be gambling almost every weekend and Friday night and Saturday night, I'd gamble with my friends and I guess you get caught up, drinking, losing too much money." For her, drinking was part of the gambling routine, and while the alcohol itself was easy to "get caught up in," its effect on her also made it easier to get caught up in gambling.

People like Nick and Patty who enjoy drinking and gambling simultaneously are targeted by gambling venues like casinos and racetracks, both of which sell alcohol on site. Everyone knows that alcohol lowers people's inhibitions, and this can lead to more, longer, or higher-stakes gambling. So, gambling venues have encouraged drinking onsite to make a greater profit. For their part, gamblers eagerly go to venues where alcohol is available, to have a good time and forget about their daily stresses. The 50 percent overlap in alcohol and gambling addictions are easily founded.

Substance abuse and gambling reinforce each other, allowing many participants to enjoy themselves more thoroughly because they have more successfully banished their stresses and anxieties.

Gambling as a Coping Mechanism

Here, finally, we will clarify how gambling serves as a coping mechanism in adulthood—for present-day gamblers as it did for Dostoevsky. Whether participants gamble to avoid thinking about their problems, to solve their problems by winning money, or to add thrills and sociability to their lives, all the study participants we spoke to gambled to relieve stress in their lives. Many realized and openly admitted that gambling was their main way of coping with the problems, though many others did not.

Grace illustrates the way many participants see gambling as an opportunity to take a break from their problems:

> What I like about it [gambling] is tuning the whole world out. That's peace and serenity to me. It's [the casino] the one place that people can't find me on cellphones. I like the excitement so I watch it. It's the unknown. I like watching it and hearing the bells go off. I like the excitement too. . . . It's a place where I go and I am alone and no one is there to bug me. If I want to go by myself, it is an escape.

Remember Nancy, whose parents died when she was a teenager? Nancy admits she gambles to blot out the sadness associated with her parents' deaths. Yet the "escape" she experiences from gambling is short lived, and she is still traumatized by their deaths "to this day." Thus, gambling proves to be an ineffective way to deal with emotional problems. It merely allows people temporarily to forget about their problems, without providing any long-term relief from the emotional pain these problems cause.

Evan also uses gambling to cope with his problems and recognizes his gambling is a form of "escapism," similar to the way he had run from his problems as a child:

> I had problems [in university], like not being able to get stuff done, not being able to go to class, stuff like that. I did that for three years of undergrad. During my second and third year, [to escape] I used food and gambling.

Gambling probably interfered with Evan's ability to "get stuff done" and consequently caused him more stress than it relieved. Still, he felt it provided him with an opportunity to escape from and forget about the pressures that school placed on him.

Joshua, too, realized that he had relied on gambling to help him escape from his problems. What distinguished him from Evan was that he didn't want to use gambling to deal with his problems anymore.

> Gambling has become an addiction and it shouldn't be an escape. It used to be fun and it's not fun and it's something I have to do to cope. I hate having anything that makes me feel like I have to use it to cope. I don't like that feeling. . . . That to me is an addiction; if I need that to cope in my life, that's an addiction to me.

Joshua recognized that he had become addicted to gambling and was using it as an unhealthy coping strategy. However, his habit had gotten so out of control that he couldn't break it. He continued to gamble to relieve his stress because he wasn't aware of healthier ways to do so or because other methods hadn't provided the same amount of relief that gambling did.

Other participants used gambling to deal with their feelings of boredom. Marcel, for example, mentioned the feelings of excitement he got from gambling. He said that everyone should go to casinos because that was where you could "let your hair down . . . you're out of the house." Marcel felt gambling allowed him to escape from his boring, routine domestic life. It also gave him a chance to experience the excitement that he lacked at home.

Similarly, gambling appealed to Janice for its excitement. When we asked what kept her coming back to the casino, she said:

> Gambling is just the excitement—the excitement of everything around, the surroundings. It could be for example the slot machines, all these music, and all these lights . . . all the excitement that goes into it. That's where the addicting factor is for me.

Graham expressed similar views when describing the feelings he got playing poker: "You take chances and it's exciting—exciting when you are winning." The thrill of gambling is what enticed Janice and Graham, and many other participants, to use gambling as a means to escape from what they considered to be boring, mundane lives.

Zachary also thought gambling provided a thrilling, exciting escape from a confined and boring life:

> There's not enough entertainment for young adults here. There's nothing much to do if you're really bored or you feel stressed. Sometimes you like to go to release some stress. Different people will do different things. When you have limited choices, then gambling is one of the big choices that people go to.

Unlike Joshua, who saw his escapist gambling as a troubling addiction, Zachary saw gambling as a conventional leisure activity that most people would enjoy. For Zachary, gambling was a fallback option, given the lack of other ways to "release some stress." (Keep in mind that all our participants were screened and met established criteria for problem gambling.) Rather than seeing it as an addiction or something he depended on to help him cope with the boredom or stress, Zachary saw his gambling as a form of "entertainment" that was popular among the "young adults" in his area. He therefore felt that gambling could function as an exciting leisure activity. Moreover, he thought it was one of the trendier forms of entertainment, so by participating, he could feel like he was a member of the socially accepted "in-crowd."

Many other participants found themselves in need of quick, easy money and hoped that gambling would supply it. Lawrence's gambling became worse after he was laid off his job and he hoped to win enough money to invest it and turn a profit:

> I got laid off from my job and stuff like that. Tough times. So I was like, "If I win a few hundred dollars, I can go invest it." There were times I was lucky too. Even if I just made two hundred dollars, I would feel good.

After being laid off, Lawrence tried to make a living from gambling, but he was unsuccessful in this.

Similarly, Janice was drawn to gambling by her financial worries, and tried to solve them by gambling but failed:

We had financial problems—not enough to pay the bills. I'm trying to win some money to pay the bills; that's the bottom line, you know. But it just gets worse so, yeah, it ran into problems, definitely.

Though some participants said they only gambled because they needed the money, notice how Lawrence says he "would feel good" even if he just made a little bit of money. This suggests that gambling filled the need to relieve stresses—to give a sense they were dealing with their problems, even if these efforts were unsuccessful. Janice's admission that "it just gets worse" reminds us that gambling to relieve stress usually has the opposite effect, heightening the stress by causing larger financial problems.

Stephen, who lost his managerial position and the highly valued social status that went along with it, turned to gambling to gain back this status. When he gambled after losing his executive position, he could feel like a "high roller" again. The wins reminded of the times when he did not have to worry about casually spending a couple thousand at the casinos in Vegas. Thus gambling became a way for him to feel, and to suggest to others, that he was still wealthy, prestigious, and high-class; it was this feeling that he continued to chase down the rabbit hole of problem gambling.

Besides serving to cope with the monotony of everyday life, gambling also helped some participants cope with their feelings of loneliness. Ingrid, for example, didn't feel that she interacted much with others, so gambling appealed to her because she thought it offered some social excitement. She had much more fun when she was out gambling than when sitting alone at home. In fact, she said that gambling drew her in instantly during her first experience at the casino:

I won that [first] time and I felt . . . that going there, the people were friendly . . . sometimes. Even if they're not [friendly], there is still something about the place—I don't know, maybe . . . subliminal, maybe the meal—but it was just better than the rest of my life.

Gambling gave Ingrid the social atmosphere she craved: "friendly" people who were willing to socialize with her, even if only occasionally. She idealized the casino as a sort of alternate existence that was "better than the rest of my life." Many other participants shared Ingrid's desire for "something" more than their current lives offered them, and they thought they could find this "something" gambling or at gambling venues.

For these people, the chance to win money was not what attracted them to gambling. Instead, it was the chance to escape from their troubles or boredom. Playing poker, the slots, or betting on racehorses briefly offered them this vacation from reality. This is consistent with the themes discussed throughout this chapter.

The coping strategies that many participants used were unhealthy and ineffective ways of handling their daily stressors. Gambling was one of the means by which some of them tried to internalize or avoid their problems. By going to the casino or another gambling venue, they could be alone to deal with their problems in private. They could busy themselves in their gambling to the point that they forgot about whatever was bothering them. And, if they wanted, they could enjoy vicarious sociability.

However, their reliance on gambling ended up creating more problems for these people: financial problems like Mae experienced, or relationship troubles like Greg experienced, for example. As a result, these participants often turned to the ineffective neutralization strategies we discussed in efforts to downplay the extent of the problems that gambling had created, making them seem more manageable.

Other people we spoke with dealt with their stress and anxiety by drinking excessively, which, like gambling, made their problems worse. Both alcohol abuse and excessive gambling served as substitutes for healthy coping strategies these people had never learned. The poor coping skills they employed were often carried over from childhood, often even techniques they had seen their parents using (unsuccessfully) to handle their own problems—a process known as learned coping that, once again, highlights the importance of the family environment in childhood.

Ultimately, gambling represented an escape for most participants. The search for something "better than the rest of my life" was a theme that came through in many participants' interviews. For these participants, gambling was not a means to make money (since they rarely made any) or a way to improve their lives (since their lives didn't improve). Instead, it was just an escape—a temporary relief from the many problems that bedevilled their lives. But this backfired: gambling actually made their lives worse in the long run. The consequences of problem gambling form the content of our next chapter.

8

How Gambling Makes Life Worse

Adopting gambling as a coping strategy creates new challenges in gamblers' lives—new or aggravated problems with finances, relationships, health, and occasionally, legal problems too. Some problem gamblers fail to recognize this, and for these folks, Jane has some advice:

> If I were to give any gambler a message, it would be: you're not just hurting yourself. You're hurting your partner, you're hurting your kids, and you're hurting your kids' kids because the cycle continues. You're not being a parent: you're absent. You're not being a partner: you're absent. And in that absence, you're forcing your partner . . . you're not allowing your partner to be a mother, or to be a father, whatever. That translates into . . . not being a good role model, not giving your kids the security and confidence they need to be good parents themselves, and that's going to cycle down. So you're hurting a lot of people for generations to come.

Compare a gambler who has lost everything—job, home, relationships, credit—with a substance abuser in the same position: the gambler is driven by the (slim, albeit) possibility that a large amount of money can be won that will at least allay unemployment, housing, and financial difficulties; a substance abuser knows that one more "hit" may ease stress, but it certainly won't bring any material gain, so the substance abuser has far less hope of emerging from the situation. Whereas hopelessness encourages other types of addicts, hopefulness encourages the gambler. This is a particularly salient point that distinguishes gambling from other addictions, behavioural or substance-based: the very fact that the behaviour of chasing losses that perpetuates the addictive cycle is the same behaviour that offers a potential solution to their life's problems (i.e., winning a large sum) makes gambling dangerously difficult to escape.

Financial Difficulties

Financial well-being is probably the most obvious and most significant target for gambling consequences. Not surprisingly, as a result of their gambling and their accompanying lifestyles, many of our participants faced serious financial difficulties brought about by gambling losses, unstable employment, and insufficient income. Many of them held a strong conviction that continued gambling would eventually provide them with extra money that could help in paying off debts and expenses. When they, naturally, lost large sums of money instead ("the House always wins"), they typically felt compelled to try to win that money back. As a result, they lost even more money. This pattern of "chasing losses" was observed among many participants.

For example, Craig said, "I will tell you what it [gambling] has messed with significantly, is my credit. That has been impacted significantly by gambling. That one hurts."

Anthony explicitly planned to gamble and use his winnings to pay off existing debts. When asked what he wanted to do with the money he believed he could win, he said:

> Pay off my credit card. That kind of thing. My winnings right now aren't substantial enough to pay for anything significant. I'm not buying booze or anything like that. I don't do any of that. It's usually right into the chequing account, and then it usually goes toward the typical university kid expenses.

Anthony was trying to justify his gambling by saying the money he won would go to a good cause: paying for his university tuition. Because he wasn't "buying booze or anything like that" with his winnings, he felt like his gambling was a solution to his financial problems, not a cause of them.

Similarly, Janice hoped that a big gambling win would help her pay her bills. Unlike Anthony, however, she understood the problems she was creating for herself, when she said, "I'm trying to win some money to pay the bills—that's the bottom line, you know. But it just gets worse, so yeah, it [gambling] ran into problems, definitely." Despite plans to make a profit by gambling and use that money to pay for necessary expenses, both Anthony and Janice lost their money to gambling. They would have been better off focusing on their respective jobs, but they kept returning to the casino because of the appealing thought that they might win a huge amount of money in little time, and with little effort.

Other participants were well aware of the vicious cycle they created by trying to win back losses. Of this, Joshua said:

> I had a problem with money because I was trying to bet and bet and win back money, and I couldn't. I went back next day to the same game and I lost more. In this case it was kind of complicated.

Most shared Joshua's feeling that "it was complicated"; by chasing their losses in an effort to regain what they had lost, these people found themselves losing everything. Yet, they found it hard to do otherwise. Many participants were thus forced to continue gambling because they felt obliged to win back the money they had lost.

Hannah said she started gambling online for fun, but once she started losing, she became determined to win back what she had lost. That's how her gambling turned into problem gambling. "Earlier on in online gambling, I just wanted to pass the time, I had nothing else to do. As I started to lose, I felt like I had to get it back. And the more I put in, the more I had to get back and the more desperate and frantic I felt." Hannah's inability to stop betting drained her not only financially but also mentally and emotionally, as she became "desperate and frantic." She elaborated further on the emotional effects her habit had on her:

> Being completely depressed! . . . If I play a high stake, then I just need to win once and then I'll get it back. So I want to play high stakes, so I'll win it quicker, so I [can] stop. But it never got to a point where I could stop, [and] I never felt comfortable. I always felt worse when I played.

Having lost too much money to give up, Hannah believed that her next big bet might win her back her losses, plus some. Consequently, Hannah was afraid to stop gambling: she didn't want to miss out on placing the bet that could finally get her out of the hole.

Like Hannah, Ingrid also felt trapped by the need to continue gambling because she had lost too much money to stop. She had been borrowing money from her friends and family and had also taken out a loan from

Money Mart. This loan was putting her under a huge amount of pressure because of the high rate of interest on it—interest that was growing because she was taking so long to pay off the loan. Finally, she lost all the money she had borrowed. Not knowing any other way to get it back, Ingrid started buying lottery tickets to try to fix her financial situation. That didn't work either:

> I spend too much money on these things [gambling], and my pay [only] comes once a month. . . . I was borrowing money before and then paying off it. . . . I tried to get into . . . doing something constructive with my own money but it's not [easy]. It's a total failure, totally stupid behaviour.

Ingrid was caught in a cycle of borrowing and owing, which she knew was "harmful," but from which she couldn't break free. The stress of being unable to pay her bills, combined with feelings of guilt about having lost so much money gambling, made Ingrid feel "stupid"—as though she weren't competent enough to manage her own finances.

Wan lost control over his finances because of his gambling habit as well. Rather than prioritizing necessities like food, Wan spent every dollar he earned immediately at the slot machines. He took out a line of credit to pay off the credit card debts that had followed his gambling losses, borrowing more money to feed his addiction. This pattern of borrowing, losing, and borrowing was another common pattern among study participants who were similarly in debt.

This willingness to borrow money to cover losses also reflected an avoidance coping strategy. Wan remembered, "I was too naive and I just ignored it. But it just felt good to not worry about it. I mean, why worry about something that you can't control?" Rather than monitoring and limiting his spending to remedy his financial situation, Wan ignored his financial problem because it "felt good" to do so. Moreover, he felt certain he could continue borrowing the money he needed until he was debt-free, via gambling wins. Wan translated this carefree mentality to his gambling, relying on chance for big wins and refusing to worry about his losses, because he didn't think he could control them anyway.

Not everyone borrowed the money they needed from lending institutions. Many problem gamblers borrowed money from relatives, stressing their family relationships as a result. Rachel, for example, borrowed money from many of her family members to fund her gambling and pay off the debts that gambling had created:

> I have borrowed money off my sisters, both of them. . . . I borrowed five hundred dollars off my brother once and it was for gambling to pay off one of my debts 'cause I was in debt and I did pay him back one hundred dollars a month.

Similarly, Blake borrowed from his brother to pay for the basic necessities he could no longer afford because of gambling losses. Blake admitted to feeling guilty about this:

> I started borrowing money from my brother for basic needs, for stuff I should have been able to afford—for rent, for food. Not for gambling specifically, but because of gambling. . . . Borrowing money from my brother was not easy, because . . . I had to admit it to him. I said, "Brother, I am not in a good way, I need help. I have no money." I mean I was working, and I had no money.

His inability to pay for things he needed to survive made Blake realize how serious his financial problems had become. Having to turn to his brother for help, rather than a large institution where no one knew him personally, made him feel ashamed that he had let his gambling get out of control.

Some people we spoke to were not able to ask their family members for help, so they borrowed the money they needed from friends. Rhonda said that borrowing money from her friends made her feel as though she had hit rock bottom, and she still feels guilty today for having asked her friends to help her:

> Sometimes I borrowed money [after] having lost. It wouldn't be very much money—maybe a few hundred dollars from some friends . . . but I felt awkward. . . . They were a little surprised. . . . I felt really stupid . . . [but] I had to pay necessities. . . . Once I gave them [back] a hundred or two hundred dollars—they just let it go. But I did feel guilty about that too.

When asked for the money the gamblers needed, friends and family members usually gave them the money they needed. Yet, despite this willingness to help, many participants who borrowed money from their friends and family felt guilty and embarrassed afterwards, which led them to distance themselves from friends and family. In this way, their financial problems negatively affected their personal relationships with the people they cared most about.

The loss of large sums of money also created mental and emotional instability. Even those who were emotionally stable before they started gambling began to feel overwhelmed and ashamed by their addiction. Carol was one problem gambler we spoke to who felt her habit had caused her a great deal of new emotional stress. By continuing to gamble past her limit and losing a lot of money in a short time, she became highly distressed, even over what some people would consider a small amount of money:

> I felt pretty bad for a couple of nights when I lost, say, five hundred to six hundred dollars one night. I didn't sleep very well because I lay awake worrying about it. How stupid can you be? So, it has affected my mental health because I get really angry at myself.

Carol's gambling losses made her feel angry and disgusted with herself, and she consequently formed an opinion of herself as a "stupid" person without any self-control. Many other participants expressed similar feelings: losing large sums of money and racking up debt made them feel guilty, ashamed, and even worthless. In order to forget these feelings, or at least distract themselves from thinking about the losses, many people we spoke to continued to gamble.

Thus, a cycle emerged: people gambled to try to ease the pain their gambling had caused, but when they lost more money, the pain worsened, intensified by the very strategy they were using to try to handle pain. A similar cycle was seen among people who gambled to win back their losses: financial stress that resulted from gambling encouraged them to gamble more, which led to even more losses. Participants' gambling spun out of control, as they became trapped in these vicious cycles of gambling, losing, and gambling.

Though gambling made the people in our study lose significant amounts of money, it also kept alive the hope they could win it back. They understood that chasing their losses was often the cause of their financial problems, but they also saw chasing as potentially part of the solution, which continually kept them coming back for more and thus stuck in the vicious cycle that is problem gambling.

Relationship Difficulties

Most of the problem gamblers in our study created relationship problems by their gambling. Their gambling often acted like a wedge, splitting their relationships apart. Typically, loved ones disapproved of their gambling, so the connection between them became strained and uncomfortable.

More than half of the participants said their gambling problem made it hard for them to maintain family or romantic relationships. As with their financial problems, they found themselves in a vicious cycle, in which gambling losses and poor relationships fed each other. Problem gambling weakened ties between gamblers and their family members, so they gambled even more to ease the pain those ailing relationships were causing, losing more money and further weakening the relationships.

Not only did this vicious cycle interfere with previously established relationships, it also prevented gamblers from seeking and building new relationships. Nick, for example, said that he had a girlfriend who did not like the amount of time he spent gambling. She resented the fact that he played poker about five times a week and this resentment put a huge strain on their relationship. After this relationship disintegrated, likely due to his girlfriend's disapproval of the gambling, Nick didn't feel he had the time to find a new partner, as he was constantly occupied with playing cards. His gambling distracted him from both the relationship he had previously had, and from finding a new girlfriend afterwards:

> It affected them [relationships] . . . because I was gambling, I had less time, less motivation, and less interest in developing relationships. Instead of dating five nights a week, I was playing cards five times a week. It affected the relationships I did or didn't have.

At the height of his gambling problem, Nick valued card-playing over his relationships with others. Putting gambling first in this manner was common among many of the problem gamblers we interviewed.

Paulo said that gambling even led to his divorce:

> Gambling had a lot to do with the first divorce 'cause I spent more time gambling than I spent at home. And it had nothing to do financially in a sense. We had a house, bills were paid, I was just never around. In the evening I would spend time at a card table, or in the afternoon I was at a track or something. I earned a really good living. At times I made $150, $160 grand a year, but I was blowing half of it gambling. So the house and everything was paid for, so it wasn't like the kids weren't fed or wife didn't have money, I just wasn't helping her with the kids, you know.

Paulo didn't resent his wife for leaving him. Rather, he sounded almost relieved, as though he realized he would have more time to spend at the racetrack as a single man. A characteristic of the gambling subculture is that it leaves little time for anything (or anyone) outside of it. In fact, the disapproval his wife expressed for his gambling seemed only to fuel Paulo's desire to gamble:

> The more my ex-wife hated my gambling, the more I wanted to gamble— 'cause she just totally used to piss me off and I would make excuses to gamble. The less she hated it, the less I wanted to gamble.

Gambling caused tension between Paulo and his wife because the ideas she held about gambling clashed with his own beliefs and desires. Recall our discussion of coping strategies such as denial and neutralization. We argued that these were born from childhood and carried through into adulthood. With Paulo, we can see just how entrenched those coping strategies are, to the point where they vehemently manifest themselves in unassailable beliefs that gambling is acceptable and anyone who doesn't accept it is in the wrong and thus unacceptable.

Many other problem gamblers we spoke to confessed that their relationships were strained by gambling. When their partners disapproved of their gambling, whatever their reasons, tension in the relationship resulted.

Other participants strained the relations with their friends because of their problem gambling. Samuel, for example, lost some of his closest friends because he was more interested in gambling and drinking than he was in spending time with them. His gambling drew him closer to friends who also gambled but destroyed his relationships with non-gambling friends:

I stopped seeing a lot of people. I would only have two or three close friends that I would often see and they would be hard-core gamblers too. And then people who aren't as much [into gambling], you sort of lose contact with them, you know.

Samuel also talked about how he pushed his family away: "I already had family problems because I would always go out. . . . I was at a casino." He never spent any time at home with his family because he preferred to spend his free time gambling. As a result, the bonds he had once had with his family and friends deteriorated.

The amount of time that Samuel, Paulo, and Nick spent gambling defined their priorities and made it hard for them to develop and maintain lasting relationships. Putting most of their time and energy into gambling, they grew uninterested in personal relationships. They felt restless and irritated when socializing with non-gamblers, since it cut into the time they could spend at the casino or the racetrack. However, as their relationships disintegrated, their risk for worsened gambling increased, as we know healthy personal relationships to be protective against gambling.

Another way gambling harmed relationships was through dishonesty: the lies problem gamblers told their friends, family members, and partners eventually made their loved ones mistrust them. Most of the gamblers in our study reported this pattern. They had often found it necessary to lie about their gambling to the people closest to them, and eventually these people no longer trusted them and they would begin to feel isolated in their habit and alienated by others.

The desire to avoid conflict was a frequently cited reason for lying to loved ones. Many participants knew their partner or family did not accept, let alone approve of, their gambling, so they simply lied about it. Vedran, for example, displayed this behaviour. He kept his gambling a secret from his parents and siblings because he did not want to deal with their disapproval. When asked how his family would have reacted, he said,

My parents would absolutely hate it and my siblings would hate it as well, except for maybe, one or two. My family, some of them are very conservative and religious. So in both instances, gambling is bad and something that they don't want to be associated with.

Many other participants behaved similarly, distancing themselves from the people who were closest to them, to avoid facing the shame of telling all about their addiction. Because of this detached, standoffish behaviour, the friends and family of these gamblers came to believe that they were unwanted or unloved, and their relationships with the gambler eventually disintegrated.

Often, the problem gamblers we interviewed blamed themselves and their gambling for these failed relationships. Consequently, they felt depressed about the loss of a loved one and ashamed that they had let gambling destroy their once strong, loving relationships. Along these lines, Naveed said, "I guess I have let a lot of people down. 'Cause I wasn't as good a father as I should have been or as good a husband as I should have been either. I've started paying for it now."

One of the ways he had let people down was by being absent, due to his constant need to gamble. It kept him from being there for his wife and children when they needed him. Even the rare occasions when he spent time with his family were made uncomfortable, since his wife and children badgered him about his gambling. Naveed claims they were bothered by it because they were jealous of the money he had won. More likely, they were upset because he spent more time gambling than he did with them.

Despite the regret he voiced in saying "I have let a lot of people down," Naveed blamed his wife and children when their family fell apart. Gamblers are always looking for an excuse to justify their behaviour (a characteristic of all addicts—see Chapter 7 and the discussion on neutralization), and Naveed used this reasoning as a way to both justify continued gambling and to cope with losing his family due to his addiction. Irritated that they "hated" his gambling, he accused them of being jealous because he "won all the money." Like many of the gamblers we have discussed, Naveed remained unable to value his relationships more highly than gambling, even when his loved ones told him how much his habit was hurting them.

Naveed's family was aware of his gambling and disapproved of it. By contrast, Samuel's family knew little about his gambling, yet it still caused relationship problems:

> They don't even know I gamble so much. . . . They would bitch at me, saying, "Why are you spending so much money?" And then I can't always tell

them that it was gambling. It does affect me somehow, but they just don't know it's because of gambling.

Samuel's gambling caused his family financial problems. Worse still, it became a source of shame and embarrassment so intense that he couldn't bring himself to tell them the real reason he was spending so much money. Samuel's inability to reveal the nature of his problem drove a wedge between him and his family. Samuel and Naveed, among others, strained the bonds with their wives and children.

Other participants were in a similar conflict with their parents. This latter kind of conflict was common among participants who still lived in their parents' home, especially if their parents were not gamblers themselves. The conflicts worsened whenever a parent tried to control his or her child's gambling behaviour. Tim, for example, said that his parents—especially his mother—tried to insult him to the point where he no longer wanted to gamble. She often called him "retarded" when speaking about his decision to gamble. However, in this case and others, name-calling and other degrading behaviours rarely had positive effects. Instead, they caused lasting damage:

> My mom was more frustrated with me than anything, to see me go and blow that money and not think anything of it. She said, "What are you, re-tarded?" "What is wrong with you?" I said, "Don't worry about me, mama, I'm okay." She said, "Oh I worry about you. I think you're retarded so I'm going to make an appointment for you."

The "appointment" Tim's mother planned to make was with a doctor who could have offered him help and guidance for his gambling problem. When we asked Tim if he had ever considered following his mother's advice and going to see such a doctor, Tim just laughed and said, "Hell no." His mother's comments did not have the effect she had intended. Rather than bringing him to his senses about the damaging effects of his gambling, her pestering served to push Tim farther away from her and, perhaps, away from a potential opportunity for treatment.

The conflict between Tim and his mother reflected their differences in the values and ideas they held about "normal" and acceptable gambling behaviour. Living at his parents' house made the conflict more intense.

There, Tim felt, his parents continuously judged his behaviour, but he didn't have anywhere else to go to escape their negative judgment. As the relationship with his parents became strained and then distant, Tim felt better about excusing his gambling problem, as he came to believe that he was only hurting himself. He refused to recognize that his gambling had a negative effect not only on himself, but on his parents too. To those looking in, however, Tim was not only hurting himself with his gambling, he was also distressing his mother, and his gambling was having a ripple effect with major negative impacts on both their lives.

Problem gambling did not only disturb established relationships, it also prevented many of the people we interviewed from developing new relationships. Though gambling allowed some participants to interact with others in a social setting, it inhibited other participants from developing real friendships. Jonathan experienced this kind of situation, saying, "I don't really have too many friends. I don't really socialize anymore."

Liam claimed that gambling gave him an opportunity for social interaction, but it was a shallow kind of interaction, providing him with only "acquaintances," not true friends. He described his dismal social life as follows: "I got a group that I went to high school with. . . . A few of them were acquaintances. Over the last forty years there is virtually no contact with anybody." Gambling often prevented people from becoming involved in close relationships, thus limiting their network of social supports.

This, in turn, created yet another cyclic condition that perpetuated problem gambling behaviour. In Liam's case, the cycle began when he lost contact with people who had once been friends, leaving him feeling bored and lonely. He responded by beginning to gamble to fill his endless spare time and distract himself from feelings of loneliness. The gambling, in turn, kept him from developing new, non-gambling relationships that could have encouraged him to adopt a healthier lifestyle.

Many of the problem gamblers we interviewed experienced similar downward spirals brought about by the disintegration of relationships and failure to form new ones that could otherwise have offered the possibility of protection from further gambling. Relationships can encourage positive behaviour and lend social support, both emotionally and instrumentally, to those seeking treatment and trying to maintain a healthy lifestyle. The role of relationships, role models, and social support will be discussed more in Chapter 9.

Legal Difficulties

Financial, interpersonal, and emotional problems were common and openly discussed among the gamblers we spoke to. Additionally, every now and then, legal problems were mentioned, and several participants revealed they had run into problems with the law because of their gambling. These occurrences were relatively rare within our sample. They tended to occur among our male participants and to be correlated with gambling severity. These legal dilemmas often made it harder to get a job, which in turn created financial difficulties. Since these financial difficulties encouraged people to continue gambling, legal troubles played a part in yet another downward spiral.

Jeremy, for example, was charged with illegal gambling when he was young and found it difficult to get a good job because of his legal record:

> When I was seventeen, they actually raided an apartment and I got charged then. Then I was [placed] on probation, and my probation was to come home [by] at least at nine o'clock and check in with my sisters . . . and I went out gambling again, but they caught us again. . . . Right now I work at [a hotel chain]. My cousin's friend, his parents worked at the [hotel] prior to when I was working there and they recommended me; but once I got an interview there, they looked at my criminal record and they just wanted to discuss it with me. My cousin's friend was there with me, telling them that's okay, that's when he was a kid. So, the controller of where I work, he was just like "You're lucky you have a good friend, because if it was my decision, I wouldn't hire you just because you have a criminal record."

Despite the repercussions from his run-in with the law, Jeremy did not quit gambling. In his view, the damage was already done. Jeremy felt that he would always encounter problems because of his criminal record if he ever looked for another job. By that reasoning, there was no need to stop gambling: the situation would not get better if he did. He was upset that he had been caught gambling, but failed to acknowledge the problems that gambling was causing.

While a few participants were caught gambling underage, most of the problem gamblers who got into trouble with the law in our sample had stolen something. More than half of these people reported that they stole to support their gambling problem. Some embezzled money to support their habit, and, occasionally, they were imprisoned for their crimes. One recovered problem gambler, Paul, described his use of embezzlement to fund his gambling:

> I systematically stole from my employer [a casino] over a period of two years to perpetuate my gambling problem. I rose to a level of trust within my position with the casino and abused that level of trust so I could gamble. When it was all said and done, I embezzled nearly $500,000 from my employer and I spent nineteen months in [jail].

Paul's desire to gamble was so strong that he violated the laws and the trust others had put in him, so he could continue to gamble. Paul's case was extreme; however, many of the problem gamblers in our study admitted to stealing money from family or friends so that they could gamble. For obvious reasons, their relationships became strained when the theft was discovered, further isolating the problem gamblers from social support.

Health Problems

Many of the gambling-induced problems we have discussed—the financial troubles, relationship troubles, and legal troubles, among others—caused stress and undermined the well-being of the people involved. Some problem gamblers we spoke to even reported significant declines in their health as a direct result of their gambling, and causality distinguishes this section from our discussion of external physical health problems in Chapter 6. The most common health problems our participants discussed that came about specifically from their gambling behaviours included fatigue, the development of unhealthy eating habits, and being in poor physical condition.

Yarina, for example, experienced problems with her diet and then with her weight. She often ate fast food while she was at the casino and her weight went up dramatically as a result. In addition, she spent much of her time sitting and gambling, rather than engaging in any sort of physical activity:

> Gambling makes you put on weight. Trust me. I was only one hundred and fifty pounds and I went up to two hundred pounds because [when you

gamble] you are sitting all day. You are having a good time [and] it's a good place; but in the process you are drinking and eating.

Yet, Yarina's unhealthy eating, and the resulting weight gain, did not motivate her to stop visiting the casino and start hitting the gym. Instead, she became even less interested in her health and gave gambling her full attention. When feeling stressed about her weight gain and other upsets, she gambled to distract her from her worries—a theme we have seen throughout this section. Thus, yet another negative cycle emerges, in which gambling encourages an unhealthy lifestyle, which in turn causes stress that is handled by gambling, and so on, ad infinitum.

Gambling also caused the problem gamblers in our study troubles with their mental health. Gambling was on their minds constantly, and even when they weren't gambling, they couldn't stop thinking about placing their next bet. In fact, these intrusive and obsessive thoughts are a characteristic of problem gambling. Many said that these obsessive thoughts interfered with their work and made them less productive. Others found it undermined their ability to interact with friends and families, causing their relationships to disintegrate.

Emotional problems also stemmed from problem gambling. Many study participants reported feeling ashamed of their behaviour and regretted decisions they had made. Such feelings did not necessarily motivate them to alter their gambling pattern. Instead, many simply worked harder to conceal their gambling from people who were close to them, as already noted. This deception led to other interpersonal problems, which made these people feel even more ashamed, stressed, and anxious than before. Many were ashamed to admit that, during hours they spent hiding their addiction in the company of friends and family, trying to appear normal, they couldn't stop thinking about getting back to the casino, to win back the money they had lost.

Brianne told us she had often felt this way, until the downfall:

Gambling is something that makes you lose everything, lose your husband, your kids. Everything. You don't want him [your husband] to know if it's too frequent [because] then the man doesn't like it. Hopefully the idea was to go back and win back what I lose, but it doesn't happen this way; instead it gets worse. And it gets worse and worse and worse until it collapsed, and that was it.

As Brianne and other gamblers became increasingly preoccupied with gambling, their stress levels increased, as did their annoyance with themselves and others. They found that gambling—more gambling—was one of the best ways to comfort themselves and ease their minds. Like the people addicted to alcohol or drugs, the gamblers in our study needed to get their fix in order to calm their nerves.

More serious mental health problems like depression also emerged in our sample of problem gamblers, which is expected in relation to findings of high levels of depression among problem gamblers (Clarke 2004). As we mentioned in Chapter 6, we also know depression is directly related to gambling severity, in that the more depressed somebody feels, the stronger the urge he or she will feel to gamble to relieve that depression and the longer he or she will want to put off those depressive feelings via increasingly longer gambling sessions (Romer et al. 2009); the end result is further increased gambling severity, which only restarts the cycle when it causes consequences that drive the individual further into depression, causing them to seek out relief through gambling once again.

Usually, gamblers began to feel depressed because they had lost so much money and so many friends or family because of their gambling, leaving them lonely and full of despair. Some participants said their feelings of depression stemmed from debts their gambling had created.

Mae described a troubling financial situation she had been in and the state of depression she sank into as a result:

> I was heavy into online gambling, and it was just brutal. I lost maybe two thousand dollars over the course of less than six months. It was all intertwined with my school debt, student loans. I wasn't in school then, I don't think. . . . And it just got so out of control, because it wasn't cash, and I couldn't keep track of what I was spending, and I didn't realize how much I was spending. And the deeper I got into credit card debt with online gambling, the more I panicked and wanted to dig myself out. But I had no clue how to do it, other than more online gambling. I went into deep depression because of it. Bailing me out was just so tough, just so difficult. Taking control of my finances and addiction, at least to the point I am now, was very tough.

Many participants who felt depressed because of their gambling problem sought professional help. However, usually they only wanted to be treated for their depression—not for the problem gambling at the root of the depression. Here, we see the issue of stigma come into play again. Most participants said they were afraid they would be judged harshly if they admitted to having a gambling problem, and this fear kept them from admitting their problem and seeking treatment. Further, they usually felt they were entirely to blame for situations they had gotten themselves into, and this sense of blameworthiness and shame further discouraged them from seeking help.

However, without addressing the underlying cause of their depression, they could never truly get over their feelings of despair and loneliness. Thus, Mae and many other participants who became depressed because of their gambling and its consequences experienced barriers to receiving the help they needed to overcome such feelings of despair, since they didn't feel they could be fully honest about their gambling behaviour.

The problem gamblers in our study undoubtedly faced serious problems, from relationship fallouts to financial ruin to poor mental and physical health, and they coped via maladaptive strategies that only seemed to perpetuate further negative consequences to their actions. These problems were aggravated by the anxiety they caused, which led people to gamble even more. Losing a lot of money, for example, made people feel guilty and ashamed, driving them to gamble in an effort to cope with these negative feelings. As well, they felt obliged to win back the money they had lost, driving them back into the casino for another round of desperate losses.

We noticed similar cycles—downward spirals—in people who experienced relationship problems with their friends, family, or spouse. Some were often absent from their partner and children, and often lying to loved ones about their gambling. Both the absences and the lies weakened the bonds between the gamblers and their families. Again, many gamblers returned to gambling to cope with the pain of failing relationships.

Friendships, too, were torn apart by problem gambling. Without anyone to keep them company or entertain them, our lonely, bored participants often went to the casino in search of company, noise, and activity. Yet, passing their time gambling kept these people from developing the deeper relationships that might have helped them develop a healthier lifestyle. So, in the end, they had to continue to use gambling to quell their boredom and loneliness.

Regardless of which factors caused a problem gambler to continue feeding his or her addiction, gambling perpetuated an unhealthy spiral that was hard to break. By trying to handle their stress by gambling, these people merely caused themselves more stress and pain, making it increasingly difficult for them to break their habits, and this failure prompts them to once again turn to gambling. The result is a vicious cycle that consumes not only the gambler, but also his or her family, friends, and loved ones.

Some Concluding Thoughts

In his meta-analysis of two twin studies and seventeen family history or family method studies, Walters (2001) concluded that the genetic heritability of problem gambling is approximately 16 percent, which is considered to be a relatively low genetic influence. Medical models of problem gambling that extend beyond genetic determination tend to emphasize individual trait and biological differences in the brains of problem gamblers, with well-known gambling researchers reporting findings, such as endogenous opioid differences in the brains of problem gamblers, and personality variables, such as sensation seeking and impulsivity (Blaszczynski et al. 1986a, 1986b).

While genetics and psychological factors certainly play a role in the intergenerational transmission of problem gambling, they do not explain how vulnerabilities in these areas are created or triggered to result in problem gambling. In support of this point, Wensley and King (2008) suggested that researchers who pronounce findings supporting a genetic cause for a behavioural characteristic such as problem gambling should include a discussion of the environmental, cultural, and socioeconomic influences on the behaviour. Particularly since genetic and psychological approaches cannot explain 100 percent of the variation in the intergenerational transmission of problem gambling, it is all the more important to acknowledge the role of the family and the social environment in this transmission, and the social processes (such as stress and coping) involved in each. Given Walters's (2001) finding of 16 percent heritability and his conclusion that the additional variance in problem gambling is thus non-genetic, it was our intention in conducting this study and writing this book to contribute to the understanding of problem gambling by determining which sociological factors help explain the remaining 84 percent variance.

As a result, this part of the book has showed how childhood trauma, adult stresses, and faulty coping combine—in the case of present-day gamblers and as in Dostoevsky's case—to initiate a downward cycle of increased stress and increased gambling to deal with that stress. In the chapters in Part III, we discuss a different set of influences on gambling: influences no less important to present-day gamblers in our sample but that played a much less important role in the gambling of Fyodor Dostoevsky. For this reason, we refer to these as "non-Dostoevskian processes."

Part III

Non-Dostoevskian Processes

Opportunity and Acceptability

Problem gambling is influenced by a wide variety of factors. As outlined in the previous section, some of these factors include childhood trauma, adulthood stresses, and poor coping behaviours. However, there are also other influential variables that contribute to the development of a gambling problem, such as having parents who gamble problematically, perceiving gambling as being acceptable, having many opportunities to gamble, and "learning" gambling as a child. These factors cannot be classified as being part of the Dostoevsky Effect because they did not encourage the development of Dostoevsky's gambling habit.

In fact, Dostoevsky's gambling behaviour and the variables that influenced it were largely at odds with those of his fellow Russian gamblers. As we saw in Chapter 2, gambling at games of skill was considered to be an effective way to demonstrate high social status, class, and manliness among Russian aristocrats in the nineteenth century. Yet Dostoevsky did not gamble in an effort to display these characteristics, did not play games of skill, and did not gamble with Russians in Russia. Instead, he travelled to Germany, where he gambled in an alien "European" mercenary environment in order to make a profit. Perhaps Dostoevsky exhibited these abnormal gambling practices because he was not exposed to gambling in his family home as a child, or in adulthood, as he had neither friends nor relatives who gambled. As such, he was not merely responding to parental problem gambling, a local gambling culture, or social learning when he embarked on his ten-year gambling binge.

However, although these factors were not influential for Dostoevsky and his gambling habit, they are important for understanding how many present-day problem gamblers develop their addictions. Our model of the development process, as discussed at the beginning of Part II, argues that gambling opportunities, gambling acceptability, and childhood learning all influence adult gambling and particularly problem gambling. Further, many of these factors are heavily influenced by parental problem gambling.

The general argument is that these non-Dostoevskian factors (that is, particular aspects of our social context) influence people's decision to begin and continue to gamble. On the other hand, the Dostoevsky Effect variables (specifically stress and poor coping strategies) increase the chances that people will gamble problematically.[1] It is therefore import-ant to keep in mind that the factors we will be discussing in this section explain why people begin to gamble in the first place, and not necessar-ily why they gamble to excess. The variables concerned with social con-text that we will be looking at here explain step one in the process (that is, why an individual decides to gamble), while the Dostoevsky Effect explains why some of these individuals progress to step two and become problem gamblers.

It is important to note that some of these factors involving social con-text were not present in our original model of the developmental process, but emerged in our interviews. Specifically, we categorized both gambling opportunities and acceptability as being parts of a social learning pro-cess that occurs in the childhood home, wherein parents model certain behaviours and help to shape their children's perception of these activities accordingly. However, gambling opportunities and acceptability can also be learned from sources that are outside of the household and can there-fore be influential factors in adulthood.

Through the interviews we conducted with our participants, we found that siblings, members of the extended family, peers, and the wider gam-bling culture can all play a part in determining whether an individual will see gambling as an "acceptable" activity. Further, these interviews revealed that a pro-gambling culture; proximity to gambling establish-ments; and the gambling behaviour of members of the extended family, siblings, and peers contribute to reducing or increasing the opportun-ities people have to gamble. Finally, we discovered that gambling can be "learned" not only from parents, but from extended family members, peers, and the media. In addition, this social learning can occur in adult-hood as well as childhood.

In the next two chapters, we explore how these non-Dostoevskian pro-cesses encourage or discourage gambling and problem gambling among people who fall within the following four groups: (1) both the individual and his or her parent(s) have gambling problems; (2) the individual does not have a gambling problem, but his or her parent does; (3) the person's parent does not have a gambling problem, but he or she does; and (4) neither the individual nor his or her parents have a gambling problem. We spoke with problem and non-problem gamblers to see how their experiences differed. In this chapter, we will examine the ways in which our participants' role models and peers had an influence upon their gambling behaviour. We will also examine the opportunities they had to gamble, as determined by their close proximity to gambling establishments, and the cultural acceptability of gambling where they grew up. In the following chapter, we will see how many of our participants learned their gambling behaviours and attitudes both at home and in the wider community.

Gambling Culture

Within any given culture, either a favourable or an unfavourable outlook on gambling exists. Our Canadian culture is predominantly pro-gambling, as the majority of Canadians support the activity as a legitimate and legal recreational pastime.[2] Opportunities to gamble in Canada are numerous, and a large percentage of the population gambles, contributing to this pro-gambling atmosphere. Many of our participants grew up in this or another culture that supported gambling, which effectively encouraged their gambling behaviours. In contrast, anti-gambling cultures discourage gambling and make related activities less widely available, thereby hindering the development of gambling problems among inhabitants.

Both pro- and anti-gambling cultures can be "passed down" through generations by parents who teach their children gambling behaviours and attitudes.[3] For example, many of the people in our study were of Chinese background, often first- or second-generation immigrants. They pointed out that gambling was traditionally common and widely accepted in Chinese culture (although casinos were outlawed by the communist government in mainland China until recently). Growing up in an environment that accepted gambling as normal behaviour, these participants were more likely than other Canadians to take up gambling themselves. This, in turn, made them more susceptible to becoming problem gamblers.

For example, one of our respondents, Zachary, described gambling as a normal part of his family life:

It's part of Chinese culture and even when you grow up in Hong Kong, almost everyone will teach the next generation while they are playing during the Chinese New Year. While they are playing, the children just learn by themselves and their relatives and family members will demonstrate how to play it. You just learn from the family.

Because gambling was part of the Chinese New Year celebration, playing these gambling games became associated with celebration and festivity for Zachary. He felt that gambling brought his family closer together by providing an activity they could bond over. In short, his childhood experiences at Chinese New Year led Zachary to form positive opinions about gambling, which correspondingly encouraged his gambling behaviours.

However, these types of pro-gambling cultures not only promote gambling as a celebratory activity, but also as everyday entertainment. For some participants, mah-jong was played with the family on a regular basis:

It is like the national sport—[the] national game of China. I remember every weekend, my family would visit another family friend and the four parents would sit together and play at least four hours of mah-jong every week, and me and the other kid would play some sort of game by ourselves. We [too] would play mah-jong sometimes.

The frequency and prolonged duration of play made mah-jong equivalent to a "national sport" that was acceptable for all ages, since even the children were invited to join in. In this sense, Chinese culture framed gambling as a normal, harmless pastime and encouraged frequent play.

Sometimes, this kind of pro-gambling culture is so widely accepted that it's difficult to pinpoint the source of or motivating factors behind gambling behaviours. According to one participant, "Everyone bets on games, you know what I mean. So it would just come natural. I am not really too sure who initiated it, right. We all knew what it was all about though. We were [all] going to lose or we were going to win." As such a widely accepted activity, gambling comes to seem like the "natural" thing to do; it becomes an ingrained, almost inherent part of the culture, so no one thinks twice about how or from whom they learned it, or whether it will be beneficial or useful to pursue.

Of course, Chinese culture is not the only pro-gambling one. Our content analysis of online and print biographies revealed that people of Vietnamese backgrounds have similar celebration experiences that are tied up with gambling activities. One woman wrote:

> Gambling has always been a tradition in our family, as it is for many Degar and Vietnamese. Because I grew up in the States, I don't know much about the games the men played back in the village, but we follow the Vietnamese custom of gambling at Tet, our New Year. We play *Bau cua ca cop*, a dice game. The dice are very beautiful, not like the numbered ones. The six sides of the dice have pictures of a fish, prawn, crab, rooster, calabash gourd, and stag—sometimes I dream of them and of my parents' hands holding them.

Cultural gambling heritage can thus be so powerful that it can even influence people who are raised in a different country and are not entirely submerged within this culture.

The culture in Trinidad is also pro-gambling, as gambling activities are considered to be very social and are correspondingly played both inside and outside of the home. One of our participants said that various forms of gambling were freely available to him as a child:

> I remember a lot of people in the neighbourhood were into gambling. People would have illegal card games at their homes; people who lived opposite us would play craps on the street. Guys would play cards—illegal games. So it was cards, craps, horses. . . . It was something people in the neighbourhood did a bit of. I don't know personally how deep some of them were involved. Destructive it was. I was an observer of it. If this was getting the better of some of them, it was all around—lotteries, craps, illegal card games.

Gambling was thus entrenched within Trinidadian culture, and consequently, children growing up in such neighbourhoods are highly exposed to both legal and illegal forms of gambling. Despite the widely recognized destructive outcomes of gambling, its widespread availability and perceived normalcy encouraged people to continue playing.

On the other hand, some of the people we interviewed grew up in societies in which gambling was frowned upon. These individuals were much more likely to abstain from gambling in their adult lives because of the widespread social disapproval of gambling they witnessed as children. One respondent named Shirin, for example, grew up in Saudi Arabia, where cultural values and religious beliefs portray gambling as a negative, permanently damaging activity: "Risk taking like gambling can destroy one's life. Sometimes, interest is one thing that consumes people." Another participant, Manpreet, was also raised in a culture wherein the majority of people disapproved of gambling; the dislike of gambling activities was so extreme in her home country of Kuwait that they were entirely prohibited: "It was a closed society in Kuwait, they never had casinos or anything there. So it was a forbidden type of thing." Because gambling was either frowned upon or illegal where they grew up, neither Manpreet nor Shirin were exposed to the lavish gambling venues or positive attitudes toward gambling that are characteristic of pro-gambling cultures. Because gambling wasn't a part of their upbringing, it didn't become part of their adult lives.

The reasons for this kind of deep, long-lasting socialization are obvious and well-understood. As a general rule, it is easier to accept and abide by our home society's beliefs than it is to go against them, and suffer ostracism and ridicule as a result. In addition, these cultural beliefs and values are normally so deeply ingrained that they often survive and persist after immigration to Canada and a change of cultural context. So growing up in a culture with a negative view of gambling protects a person against problem gambling in adulthood by discouraging participation in gambling activities and preventing the development of positive memories of or attitudes toward gambling. But these findings also hold true for people who leave their original anti-gambling cultures and settle in pro-gambling ones; the values and norms of their home societies continue to influence their gambling behaviour, even when they are no longer surrounded with negative attitudes toward gambling.

Proximity

Cultural beliefs about the acceptability of gambling are particularly influential in affecting the availability of gambling opportunities. In societies where gambling is largely accepted, gambling opportunities are common and widely accessible. Parents, relatives, and peers are more likely to approve of a variety of gambling activities, and many may even participate.

Moreover, people within these pro-gambling communities are more likely to live near a gambling venue or have friends and family who provide gambling opportunities, simply due to the general perception that gambling is normal and acceptable. Occasionally, positive inducements are even offered to encourage people to participate in gambling activities, such as social acceptance.

In most of Canada, gambling opportunities are widely available in the form of casinos, racetracks, and various other formal gambling establishments, as well as in more casual, personal settings. Research has repeatedly shown that physical closeness (or proximity) to these gambling opportunities increases an individual's chances of becoming a problem gambler.[4] This proximity factor plays a particularly important role in explaining why those of our participants with non-gambling parents became problem gamblers or took up gambling in the first place; they would not have learned gambling behaviours as children, because their parents did not gamble themselves, but the nearby gambling establishments exposed these individuals to a variety of gambling practices. Nearly 70 percent of the gamblers we spoke with whose parents did not gamble told us they had lived near, or were aware of, gambling venues when they were growing up.

Proximity to gambling venues and other opportunities encourages gambling and ultimately problem gambling in three important ways. First, it makes gambling easily accessible, lowering both the travel time it takes to reach the gambling establishment and the monetary cost for making the trip. Second, it familiarizes gambling as a local institution, contributing to a general perception of gambling as being a normal and acceptable pastime. In our study, the ease with which some adolescents could access gambling venues made participation easy for those who were already interested in gambling, and also gently encouraged others to try it if they weren't already involved. Nearby gambling opportunities were found to be particularly enticing in terms of their entertainment value, as many of our participants chose gambling as their go-to activity when looking to occupy their spare time. One of our participants told us that his close proximity to the racetrack played a role in encouraging him to gamble at a young age:

> I just would play with my buddies mostly, and then at thirteen I started gambling. I would fill out the racing forms at home all the time, and then I would go down to the track, it was just fifteen minutes away from my house.

So I would always go there in my spare time and then be home by nine. I started working part-time at a car wash when I was fourteen, so I started getting money [and] then I got into gambling.

Easy access to the racetrack, in addition to a disposable income and an excess of "spare time," were potent inducements to gambling. But further, when adolescents use gambling as a time-filler in this manner, the habit often continues in adulthood.

The third way in which close proximity to gambling opportunities encourages gambling is by repeatedly exposing people to the excitement and glamour to be found within these venues. Adolescents have been found to be particularly vulnerable to flashy, visually stimulating gambling establishments; not only does the sparkly bustle of a casino front make the interior seem mysteriously desirable, but the conception of gambling as being a mature activity, for adults only, makes teenagers want to immerse themselves in this exhilarating grown-up atmosphere.

This kind of mentality is exemplified by our respondent Brent, who described his childhood fascination with Fallsview Casino in Niagara for us: "I remember walking by and seeing all the people dressed up in fancy suits, and the lights and everything. It was appealing in that [way] when I was younger." The seeming "classiness" of the people who frequented the establishment suggested to Brent that people of wealth and high status gambled regularly at this venue. Likely, Brent felt that he, too, could become wealthy and lead a glamorous lifestyle by going to this alluring casino. These beliefs ultimately encouraged him to take up gambling once he was of legal age.

The conception of gambling as a glamorous and thrilling pursuit may be supported when a parent works in the gambling industry. For example, one of our participants was exposed to gambling through her father's job on passenger ships:

In the 1980s, there were passenger ships going from Kuwait to India a lot of the time, and my father happened to work on these ships, so we were always invited for parties. That was the time we could see the machines we had never seen on the land. On the ship, it was a different thing; we could do anything. My friends would say, "Oh, you can go and enjoy," whereas some of my friends never saw the slot machines in their life.

This secretive glimpse of gambling made slot machines all the more seductive for this participant, as her friends were denied this privilege and consequently envied her access to this unfamiliar form of gambling. In this way, she developed a positive image of gambling as a secretive privilege for a select few and subsequently gambled at casinos as an adult due to this attractive perception.

In opposition to these individuals who were raised with the ability to easily access gambling venues, several of our participants were not so highly exposed to gambling activities. A lack of proximity to gambling opportunities has much the same effect as living in a culture that does not perceive gambling positively: it makes gambling less accessible and less attractive, and correspondingly discourages people from participating. Our respondent Laura, for example, was neither aware of, nor had access to, gambling until she was "much older." When she did start coming across gambling venues as an adult, they did not appeal to her because she recognized the tricks being used to draw people in, such as extravagant, glamorous venues. Her restricted access to gambling activities and establishments as a child therefore protected Laura against becoming involved with gambling as an adult.

Role Models

A large body of research shows that "significant others"—including peers, friends, and relatives—can influence a person's gambling behaviour in several ways. These can include providing gambling opportunities, conveying the acceptability of gambling, and teaching the benefits and skills needed to gamble. We will discuss the first two factors—opportunities and acceptability—in the next two sections, paying particular attention to the influence of role models and peers. The third factor, concerning the teaching and learning of gambling, will be explored in the next chapter.

To begin, a role model is someone in a child's life whose actions and opinions affect the values the child develops. Our study found that role models played an important part in the lives of our participants by shaping their opinions about the acceptability and attractiveness of gambling. As such, these role models either influenced participants to gamble or discouraged them from doing so. Parents often served as role models for the people we spoke with, but our respondents were also influenced in the same ways by their extended family members and siblings. Overall, the majority of our participants normally found their role models close at hand, among parents, older siblings, or other kin, such as uncles or cousins.

If these role models were gamblers themselves, participants in our study often gambled as well, emulating their behaviour. Having a role model who gambled meant that their game of choice, or even the concept as a whole, came to be seen as acceptable, available, and attractive. Those of our participants who became problem gamblers were typically exposed to gambling by their parents, aunts, uncles, grandparents, or siblings—and in some cases, by all of these family members.[5] Exposure to gambling within the family household was found to be particularly powerful, usually causing participants to associate gambling with an opportunity for intimate bonding. Because gambling within the home can be seen as quality time spent with other family members, it often came to be thought of as an acceptable type of family leisure.[6]

One of the people we spoke with, named Evelyn, revealed that her childhood experiences with gambling were intimately tied to the close relationship she was able to develop with her father. She fondly remembered her father's participation in the lottery, and the way that it allowed her to spend time with him when they would buy tickets together: "It was also bonding. 'Cause we'd go to the bank and then we'd get lottery tickets and then go to McDonald's. So it was more of the bonding aspect." These pleasant memories were especially valuable to Evelyn because she lost her father to Lou Gehrig's disease when she was still in high school. This precipitous death meant that she had few memories of time spent with her father in which gambling was not involved. Perhaps because of these fond memories, Evelyn came to develop a positive perception of gambling and began buying lottery tickets herself as an adult.

In much the same way, our participant Chase's views on gambling were highly influenced by his mother's gambling habit. As a child, he looked forward to weekly "mother and son outings," which always involved going to what Chase saw as the thrilling and exhilarating bingo hall. When asked to describe his experiences there, Chase revealed that there was always:

> Lots of excitement . . . the girls get really excited and jump up and down when they win. They really get involved in the game. That's what I can remember from it. There were all kinds of excitement.

Chase thus saw gambling positively from a young age, as he was regularly surrounded by enthusiastic players within the "excitement" of the bingo hall. But like for Evelyn, for Chase these outings were mainly important because they allowed him to bond with his mother. Since she worked full-time and was occupied at home with most of the housekeeping, Chase was only able to interact with her privately when they went to the bingo hall together. This quality time was all the more important to Chase because of his distant relationship with his father. During our interview with him, Chase revealed that he felt left out of the gambling that his father and brother shared, so he "did everything with mom," including playing bingo. So Chase looked forward to these gambling outings as an opportunity to bond with his mother, as well as a chance to overcome the feelings of exclusion created by his father and brother's gambling ventures. Because he developed these positive associations with gambling as a child, Chase continued to gamble as an adult, perhaps with the hope that he would still be able to achieve the same feelings of inclusion and excitement as a result.

Parents thus played an important role in creating a positive image of gambling as being acceptable and attractive. The second most influential role model within the family were uncles, whose gambling habits had a similar normalizing effect on our participants' perception of gambling. Our respondent Bill revealed that one of his uncles played a key role in the development of his own gambling habit. Bill told us that his parents did not have much to do with him when he was a child: "My parents [were] working or . . . drinking, so they wouldn't really come out and play with us. Like, we would still go to the [Toronto] Island or something, but they would still be drinking and sitting around." Unlike his parents, Bill's uncle took interest in him, and they frequently gambled together: "I was . . . excited, you know, going out with my dad's brother, [him] taking me out somewhere." Bill appreciated his uncle's willingness to spend time with him, and consequently he began to distance himself from his less attentive parents, choosing instead to look up to his problem gambling uncle as a role model. Bill's continued participation in gambling activities during adulthood is therefore due in large part to his childhood admiration of and appreciation for his uncle.

Another one of our participants, Jonathan, also demonstrates how extensively role models within the family can influence gambling perceptions and behaviours. His father's frequent absences drew him and his mother together more closely: "I was very close to my mother because [my father] travelled a lot. He was always away from home." Jonathan's mother and her brother were very close themselves, so when he spent time with his mother, he was usually spending time with his gambling uncle as well:

> When I was around him, there was always some form of gambling—like at the racetrack or playing cards, or something. Well of course, I didn't gamble with him when I played cards. But if I was around him, we'd always be at the racetrack, and if I was with my mother, because they were very close, we'd [all] be at the racetrack.

These trips to the racetrack with his mother and uncle were a weekly occurrence for Jonathan when he was a child. Considering the poor relationship he had with his largely absent father, these gambling-focused outings stood out as enjoyable times with respected and loved family members. Further, because Jonathan's father was very strict and enforced extreme rules, Jonathan eventually took up gambling and some of the other activities his father discouraged in an attempt to undermine his harsh parenting style. In explaining his behaviour, he told us, "It was like because [the rules] were so square, that you kinda wanted to have some fun." Ultimately then, Jonathan's family played a large role in shaping his view of gambling, encouraging him to think of it as a fun, carefree opportunity for familial bonding.

In addition to the influence of parents and particularly uncles on our participants' perceptions of gambling, we found that older siblings often contributed to the development of positive feelings toward gambling. Usually, our respondents were much younger than their siblings, so they tended to view them as other, often "cooler," parents. As such, these participants often looked up to their older brothers or sisters as models of the kind of adult they wanted to become. But further, they saw gambling as an opportunity to forge a closer bond with the sibling(s) they looked up to so much.

One of the people we spoke with, named Luca, learned about gambling from his brother, who was twenty-four years older than himself. Despite the large age gap and despite having grown up in separate households, gambling was something the two brothers did together, even when Luca was very young. Luca told us:

I grew up around gambling. My brother was a heavy gambler. He lives in Chicago now, but when I would visit him or he would visit, it was always a source of interest. Sports gambling primarily, some card playing, racetrack, primarily sports events. Betting—that sort of thing.

By participating so extensively himself, Luca's brother made gambling seem acceptable. Moreover, he created gambling opportunities for Luca that he may not have had in his brother's absence. Gambling thus established a connection between Luca and his brother that would have been otherwise non-existent because of the years and distance that separated them. This kind of companionship that Luca was able to experience while gambling with his brother contributed to his development of a favourable view of gambling that persisted into adulthood, and he continues to associate gambling with these positive feelings of brotherhood and friendship.

Whether they gambled in order to spend quality time with their loved ones, or to rebel against their parents, many of the participants in our study learned their gambling behaviours from family members whom they considered role models: a loved parent, a "cool" uncle, or a grown-up sibling, among others. Because they looked up to these role models, our respondents came to see gambling in the same light as their role model did: positively if the role model participated, or negatively if they disapproved. Moreover, these role models could even overcome the effects of parental influence. Non-gambling role models who were family members—such as siblings, uncles, or cousins—were most likely to gain our participants' trust, help them to discover new skills and ideas, and to build their confidence. These tools helped some of our respondents to abstain from taking up gambling as a habit, and thereby protected them from the disadvantages of developing a gambling problem. In fact, every single participant in our study with a problem gambling parent who managed to avoid "inheriting" his or her parent's problem had a role model who disapproved of gambling. Having this kind of positive role model and being able to refrain from participating in the destructive gambling behaviours modelled by parents are thus strongly connected.

Sometimes, a non-gambling parent can act as this positive role model. Those of our participants who had problem gambling fathers usually had mothers who explicitly discouraged them (and their siblings) from gambling. By reinforcing the negative consequences of gambling, these mothers taught their children that gambling was harmful, rather than the productive and exciting activity their husbands believed it to be. This sort of preventive action succeeded for the cases in which the child bonded and identified with their non-gambling parent and blamed their gambling parent for their negative childhood experiences.

Our respondent Brigit exemplifies this trend. Despite the fact that she grew up with a gambling father, her mother's disapproval of gambling played a part in discouraging her from becoming a gambler herself. She explained her childhood experiences to us as follows:

> My mom doesn't like it 'cause she thinks my father is losing too much money on that. She thinks that instead of that, he should work and then we'd have more money and we could be a lot better off. She's never approved of it because that's the primary reason [for] the money and the financial problems.

The emphasis that Brigit's mother placed on maintaining control over the family's finances helped Brigit to recognize some of the concrete disadvantages of her father's gambling habit. As a result of these discussions about the value of money and the importance of financial stability, Brigit was able to avoid inheriting her father's problematic gambling behaviour. This kind of experience tends to hold true, as a general rule: non-gambling parents who discuss the financial risks of gambling with their children reduce their risk of becoming gamblers.

In a similar case, our respondent Todd had a gambling father but a mother who encouraged a healthier, non-gambling lifestyle. Todd told us about the memories he has of his mother urging him to stay in school. "She would be like, 'Stay in school so you won't have to work this kind of job,' when she was working in manufacturing and even now, she's like, 'Yes, stay in school! Do a designation, be a professional [or] be a manager!'" Despite the negative influences of his father's gambling problem, Todd's mother provided him with the direction he needed to refrain from following in his father's footsteps. She encouraged him to occupy himself by becoming involved with his education and participating in sports, rather than filling his time by gambling. Todd therefore avoided "inheriting" his father's habit largely due to his mother's ability to teach him that gambling is not a productive pastime.

Non-gambling parents, however, are not the only people capable of being positive role models; other family members are also particularly influential in this role. In some cases, our participants suggested that finding guidance outside of their immediate family helped them to counterbalance the pro-gambling atmosphere they lived in at home.

For example, our respondent Louisa got the support she needed from extended family members, who cautioned her against gambling when she was growing up and encouraged her to invest her energy elsewhere. She recited their warnings during our interview with her: "'It's not a good habit. It can become a big addiction problem. People can lose everything if they go too far.' [They said] things like that." By making her aware of the potentially disastrous effects of gambling, Louisa's relatives helped her avoid developing a gambling habit as an adult.

Another participant, named Rochelle, was also fortunate enough to have an extended family member who helped her avoid following in her problem gambling mother's footsteps. The financial losses that her mother's gambling brought about were significant parts of Rochelle's childhood, both in terms of the monetary strain they placed on her family, as well as in terms of the conversations they sparked between her and her aunt: "She tells me I should always go to university, so I don't end up [in financial trouble]." Rochelle's aunt thus taught her to value financial stability and post-secondary education, but she was also a source of emotional support who helped Rochelle cope with her mother's gambling problem in a healthy, positive way. When we asked her what she used to do when things got bad at home, Rochelle said, "Talk to my aunt. She is really cool, she's my uncle's wife so I see her every day. I always go over there. . . . That's where I go when I'm not sleeping at my house." By supporting her emotionally, and by teaching her positive values like financial stability, Rochelle's aunt played an essential role in helping her to navigate her way through a childhood full of negative influences that could have led her to develop a gambling problem of her own.

In short, these positive role models were lifesavers for many of the people who took part in our study. Without their support and positive influence, many of our participants might not have been able to avoid developing a gambling habit of their own. Considering that people frequently learn and adopt the gambling behaviours of their addicted parents, or begin gambling in order to cope with the stress and hardships these gambling addictions cause, positive role models have the potential to exert a considerable amount of influence. The wide variety of our participants whose gambling behaviour has been affected by a role model shows, once again, that problem gamblers are made, not born. If gambling addictions were primarily the result of a genetic predisposition, positive role models could never prevent the child of a problem gambler from "inheriting" their habit. Yet they do so with great regularity, demonstrating that a wide range of factors contribute to shaping perceptions of and participation in gambling activities.

Peers

While we have been focusing on the strong impact that family members can have on gambling behaviours, friends and peers are also important sources of influence, as we spend a great deal of time in their company and tend to share many qualities with them. Our interviews revealed that friends and peers often play a significant role in forming people's perception of gambling as acceptable or unacceptable, fun or boring. As a result, peers also influence gambling behaviour and ultimately have the potential to determine whether a person begins to gamble problematically.[7]

We found that those of our participants who were part of a close group of gambling friends were more likely to participate in gambling activities themselves. Many of these individuals told us that their friends organized social events around gambling and supported each other's gambling activities: they went to gambling establishments together, let each other know about gambling opportunities, and lent each other money to gamble. Unsurprisingly, many of the people we spoke with would include themselves in these outings rather than stay home alone. Because they participated together, on a regular basis, and facilitated the process for each other, these groups of friends characterized gambling as a normal, acceptable pastime that encourages bonding between peers. Simply having a group of friends who were interested in gambling thus strongly encouraged our participants to gamble as part of their social routine.

This trend is a form of social contagion: people "caught" the gambling bug from their friends, simply by spending time with them, watching them, and seeking their approval. They came to adopt their friends' views that gambling was a normal and desirable way of spending time (and money).

In many cases, this was the extent of the incentive in the development of a gambling habit.

Though most of the family role modelling we discussed in the previous section took place during childhood, a great deal of peer role modelling occurs in early adulthood. It is during this period of late adolescence—which we will define as being roughly between the ages of fifteen and twenty-five—that people sort themselves into groups, with gamblers collecting in one type of group and non-gamblers in another. Thus, those of our participants with gambling problems tended to have friends with gambling tendencies similar to their own. Graham, for example, said that his friends "are all gamblers. Big time." Another respondent, named Tina, also had friends who gambled a lot: "All of them gamble more than I do. We always go together; I don't think they go more often than I, but they usually spend a lot more. I don't think anyone has gone bankrupt, but losing seven hundred or eight hundred dollars for one night, that's a lot."

Graham and Tina were two of the many people we spoke to who surrounded themselves with friends whose gambling had gotten out of control. These types of friends obviously did not discourage risky gambling behaviours, because they were engaged in these very activities themselves. Because no one in Graham or Tina's group of friends was suggesting that they develop some limits to their gambling, their irresponsible, out-of-control behaviour flourished.

However, peers with problematic gambling habits are not the only negative influences; sometimes, non-gambling friends support a perception of gambling as an acceptable pastime, and thereby encourage participation in gambling activities. One of our participants told us that his friends were never concerned with the negative consequences of his habit, but, rather, that they were impressed with his gambling abilities: "Their attitudes are amazement at the fact that I have won so much sometimes, but never, 'Oh, you have a problem.' It's more like, 'Dude, you are doing awesome, can I get in on it?' type of thing."

This kind of praise and awe made gambling seem like a desirable activity that requires skill and competence, and correspondingly made this individual believe that he was capitalizing on a special talent. In this case, it was the very inability of his friends to gamble, rather than their regular participation, that encouraged our respondent to continue with his own gambling.

We spoke with many others who felt that their non-gambling friends sometimes gently encouraged their gambling, particularly by focusing on their winnings:

> They like when I win because . . . I tend to give away some money when I win to people I know. I come down the street and I go, "Here is ten bucks, twenty bucks." Maybe I will give away fifty or sixty bucks. I feel good about that. I do that most of the time, if I win some.

The potential for financial gain without any risk caused this individual's friends to support his gambling habit. In response to their encouragement, his own sense of pride and self-worth became tied to his gambling abilities: sharing his winnings became a way to show off his skills, in that he could produce concrete evidence of his gambling success. This boasting, in turn, would increase his friends' interest in getting a cut of his winnings, leading them to encourage—and maybe even rationalize—his gambling. So again, rather than gambling in order to spend time with his other gambling friends, this respondent's behaviour was encouraged by people who did not gamble themselves.

So far, we have looked at people who gamble due to their membership in a group of gambling friends, and people who gamble because their non-gambling friends encourage them to believe they possess the (supposedly) necessary skills or talent to win. We also found that some of our participants were friends with other gamblers, but that they preferred to gamble on their own. Rhonda's experiences exemplify this third type of peer influence, as a discussion with one of her friends drew her attention to the casino, but they never gambled together:

> A friend of mine, she goes like, "I went to the casino" and she won. She is like, "You are lucky [too] you know; you are going to have to come, because you are a lucky person, and if you come with me you are going to have luck." . . . I never went with her, but I went on my own.

Two factors combined to pique Rhonda's interest in gambling, eventually leading to her decision to go to the casino herself. First, hearing about the time her friend spent there made gambling sound exciting and made Rhonda want to experience it herself. Second, her friend's big win proved to Rhonda that such luck was possible and potentially within her reach. She confirmed this mentality with us, saying, "When you hear people's stories and you hear the winners' stories, it makes you get encouraged and want to go, and that's how I started." Ultimately, this conversation with her friend made Rhonda believe she could win big, establishing the main attraction of the casino for her.

One of Rhonda's other friends further encouraged her new interest in gambling by making it easily accessible. In particular, she provided information on a certain gambling venue, as well as giving her the route to get there:

> Just a few years back, this other friend came by and she was telling me, "You live close to Woodbine casino now, the bus takes you." So I went there and that's where I started to go very often, 'cause I am close to the casino.

Rhonda was thus made aware of the nearby casino due to her association with other gamblers. Had her friends been non-gamblers, she may have never come to believe that big wins were possible, or she might not have discovered just how easily she could access gambling venues. So even though she didn't go to these establishments with the people who introduced her to them, Rhonda's original interest in and access to the casino were due in large part to the gambling experiences of her friends.

Our discussions of pro-gambling friends and pro-gambling family members have so far led us to similar conclusions. That is, spending a lot of time with friends who gambled encouraged the same positive feelings about gambling that spending a lot of time with family members who gambled did. This positive attitude, in turn, led to our participants becoming involved in gambling activities, usually in the company of the relative or friend who introduced them to gambling. Because they would gamble with the people they were closest to, our participants came to see this time as an opportunity to catch up and bond with their friends and family members. These positive social experiences made them more likely to return to casinos, racetracks, or other gambling venues because they remembered the fun and pleasant company they had enjoyed there.

One of our participants, Chris, recounted some of the experiences he had enjoyed with his friends at the casino. He described one of their particularly successful trips as follows:

> One day with two of my friends, we went there and we said, "We'll just give twenty bucks each. There's three of us, so that's sixty bucks." We stuck it in a machine, we won over seven hundred bucks, and we cashed it out right away. Then we tried another machine, the same, and we won another seven hundred and seventy bucks on the same money we had won, on this different machine. So we had almost twenty-four hundred bucks.

This experience made Chris want to return to the casino, not only because winning had encouraged him to believe that something similar could happen again, but also because sharing the excitement with his friends made this trip particularly memorable and attractive.

While Chris's big win made his visit to the casino even more appealing, some of our participants weren't concerned with money at all when they were gambling with their friends. What stood out most for people like Tysen was the fun he was having as a result of being in good company—not the huge sums of money he was losing. During our interview with him, Tysen smiled while recounting the bets he and his buddies had placed, saying, "You share that whole experience with them. It's not just you on that high, but rather you're sharing it with everyone else and there's that fun factor. That's always nice." Gambling together made Tysen feel more intimately connected to his friends, which led him to associate gambling with positive qualities like solidarity and camaraderie.

In this sense, some of our participants came to see gambling as an opportunity for social interaction. Having friends who gambled made the activity seem like a normal, acceptable social pastime, and provided our respondents with many chances to participate. People with friends who frequented casinos and other supposedly glamorous gambling establishments were often quickly caught up in the thrilling, exciting atmosphere. However, when they began to recognize the extreme financial costs of these friendly outings, most of these individuals began to focus more on gambling itself, forgetting about the opportunity to socialize that had originally attracted them. Soon, they were not just gambling "for the fun of it" anymore.

On the other hand, we spoke with many people who were aware of gambling and their peers' participation in it, but who remained uninterested and uninvolved. Some of them knew that their acquaintances were gambling, but because it didn't interest their closest friends, it hadn't drawn their attention either. For example, when asked if she knew of any students at her school who gambled, Laura told us: "No close friends, no; friends, yes. My close friends didn't really gamble, but [some of] my classmates, yes." She then added, "It just wasn't interesting to [my close friends]." Laura also revealed that her adult friends were uninterested in gambling, and in response to our asking if any of her close friends gambled, she said, "No, not really. I don't think so. We prefer to go to movies and stuff, go out bike riding and stuff." Because she spent most of her time in the company of non-gamblers, Laura was never tempted to give the activity a try.

In a very similar case, our participant Marisa avoided gambling mainly because her friends weren't interested in it. She became particularly close with another girl named Jenn, largely due to their similar interests: "Jenn and I were somewhat loners, we didn't really play. We were more book-ish. We would read and write. We thought we were going to be writers, so we'd write stories." Marisa was never part of the "cool group" who gambled, so she never felt like she had to gamble in order to fit in or be appreciated. Later on during our interview, Marisa mentioned that she and Jenn have remained good friends. Throughout their lives then, these two have encouraged each other to direct their energy toward more posi-tive activities, rather than investing it in gambling.

Another common trend we observed throughout our study was the ten-dency for groups of friends to exhibit similar gambling habits. As we men-tioned earlier, not all gamblers are excessive or out of control. The ability to gamble in moderation depends (in part) on the behavioural influences of family and friends. That is, having friends who gamble within their means can help a person stay within his or hers. One of the more casual gamblers we spoke with told us that her friends also gamble, but moderately, like she does:

> Generally [my friends] are like me, casual visitors. They don't carry much cash, like me. And we do go in groups, but we know our limits, when to play, when to just say "Bye" to the casino. So . . . when we go, we enjoy it and that type of thing, going to the casino, and then going for dinner.

When a group of friends, like this one, collectively defines how much gam-bling is "too much," and when each member implicitly agrees to watch out for the others, it's easier for everyone to remain in control and within the set limits. In this way, playing with a group of friends or family members can actually encourage more moderate gambling.

Overall then, the participants in our study have shown that friendships and peer networks—just like families—can either promote or discourage gambling behaviours. For many of the people we spoke to, gambling with close friends made the activity even more fun and exciting. Some of these individuals who discovered gambling through their pursuit of thrills and fun in good company eventually developed a reckless, compulsive need to gamble, rather than continuing to visit venues "in good fun." Other participants in our study had developed friendships with people who did not see the appeal of gambling, and who were less likely to gamble or develop a gambling problem as a result. Thus, we found that role models and peer groups played a crucial role in shaping the views that our participants held about gambling. Whether these individuals acted on those opinions and values and began to gamble themselves depended in large part on how easily they could access gambling venues and other opportunities. These two factors of role models and proximity to gambling opportunities thus combine to exert considerable influence upon people's perception of and participation in gambling activities.

A person's idea of how acceptable or normal gambling is, in addition to the ease with which he or she can access gambling venues, both contribute to determining whether he or she begins to gamble, or eventually develops problematic or addictive gambling tendencies. As we have seen, gambling's acceptability—at the cultural, role model, and peer levels—can either positively or negatively influence a person's opinions toward gambling, and thereby affect the decision to participate or not.

In pro-gambling cultures, gambling is considered a natural pursuit that is appropriate to engage in both as an everyday pastime and as a way to celebrate special occasions. In these types of societies, gambling is encouraged by widespread participation, easy access and close proximity to gambling establishments, and positive attitudes toward gambling. Because such cultures normalize gambling behaviours, venues and opportunities are not seen as problematic, and are therefore widely established and readily available. As such, people are repeatedly exposed to a glamorous, exciting depiction of gambling that makes them want to experience the thrill and lavishness these venues promise. Pro-gambling societies thus encourage gambling, thereby increasing the risk that their members will develop compulsive gambling habits. On the other hand, anti-gambling cultures exhibit widespread social disapproval of the behaviour that inhibits people from engaging in it. Forms of social control like stigmatization and exclusion can also be reinforced in these societies by more concrete types of legal control, such as banning gambling, or making it illegal. Ultimately, people who live in cultures that hold negative perceptions of gambling are much less likely to take up the habit or become problematic gamblers.

In addition to these cultural influences, role models, family members, and peers play a large role in encouraging or discouraging gambling. Role models who gamble suggest that their habit is an acceptable pastime and make it accessible to the people who look up to them. Non-gambling role models, on the other hand, can help prevent problem gambling by teaching and exemplifying healthy, productive coping strategies and hobbies. In much the same way, peers who gamble encourage the activity by making it appealing and available, but non-gambling friends create interest in and offer access to alternative values and activities.

Our discussion of each of these variables demonstrates that people do not develop their gambling attitudes and practices in a vacuum—these perceptions and behaviours are conditioned through the social interaction and social modelling that occur from childhood into adulthood. While our model acknowledges the significant role of the immediate family environment in this process, our interviews show that gambling attitudes and behaviours are also largely influenced by the wider gambling culture, members of the extended family, friends, and peers. Childhood trauma and adulthood stress help to tip the balance, putting the people who experience these factors at a greater risk of becoming problem gamblers by making them more or less susceptible to the social influences around them. Gambling acceptability and availability help to explain why these people choose gambling in favour of alternative, potentially healthier, activities: that is, by supporting a perception of gambling as a fun pastime to be shared with loved ones and by making it easy to access and participate in gambling activities. Overall then, the experiences of our participants serve as clear evidence that problem gamblers do not merely inherit their addiction; rather, a wide range of social factors combine to determine their attitudes toward gambling, and correspondingly, their gambling behaviours.

Learning at Home and in the Community

As we just discussed, people who have gambling opportunities readily available to them at several levels—meaning that they live within close proximity to venues and/or have family and peers who make them aware of upcoming events—are at higher risk for developing problematic gambling habits. We have already seen that culture, role models, and peers make gambling more widely available and make it seem acceptable or normal. Individuals who develop positive attitudes toward gambling, usually as a result of being submerged within a pro-gambling culture, and who have many opportunities to gamble are more likely to become gamblers. In addition to these factors, however, problem gamblers do not reach the level of compulsiveness that defines them as such without attaining certain skills and knowledge. In this chapter, we will be examining how family members, friends, and the media teach gambling behaviours and frame them positively, as being beneficial and advantageous. We will also be applying social learning theory to these processes as a way of explaining how and why our participants learned about and eventually began to participate in gambling behaviours.

To begin then, we would like to outline the main arguments of social learning theory. This sociological approach argues that both environmental and cognitive factors influence people's behaviour; we "learn" behaviours from one another by observing and imitating the things we see other people do and say.[1] Further, we choose the kinds of behaviours we want to adopt as our own based on our observations of the reactions to and consequences of other people's behaviours. As such, good outcomes such as admiration or rewards make us want to imitate the behaviours that lead to these outcomes. On the other hand, witnessing bad consequences like negative reactions and punishment makes us want to avoid engaging in the conduct that produced these responses. Further, when we admire or respect somebody, we are also more likely to imitate and adopt his or her behaviours as our own.[2] This pattern occurs mainly because we can imagine receiving the same rewards—like acceptance and admiration—if we behave in the same way as the person we admire. Because many people look up to or identify with their parents, siblings, and friends, they learn much of their behaviour from these people.

In our study, this kind of social learning was a key factor in predicting whether our participants became gamblers, and whether this habit progressed to a problematic level. As we have seen in the previous chapter, exposure to gambling increases the chances that an individual will become a gambler. But more specifically, learning to expect rewards from gambling, or discovering that gambling can be a way to make easy money, put people at an even higher risk for becoming problem gamblers. In fact, 64 percent of the problem gamblers in our content analysis of online and print biographies "learned" gambling in the way we have been describing when they were children. This concept of social learning thus helps to explain the high rate of transmission of problem gambling from one generation to the next, as the children of problem gamblers are usually highly exposed to problematic gambling behaviours while they're growing up, and are therefore extremely likely to learn and adopt these behaviours as their own.

The other interesting and important thing to note here is that Dostoevsky, once again, is an exception to this part of our theory: he did not become a problem gambler due to exposure to and learning of gambling behaviours. This led us to hypothesize that people whose induction into problem gambling is least "normal" or customary in that it is not learned—people like Dostoevsky, for example—are likely to have a higher level of precipitating pathologies (like childhood trauma). For this reason, they are also more likely to have difficulty recovering from their gambling problem.

Understandably, those of our participants with a parent who was a problem gambler were more than three times as likely to gamble as a result of social learning. Further, social learning theory also explains why some people became problem gamblers, even though their parents were merely casual or moderate gamblers—they were able to learn compulsive gambling behaviours at some point from another source who exhibited this conduct. People who didn't experience this kind of social learning—who did not learn how to gamble at all, or were taught negative views about gambling—were much less likely to become problem gamblers, for a variety of reasons that we will discuss throughout this chapter.

The First Step of Social Learning: Exposure

Family

In order to imitate or adopt someone's behaviour, we have to observe it first. People with problem gambling parents are the most likely to be exposed to gambling as children, since their gambling parent(s) might gamble within the home, create gambling-related issues that trouble their home life, or a combination of both. Many people are also accustomed to using gambling games as forms of entertainment at family gatherings, or to celebrate special occasions, as we discussed earlier. For others, gambling in the home was not meant for special occasions, but was a natural, regular part of family life. By being exposed to gambling in these ways, children learn to see it as an exciting, acceptable way to make easy money or bond with loved ones.

Some of our participants also told us that their childhood experiences with gambling were not contained within the home; rather, their parents would bring them along to the casinos, bingo halls, horse racetracks, and underground gambling establishments they frequented. Our respondent Carol, for example, frequently tagged along to the racetrack, where she witnessed her parents betting and was immersed in the high-energy environment. What Carol remembered most about these trips was: "It was fun to watch [the horses] run around, and see the people get excited about stuff, and yelling at the horses. I don't know why they do that, it doesn't make them go any faster." Even before she could fully understand what was happening around her, Carol experienced the "excitement" that gambling venues could offer. In turn, this alluring atmosphere continued to attract her as an adult, encouraging her to continue making visits in order to participate herself.

Many of our other participants recounted similar memories of gambling establishments as being full of sensory stimuli like bright lights and lots of noise, all of which led them to characterize these venues as exciting, glamorous places. This perception of gambling venues as fun, exciting, and alluring left a lasting impression on these individuals as children, making them yearn to experience the thrills of such establishments themselves once they reached adulthood.

In addition to seeing the glamour and excitement of these venues, gambling trips with their parents allowed many of our participants to learn about the potential to earn money quickly and easily. Jeremy, for instance, attended underground poker sessions with his father, whose friends would give him money.

> Then [his father and his father's friends] used to say, "Come over here," and I used to hate that, they used to squeeze me like I thought they were going to kill me. Then they'd give me fifty dollars here and there, so I made about a hundred dollars before I walked out the door.

Money seemed to be free-flowing during these gambling sessions, so even though he himself wasn't earning this cash as a direct result of gambling, Jeremy came to connect poker with financial gain.

As we saw in the previous section, parents are closely followed by uncles in their ability to influence gambling attitudes and behaviours. One of our participants communicated the impact he believed his uncle had on his own gambling habit as follows: "I remember my uncle used to treat us children with ice cream. So we'd always think, 'Oh, my uncle won so much' and all that, so maybe that has influenced my gambling, 'cause of the winning." Many other individuals also learned to associate gambling with financial gain in this way. This mentality eventually encouraged them to gamble later in life, since they came to believe that they, too, could attain a similar level of monetary freedom.

However, believing that gambling is an *easy* way to generate money is particularly harmful. One of the people we spoke with explained how he learned to think this way by witnessing his grandfather's successful gambling ventures:

> I watched my grandfather place a bet for twenty dollars and he won. He placed a few bets for twenty dollars one night and at the end of the night, after placing one hundred dollars he won about a thousand dollars. He was empowered with this sense of great wealth, even though he earned a good chunk of money. So, a thousand dollars wasn't so much, but the fact that he won it without any real effort—just like he took it from some big casino—brought so much joy to him. My grandmother went on this shopping spree and it was very crazy.

This incident taught our respondent that gambling allows people to make quick, easy money, without investing a great deal of time or effort. The sense of "empowerment" he saw his grandfather experience as a result of this win encouraged him to gamble later in life, as he yearned for his own big win and his own corresponding wealth, "empowerment," and joy.

This kind of social learning of gambling from family members is indirect; that is, it occurs via exposure to and observation of other people's engagement with gambling activities. Though it may seem less potent, indirect social learning still makes gambling seem acceptable and attractive. One participant in our study demonstrated just how influential this form of learning can be through his response to our asking who taught him to gamble:

> My father did. I mean, he would go with his friends and play poker, all kinds of things. I wouldn't say he introduced me, 'cause he didn't come and physically introduce me, but he was doing it and I seen the stuff. And I thought, 'Maybe that's the right thing to do,' so I start doing it myself. Not with him though. I couldn't dare go with him to do it, but with my friends. That's how it becomes a habit afterwards.

For this individual, and many others like him, explicit instructions were not necessary in order to be able to gamble; mere exposure to other people's behaviours and reactions were sufficient to convey the attractive qualities of gambling.

While this kind of indirect exposure to gambling was more common among our respondents, some of the people we spoke with learned about gambling through direct exposure. For instance, some of our participants had parents who would buy lottery tickets for them. As one individual explained, "He'd [the father] start buying them for me [when I was ten] and then afterwards I'd buy a couple here or there." This finding is neither new, nor surprising: many other studies have also reported this kind of direct promotion of gambling, and some research has found that gambling with parents is quite common.[3] Even though only a few of our participants gambled with their parents, the effects of this kind of direct exposure can be quite troubling. In some cases, parents would even give their children specific instructions and tips on how to gamble, as one individual told us. "For cards, he will say you know, 'This is how to play this, how to bet,' and all this type of stuff." The children who received this kind of special direction not only learned that gambling is acceptable, they also developed the knowledge necessary to play certain games successfully. Having this knowledge base effectively encouraged these individuals to gamble in the future, since they were made comfortable with particular games and confident in their gambling abilities.

In this way, direct social learning can be particularly effective in encouraging gambling, since it explicitly condones the activity. One of the individuals who experienced this type of learning told us: "My father would get upset because we would play twenty-five-cent ante with a twenty-dollar limit and he would say, 'I can't afford those amounts.' But he would play those and bring forty or fifty bucks. I liked the limit because I was very good." Playing with parents thus allows children to hone their gambling skills, since they can learn from more experienced players. Because parents set the example and guide their children's gambling experience in these cases, they are teaching their children gambling behaviours in a more concrete manner; the parent specifies exactly what he or she wants the child to absorb, and the child focuses on the aspects of the game that the parent guides the child's attention to. Though this kind of direct social learning is less frequent, it is more likely to encourage the development of a gambling habit than indirect learning, since it frames gambling as an acceptable behaviour in such an explicit manner.

One of the participants in our study gained particularly extensive direct and indirect exposure to gambling from his grandfather, father, and siblings. His problem gambling grandfather started teaching him how to play poker when he was only five years old, which he described to us as follows:

> He would always guide me. We would play almost like a kid is learning the ABCs: it's all very gradual and at its own pace. So, too, with poker: he would play very simply and with so much encouragement that my grandmother was very happy that my grandfather was spending time, 'cause he was always more of a tough kind of guy. Here, he was showing his softer side.

Learning how to play poker at such a young age both normalized gambling for this individual, and characterized it as an activity that allowed him to bond with his grandfather. His father contributed to this positive perception of gambling by purchasing books on skills and strategies for him when he was ten. He also actively encouraged this individual to go to the casino, and helped him get a fake ID so that he would be able to do so. As such, our participant was directly exposed to gambling through the poker lessons his grandfather provided, as well as through the instructional books his father bought for him.

In a similar case, we heard about the lessons and values children take away from these types of experiences wherein role models support their participation in gambling activities:

> When I turned sixteen and I got my fake ID, my grandfather and I would go to the casino every other night. He would always give me forty dollars of his money and he said, "If you win and come back with fifty dollars, you give me back the forty that I gave you and keep the winnings. If you lose, don't worry about it. I will foot the bill." This—although there was other times— this was a major time when I started to [think] I always win or if I lose forty dollars, it's not mine. It gave [me] a very false perspective on addictiveness and on the loss of money gambling.

In accordance with social learning theory, this participant's childhood experiences and the behaviour of his role models taught him three main things about gambling. First, he learned that gambling was an acceptable activity, since his grandfather participated in it and encouraged him to do the same. Second, he gained knowledge of the rules of the game and the relevant skills he needed to be able to gamble. Finally, he learned not to concern himself with the money he lost—that these losses were inconsequential and shouldn't deter him from continuing to play. Because he had not had positive qualities like responsibility or restraint modelled for him, these learned perceptions and skills remained unchecked and eventually drove our participant to gamble to excess.

Peers

As we discussed earlier, people can also be exposed to gambling through their peers. Many of the people we spoke with said that their first gambling experiences consisted of playing pogs, marbles, card games, quarters, or other children's games with their friends. Those who eventually developed gambling problems typically reported having gambled with their childhood friends while they were growing up, or having friends who gambled.

For example, one of our participants told us: "We did it every week, and when we would play it would often go like five or six hours, all night, and the thrill of playing and the skill and trying to beat each other—three or four close friends—was very addictive." In these ways, exposure to gambling from peers is similar to exposure from family members: it can be frequent and lengthy, and can teach both the benefits of and knowledge necessary for gambling. While both family and friends tend to convey that gambling is a source of money, friends are more likely to teach each other new games. As such, exposure to gambling through peers supplemented or compounded the social learning that many of our participants were experiencing as a result of having parents who gambled. In other cases where participants did not have gambling parents, and were therefore not continuously exposed to gambling within the home, friends who gambled could serve as an introduction to the behaviour. Either way, those of our participants with gambling friends were at a greater risk for beginning to gamble and for developing a gambling problem.[4]

As we just mentioned, gambling friends most often introduce their peers to new games. For example, our respondent James had friends who taught him how to play poker:

A couple of my friends were over at my place one time and we were watching some videos or whatever and then they said, "Hey, man, come over here, let me teach you how to play this game." I said, "First of all, I'm not into card games," but then I played anyways and I got into it. Then I started to play more and a little bit more. I actually started going online to learn different strategies and I got really into it after a while. Then after a while I got deeply into it, almost addicted to it, 'cause I was spending so much money on it.

James thus found himself addicted to a form of betting he had never even considered before his friends introduced him to it, demonstrating just how strong peer influences can be.

In a similar case, we spoke with a Russian immigrant who told us that his friend had introduced him to gambling after he arrived in Canada: "I think we went to the Niagara Falls and he was like, 'Let's go to the casinos here and we will have good luck,' and he showed me how to play—showing me the tables and everything else." The experiences of these two participants in particular demonstrate that exposure to gambling from friends is often more direct than it is from family members. Often, peers are directly responsible for introducing each other to new games, willingly teach

each other the skills and knowledge necessary to play these games, and organize their time together around gambling. Those of our participants who were friends with gamblers while growing up were thus encouraged to gamble and were correspondingly placed at a higher risk for developing a gambling addiction.

In much the same way as parents, peers can teach each other that gambling may lead to material gain. Often, this happens as a result of incorporating mutual interests into gambling activities. Our respondent Dharshan, for example, began to gamble with other children in his neighbourhood because they played for toys. He told us: "We had neighbour's kids that would come over and we would play together. They knew more than I did, basically." These knowledgeable friends taught Dharshan the skills he needed to win the toys he desired. Other participants in our study were also driven to gamble because they were interested in the particularly appealing winnings. One such individual revealed, "We played cards for pogs, and we used to play pogs for Halloween candy." By playing for toys or candy as children, our participants learned that gambling can have material benefits; as adults, their desired winnings changed, but their learned ability to gamble for these winnings persisted.

Media

The media are yet another source from which children can learn gambling behaviours and attitudes. They generally depict gambling as an acceptable and glamorous pastime.[5] Further, they tend to teach audiences how to play certain games—for example, by highlighting poker championships—and encourage the belief that gambling leads to financial gain. Some of our respondents, like Ned, were first exposed to gambling through the media. When he was about fifteen years old, Ned "was watching poker on TV, so TV did this [inspired his problem gambling]. That's how it happened." As a result of his discovery of the game, he began to play poker regularly with friends at school, and this habit later spiralled into a full-blown gambling problem.

For others, TV simply renewed a fascination with gambling that had been sparked elsewhere. One of our participants said that he started betting on horses again after he saw advertisements for a special race:

Days before, there were ads in the paper, a list of horses, so I was reading through the list and I was doing my own handicapping. I picked a horse. . . . I made a two hundred dollar bet and I won nine hundred dollars. So I felt pretty good about this. Then a friend . . . who was going to the track . . . started talking about the other upcoming races and he told me about another horse. I played again and I won again. So if you want to say that I started getting bitten by the bug.

Later in our interview, this same respondent said that he bet on this race because he wanted to be part of the excitement surrounding this special event, which had been prominently displayed on television and in the papers. Had the media not informed him of the details of this event, or depicted it as an exhilarating experience, this individual might have been able to maintain his distance from gambling.

Most often, the media is one of several sources of exposure. One of the gamblers we spoke with, named Kieran, said that he learned his gambling habits from various sources: "I guess it was a combination of things: talking to people at school, reading about it, seeing ads, and kind of forming my own opinion and wanting to know more about how this works." Media advertisements for and depictions of gambling thus sparked Kieran's curiosity and initial interest in gambling, which was then fed by his own research and experimentation.

Movies were particularly influential sources of exposure for some of our participants. Often, leading actors are portrayed as being cool and powerful while they gamble, or because they gamble. These types of gambling-friendly movies typically fail to depict the real odds of winning, or the negative consequences of problem gambling. Impressionable viewers who look up to the leading actors as role models internalize this glamorous, idealized view of gambling and, in line with our previous discussion of social learning, may follow their example and adopt these behaviours as their own.

One of our respondents, Eddie, told us that he had been influenced by gambling movies in this way when he was a child. He said, "I think [my parents] first talked to me [about gambling] when we watched *Boiler Room*. I forget when that came out. Around that time I was like, 'Oh, these guys are really cool. I want to be one of them.'" Eddie idolized the heroes in this movie, and he consequently tried to imitate their behaviours in his efforts to "be one of them." Eddie also revealed that he directly imitated the actors in another movie that was centred around gambling. "There is this movie called *Bookies*, so I wanted to do that—I wanted to be the bookie. So I took bets from people. It was just a lot of hard work. It's control." His experiences are particularly relevant to our model, since he came from a stable background and enjoyed a relatively stress-free childhood, but still developed problematic gambling tendencies. The clear desire he expressed to emulate gambling film actors thus helps to explain his own gambling problem.

As we have seen, social learning—whether through family members, friends, or the media—can teach people that gambling is a natural, attractive, entertaining, and empowering way to make quick and easy money. These kinds of social learning do not guarantee that people will become problem gamblers, but they make it significantly more likely. This is largely due to the positive perception of gambling that social learning fosters, in that it demonstrates how gambling can be a source of excitement, as well as an opportunity to make money. Social learning also makes gambling accessible by teaching the rules and skills necessary to play certain games, and by generating opportunities to play. As we will see in the next section, social learning can be a main contributing factor to the development of a gambling problem if it encourages people to believe that gambling is emotionally or financially rewarding.

Minimal Exposure as a Protective Factor

Although exposure to gambling is more common in families with a parent who gambles, not all children of problem gamblers are exposed to this gambling. In fact, minimal exposure to parental gambling is a key factor in explaining why some of these children did not inherit their parent's addiction. About 40 percent of our participants who were able to avoid following in their gambling parent's footsteps said they had not learned about gambling when they were growing up. Their parents had kept their gambling hidden, or at least, they had only gambled outside of the household. In some cases, the parent(s) only gambled after the child's formative years, when they were no longer as susceptible to the influence of social learning. Since they weren't exposed to their parent's gambling behaviour, these children were unable to observe it, and therefore had no desire to imitate it. As a result, they did not participate in gambling activities.

This kind of limited exposure is exemplified by the upbringing our respondent Wanda experienced, which she discussed with us during her interview: "I was never sitting at the same table when [my parents] were [gambling].[I heard things], but I was never present when they were playing or anything like that." She went on to explain, "My mom had a restaurant back then, so they would play there sometimes, but it was never in the house." By gambling only in their daughter's absence, Wanda's parents reduced her ability to learn and adopt their attitudes toward or participation in gambling.

Another one of our respondents, Tim, was also minimally exposed to his father's problem gambling. He did not know how, when, or where his father gambled, since it never happened at home: "I knew my father and his friends, they gambled . . . but it was never done at our house." Both Wanda's and Tim's parents thus prevented their social learning of the benefits or techniques of gambling, thereby contributing to their ability to avoid inheriting their own gambling addictions.

In some cases, limited exposure was the result of parental separation. Many of the people we spoke with grew up away from their gambling parent, which significantly decreased their exposure to gambling. When asked if he had been exposed to his father's gambling, one participant said, "No, because my parents got divorced—there was a contentious breakup and there was a custody battle, so I didn't really spend that much time with him. I was living primarily with my mother during this period, so I guess I would hear of my father more than I actually experienced it." Because his father was never present within the household, this individual was not at risk of learning or adopting his negative gambling behaviours.

Other respondents told us that they weren't made aware of their parents' gambling until later in life. Matthew, for example, said he was completely unaware of his mother's gambling as a child: "She never told me anything about [her gambling problem]. She just told me that she worked at a casino, that she was a dealer. That was it." By the time Matthew discovered that his mother was addicted to gambling, he was no longer in his formative years and was therefore considerably less susceptible to the effects of social learning. His complete lack of exposure during these formative years thus prevented him from picking up his mother's habit.

Similarly, our participant Tanya didn't become aware of her mother's gambling problem until she was a teenager: "My parents started fighting a lot when I was in grade seven. So that was [age] thirteen. And then I actually found out it was gambling, maybe a year later, when I was in grade eight, so still [age] thirteen, maybe fourteen." At that age, Tanya would have been past her most influential childhood years when she realized that her mother's gambling habit posed a significant problem. Both Matthew and Tanya were therefore able to avoid "inheriting" their mothers' addictions because they were completely unaware of these habits while in their forma-tive years. Consequently, they had the opportunity to form their own views on and beliefs about gambling, rather than learning to see it as an enjoy-able, exciting, or normal activity.

Just like the lack of exposure to parental gambling is protective, limited exposure to gambling peers also reduces the risk of becoming a problem gambler. When we asked one of our participants, named Marcus, if any of his friends gambled during his childhood, he told us: "I do not know what you consider [to] be gambling. I notice a lot of kids playing cards, and sometimes if they lost a game, they lost ten cents. I don't know if that's gambling or not. That's gambling?"

Marcus' uncertainty about his peers' gambling habits illustrates his lim-ited exposure to the activity. As with limited exposure to parental gam-bling, children who are not exposed to the gambling habits of their peers are less likely to learn gambling behaviours and beliefs. That is, they don't learn how to play gambling games, they don't see any appeal in playing these types of games, and they don't come to view gambling as a way to have fun or cope with stress. As a result, they are less likely to become gam-blers or problem gamblers, since they haven't undergone the social learn-ing process that increases this risk so significantly.

The Rewards of Gambling

In this section and the next, we will discuss the two factors that are most important in distinguishing the social learning processes of problem gam-blers and non-problem gamblers. These consist of being rewarded for gambling, and learning that gambling is an easy, quick way to earn money. As we mentioned in our earlier discussion of social learning, people gen-erally imitate behaviours that are well rewarded. In addition, role models and peers can make gambling seem like an acceptable pastime simply by expressing their positive feelings toward it. By encouraging others to play with them, role models create positive memories of and feelings toward gambling. As such, people feel as though they are being rewarded for gam-bling in the form of fun, excitement, bonding time with their friends, and perhaps financial gain. These rewards become particularly tempting for individuals who are at high risk for developing gambling problems, due to a variety of factors we have discussed earlier, such as a troubled childhood and adult stressors.

Another example of a reward that gambling can sometimes produce is a self-esteem boost.[6] In our content analysis of online and print biographies, we came across the story of a Singaporean homemaker who suggested that she was bored with her daily routine and received little social support. When she gambled, however, "her self-esteem soared as she saw herself as a smart and lucky gambler, [for this reason] increasing her bets and frequency of gambling." Because gambling made her feel more confident, this individual was encouraged to continue and even increase the frequency and intensity of her gambling. In this sense, gambling problems can develop out of a search for emotional fulfillment.

One of our interview participants, named Craig, told a similar story about the way gambling influenced his self-esteem. Because his parents organized family time around horse racing, Craig was already involved with gambling at the age of seven. He told us about a positive experience he had at the racetrack with his family: "I was seven years old. I won [a bet]. [My mother] told me to pick a horse so I picked one and it won. 'Oh, I am Mr. Lucky.' The whole family was like, 'Oh yeah!'" Both his win and his family members' response to it reinforced Craig's desire to gamble, making him feel that gambling offered a positive, rewarding experience with outcomes that made him and his parents proud. Craig also told us that as he grew older, he started feeling "anxious" about picking horses on these family outings because he was afraid of disappointing his parents if he lost. Craig's concern with losing this sense of pride and confidence shows how powerful the rewards for gambling can be.

Yet another one of our participants also told us about the ways in which his childhood gambling experiences increased his self-esteem. His grandfather put him in charge of the family gambling events, encouraging him to act like a bookie:

> Even more memorable than winning here or winning there was this feeling of [being] ten years old and all these people come to me, asking questions about odds, questions about betting, and then they have to come to me before the betting time, the betting window closed and I was in charge of the whole thing. My grandfather would watch over me and would be like, "Hey, how are we doing?" Then he would give me money to distribute. . . . Being a bookie is so much fun and exciting. I wouldn't go anywhere and people would run to me with their bets. It was very exciting as a kid to do and have

> this authority over the entire family. That was probably the best experience. Not winning this or losing this, but more the knowing everything and being in charge of other people's gambling and being respected.

This individual's prolonged involvement in gambling was due in large part to the rewards of approval and respect he received from his grandfather and the other involved members of his family. He was also rewarded for acting as a bookie in the sense that he gained some degree of power over his siblings and the other participants. Most young children value these emotional or psychological rewards more highly than material winnings, since their parents or guardians (usually) take financial responsibility for them. When gambling boosts children's self-esteem and confidence, as it did for this individual, they are more likely to continue to participate because they want to continue to experience these rewards.

Social approval from friends and peers is another type of reward that gambling can generate.[7] Our respondent James told us that his circle of friends regularly spent afternoons in the casino, lending money to and borrowing money from each other. As a result, they were able to stay for extended periods of time, gambling continuously. On one occasion, James lost fifty dollars almost immediately upon arriving at the casino and told his friends that he was "ready to quit." Since they were not yet ready to leave, his friends encouraged James to stay at the casino and continue gambling with them, and consequently, he lost more than one hundred dollars that day. Instead of losing the approval of his friends, James chose to continue gambling and endure the financial consequences.

James's experiences are somewhat uncommon, however; often, peer pressure is less overt. Sometimes, an explicit statement of gambling's "coolness" or "glamorousness" is not necessary, but, rather, friends come to a general understanding that participation in gambling activities is associated with social status. One of the participants in our study, now in his mid-sixties, fondly remembered the positive, non-financial consequences of winning at gambling:

> As a kid growing up, [if] you had two bucks [from winning at gambling], you could take your friend, he or she, to the ice cream store, buy them an ice cream, and take them to a restaurant and buy them a cold pop or somethin', they thought you were "it." Like you were their crowd.

Gambling allowed this person to "buy" social status and inclusion as a child. Knowing that gambling offered a way to be part of the "it" crowd was sufficiently enticing; this individual continued to gamble into adulthood in his efforts to attain approval and praise from his friends.

Several other participants told us similar stories about their early participation in gambling as a form of social interaction with their friends. Wan, for example, began betting on sports with his friends in his early teens, "because everyone else was doing it, for social activity." Teenagers in particular feel a lot of pressure to fit in with and be accepted by their peer group. By taking part in the same activities as everyone else, adolescents can achieve this sense of belonging. One of our respondents put it this way: "When your friends are all into one thing, then it kind of becomes contagious." By suggesting that it is a "contagious" activity, this individual suggests that adolescents will inevitably adopt the gambling behaviours of their friends and peers.

But this susceptibility to peer pressure is not limited to teens; adults often experience the same pressure to fit in. One of our participants experienced this pressure from her co-workers:

> I worked at this one restaurant, and all the staff there, they were heavy gamblers. After our shift would be done, they just went to the casino. I always heard them talking about their gambling stories, and I didn't get involved for the longest time, probably a couple months after I started working there. One day they invited me out to the casino and I wasn't going into it at all, [but] I tried it out because it was just kinda like an outing, a social event, so I went.

In much the same way that childhood peer pressure can encourage kids to participate in activities that didn't originally interest them, this individual was driven to gamble by the social acceptance it seemed to promise. By failing to participate in the activity that unified the rest of the staff, she was excluded from the "it" group in her workplace; taking part in these "social events" would allow her to attain the acceptance she desired.

Peer pressure can also be exerted by family members, as well as friends. One of the people we spoke with told us that both his father and grandfather would force him to go gambling with them:

> My grandfather likes to peer pressure. It's his wish to have the family together and that includes gambling as part of the thing. To say, "I wouldn't do it" is like an offence to him. My dad says, "Let's go to the casino." To say no, it's an offence. I don't come out and say, "No I don't want to go." I just go and he likes sitting next to me. He favours me sometimes, like, "Calculate this and this." He likes when I sit next to him.

Instead of insulting his family and ruining their time together, this individual chooses to succumb to their peer pressure. In exchange for his participation in the gambling, he receives the rewards of favouritism from and bonding with his family, both of which encourage him to return to the casino in the future.

Our discussions of social modelling and the rewards for conforming have so far demonstrated that each of these factors is highly influential in driving both children and adults to gamble. Social learning that occurs during childhood seems to be the most influential, because people are more impressionable and eager to be accepted when they are younger. However, problematic gambling habits can also develop as a result of peer pressure and exposure to gambling as an adult. The rewards for gambling, on the other hand, are relatively consistent in their influence over time; that is, bonding, social acceptance, self-esteem, and social interaction remain powerful incentives to gamble throughout the life course. In one way, receiving these rewards from parents who struggle with a gambling problem can explain why some individuals inherit their parent's habit. But because these rewards can also be obtained from peers, or during adulthood, they also help us understand why people with non-problem gambling parents develop problematic gambling behaviours.

Winning versus Fun

In addition to teaching that gambling can be exciting and emotionally rewarding, social learning can also function to illustrate the purpose of gambling and therefore plays a role in motivating problem gambling in yet another way. Those of our participants who were taught that gambling could be used to make money were at the greatest risk of developing a gambling problem. In contrast, those who learned that gambling was just a form of entertainment, and that the chances of making a financial profit were slim, were less likely to become problem gamblers.

One way that people respond to learning that gambling can be used to make money is to take gambling more seriously. As children, many of our participants quickly learned from their parents that gambling could be a quick, easy means to significant financial gain. This view was particularly common among problem gamblers whose parents also gambled compulsively. None of these participants talked about learning the value of money or the skills of budgeting from their parents while growing up. In some cases, these individuals had problem gambling parents who were unemployed and even tried to make a career out of their gambling; these parents reportedly depended on gambling winnings to support themselves and their families, believing that winning could lead to a "better life" of wealth and financial stability. Chris's father, for example, held these opinions about gambling, which Chris, in turn, eventually embraced and imitated. During our interview, Chris described the influence his father's gambling "career" had on him:

> Every week, we would buy lottery tickets. In my youth, he [Father] was talking about buying a lottery ticket and maybe we're going to win and then . . . pay off all the bills without having to worry, you know. He didn't have enough money to pay all his bills every month, so I knew every week he was buying lottery tickets. That's where it influenced me.

Because Chris's family framed gambling as the solution to their financial problems, he came to believe that he could sort out his own money issues by "winning big." Those of our participants who grew up in these types of households were much more likely to resort to gambling whenever they were struggling financially. These individuals were thus taught to view gambling as an acceptable way to support their families and meet their basic material needs.

As we have repeatedly suggested, peers can also teach each other about the financial incentive for gambling. Our respondent Samuel explained that, although his family only gambled for fun, his friends taught him to gamble for "real money":

> [At first] I felt that gambling was just a for-fun thing. Then, when I grew up [I] started gambling for "real money." Maybe that's how I felt, because that's how me and my friends used to do it in the beginning. [First it's] two dollars, but then it gets bigger and bigger.

The influence of his friends overrode the somewhat more positive perception of gambling that Samuel had learned from his family. As a result, he started to believe that gambling was an easy way to make money, rather than just a fun pastime, and his gambling behaviours became correspondingly problematic.

In direct contrast to these last few examples, we also spoke with several individuals who were able to avoid developing gambling addictions because they continued to see the behaviour only as a source of fun. These participants took gambling less seriously, participated only occasionally, and played for little or no money. Our respondent Ian, for example, said that his father sometimes played card games with friends, but their gatherings were not organized or centred around gambling. "My dad would occasionally have people come over. But it was not exactly gambling, more like friends meeting up for beer, [playing] some cards to pass time, minimal money." Because his father only gambled occasionally, and just for the fun of it, Ian learned that gambling was not something to be taken seriously. Instead, he came to view gambling as a fun pastime that should be done only occasionally and at low financial stakes—not an activity that could lead to material gain.

Playing for no money at all was particularly effective in terms of ensuring that children saw gambling only a source of entertainment, and not income. For example, one of the people we interviewed, named Lila, learned how to gamble with her family, but never played for money. She told us about some of her childhood gambling experiences:

> I used to play cards, but we never bet money on it. It was more like a leisure activity when we had friends over. Even with my mother and my grandmother, we used to play cards, but we never bet any money.

Like Lila, Petar also recalled being exposed to a representation of gambling that was not centred around money or winning when he was growing up. He told us, "We played poker, but the betting wasn't for money, it was just [for] little chips and dominos." Because they didn't play for money, neither of these individuals came to associate gambling with financial gain. In turn, they weren't motivated to play because they didn't feel there was anything material to gain by gambling.

These sorts of participants, who viewed gambling as casual fun, were unlikely to gamble for money for two main reasons. First, they understood that the odds of winning were not in their favour; they knew that they couldn't rely on gambling to support them financially because the chances of actually winning were so slim. Second, they placed a high value on the money they earned outside of gambling, making them wary of spending it so frivolously.

In relation to the first reason, several people we spoke with told us that they felt that gambling was an unreliable source of income, since it is based entirely on luck and chance. One of our respondents said, "Okay, fine, you might win some money the first time you go to the casino 'cause you're lucky or whatever, but you cannot rely on that." Another told us, "Playing cards, for me, no one actually wins. It just goes from one pocket to another pocket. It's meaningless to me. You're not generating more money." These individuals both suggest that gambling winnings cannot be seen as "earnings"—unlike a salary or steady paycheque, these winnings cannot provide players with a sense of financial stability.

Similarly, we found that some of our respondents acknowledged that the odds are always in favour of the House. One such individual said, "I lose because gambling is meant for you to lose. I know you are not meant to win in gambling. If you win, you win, but in your first five or ten minutes wherever you are, after that it's a downward spiral. You are not meant to win [at] gambling. That's just how casinos are set up." By recognizing that the chances of winning are slim at best, these types of participants were able to avoid seeing or relying on gambling as a way to make money.

In this way, learning the odds of winning can demystify people's perceptions of gambling, and help them develop more realistic outlooks on what they should expect from their participation in the activity. If they know the odds are not in their favour, people are unlikely to spend much time or money chasing the dream of "winning big." Similarly, having this knowledge also reduces the likelihood of chasing losses, since they realize how slim their chances of winning back lost money are.

With regards to the second reason, many of our participants who avoided developing a gambling problem told us that they valued their hard-earned money very highly. This discouraged them from wagering it on games that were unlikely to reward them in the long run. As one of our respondents explained, "I respect the money I make too much to possibly lose it." A few of the people we spoke with suggested that even a few dollars is too much to risk on gambling: "I played, like, five dollars and then maybe two or three dollars. I mean, I could buy a lunch for that. Well, not a lunch, but a muffin, so I'll leave." For these individuals, the risk of losing their hard-earned money made gambling unattractive.

Our participants thus communicated fairly explicitly about their concern with money, and their unwillingness to spend it on gambling. These individuals learned to place such a high value on the money they earned in three ways. First, they usually had parents who did not gamble themselves, but who worked hard for their money instead. As such, our respondents' parents acted as positive role models, from whom they were able to learn qualities like dedication and hard work. In response to our question about his family's gambling habits, one individual told us: "No. My family never did it [gambled]. Not my mother, father, or uncles. Nobody. They're too hard-working people to stupidly spend money." Similarly, another one of our participants explained his lack of interest in gambling by saying, "Just the way we have been brought up. We believe more in hard work rather than chance."

Second, many of our respondents had to endure and support their gambling parent(s) while they were growing up. Sometimes, this experience would deepen their appreciation for money. When we asked her why she doesn't gamble, one of our participants said:

> I understand the value of money. I have had to work for everything I have today. Maybe if it came easy, it would be easier to gamble, but I know how hard it comes. Even when I was in my undergrad—and I know I'm not the only person who has had to do this—I know some people go to school from eight to six, and work until eleven. Then you're on the bus going home and you still have to get up and go to school [the next day], so it's tough. [That's why] I truly value money and don't throw it away frivolously.

Her difficult upbringing and lifelong struggles with money taught this individual the difficulty of making money, but also the importance of financial stability. As a result, she treasures the money she earns, rather than risking it on gambling.

The third way our participants learned to place a high value on money was by being part of a family with a small income and hard-working parents. Parents who cope with small salaries and financial instability often aim to impress upon their children the importance of hard work, and the value of money. Those of our participants who were brought up under these circumstances came to believe that money was precious and not to be spent frivolously. When we asked one of our respondents if she found gambling appealing, she replied:

> No, I have never had enough money to, and I have always worked for every-thing, so I don't have any debts and I have no credit [cards]. Every dollar you make, you work very hard for it, so I wasn't going to squander it. It wasn't part of my upbringing. I had like a very strict sort of upbringing, and my parents didn't have enough money to squander it either, so [gambling] wasn't very familiar.

The ways in which our participants' parents dealt with their own financial struggles were thus extremely influential: if they tried to solve their money troubles quickly through gambling or other shortcuts, their children learned to deal with financial problems in the same ways. On the other hand, when parents turn to hard work in order to get the money they need to support their families, their children tend to take similar steps to solve their own problems with money.

Perceptions of and attitudes toward gambling, as well as gambling skills and behaviours, are learned from role models and valued others through social learning. In order for people to learn about gambling in this way, they must be exposed to the activity. Those of our participants who had a problem gambling family member were most likely to experience expos-ure, since gambling often occurs inside of these homes, and the parent will occasionally gamble with the child. In these cases, our respondents were able to learn the rules of the game and skills that would help them win at an early age. They were also taught to view gambling as a fun, exciting, and easy way to make money. Finally, children who are raised in this kind of pro-gambling environment are also emotionally rewarded for their participation in the form of increased self-esteem and family approval. All of these factors contribute to encouraging children's engage-ment with gambling activities and to maintaining their learned gambling behaviours into adulthood.

In much the same way that children can pick up gambling through social learning, adults are also susceptible to the rewards of gambling, exposure to a variety of games and activities, positive modelling of gambling behav-iours, and peer pressure. As such, problem gambling is not simply the result of having an addicted parent who models the behaviour for his or her children; rather, a person's compulsive desire to gamble can develop due to a wide combination of factors that arise as late as adulthood.

One of these variables is the influence of peers, who can introduce each other to gambling, teach each other new games, reward each other for their participation with praise and admiration, and support the perception of gambling as a means for financial gain. Both children and adults are thus often driven to gamble as a result of peer pressure, as they feel they can gain approval, social status, and inclusion by participating. Another factor we discussed earlier is the media, which teaches its audience how to play; informs them of upcoming gambling events and opportunities; and depicts these occasions as fun, exhilarating, and desirable. Exposure to gambling from each of these sources thus helps to explain why and how individuals with non-problem gambling parents develop compulsive gambling habits of their own.

Overall then, social learning teaches people that gambling is an acceptable, normal pastime, and an exciting opportunity for financial gain. It also makes gambling more easily accessible by teaching relevant skills and the rules of the game, and by providing a range of opportunities to play. When people aren't exposed to social modelling of gambling, they are less likely to view the behaviour as acceptable or accessible. This was the case for many of our respondents who did not inherit their parent's gambling problem: they were either physically absent during their parent's gambling, or the gambling only occurred once they were already grown up. As a result, they did not develop positive attitudes toward gambling, they did not know how to gamble, and they were unaware of gambling opportunities.

However, we also saw that social modelling is not always negative, and that it does not always result in problem gambling. Simply being exposed to or learning about gambling is not the crucial aspect of social learning; rather, the rewards obtained and the values taught determine whether an individual will begin to gamble problematically. Those of our participants who place a high value on money, and learn that gambling can be a casual social activity rather than a source of material gain, were generally able to gamble while staying in control. However, the people we spoke with who felt that gambling was an easy way to attain financial freedom were at a much higher risk of becoming compulsive gamblers. So, while social learning can encourage problematic gambling behaviour, the modelling of parents and peers can also protect people from developing this kind of dangerous habit.

To summarize then, social learning helps us understand why some people come to see gambling as an attractive behaviour and become so invested in it. That is, by observing the modelling of their family, friends, and peers, people start to believe that participating in gambling is a way to gain the acceptance of their loved ones; improve their self-image; and make quick, easy money. Childhood trauma, adulthood stress, and poor coping behaviours play a different role in our model because these factors encourage serious involvement with gambling by making people more likely to use the behaviour as a means to deal with stressful situations, and to attain a sense of emotional fulfillment.

These past two chapters have thus allowed us to outline the ways in which non-Dostoevskian factors—in particular, the acceptance, availability, and social learning of gambling—help to explain why and how our participants did or did not become problem gamblers. In the next chapter, we will focus less on the differences between problem and non-problem gamblers, and more on their similarities.

11

How Do Non-problem Gambling Families Compare?

So far, we have been focusing most of our attention on families with problems—in particular, families that produce or endure problem gamblers. In so doing, we have implicitly assumed that families that do not produce or endure problem gamblers—what we will call control group families, for lack of a better term—are without problems. However, in this chapter, we will see that such an assumption is unwarranted. All families have problems, but not all problems give rise to, or result from, problem gambling. So, in this chapter, we will try to figure out how some families manage to avoid a descent into the struggles associated with gambling addiction, despite having other problems to solve.

In other words, we will be discussing the varied circumstances of non-problem gambling families today and the factors that offer these families some protection against problem gambling. In order to do so, we examined a sample of the general, non-problem gambling population. The following discussion is based on the responses of fifty-two participants who were not problem gamblers themselves, and whose parents were not problem gamblers either. What is clear from their interviews is that being part of a non-problem gambling family is by no means synonymous with having a stress-free family life. Rather, the lives of non-gamblers and non-problem gamblers are also filled with various combinations of both childhood and adult stress, and poor strategies for coping with this stress. In fact, 16 percent of the participants in this control group experienced all three of the key risk factors in our developmental model—childhood stress, learning of gambling, and adulthood stress—but they did not become problem gamblers as adults. Within this chapter, we will be trying to explain why these individuals diverged from our model in this way.

These participants reminded us that non-problem gamblers are not terribly different from problem gamblers, and that everyone is at risk of developing a gambling habit. Further, this group of individuals demonstrates that the factors that contribute to problem gambling are so complex and sensitive that it is often difficult to determine why one person becomes a problem gambler and another does not. This complexity is not a result of uncertainty or confusion—we know what the key variables are; it is their interaction with each other and their specific timing within the life course that make them complicated to model and predict.

Overall, we found that each individual in this control group usually experienced at least one factor that protected her or him from becoming a problem gambler. As such, it appears that gambling problems develop largely due to the number and severity of the problems that families struggle with, and the number and type of factors that protect them. Everyone experiences a delicate, fluctuating balance between these pluses and minuses while growing up and during their adult lives. We therefore speculated that a slight increase in the number and severity of problems, when unaccompanied by support or coupled with ineffective coping behaviours, might be enough to drive some people toward problem gambling. On the other hand, a slight reduction in the number and degree of problems, coupled with support and healthier, more positive coping behaviours, might be enough to prevent them from developing a gambling addiction.

The timing and circumstances surrounding the development of problems may also be a contributing factor. For example, being thrown into unemployment at a particularly awkward or inconvenient time, or developing a dreaded disease while his or her family members are trying to cope with other challenges, may drive that person to develop problematic gambling behaviours. In short, there are matters of chance involved in real life, just as there are in gambling: some people are unlucky enough to get sick, be thrown out of work, or suffer a death in the family at the worst possible time, while others are lucky enough to avoid these things.

In the midst of these roiling, chancy events, we find our non-problem gambling families managing to escape the hardships of problem gambling. Let us now consider what the members of this non-problem gambling group told us about their experiences with childhood distress, adult stressors, poor coping, social learning of problem gambling, and the protective factors that surrounded them in a risky, sometimes hostile world.

Childhood Distress

Our non-problem gambling participants experienced various levels of childhood distress. Some remembered having relatively stress-free childhoods, except for one or two significant traumatic events, like a death in the family, for example. Others, however, had to deal with many troubling experiences, each one adding to the stress that the previous one had caused.

Overall, eight of the participants in this control group experienced severe childhood stress (and half of these individuals experienced abuse). While the high level of childhood distress that these people encountered was not caused by their parents' problematic gambling behaviours, they still experienced troubles that were similar to the issues our problem gambling respondents struggled with. Take Norman as an example: first, his parents' marriage ended in a messy divorce when he was fourteen. This was preceded by emotional abuse at the hand of his mother, followed by unstable living situations:

> She was like, "If you guys don't watch out, I'm gonna leave both of you [Norman and his father]." And then she ended up picking me up at school the next week, saying, "We are leaving your father," and took me off to live in four different houses over the next week. Then [we] kept moving and moving until I had to tell her that I want to live with my father.

Even when he no longer resided with his mother, the emotional abuse she had been subjecting him to continued into the next year, when Norman was blamed for his parents' divorce in a letter she wrote:

> It was shortly before my birthday they split, and [her letter] said that she had seen her depression mirrored in me and she felt like she had to get me out of it. That was pretty much the end of my relationship with my mother, when she gave it to me.

Norman's mental health declined as a result of this unstable family environment: "I was suicidal at twelve and very depressed, rarely had my mood lifted, didn't want to see friends, family, eat." Norman's childhood experiences remind us that the children of problem gamblers were not the only ones to experience parental conflict and related family stresses, or the mental health consequences of these situations.

Many of our non-problem gambling participants also witnessed their parents being abusive toward each other, or suffered abuse themselves. Oliver, for example, described the violence that was common in his house while he was growing up:

> We would be left at home alone, for instance, and my brother was very mean to me. It was more my dad who would be violent, so I guess because he already had that problem, my brother would return the problem on me, or make my dad think it was me, so I would have [to take] a cold shower or something because I broke something.

In addition to being the recipient of abuse, Oliver also witnessed physical fights between his mother and father. In our interview, he told us about those fights:

> Awful. You don't want to hear about it. After a while my mom didn't want to stay with him, share what you usually share in a couple when you're my age. Of course my dad didn't accept that, so it went pretty far. I remember her having this bone broken [pointed to his clavicle].

Despite the severity and ongoing nature of this abuse, Oliver's mother would lie to doctors and nurses at the hospital where she was treated, and eventually to the police, in her efforts to cover up her husband's abuse:

> Sometimes my brother would protect my mom—of course, she was smaller and she couldn't resist—she couldn't have, with what happened to her because of my dad. My brother would call the cops, but when the cops would arrive, my mom would say, "No, no, nothing happened."

As with Norman, this domestic violence caused Oliver a great deal of distress, making his childhood similar in that sense to those of the problem gamblers we spoke with.

Abuse, however, was not the only traumatic childhood experience we heard about; other people in this control group were distressed by a death in the family during their childhood. Lila, for example, lost her mother during her early teenage years, and her sister and grandmother passed away shortly after. This traumatizing series of events pushed Lila to immigrate to Canada—which was merely another source of stress—because she no longer had immediate family in her home country. She explained her decision as follows:

> I was fifteen when I lost my mother, and I was twenty when I lost my sister, and I was twenty-two when I lost my grandmother, so all my pillars of life are gone. Actually that's the reason I'm here [in Canada] too. I just couldn't live there anymore.

She went on to describe the situation as "devastating," adding, "When I first came here I was really depressed, so it took me a really long time to get over it." This emotional instability that troubled Lila throughout her teenage and early adult years had nothing to do with problem gambling. Her experiences, and those of many others within this control group, did not drive her to develop problematic gambling tendencies.

Yet another source of childhood anxiety for close to half of our non-problem gambling participants was having a distant and unsupportive relationship with one or both of their parents. These negative relationships caused them long-term stress while they were growing up and continued to affect them as adults. Brandon, for example, described the relationships between his family members as being cold and tense.

> [I] didn't think that my father and mother were suited for each other. It was just kind of an odd feeling. You never thought of divorce at the time I was growing up, it was never spoken of or mentioned at all, but you knew there was a lot of tension.

Due to this "tension" between his parents, Brandon felt like he didn't get the attention from them that he deserved. He told us that his parents did not "provide him with what he needed," since they were too wrapped up in their own problems to offer him any emotional support.

Though none of these weak or strained family relationships were a result of gambling problems, they were occasionally the result of other parental addictions. One of our participant's childhood problems were due, in part, to parental alcoholism and her immigrant background:

> We didn't do leisure activities. My mother and father were Italian, hardly
> spoke English. My father was a little older, an alcoholic. We didn't do any-
> thing, we didn't go out. The only thing I can remember is going to visit my
> father's family, his sisters, because he had a big family. But I don't remember
> any [other] family activities—going anywhere, doing anything—no, none.

The communication barrier created by her parents' background, and the troubles associated with her father's drinking problem, limited this individual's ability to bond with her family and establish a sense of emotional connectedness with them.

Much like those of our participants who grew up with problem gambling parents, a number of the people in this control group also experienced some degree of parentification as children, though it did not stem from the troubles associated with having a gambling parent. This parentification was the result of various other childhood stressors. One individual told us about the struggles of his single mother and the challenges he faced as a result of being brought up in a single-parent home: "She worked two jobs and she was never there, so I was basically left to my own devices all the time, right? And then she would come home and wouldn't ask me what I was doing." Taking care of domestic chores and duties was an ongoing source of stress for this participant, who continued to perform most of the housework when he was in university. Though he did not experience parentification due to a parental gambling addiction, he suffered similar emotional consequences as those of our participants who were forced to take on the responsibilities that should have fallen with their problem gambling parents.

Adult Stressors

Just as their childhoods were characterized by differing amounts and sources of anxiety, our non-problem gambling participants also experienced varying levels of adulthood stress. While most of them told us that they were or had been only mildly or moderately distressed in their adult lives, a few reported that they experienced severe anxiety. The most common sources of this stress were financial strain, pressures from their work or home lives, and having to care for a sick family member. However, despite being troubled with adulthood stressors similar to those experienced by people who became problem gamblers, people in this group experienced protective factors that may have played a role in preventing them from developing a gambling habit.

Financial pressure negatively affected many of the people we spoke with. Often, the stress caused by these monetary issues was intensified by pressures from work or home. This was the case for our respondent Prya, a single mother who worked long hours to support herself and her daughter. "I have two jobs, so yeah, I work quite a bit," she told us. In addition to being solely responsible for earning the income that would support her entire household, Prya had no help carrying out her household duties:

> Sometimes I work fifteen hours a day. . . . I come home and I'm so tired, but if I don't cook I have nothing to eat; I would love to have a chef. I'm okay with cleaning, [it's] just cooking and grocery [shopping] I don't have enough time [for].

Often, what distinguished non-gamblers like Prya from their problem gambling counterparts was that they had taken on extra work to support their families, instead of gambling in their efforts to solve their money problems. People like Prya had learned to work hard and value money from a young age, and were therefore protected against developing a gambling problem, despite having been exposed to certain adulthood stressors that drove many of our other participants to become addicted to the habit.

Another person we spoke with, named Maggie, told us that her caregiving responsibilities caused her a great deal of stress. In our interview, Maggie revealed that she felt very anxious about her mother's condition because, "her health is deteriorating and she's not doing anything about it." Due to this lack of agency on her mother's part, Maggie took on a variety of caregiving responsibilities, one of which included looking out for her mother's safety: "I'll probably call [my mother] every day. I like to make sure she gets home, 'cause now she works nights, so I always want to make sure she gets home all right and stuff like that." Maggie also talked about the frustration she experienced while trying to get her mother to adopt a healthier lifestyle. Quoting her doctor, Maggie said, "'[Mother's] going to be diabetic if she keeps eating like that, and she doesn't listen.' So he's like, 'You try.' I'm like, 'Well, if she's not listening to you . . .'" Though this situation was certainly stressful for her, Maggie was able to reduce its effect on her by acknowledging that she could only do her best, and that ultimately, the choice was up to her mother: "I kind of throw my hands up at this point, right?" Maggie was therefore able to recognize that she wasn't responsible for the lifestyle choices her mother made, whereas other individuals may have turned to compulsive behaviours (like gambling) in order to cope with the frustration caused by this kind of stressful situation.

Another one of our participants, David, reported similar feelings of stress because of the caregiving responsibilities he took on for his father, who was diagnosed as depressed and bipolar:

> When I was living with [my father], especially when I came back at night, it was like pretty stressful. Because he was threatening to almost kill me, well, he was delusional. He said that he knew people in the mafia, he told me that he would kill me and etc. He was threatening me, saying, "If I was a younger man I would attack you for the stuff you're doing."

Managing his father's threats was so stressful that it compromised David's own mental health. As he said, "I think I had mild depression and mild anxiety at that time, and I was seeing a psychiatrist." He was affected physically by his father's behaviour as well:

> I've had indigestion, and vague general symptoms of anxiety or depression, like diarrhea, but I haven't had any severe physical illnesses. Anxiety—well I've just had very nervous thoughts, heart racing at times, [and] stomach issues would be result of anxiety.

Although his feelings of stress were intense enough to cause mental and physical suffering, David was able to cope by exercising or by spending time with his girlfriend. His ability to handle the anxiety his father produced in a healthy, productive way contributed to David's ability to avoid problematic gambling behaviours. This brings us to the central question we will be addressing in the next section: how do non-problem gamblers cope with their common—though sometimes terrible—problems?

Poor Coping Behaviours

Just like the problem gamblers we spoke to, several non-problem gambling participants employed poor coping behaviours to deal with the stressful events they experienced. These included using alcohol in their efforts to escape from or forget about the issue that was troubling them.

Our participant Oliver exemplified this coping strategy. Instead of addressing his problems directly and trying to come up with a solution, he chose to drink in order to forget about what was bothering him. In our interview, Oliver described how a friend reacted to his new alcoholic tendencies:

> She was just like advising me at first, she was following me around. "[Be] very careful about who you are going out with," [she would say]. But at that age, I was just thinking of changing my mind, leaving my mind, having fun; and it was easy for me to follow bad influences and do other things which were not good at all. She was just like: "You are disappointing me," but she wouldn't have done anything else.

Despite the positive direction his friend was attempting to lead him in, Oliver believed that drinking, and the accompanying sense of literally having left his mind, was the most effective way to manage his stressors.

Other people we spoke with also tried to forget about their problems, but rather than turning to alcohol, they simply avoided thinking about or dealing with their stressful situations. In the hope that they would resolve themselves, these participants completely ignored their issues. Miles said that this was his behaviour of choice: "It keeps me up all night thinking about it—an alternate solution to problems—and yeah I just don't deal well. I would rather not think about it at all." Interestingly, Miles learned this coping technique from his mother and maternal grandmother, both of whom employed this strategy in their efforts to deal with their own problems. His experiences thus demonstrate that both non-gamblers and gambling addicts can exhibit the same poor ways of managing their stress, and that each group can learn these techniques in the same ways.

Social Learning of Gambling

The participants in our non-problem gambling control group also experienced different levels and types of social learning. Twenty-nine individuals, or just more than half of the members of this control group, had limited or no exposure to gambling while they were growing up. The remaining twenty-three individuals experienced some (but not extensive) social learning of gambling as children. Though none of these people became problem gamblers, those who experienced social learning of gambling were more likely to gamble casually, or within their limits.

Those individuals who gambled the most often had childhoods that were most similar to the problem gamblers we spoke with. Many of these non-problem gamblers played for money with their family while they were growing up. For example, one of our participants said he began gambling at the age of nine during family gatherings and on special occasions:

> We would have Christmas parties when family would come from out of town and . . . we played blackjack, sometimes for nuts but usually for change. It was like five bucks here and there, but it was for money and my family would teach me how to play. We'd play twenty-one and all these games, a lot of the games they'd learned growing up.

While these childhood experiences provided entertainment, quality family time, and pocket change, all of which encouraged him to continue gambling when he grew up, this individual never learned that gambling was to be used solely to make money, and he never witnessed frequent, repeated, compulsive gambling behaviour. Because gambling was always framed as a tame family event that was to be played only rarely, our participant was able to gamble casually and without losing control.

For other members of this control group, gambling wasn't only meant for special occasions, but occurred on a regular basis. One of our participants described how watching his mother play cards had gradually transitioned into his own playing:

> My mom played the painted card with her friends at home when we were young. We [children] just watched them play. They played with coins and we counted the coins for them. And when we grew up, after we got to fifteen or sixteen, I played cards together with my friends.

Another individual told a similar story:

> It was just twenty-one—just counting—so I'd look at the cards and hit and [it was] just jokes and it was fun. When my parents were making drinks for

the table, [they'd say,] "Play a couple of hands for me while I'm gone," so that's what we did.

As with those of our participants who became problem gamblers, some of the members of this control group recounted trips to gambling establishments they had taken with their families. One such individual said that since he was under the legal gambling age, his mother had to place bets on his behalf:

> We [his family] would all get together and play blackjack and stuff like that, and occasionally we went to horse races; and even though I was underage, my mom would put a two-dollar bet for me.

Despite these early gambling experiences that made the behaviour seem acceptable and attractive, these participants did not develop gambling problems. For the most part, this was because the other precipitating conditions, such as those included in the Dostoevsky Effect, were missing from their lives while they were growing up.

However, non-Dostoevskian factors like peers and the media also acted as sources of social learning for members of the control group. One of the people we spoke with said that he began and continues to gamble because he is trying to emulate his friends: "I've seen a lot. . . . I continue to do it 'cause I have friends who do well. I try to shadow them, try to see if I can be as good as them." Another one of our participants said that he took up gambling because of the television commercials he watched: "I saw it on TV, in the commercials, and I was like, 'Okay, I'll try that.' And then I was winning, and I put [in] twenty dollars of my own money. And then I won a hundred dollars, and I just kept using the same money." Our interviews with these individuals therefore revealed that both problem and non-problem gamblers can be influenced to gamble by peers and the media. However, it seems that exposure to these types of factors alone is not enough to drive people to gamble compulsively; without the influence of the variables we discussed earlier, these control group members were capable of refraining from gambling to excess.

Overall then, the members of our control group "learn" gambling in much the same way as those of our participants who become problem gamblers. Clearly, other factors in their lives contribute to protecting them from becoming addicted to gambling, allowing them instead to gamble only casually. Within the next section, we will outline why and how these factors play such a pivotal role in determining which people will gamble excessively, and which will gamble within their limits.

Protective Factors

Many of the people in our non-problem gambling control group experienced some combination of childhood distress, social learning of gambling, adulthood stress, and poor coping habits, but were somehow able to avoid becoming problem gamblers. While the reasons for this are generally very complex, we found that all of these people had experienced certain protective factors: many had had pleasant childhoods, most had only been minimally stressed as adults, and the majority exhibited healthy coping behaviours. Significantly, many of these individuals' exposure to gambling had been limited: it simply wasn't prominent in their childhood households, venues and establishments were not close by, and their friends did not participate.

Those participants who did experience social learning of gambling learned that it provided few, if any, certain rewards; that hard-earned money held high value; and that gambling was only a source of fun, rather than a way to make a profit. Since we have talked about most of these protective factors earlier, we just want to touch on pleasant childhoods and positive coping behaviours.

The majority of our control group—thirty-one of fifty-two participants—grew up within a positive family environment. They told us that they had often spent special occasions, such as birthdays, anniversaries, and holidays, with their families. For example, our participant Heather said that she and her family:

Went [out] every Sunday and to all the big events at Christmas and Easter. [Summer] days we used to go to the beach with my family and relatives, [and] sometimes rent a cottage. We'd often go to my grandmother's house, so there were a lot of family occasions. [Sometimes] we'd go to the movies.

Another respondent, Trevor, told us that he and his family shared similar experiences; they "would do a lot of family outings on the weekends: go to the park, have ice cream, spend a lot of time together at home, [and watch] rented movies—a lot of quality family time." Having been raised in a loving environment, Heather and Trevor were able to develop close ties with their families and feel confident that they were always there if they were needed. These two participants, along with several others in the control group, received the emotional support they needed as children and grew up in households with positive role models who displayed healthy, non-gambling behaviours for them. These positive variables combined to help Heather and Trevor avoid the descent into problematic gambling behaviours.

Some of our participants who experienced these positive childhoods had parents who fulfilled traditional family roles. These individuals told us that their mothers stayed home to care for them and the household, while their fathers worked to financially support the family. One such respondent, named Simon, explained that his family had exemplified these traditional household roles:

> My family was very traditional. My mom was the caretaker of my sister and I. I guess you could say my dad was the breadwinner [and] brought home the paycheque. [They did] very traditional roles; cooking, housework, all the rest were my mom. Disciplining us was [also] our mom, but if it got really bad, she would say that she'll tell my dad and that was really bad. We didn't want my dad to find out.

Trevor also described his family as fulfilling "traditional" roles:

> My home life was very traditional, [where] the mother stayed at home. And when my dad married my mom, she was a secretary. She worked for Irving Oil, and as soon as he married her, it was understood "No wife of mine is gonna work, 'cause I'll look after you." And [for] everyone—every mother in the neighbourhood, at school, my friends—no women worked. [A woman] stayed at home and cooked, [and] the man brought home the bacon.

We do not want to suggest, based on these experiences, that a traditional division of labour in the household invariably acts as a protection against problem gambling; recall that Dostoevsky, like a number of modern-day problem gamblers, grew up in a traditional nuclear family. That being said, something about these family arrangements allowed some of the participants in the non-problem gambling control group to assume that the "traditional" organization of family roles in their childhood households had positive outcomes for them.

For some, like Trevor, it may have been conformity to community norms that contributed to making him feel as though his family and home life had been stable and secure. Because no mother in his neighbourhood held a job, Trevor felt just like his friends, and was therefore likely comforted by the conventional arrangement. Things might have felt different for him if his mother had been one of only a handful of stay-at-home mothers in his neighbourhood.

In addition to the comfort of conformity, Trevor and Simon might also have benefited from having a parent at home throughout the day, to talk to and spend time with. However, they might not have been able to enjoy this kind of positive relationship if the stay-at-home parent had been filling that role reluctantly. This underscores our initial point that the factors contributing to—and protecting against—problem gambling are complex, sensitive, and dependent on variable social contexts.

Having a positive family upbringing likely contributed to another important protective factor we encountered among this group: it engendered healthy coping behaviours. Participants who were raised in these types of families usually learned to discuss their problems with their loved ones, close friends, spouses, or professionals: nearly half of those in our control group said they spoke with others about stressful experiences and feelings of anxiety. Moreover, they chose to confide in people whom they felt they could trust to provide honest, useful advice. In this way, our control group members were able to tackle their problems head on, engaging with positive role models and building supportive relationships.

Manpreet was one of our participants who became particularly skilled at working through her problems by discussing them with her family:

> We function a lot better as a family unit now, like, we will discuss things together. . . . I realized that you know that if my family is not working well, I'm a part of it too and I need to be involved in the discussion.

Manpreet was thus able to face her problems head-on, and to acknowledge her own role in them, within a safe and supportive family context.

Taking responsibility for one's problems, much like Manpreet was able to do, was an important theme among those in the non-problem gambling group. Their ability to do so stood in stark contrast to the problem gamblers in our study, who rarely took responsibility for the issues that were troubling them. A few of the people within our control group went as far as to seek professional help for their problems, choosing to speak with an expert instead of with loved ones out of respect for the professional's extensive knowledge and training. The expert advice they received usually directed them toward more positive ways to handle and reduce their stress, which in turn steered them away from negative coping strategies such as gambling.

In terms of the protective factors they experience(d), this group of non-problem gambling participants is similar to the group of individuals with addicted parents who did not inherit their parent's gambling habit. In both groups, a person was unlikely to become a problem gambler if he or she had been only minimally exposed to gambling activities and positive attitudes toward gambling; had a childhood characterized by low levels of stress or trauma; was living a relatively stress-free adult life; exhibited good coping behaviours; and had had non-gambling role models and peers.

Thus, we see that our general model of development sheds light on the occurrence of problem gambling among people with and without parents who are problem gamblers. Equally important, it also clarifies the circumstances in which people can avoid problem gambling, regardless of whether their parents are problem gamblers or not.

Our discussions throughout this chapter have shown that non-problem gamblers with non-problem gambling parents lead lives that are far from idyllic or stress-free. Some of the people we interviewed suffered through extremely negative upbringings, which included abuse, mental distress, deaths in the family, distant parental relationships, and parentification. Quite a few of our participants also experienced severe adulthood stress, mainly from financial strain, home or work pressures, and caregiving responsibilities. Poor coping behaviours, such as using alcohol as an escape mechanism, or avoiding stressful situations all together, were evident with a few of these individuals as well. Finally, many of these control group members were exposed to positive social modelling of gambling, where they gambled with family members, went on regular gambling outings, observed the gambling behaviours of their friends, and learned about positive depictions of gambling through the media.

Despite sharing these similar child- and adulthood variables with problem gamblers, all of these participants enjoyed one or more protective factors that kept them from becoming gambling addicts. For some, these factors could include happy childhoods and adulthoods with minimal stress and strong, supportive family relationships. Others were only minimally exposed to gambling, or learned that gambling was only a source of entertainment that provided few other rewards. The majority had learned how to cope with stressful situations in a positive way by speaking about their problems with loved ones. Although all of those in our control group shared something with the participants who became problem gamblers, there was always at least one factor that protected them from following the same route into compulsive gambling.

What is perhaps most interesting of all is the evidence that anyone is potentially one risk factor away from becoming a problem gambler, because the lives of compulsive gamblers and non-problem gamblers are not always very different. The crucial distinction is a matter of degree—especially, degree of stress—and the specific constellation of social circumstances in which the crucial stress occurs.

Part IV

Conclusions and Implications

12

The Gambler, Then and Now

If you flip back to the beginning, you'll remember that this book grew out of an interest in the social and psychological factors that contribute to the transfer of problem gambling across generations. As researchers, we set out to explore the mechanisms that transferred the problem from one generation to the next, and it quickly became apparent that these mechanisms of transfer are understandable from a social learning perspective.

Some researchers have offered genetic or biochemical accounts of the problem (Shah et al. 2005; Perez de Castro et al. 1997). However, most of these explanations of transmission are lacking in the consideration of social conditions that predispose or trigger the genetic potential. Further, it has been argued that the genetic heritability of problem gambling is low, at roughly 16 percent (Walters 2001). Apart from the small portion of variability attributable to genetic inheritance, inclinations toward problem gambling tend to pass from parent to child through social mechanisms—through parental modelling and encouragement of gambling behaviours and attitudes and the creation of a gambling-focused family lifestyle, for example. It was not at all surprising to us, then, to find that children of problem gamblers are much more likely than children of non- or moderate-gambling parents to develop a gambling problem themselves. Likewise, it is easy to understand why the children of non-gamblers did not become problem gamblers themselves: they learned to do otherwise.

After confirming our intuitions, we became intrigued by the non-intuitive, non-diagonal cases encountered in our study, namely, the children of problem gamblers who did not become problem gamblers themselves, and the children of non-gamblers who did become problem gamblers. We found ourselves particularly puzzled by those participants who developed a gambling problem seemingly "out of nowhere," in respect to our social learning model.

This is how the comparison to Dostoevsky eventually emerged. Dostoevsky, that famously dysfunctional nineteenth-century Russian novelist, not only wrote insightfully about problem gambling in his novel *The Gambler*, but, as an adult, he also had a gambling problem himself. Most interestingly for us, he did not inherit this gambling problem from his parents: not from his passive, sweet-tempered mother and not from his mercurial, despotic father.

As our knowledge about these non-intuitive, or "non-diagonal," cases increased, so did our interest in understanding the non-inherited factors that led Dostoevsky to become a problem gambler. Combing through the more than two hundred transcripts of interviews with our participants, we noticed that many participants shared numerous biographical and social characteristics with the great nineteenth-century Russian novelist.

Consequently, throughout this book, we've referred to this combination of non-inherited factors as the Dostoevsky Effect, a developmental model of gambling that applies to both Dostoevsky's experience and the experiences of gamblers in present-day Toronto. This model proposes a range of non-inherited social and environmental factors that interact throughout one's life to produce negative outcomes for a person's mental health.

Without instruction, the troubled person struggles to relieve these negative feelings, and in the absence of positive and healthy coping strategies, turns to gambling as both a solution to and escape from her or his troubles. The choice of a particular addiction—gambling as opposed to drugs, for example—is often the result of exposure or availability. The Dostoevsky Effect, as we have seen, begins early in life, with a stressful childhood setting the stage for long-term psychological problems and stunted coping skills. Confronted with adult life stresses that challenge their mental health and well-being, people are forced to call on the coping strategies they've developed throughout their lives, the large majority of which are rooted in childhood.

But when the person's learned coping strategies are stunted and maladaptive, the outcome is more harm to the person's mental health, in the form of increased anxiety and increased depression. As we have seen, the result is an often-endless cycle of attempts to use failed coping strategies to relieve negative feelings. As failure mounts, desperation ensues. Anxiety grows and depression deepens. This is when participants are most likely to turn to gambling to cope with stress.

In the rest of this chapter, we'll draw more explicit comparisons between the lives of Dostoevsky and our present-day problem gamblers, showing the roles played by childhood stress, adulthood stress, and maladaptive coping strategies in the development of a problem gambler.

The Role of Childhood Stress

Neither of Dostoevsky's parents was a problem gambler; in that sense, he grew up in a "normal" family. Yet, growing up, Dostoevsky was exposed to a range of factors that triggered poor coping strategies, and consequently, compulsive behaviours that included problem gambling. Like some of our participants who also became problem gamblers, Dostoevsky suffered from childhood adversities that made him anxious and distressed, the effects of which followed both Dostoevsky and our study participants into adulthood.

As we know, Dostoevsky's father had a volatile temperament and suffered from severe bouts of depression and irritability, contributing to the emotional abuse Dostoevsky suffered. Many present-day participants also reported abuse at the hands of difficult parents. Whether it was physical, sexual, or emotional abuse, the experience always led children to feel degraded, betrayed, and unloved. Fear of punishment meant these children, including Dostoevsky, had to tiptoe around their abuser; they felt they were being held captive in their own homes and unable to express themselves. As we know from the case of Dostoevsky, these children would have also felt considerable anger, shame, and guilt.

Understandably, many participants lost their confidence and self-esteem, and they were unable to develop their own identities, even outside the home. Consider Dostoevsky, who so desperately sought to pursue writing, but whose father insisted on his becoming a military engineer, sending him to a military academy where he had no choice but to comply. Our study found that victims of childhood abuse were more likely to resort to abusive and maladaptive coping practices in their adult lives—practices that included problem gambling and, often, co-occurring substance abuse.

As we know, Dostoevsky used gambling to deal with his adult stresses—especially those connected with a shortage of money. However, we agree with Freud in thinking that the problem of gambling started far earlier, with the emotionally abusive upbringing he experienced at the hands of his father. For both our participants and Dostoevsky, gambling became a way of rebelling and avoiding a tumultuous home environment. It is not surprising that, like many of the people who participated in our study, Dostoevsky learned to cope with his problems through (self-)abusive behaviours, as this approach had become normalized to him via his father throughout his childhood.

Several of the problem gamblers who participated in our study shared the traumatic experience of losing a family member, like Dostoevsky, whose mother died when he was still young. The death or illness of one parent could have led the other to become abusive, or, as Dostoevsky experienced, the death of someone's non-abusive parent could leave them in the care of the abusive one, compounding the negative effects of this mistreatment. Thus, the loss of Dostoevsky's mother was made all the more traumatic by the fact that it left him in the care of his abusive and explosive father, who was unfit to provide a safe, supportive, and caring environment for his son.

This undoubtedly difficult loss, in combination with the harsh treatment Dostoevsky experienced from his father, contributed to making his childhood, which is such a formative period, a stressful and upsetting time in his life. Likely, he remained troubled by these problems well into his adult years, contributing to the other stresses he encountered in adulthood, around finances and caregiving responsibilities. Consequently, Dostoevsky and many of our study participants who also experienced the death of a loved one were eventually driven to gamble in their efforts to handle the feelings of stress and loneliness that accompanied their loss.

The loss of a loved one was not the only traumatic experience that participants shared with Dostoevsky. Consider the comparison between him and those participants who were forced to deal with constant moves from one place to another. With each move, they had to deal with the difficulties of saying goodbye to their home, friends, and neighbourhood, and then with the challenges of establishing new friendships and adjusting to a new school and neighbourhood dynamics.

Remember Ted, whose parents enrolled him in a school for gifted children, where he was lonely and unhappy. The fact that his parents kept him enrolled in the school despite his negative feelings about it made him think that his parents did not care about his happiness. This is similar to Dostoevsky's experience with his father sending him to the prestigious

Academy of Engineers rather than encouraging Dostoevsky to pursue his passion for writing. Instead, at the academy, he felt socially alienated from his peers, who did not share his interests in reading and writing; this, in combination with adjusting to the harsh regime of barracks life led Dostoevsky to become increasingly lonely and withdrawn.

One reason for strain in the Dostoevsky household, and in many participants' households too (especially those with gambling parents), was the propensity to overspend family finances, leaving the family in a state of relative poverty. Curiously, this existed for Dr. Dostoevsky alongside a preoccupation with the importance of money and associated prestige. His constant reminders to his sons to choose well-paying professions over anything reinforced the idea that acquiring money is more important than maintaining healthy relationships with family.

Not surprisingly, we found the same lesson was learned in childhood among our own participants, inevitably influencing how they prioritized their gambling over their relationships as adults. A further example of traumatic change encountered by both Dostoevsky and participants is that of parental divorce or remarriage. Having to witness unstable family relationships as children biased both Dostoevsky and participants who dealt with such a traumatic experience by being unable to form healthy relationships of their own as adults. This is evident in Dostoevsky's relationship with his first wife, and in the lives of participants, as evident in our discussions of their strained relationships.

Although they lived centuries apart, the links between childhood adversities and the development of problem gambling for both Dostoevsky and participants are evident, as are the ways in which the effects of such experiences contribute to future anxiety and depression, and consequently, a need to cope with such feelings. For this group, coping emerged in the form of gambling.

The Role of Adulthood Stress

Having a stressful and traumatic childhood and consequently lacking opportunities to develop mature and effective coping skills is not enough to surely predict a gambling problem later in life. According to the Dostoevsky Effect, theoretically, stressors encountered in adulthood should call on or initiate coping strategies that were conditioned in childhood.

However, resorting to gambling as a coping strategy required that these people first encounter adulthood stressors, and the results of our study agreed. Our qualitative analysis strongly supported the notion that participants experienced significant stress in their adult lives, and to provide some statistical leverage, our quantitative analysis showed that the chances of a participant becoming a problem gambler increase nearly three times with every additional stressful event encountered in adulthood.

Dostoevsky was no stranger to stress as an adult. Fraught with the distress of his childhood, Dostoevsky experienced significant health problems like those experienced by our study participants. He was plagued by chronic illnesses—emphysema, epileptic seizures, and insomnia were frequent complaints, in addition to neuroses, depression, and suicidality. Not only were these health challenges stressful in and of themselves, but they also predisposed him to experience additional stressors, such as strained relationships and financial difficulties, and rely on nationalistic and religious beliefs as one form of coping. His eventual arrest, time spent in solitary confinement, and exile no doubt further compounded his mental health problems.

In addition to the traumatic loss of his mother in childhood, and in adolescence of his father, Dostoevsky also lost his first wife and brother in adulthood. Despite the fact that his relationship with his first wife was tumultuous at best, this was nonetheless a distressing loss for him. Further, the death of his brother put Dostoevsky in a position of care for both his own and his brother's family. Just as they were for participants, Dostoevsky found the caregiving responsibilities stressful, particularly in terms of financial support.

A person's financial standing and profession have a profound impact on the way the rest of society looks at them and ranks them within the social hierarchy. At the same time, a person's subjective interpretation of how important, dire, or stressful something is is very important in determining how they will react and cope. Dostoevsky was constantly in a state of distress regarding his financial problems.

Despite some recognition for his writing during his life, Dostoevsky lived most of his adult life impoverished, unable to cover his own or his family's basic necessities. In addition, he was forced to support his brother's family along with his own, all on a meagre salary, after his wife and brother passed away. The stress that resulted from this kind of financial strain most likely encouraged Dostoevsky to gamble so that, with the prospect of a big win, he was better able to forget about his troubles, if only temporarily.

However, using gambling to cope with his financial problems only made those financial problems worse—something that many participants experienced as well, as evident in our discussion on the implications of gambling and chasing wins and losses. Like Dostoevsky, when some of our study participants lost large sums of money, they felt compelled to try and win that money back, which in turn encouraged them to continue gambling, leading them to lose even more money. The result is that study participants—not unlike Dostoevsky—found themselves right back where they started, or worse off than before, and without the appropriate strategies to handle such situations.

The Role of Maladaptive Coping

Commonalities between the study participants and Dostoevsky begin with their stressful and traumatic childhoods, regardless of whether their parents were problem gamblers. Having to experience stress at an early age often robs children of the opportunity to develop positive, effective coping strategies. When faced with the kinds of experiences we've been discussing, both the participants and Dostoevsky, as children, found themselves thrown into situations for which they were not developmentally ready to cope. They were deprived of the chance to gradually build developmentally appropriate coping skills over the course of their childhood, and as such failed to develop mature, appropriate coping skills. This left Dostoevsky and some of our study participants predisposed to experience a wide range of stressors in adulthood, with no effective way to cope.

As suggested by the model, these poor or insufficient coping mechanisms only aggravate gambling behaviour in adulthood. Without other means to relieve stress, participants turn to compulsive gambling to cope.

As we discussed in previous chapters, maladaptive coping strategies begin in childhood. Participants reported acting out as children as a way of dealing with their stress. This kind of acting out included drinking excessively at a young age or engaging in other risky behaviours, such as using drugs or sexual promiscuity. For those who began gambling in their teenage years, like Dostoevsky, it was a way to cope with stress, to rebel against parents and their expectations, or to avoid an unstable home environment. These ineffective coping strategies were carried through to adulthood.

As we saw with our participants, and with Dostoevsky, their childhood experiences and their tendency to choose ineffective coping strategies often prevented them from developing healthy and supportive social relationships with others. This is truly unfortunate, because our quantitative analysis found that when participants coped with problems by seeking social support from reliable and healthy relationships, the likelihood of having a gambling problem decreased by 56 percent.

In Dostoevsky's case, he managed to emerge from his downward gambling spiral, at least in part, because of his intense guilt over the impact his behaviour was having on his second wife, Anna, who seemed to faithfully support him through his addiction. For Dostoevsky, a supportive relationship may have saved him. However, for study participants whose relationships were strained, gambling seemed to serve as an alternative source of social interaction. Thus, in the absence of a healthy support network, gambling seems to become a primary coping mechanism, which only perpetuates further distress. The result is often a never-ending cycle.

A Few Present-Day Dostoevskian Gamblers

In order to more specifically show the general usefulness of the Dostoevsky Effect for understanding modern gambling addiction, we now briefly look at present-day gamblers who are similar to Dostoevsky in the general story that led them to problem gambling. (Needless to say, none of these present-day problem gamblers is an author, much less an eminent author.)

To identify Dostoevsky-type gamblers, we searched the stories told by our third group of respondents—those who are problem gamblers but whose parents are not. We looked for people who had a stressful childhood due to poor parental relationships, experienced no social modelling of gambling during childhood, had stress in their adult life, and used poor coping behaviours to deal with stress. Of the sixty-one individuals in this group, five told stories that fit nicely with Dostoevsky's experiences.

Our first modern-day Dostoevsky is Rachel. As discussed in Chapter 5, her childhood was stressful because of the severity and unpredictability of the violence she suffered, including the time when her mother threatened to cut off her arm with a butcher knife.

Rachel's childhood was also complicated by her parents' high expectations, which echoes Dostoevsky's experiences with his father. Though stress was present in her childhood, social learning of gambling was not. Rachel's parents were strongly against most forms of gambling, though they purchased lottery tickets on occasion.

Like Dostoevsky, Rachel was only exposed to and began gambling as an adult. She started to gamble once she got to university, where she entered a poker tournament. She continues to play casino games, namely, poker and slot machines. For Rachel, gambling is both a cause of and way to cope with stress in her adult life. At present, she is involved in a poor relationship with her boyfriend, who is also a gambler, and they are experiencing money problems as a result of their combined gambling habits. When asked about her most negative gambling experience, she replied,

> It probably was with my boyfriend 'cause one time he lost two hundred dollars. It wasn't my money, but it was his money and he went down two hundred dollars 'cause he kept trying to punch out money, but I didn't want to. He said, "Oh come on, just go punch some more out with your debit," and I said, "No," and he said. "Well, we have to win it back," and we were arguing. So I eventually caved in, but we just lost it. So all together that day it was two hundred, two hundred and fifty dollars.

Her relationship with her boyfriend causes Rachel further stress because her parents disapprove of his gambling and marijuana dealing. Rachel copes with these various sources of stress through avoidance. She avoids confrontation with her boyfriend by caving to his requests. She avoids upsetting her parents by keeping her losses from them. Overall, she deals with stress by using gambling as a source of stress relief.

Niraj also tells a life story similar to Dostoevsky's. As a child, his immigration from India to Canada was a source of stress for the whole family. His parents fought frequently, though they made attempts to keep this from the children. Niraj felt severely limited as an immigrant child, because his family lacked money and his parents held views that were inconsistent with Canadian culture. As an adult, the stressful family circumstances continued for Niraj, who became his mother's caregiver and experienced a stressful first marriage. As with Dostoevsky, Niraj's gambling only began in adulthood. During his childhood, Niraj's parents strictly disapproved of gambling and he received little exposure to gambling while in India. Niraj described his entry into gambling as follows:

> As an adult, I started to gamble, I never gambled as a kid. And when I started to gamble, I think one of the reasons was I never really had any money as a kid and I figured, Oh wow, it says if you got a hundred dollars you can make a couple thousand dollars? Let's go, where is this place?

As with Dostoevsky, a childhood of strained finances and adulthood caretaking responsibilities made gambling attractive to Niraj because he saw it as an easy source of money. Gambling also served a coping function for Niraj, who would flee from his domestic problems:

> The more my ex-wife hated me gambling, the more I wanted to gamble. 'Cause she just totally used to piss me off and I would make excuses to gamble. The less she hated it, the less I wanted to gamble.

Niraj's coping behaviours created a vicious cycle—he would gamble to escape problems, which would create more problems since his wife disapproved of gambling. This vicious cycle allowed the gambling to continue.

Sharon also tells a story of stress and gambling. As a child, she suffered physical abuse at the hand of her father and sexual abuse from her piano instructor. Her home life was further complicated by her brother's long history of mental health issues and her father's insistence that the son was not his child. As an adult, Sharon continues to receive abusive treatment from her father. This problematic paternal relationship echoes Dostoevsky's experiences. Sharon suffers further adulthood stress in the form of financial difficulties, caretaking responsibilities for her brother, and physical health problems—all problems shared by Dostoevsky.

Despite not being exposed to gambling as a child, Sharon learned to use gambling as a way to alleviate her boredom as an adult. She first gambled during a medical leave from work. She continues to gamble out of boredom, recently retreating to the casino to avoid her apartment renovations. Sharon also gambles as a way to remedy her financial difficulties. She explains how she hopes her gambling will solve her money problems as follows:

> People are paying more than half their money on rent just to live half decently in a place that's safe. People think with the 6/49 or Pick-4, if they don't have one ticket, then they know they're going to lose. And that's depressing to them, whatever status they have at that point, but if they don't even have one it's like, how am I going to dig myself out of this without even one? But if you still have one you can limit. With slot machines it's hard to limit yourself if you haven't won already.

Sharon hopes that betting on the lottery will eventually get her the big win she needs to get herself out of financial trouble. However, because this is unlikely and because she also relies on payday loans, Sharon keeps worsening her financial situation.

So only five of the sixty-one present-day problem gamblers who did not inherit their problem shared stories that are consistent with Dostoevsky's. As indicated by Rachel, Niraj, and Sharon's accounts, these five individuals experienced stressful childhoods and adulthoods and had poor coping behaviours but did not experience social learning of gambling during their childhood. The majority of the problem gamblers in this category did experience social learning of gambling as children from family, friends, or relatives. The relative rarity of cases that lack childhood exposure to gambling suggests that Dostoevsky was an exception to the general pattern. It also suggests that important information about his childhood exposure to gambling may be lacking. Further research is needed to confirm Dostoevsky's lack of childhood exposure to gambling.

Conclusions

In sum, the life of Dostoevsky, like the lives of some of our study participants, provides insight into understanding the complex connections between childhood stress, its contribution to the development of poor coping strategies, and their impact on and interaction with adulthood stress. While none of these factors on their own are sufficient to explain gambling addiction, together, they provide us with insight into how problem gambling may develop among those whose parents were not themselves problem gamblers.

We discussed several troubling stressors as examples, all varying in cause and severity, but several proved most important for our study, namely, participants all subjectively found their lives stressful, both as children and adults, and they lived with continuous worries, in a state of uncertainty. Since Dostoevsky and study participants experienced varying combinations of stressors throughout their lives, they were each driven to gamble for a variety of different reasons. Although each individual's gambling is intensely personal, nonetheless it results from an array of combined stresses in both childhood and adulthood that are mediated by poor coping skills.

In many respects, Dostoevsky was different from present-day problem gamblers. Equally important, in his gambling addiction, he was also different from many of history's other great thinkers and artists. That said, as noted earlier in this book, Dostoevsky was not the only artist to be fascinated by gambling and casino life. Famous painter Edvard Munch, travelling to France in 1908 from his native Norway, was strongly affected by his visits to casinos. Indeed, he reported a strong physical reaction to the casino atmosphere, which he described as a kind of fever. And like Dostoevsky, Munch marvelled at the crassness and posturing on display, the preoccupation with winning and wealth. Recall that, in a brief note, Munch referred to the casino he visited as "an enchanted castle—where the devil is throwing a party—the gambling hell of Monaco" (quoted in Stang 1977, 86). Yet despite this fascination, or perhaps because of it, Munch only painted what he saw there—he didn't gamble. By contrast, Dostoevsky came, saw, and gambled.

The vast majority of extreme gamblers, so far as we can tell from other studies and from published accounts, have been ordinary people, mixed with a sprinkling of famous entertainers (like Ben Affleck), criminals (like Al Capone), sports figures (like Charles Barkley), and aristocrats (like the Duchess of Devonshire)—typically, people who inherit (or marry) fortunes or earn large amounts of money for a time.

Greatness in most enterprises requires daily dedication for decades—the famous ten thousand hours of continuous practice that author Malcolm Gladwell has famously written about. The interruptions of diligence caused by a gambling addiction may be compatible with an aristocratic lifestyle or the life of a celebrity, but seemingly not with the life of a productive—much less a great—artist, scientist, scholar, or everyday worker. So a particularly severe pathology must have driven him to this life-changing addiction. On this matter, Freud was likely correct in his diagnosis of an Oedipal rage toward an abusive father, though Freud's take on infantile sexuality seems very much off the mark.

While they seem to provide an unusual comparison, we continue to believe that Dostoevsky and the participants of our present-day study offer a series of lessons and insights into understanding problem gambling today.

13

Lessons from and for Dostoevsky

In this chapter we continue to bring together the two halves of the book and make good on the claim that something important can be learned from this comparison of Dostoevsky and present-day problem gamblers. In the brief pages that follow, we outline a few of the benefits of this comparison; no doubt, the careful reader will be able to imagine others.

From the standpoint of this book, Dostoevsky was not simply an author who gambled, he was also a gambler who wrote great books. He was that one gambler in a million who could translate his pain, shame, and anger into eloquent words and not merely gambling losses. Obviously, there are important differences between Dostoevsky and the present-day gamblers we studied in Toronto. On the whole, our present-day gamblers lack Dostoevsky's analytical intelligence, artistic daring, and literary eloquence: none had written an important novel or was likely to do so. None lives in the nineteenth century, let alone nineteenth-century Russia; so none has contributed to, or likely even considered, the important philosophical issues that animated intellectual life in nineteenth-century Russia.

Still, there are important similarities between Dostoevsky and the present-day gamblers we studied in Toronto. They were all fascinated by; animated by; and, for a time, preoccupied by gambling. For all of them, gambling was a central life activity at some point in their lives. This gambling affected their lives in important ways: it impoverished them, damaged relationships, and undermined the routines of normal everyday life.

Most important, all of them—Dostoevsky and the present-day gamblers—rationalized their engagement with gambling: they explained it, excused it, justified it, dreamed about it, talked about it, and made plans around it. Whether their denials of harm were simple and simple-minded, or complex and philosophical, they (almost) all presented gambling as a worthy activity. All of these gamblers felt enlivened by gambling; and since they gained something from gambling, they felt they owed it something—at least, praise and justification.

This being so, we learn something important about problem gambling by comparing the views of Dostoevsky with the views of other problem gamblers who happen to live in Toronto today. Such a comparison has as much value as a comparison of the views of Canadians and the French on the nature of the family, if our goal is to learn something important—something universal—about families; or a comparison of the views of ancient Romans and present-day Italians on the nature of politics, if our goal is to learn something important and universal about politics. So, what of importance have we learned from this book-long examination of Dostoevsky and present-day gamblers, and their similarities?

From the Dostoevsky case, we learn, first, that problem gambling—gambling addiction—is no respecter of talent and ability. Even the most intelligent, insightful, and dedicated people—even remarkable people like Fyodor Dostoevsky—can fall victim to a gambling problem. No doubt this has always been true, and it remains true today. Even intelligent people like Dostoevsky can embrace mistaken notions that they control chance or can devise systems to eliminate the risk of loss when gambling. This means that we researchers can never approach present-day problem gamblers as though they are deficient in important ways. Everyone is at risk of a gambling problem, under the right circumstances, and we have striven in this book to describe the "right circumstances."

Second, we see from the study of Dostoevsky's critics and interpreters that understandings of gambling vary widely. Indeed, understandings of gambling and problem gambling change over time, to reflect changing beliefs about addiction, mental health, good manners, courage, social standing, and so on. This means that we cannot fully understand gambling or problem gambling without understanding the social and cultural context in which it occurs. Studies of gambling need to be grounded in a specific historical and cultural setting, ideally a setting that is studied through direct observation.

Third, as Dostoevsky biographer Joseph Frank seems to suggest, people express their personal troubles through an interaction and struggle with dominant cultural issues of the day. Thus, there is a connection between personal turmoil and social turmoil—or personal troubles and public issues—that we need to consider, even in studies of present-day problem gamblers. For example, Dostoevsky viewed (and rationalized) gambling as a struggle of free will against external control—a topic of particular interest in nineteenth-century autocratic Russia. There is no evidence that present-day Canadian gamblers think in these terms. However, we know from earlier research (for example, Tepperman 2009) that they see their own gambling in terms that reflect the concerns of their ethno-cultural group and economic class. So, in studying gamblers, we must always ask people what they think they are doing when they gamble, even to excess. Their behaviour is motivated by their ideas and experiences, not merely by their passions.

Fourth, from the study of Dostoevsky we see the value of longitudinal (historical or biographical) research. Recall that problem gambling was only one of Dostoevsky's relatively short-lived adaptations to difficulty and turmoil. Others included political radicalism; religious devoutness; romance; and, of course, writing. So, it is important for researchers to remember that problem gambling is often only a part of people's lives. We must see it against the backdrop of a person's entire history. We cannot fully understand Dostoevsky's gambling without knowing about his earlier failed efforts at coping with stress and depression. For similar reasons, we would do well in our present-day research to seek longitudinal data on problem gambling, even if it is only retrospective information about the past. The mere snapshot of a person's life is rarely sufficient if we want to understand the meaning and current importance of an invasive behaviour like gambling.

Fifth, from the study of Dostoevsky, we see the research value of public, carefully crafted documents. In Dostoevsky's case, we have a treasure trove of fictional writings to help us see into Dostoevsky's mind—his loves, hates, fears, and aspirations. There is even a novel specifically devoted to gambling problem for us to study. Rarely in the study of addictions—whether gambling, alcoholism, or drug addiction—have we had such a clear, eloquent window into the mind of an addict. So, in studying the lives of present-day problem gamblers, we might solicit stories, blogs, or drawings to supply similar information about their thought patterns.

However, we also learn from the study of Dostoevsky's fiction that public, carefully crafted documents put forward a particular vision of the world and a particular image of the author. They are designed to highlight only certain features and obscure others. That means the researcher must always interpret these documents with care, whether the subject of study is a great nineteenth-century author or present-day blogger.

Sixth, and along similar lines, from studying Dostoevsky we learn the importance of metaphorical communication. All artists communicate their ideas in this roundabout way, in a sense hiding the truth "in plain view" behind ideas, plot lines, and characters that may (or may not) correspond directly to their own ideas, lives, and personalities. There is no doubt that we learn a great deal about Dostoevsky from his novels; it is no accident that he wrote *Crime and Punishment*, not *Sleepless in Seattle*. He was not a light-hearted, humorous, or superficial person, given what we know of him from novels and biographic sources.

Yet we cannot assume that everything in Dostoevsky's novels is a direct expression of his own feelings and ideas; for example, that the novel *The Idiot* directly reproduces Dostoevsky's own experience as an epileptic. One reason people write fiction is so they can freely explore personal events and ideas without revealing deep personal secrets. So, whenever researchers examine accounts of a life—whether real or fictional—they need to look for signs of metaphor and allusion. Everyone uses these techniques of expression, even in everyday conversation, though few people use them as often or artfully as great novelists like Dostoevsky.

Now, let's consider benefits flowing in the other direction. From our study of present-day gamblers, we learn the following that can be usefully applied to understanding Dostoevsky. First and most important, we have learned there is rarely a gambling problem without childhood trauma in the background. Therefore, we need to know more about Dostoevsky's childhood than we do today—though at this remove we may never know as much as we need to. Likely, Freud was on the right track when he looked for signs of childhood trauma in Dostoevsky's life and writing. However, his analysis was flawed by a single-minded focus on infantile sexuality and on the belief that everything had symbolic significance; for example, that Dostoevsky's epileptic attacks were signs of guilt, not of physiological malfunctioning.

Whether in the past or the present day, the Oedipal conflict is not the only kind of childhood trauma that may play a part in problem gambling, contrary to Freud's analysis. Our data have shown a wide variety of abuses and neglects producing the same result in present-day problem gamblers. Likely, they played a part in Dostoevsky's problem gambling as well.

Though the truth about personal pathology is obscured, sometimes it is in plain sight.

Second, we learn from present-day gamblers that there is rarely a gambling problem without some childhood exposure to gambling. This means that, to understand Dostoevsky's addiction fully, we need to know much more about gambling in Dostoevsky's childhood environment—in his home, school, and community—than we do now. This should send us back to the original sources for more information about his father's gambling experience, for example. It is hard to believe that Dr. Dostoevsky—a member of the nineteenth-century Russian gentry and former military man— had no experience of, or interest in, gambling. The evidence we collected from present-day problem gamblers has intensified this conviction, not laid it to rest. There may be many routes to problem gambling, but few of them include a complete absence of gambling experience.

Third, since early and frequent exposure to gambling is apparently a common part of a gambling problem, people who become problem gamblers without this childhood exposure may be far more troubled psychologically than other problem gamblers. To state this idea in other words, it is likely that problem gambling signals far more personal pathology when local opportunity and acceptability are lacking—when, for example, a gambler has to travel thousands of miles to lose all his money, as Dostoevsky did repeatedly. Such diligence—such devotion to causing a personal tragedy—suggests the existence of a pathology and helps to explain why Freud was convinced that Dostoevsky was deeply neurotic. While many today can travel to Vegas to do the same, this is a far cry from the average person who "falls into" problem gambling through convenient habituation—for example, present-day people who spend a little too much on bingo games or lottery tickets they can acquire just around the corner or online gambling done in the privacy and comfort of their own homes.

Fourth, from our study of present-day gamblers, we learn the value of a cross-sectional survey sample. Though lacking the advantages of a longitudinal study, the sample survey has its own merits. For example, it sets a benchmark for "normality," shows the many ways people cope with stresses to avoid gambling, and examines the extent of co-morbidity among people with a gambling problem. Against this backdrop of "average people" and "average addicts," we are better able to assess the pathology of individual addicts like Dostoevsky. We are also better able to see the typical "career pattern" of a gambling problem, which also helps us see deviations from that pattern. In short, the sample survey washes out unique features to reveal the major contours of similarity among problem gamblers. That is why a sample survey provides certain advantages over case studies, such as Freud depended on for information about gambling.

By these standards, Dostoevsky was likely an odd gambler, even in his own time. He did not gamble for honour, though he came from a middle-class family and was highly educated. He gambled for money, though he never succeeded in winning much or keeping what he won. He (apparently) came to gambling later in his life and left it after about a decade, embracing it briefly and explosively as he had embraced his other passions in life. Like the characters in his novels, and unlike most people in real life, Dostoevsky did nothing in moderation. And despite his belief in "a gambling system," he was chaotic and unsystematic in his gambling as in other activities.

In only one important respect was Dostoevsky like many of the problem gamblers we see today: he required and relied on a loving, long-suffering wife to settle him down, so he could escape his gambling problem and enjoy domestic peace.

Fifth, from our survey of present-day gamblers, we see the value of relatively spontaneous, private communications—for example, the information gained in face-to-face interviews. People are likely to reveal things in interviews that they are less likely to reveal in more structured formal communication, such as found in books or stories. So, we can often learn a lot from personal letters, emails, and conversations that we cannot learn in any other way—certainly not from highly polished novels. This suggests that, in studying the life of Dostoevsky for clues to his gambling problem, we need to rely less on his novels and more on other sources of information, such as reported conversations and personal written correspondence. These casual communications are of less literary interest precisely because they are less polished and more casual. However, as we see in the study of present-day gamblers, they give us an understanding of everyday life that is hard to match in even the best novels.

Sixth, we learn from the Toronto study that problem gambling follows a pattern in which, typically, adult stresses awaken childhood traumas, calling for strong coping strategies. The childhood traumas may come in many forms, as we have seen; likewise, the adult stresses can come in many forms, over an extended period. Some resilient personalities are able to endure these continuing stresses for much longer than others. In the end, however, healthy functioning comes down to healthy coping strategies. People who cope effectively with their adult stresses are best able to resist various kinds of addiction, including gambling addiction. When their strategies and their adaptations to stress are exhausted, they are then most likely to fall into problem gambling.

Why gambling? Likely, this addiction is "selected" because it is available and (mistakenly) promises relief from financial worries. Thus, to judge from information about present-day problem gamblers, Dostoevsky's fall into problem gambling was far from unusual, let alone unique, given his childhood trauma, adult stresses, and faulty coping strategies.

Seventh, we have seen in the Toronto study no evidence that problem gamblers have a desire to lose money and/or punish themselves. This is important because it contradicts the major conclusion, or assumption, of psychoanalytic analysis—including Freud's analysis of Dostoevsky. It is important to highlight this, because Freud offered the first and best-known analysis of Dostoevsky's gambling; so our divergent interpretation needs to address it. Second, Freud's interpretation—that addictions are purposeful self-punishments—lies at the root of all psychoanalytic understanding of neurotic repetitions, addictions or otherwise. Thus, our results take issue with a central tenet of psychoanalytic therapy, as well as Freud's specific interpretation of Dostoevsky's gambling.

As a result we believe that on its own cognitive therapy would not likely work well with someone like Dostoevsky—indeed, work well with anyone with a long history of childhood trauma, adult stresses, and faulty coping. Cognitive therapy might work for a while to help certain kinds of problem gamblers, to provide a temporary coping strategy. But the case of Dostoevsky suggests that, in time, this—like other coping strategies—would fail and need replacement. It is not our intention, in this book, to propose a therapeutic strategy based on our findings, however.

Our most important finding in this study is the similarity of the problem gambling histories of Dostoevsky and present-day Canadians. In both instances, we see clear evidence of what we might call a negative affect pathway. In short, childhood trauma tends to produce negative affect—anxiety and depression—throughout a person's life, forcing her or him to seek relief through coping strategies often learned in early life. When this fails to work, the person takes to gambling or another stress-masking adaptation. Without this childhood predisposition to stress, and without ineffective coping strategies dating from childhood, a person is extremely unlikely to resort to problem gambling—however much he or she might need money.

This is why we have focused so much attention on childhood traumas such as abuse, neglect, and parentification and also why we have focused on faulty coping strategies. As we have seen, some learned strategies are particularly unhelpful; in this category, we have focused attention on the tendency to avoid confronting problems, so-called avoidant strategies. These strategies are learned in early life, as we saw from the many quotes from participants who ran away from their problems by, for example, going out with their friends or hiding in their rooms—anything to simply escape the home environment they found stressful (before they had any involvement with gambling). These strategies perpetuate or intensify conditions that produce depression and anxiety. In contrast, approach-oriented coping strategies that use problem solving rather than problem avoiding offer protection against depressive symptoms.

Gambling, as we have seen, is just one of many avoidant coping strategies. As we have seen, some people fall into it because it is available or it offers false hope of financial betterment or of social interaction, whatever the case may be. If they were exposed to gambling in childhood, they have all the more reason to choose gambling as a coping strategy.

This formula is particularly helpful for understanding Dostoevsky, because gambling was just one of many failed efforts to deal with his constant feelings of stress, anxiety, and depression. In a nutshell, both Dostoevsky and our Toronto sample taught us to look, in each case, at the precipitating roles played by the childhood predisposition to experience stress, and the coping strategies learned in youth.

This realization, in turn, leads us to frame a new theory of problem gambling that we might call Diversion Theory. According to this Diversion Theory, the probability that someone will develop a gambling problem is a joint function of two things. First, there is the absolute intensity of that person's need for diversion from feelings of anxiety and depression—which, as we have seen, is determined by a combination of childhood traumas, adult stresses, and ineffective coping strategies. These three things, taken together, constitute what we have called the Dostoevsky Effect. Second, there is the relative attractiveness and availability of pleasurable diversions. Any pleasant activity can serve as a temporary diversion from anxiety and depression, but it needs to be endlessly repeated to have its continued effect, so it can become addictive.

We cannot claim ownership of this theory: it seems that Blaise Pascal, seventeenth-century philosopher and mathematician, may have come to it sooner. Meyers (2001) reminds us that

> Blaise Pascal (1623–1662) suggested, in his *Thoughts*, that faith was a wager about the existence of god and the immortality of the soul that you denied at your own risk. Bettina L. Knapp, in *Gambling, Game, and Psyche . . .* quotes Pascal that "gambling" itself is the "diversion," not necessarily driven solely by the outcome; hence the appeal of gambling to self-destructive individuals . . . who were driven by the illusory victory. (353)

Closer to the time of Dostoevsky's life, Ian Helfant (2003) quotes critic I.I. Panaev as saying that "All select, progressive men, when they are stricken with suffering, experience a darkening of heart—and [critic T.M.] Granovskii, perhaps , more than most. . . . He sought diversion, distraction from various sorts of unpleasantness—in cards." Helfant continues, "According to this view, it is precisely the most sensitive and exceptional individuals who are likely to fall into the grip of this addiction" (241).

The first set of factors in this process of diversion—the Dostoevsky Effect factors in our theory—incorporates variables that are common to all problem gamblers: variables that precipitate gambling regardless of whether the gambler had a gambling parent. The second set of factors includes variables that intensify the likelihood of becoming a problem gambler through social learning and peer influence.

In Dostoevsky's case, gambling was particularly attractive for a time (though not particularly available) because he had already exhausted other potential diversions (including politics, religion, and romance), rendering them ineffective. Adding to gambling's attractiveness was the slim possibility it held out that he might solve his financial problems while managing to ignore his anxieties and feelings of guilt. In the end, gambling failed to offer him the diversion he needed and failed to solve his problems. So, he gave it up.

If this theory is valid, it suggests that there are two ways to deal with problem gambling in our society: first, to limit the availability and attractiveness of gambling as a diversion from personal troubles and, second, to monitor family life more carefully, to reduce the incidence and duration of traumatizing childhood experiences, or to provide support when it occurs. Particularly important is monitoring children in the formative years, as this is when the stage is set for problems in adulthood. We will discuss each of these issues in the chapter that follows.

14

Implications of This Research for Gambling Policy and Childrearing

While we do not agree with Freud's interpretation of Dostoevsky's gambling problem, we do agree that childhood is a good place to begin to try to understand it.

We learned from present-day gamblers that there is rarely a gambling problem without some childhood exposure to gambling—though this has not been confirmed in the case of Dostoevsky. More importantly, we learned that there is rarely a gambling problem without childhood trauma in the background—this was true for Dostoevsky. From this comparison and juxtaposition was born our notion of the Dostoevsky Effect.

The Dostoevsky Effect begins in childhood, with stressful events setting the stage for poor mental health and stunted coping skills. A range of life stresses in adulthood challenge the individual's well-being, forcing the person to call upon (poor) coping strategies he or she acquired in childhood. Because these coping strategies are stunted and maladaptive, the individual often ends up in a cycle of using failed coping strategies to relieve negative affect.

Our model (like the models of Hirschi [1967] and Blaszczynski and Nower [2002], discussed in Appendix 1) suggests that life experience and environment contribute to the development of gambling problems. Whatever effect genes or psychoses may have on addiction, we feel that the social factors to which individuals are exposed are responsible for activating those vulnerabilities. As such, we stand by the idea that problem gamblers are not born, but made.

This book has revealed a range of non-inherited social and environmental factors that interact throughout one's life to induce problem gambling. This being the case, problem gambling can be tackled as a social issue and not merely a psychological or psychiatric one. What complicates matters, however, is our finding that "average" people—people who neither had parents who were problem gamblers, nor themselves are problem gamblers as adults—had childhoods and adult lives that are not very different from the lives of problem gamblers.

The childhoods of non-problem gamblers were by no means stress-free. Rather, they were often filled with various combinations and levels of childhood stress, learning of gambling, and adulthood stress; most simply coped differently. These findings reminded us that the "average" person is not terribly different from a problem gambler, and that anyone is at risk of becoming a problem gambler. It underscored the point that the factors contributing to problem gambling are complex and sensitive, often making it difficult to determine why one person becomes a problem gambler and another does not.

Becoming a problem gambler seems to be a matter of the number and degree of severity of the problems families experienced, and the number and type of protective factors that surround them, and so assist them in developing effective coping strategies. We speculated that a slight increase in the number and severity of problems, when unaccompanied by support, or coupled with ineffective coping strategies, may be enough to plunge some people into a gambling problem. However, a slight reduction in number and degree of problems, coupled with support and more effective coping strategies may be enough to keep them safe from addiction.

Perhaps most importantly, we noted that for each individual in the non-problem gambling group, at least one protective factor has prevented them from becoming a problem gambler. This gives us much to consider in terms of recommendations and possible steps forward.

The good news is that our findings confirm that children are not born predestined to live the life of a problem gambler. Rather, circumstances and events that take place throughout their lives shape them into the adults they become, and influence the habits they develop. The bad news is that our model suggests that problem gambling is fed by a number of forces, including: (1) childhood trauma, (2) living in a positive gambling culture, (3) having access to gambling establishments, (4) social learning of gambling, (5) having role models who gamble, (6) developing poor coping strategies, and (7) being exposed to adult stresses. Though some of these are easier to tackle than others, we believe that addressing each of these, to some degree, should help reduce the odds of someone becoming a problem gambler.

Adult stressors, too often a "normal" part of adult life in the present day, awaken childhood traumas, which call for strong coping strategies. As we discussed in detail throughout the book, childhood traumas come in many forms, but these may be limited through increased attention—through research and policy—to proper child development and improved social contexts.

Childhood Trauma

We found that present-day problem gamblers were disproportionately likely to have experienced parentification, neglect, financial instabilities, or emotional or physical abuse in their families while growing up. A great deal of this trauma was caused by parental addictions, parental un(der) employment, and other stressors in the lives of adults in the household. To assist in breaking the cycle of poverty, abuse, and neglect, some govern-ments, as in the case of Quebec, have turned to providing families with more protection through stronger, universal family policies, which include providing such services as low-fee child care.

Low-fee child care removes very young children from problem-plagued households, and provides them—even if only temporarily—with exposure to developmentally appropriate spaces and activities. Parents, too, benefit from the opportunity to seek paid employment or schooling. It goes with-out saying that, on top of this, addicted or abusive parents need access to counselling and other support programs to deal with their behaviour.

While it is extremely difficult to monitor negative family settings and so prevent childhood trauma, we know from interviews with our non-problem gambling group that any number of protective factors help to moderate the effect of trauma in a child's life. Children need access to people and activities that take them out of unhappy homes, into safe spaces and places where they can communicate freely, learn, and grow. They may then be able to model themselves after adults who are positive and supportive.

Social Learning of Gambling and Positive and Negative Role Models

Growing up with role models who gambled compulsively influenced some individuals in our study to develop the same gambling habits. Parents who gambled "modelled" the activity for their children, teaching them that gambling is a fun activity that can lead to "easy money" and can be used to manage stress. Children learn that gambling is an acceptable activity, and often carry this belief with them into adulthood.

We also found that many parents or guardians failed to set down rules for their children about acceptable gambling practices, leaving children to experiment with and form their own opinions about gambling. But even in cases where one parent strongly opposed and maybe even prohibited gambling, the influence of the other, compulsive gambling parent tended to be strong. Though in some cases, it clearly helped to have one parent disapprove of the behaviour.

In fact, we found that in some cases, children who identified more with a non-gambling parent, and who blamed the problem gambling parent for the difficulties the family was experiencing, did not become problem gamblers as adults.

We found that role models played an important part in the lives of our participants by contributing to the opinions they developed about the acceptability and attractiveness of gambling. As such, these role models either influenced our participants to gamble, or deterred them from doing so. If role models were gamblers themselves, the people in our study who looked up to them often gambled as well. These role models made gambling seem acceptable, available, and attractive. Exposure to gambling within the family was particularly powerful, because it often caused participants to associate the activity with bonding and quality time spent with loved ones.

That said, non-gambling role models who were family members had the greatest opportunity to help participants build trust, discover new skills and ideas, and gain confidence. Since having a non-gambling role model can serve as a protective factor for children, preventing them from developing a gambling problem as adults, it seems only logical to suggest that young people be given options and opportunities to interact with positive role models inside and outside their families.

When parents are unable or unwilling to be positive role models, other family members should be given the opportunity to fill this role. Reaching out to opportunities outside the home will surely help some young people avoid succumbing to the inducements to gamble that were emanating from their own homes, and we suggest that the community, with generously funded social programs, is a good place for some of them to turn.

A person's level of community involvement—whether as a child, adolescent, or adult—affects her or his vulnerability to problematic gambling. Community involvement can take many forms, including participation in conventional activities, such as community groups or sports teams. According to Hirschi's theory of social control (1967) involvement in these kinds of activities keeps people's time occupied, while also allowing them to form strong social bonds with others. Further, in a community setting, conventional social behaviours are upheld and promoted. Finally, community involvement allows children to form strong social bonds with positive role models, such as coaches, teachers, mentors, and teammates.

These social ties outside of the family are important because they can compensate for poor influences at home and/or the lack of parental attachment these children often face. This further supports our idea that people are not born problem gamblers. Children with parents with gambling problems may be able to avoid transmission, at least in part, through their participation in recreational activities and through community involvement.

Through interaction with non-gambling peers and positive role models, young people come to understand that in order to thrive and prosper they must conform to acceptable social behaviours, which do not include problem gambling. Active members of a community interact closely and frequently with each other. This, in turn, allows them to discourage certain behaviours by way of gossip, exclusion, or merely disapproving glances. Those individuals with strong social ties, including young people, are typically reluctant to sacrifice these bonds in order to engage in activities like gambling, if it is disapproved of. Having leisure activities available to them leaves young people with less time to spend on gambling and more time to do other things, if and when other activities are available to them.

We suggest that supporting the development of community-based programs may help some avoid gambling and provide opportunities to interact and learn from positive peer and adult role models. Positive peer groups could work together with positive role models, including non-gambling parents, siblings, or relatives, all of which have the potential to support and guide people away from gambling activities.

Living in a Gambling Culture and Having Access to Gambling Establishments

Gambling will likely only grow in popularity, given that it yields huge profits for governments and offers false hope of financial betterment, social interaction, entertainment, escape, and so forth for individuals with and without gambling addictions. Remember Diversion Theory—according to this theory, the probability that someone will develop a gambling problem is a joint function of (a) the absolute intensity of that person's need for diversion from feelings of anxiety and depression and (b) the relative attractiveness and availability of pleasurable, effective diversions.

In Canada, we are living in, and children are growing up in, a gambling culture. When a society promotes gambling activities, as ours does, through the media and by providing opportunities to gamble, those who live in that society are put at a higher risk of developing a gambling problem. While it will be very difficult to curb governments' promotion of gambling, efforts should be made to curb the relative attractiveness and availability of gambling.

It is especially important to limit the availability and attractiveness of gambling as a diversion from personal troubles. It will be difficult, however, to limit young people's access to gambling without making it mysterious and desirable. This would require limiting the advertising of various types of gambling, but also changing young peoples' ideas and value system surrounding gambling.

Our study found that people who were raised in societies, subcultures, and families where gambling was considered immoral or problematic often maintained those beliefs and never gambled, even when they moved to areas where gambling was acceptable and accessible. These individuals were more likely to conform to certain behaviours—refraining from gambling—if they believed in the social norms surrounding these behaviours. As noted in Appendix 1, research done by Jessor and Jessor (1973) found that teenagers' engagement with gambling is largely affected by how they perceive attitudes toward the behaviour, and by the responses of others to their participation in gambling.

When children or teenagers developed positive associations with gambling, they are more likely to gamble recreationally or problematically. But when they form negative associations with the activity, they are less likely to gamble. Since children spend a large part of their day in school, schools may be places to turn to begin to make changes in young people's value systems—through curriculum, extracurricular activities, and positive role models. Schools may also be helpful in helping to develop strong and positive coping strategies.

Coping Strategies

We saw from our findings that poor coping strategies are learned early in life. We included many quotes of participants who would run away from their problems to escape a home environment they found stressful. Because they were forced into stressful situations for which they were not developmentally ready, their strategies were ineffective and insufficient. These strategies are avoidant and thus ineffective. In contrast, young people can and should be taught, at home, in community groups, and in school, that approach-oriented coping strategies that include problem solving rather than avoidance are protective against depressive symptoms and the development of addictions.

Through school, after-school programs, and community participation, we can help children develop effective coping strategies and help them gain access to positive role models if they don't have access to them at home. Our study showed that many of the respondents who had a gambling problem also experienced low parental attachment as children. Some spoke about having emotionally absent parents, or a parent who was not around much in their childhood.

As a society we will do well to provide substitutes to absent parents though educational, recreational, and other leisure activities that put young people in contact with people and things that motivate them to work hard and live well—and perhaps avoid the stressors in childhood that lead to poor coping and adult addictions.

In this book, we wanted to better understand the "inheritance" of problem gambling and to unravel some of the mechanisms that pass the problem down from one generation to the next. Tracing through the life of Dostoevsky and through a series of interviews with modern-day study participants, we found that inclinations toward problem gambling pass from parent to child through parental modelling and encouragement and through the creation of a family lifestyle that is gambling-friendly. We identified a range of non-inherited social and environmental factors that interact throughout one's life to induce problem gambling. We end by highlighting the point that gamblers are not born but made, and as such can be "unmade" through exposure to better and different social influences and environments.

– Appendix 1 –

The Theoretical Framework

In addition to the literature discussed in the text, earlier researchers have developed theories that also contribute to our understanding of how and why people develop gambling problems. These theories help to clarify how our three key variables—childhood learning, childhood trauma, and adulthood stress—contribute to problem gambling. One such theory is Travis Hirschi's (1967) theory of social control, which states that, generally, there are two types of control that influence behaviours: informal and formal control. Formal controls are those rooted in the legal system, while informal controls are those exercised by social groups such as family and friends. These relationships are the social bonds that prevent people from engaging in delinquent behaviour, or even merely in socially undesirable behaviour (such as reckless, irresponsible gambling).

Hirschi also discusses why people conform to or deviate from social norms, using four variables: attachment, commitment, involvement, and belief. Attachment refers to the extent to which a person is attached to others; primary attachments would include a person's parents, for example, closely followed by friends, teachers and other people within their community. This variable is at work for gambling, since low parental attachment and minimal participation in the child's day-to-day upbringing is linked to an increased risk for gambling (Kalischuk et al. 2006). This is supported by our research, as many study participants with a gambling problem also experienced low parental attachment as children and adults. On the extreme end of the spectrum, participants spoke about having an emotionally absent parent, or a parent who was simply not around much in their childhood.

In many cases, they also reported experiencing instances of trauma in their childhood, which is also associated with low family cohesion and parental detachment. In addition, a majority of participants failed to establish intimate relationships in adulthood, or had adult relationships fail because of gambling or other problems. Because so many problem gambling participants experienced trauma and isolation, we can also conclude that these life experiences contribute to the development of a gambling problem.

A person's level of community involvement also affects his or her vulnerability to problem gambling. This variable refers to people's participation in conventional activities in society, such as community groups or sports teams. According to Hirschi's theory of social control, involvement in these kinds of activities keeps people's time occupied, while also allowing them to form strong social bonds with other people. In a community setting, conventional social behaviours are upheld and promoted.

Through socialization with non-gambling peers and positive role models, people come to understand that in order to stay afloat, they must conform to acceptable social behaviours, which do not include problem gambling. This is related to the idea of informal social control that we mentioned previously. Members of the community interact closely and often with each other, which allows them to discourage certain behaviours by way of gossip, exclusion, or merely disapproving glances. Those people with strong social ties are typically reluctant to sacrifice these bonds in order to engage in another activity, in this case, gambling. So while community involvement can prevent problem gambling by occupying people's time, leaving less for them to spend in the casino, it can also discourage participation in gambling by threatening a kind of social punishment for engaging in this undesirable activity.

When we discuss parentification in further detail below, it will become evident that many of the gamblers we spoke with did not have time to participate in these kinds of activities during their childhood. Instead, they spent much of their childhood caring for their parents, raising their siblings, or doing extra work around the house. While the trauma and stress of parentification itself can contribute to a gambling problem, the lack of social involvement these children endured because of their additional responsibilities increased the risk.

In contrast to these children who were unable to participate in conventional activities, we interviewed several people who were highly involved in their communities throughout their childhoods. In accordance with our previous description of Hirschi's theory of social control, we found that these people who had participated in community activities as children were the ones who had escaped "inheriting" their parent's gambling problems. As we briefly mentioned above, these kinds of recreational activities often serve as a buffer in the transmission of gambling from parent to child because they offer opportunities for positive socialization and also occupy the child's time with productive activities, instead of maladaptive ones like gambling.

Community involvement also allows children to form strong social bonds with positive role models, such as coaches, teachers, mentors, and teammates. These social ties outside of the family are important because they can compensate for poor influences at home or the lack of parental attachment these children often faced. This further supports our theory that people are not born problem gamblers. These people, who should have been genetically predisposed to problem gambling behaviour, did not "inherit" their parent's addiction, as they supposedly should have; rather, they were able to avoid this transmission, at least in part because of their participation in recreational and community activities.

A person's value system is yet another variable that influences the likelihood of developing a gambling problem. The people who are closest to a person influence the opinions that make up their value or belief systems. In order for these opinions to be sustained, they must be constantly reinforced. These value systems and the opinions that they are composed of are significant because they inform the decisions people make and the way they act—in this case, their decision to participate in potentially harmful gambling, or to refrain from doing so. This was reflected in our findings: people who were raised in societies where gambling was illegal or considered immoral often maintained those beliefs and never gambled, even when they moved to areas where gambling was acceptable and accessible. These people were more likely to conform to certain behaviours (specifically, refraining from gambling) if they believed in the social norms surrounding these behaviours.

This kind of conformity to the values, beliefs, and behaviours prescribed by society is particularly common among adolescents. According to research done by Jessor and Jessor (1973), teenagers' engagement with gambling is largely affected by how they perceive attitudes toward the behaviour, and by the responses of others to their participation in gambling. Parents and guardians are among the most important people in this respect, as they have a significant effect on the personal opinions that their children develop toward gambling. These opinions are important because they inform the way these teenagers will act with regards to gambling. When children or teenagers develop positive associations with gambling, they are more likely to gamble recreationally or addictively. But when they form negative associations with the activity, they are less likely to gamble.

Among participants, we found that these positive or negative associations were largely formed through observing the attitude of their parents toward gambling, or their participation in gambling. Parents who gambled "modelled" the activity for their children, teaching them essentially that gambling is a fun activity that can lead to "easy money," and that it can be used to manage stress. Through this kind of social modelling, participants learned that gambling is an acceptable activity, and they carried this belief with them into adulthood. For these people, gambling was a normal part of their childhood, so it makes sense that they consider it to be an acceptable activity in their adulthood.

However, many of the people we interviewed did not grow up with two gambling parents; many only had a mother or a father who was a compulsive gambler, while the other parent did not gamble, and might have even strongly opposed the behaviour. In these situations, children and teenagers receive mixed messages about gambling, so what is important is what they take away from the experience and the opinions they form about gambling as a result. The development of these opinions is not an entirely straightforward process though; many parents or guardians fail to set down rules for their children about acceptable gambling practices, leaving children to experiment with and form their own opinions about gambling. But even in cases where one parent strongly opposed and even prohibited gambling, the influence of the other problem gambling parent tended to be stronger. In our study, we found that teenagers responded to the social modelling of their gambling parent positively and developed a gambling problem of their own later in life. Thus for many participants, the disapproval of one parent who did not condone gambling was often not enough to outweigh the example the other addicted parent was setting.

Though most participants told a similar story, having a non-problem gambling parent did prevent some children from becoming problem gamblers themselves. Children who identified more with the non-gambling parent blamed the problem gambling parent for the difficulties the family was experiencing. They also sympathized with the non-gambling parent, and did not become problem gamblers as adults. So sometimes, children respond more positively to the social modelling of the non-problem gambling parent, which acts as protection against problem gambling transmission. Parents were not the only role models who condoned gambling behaviours through their own participation; friends also influenced some participants to take up gambling, even if these participants came from non-gambling families.

When gambling becomes a normalized activity among the friends and family of a person, it can become difficult to avoid gambling and also difficult to assert a personal conviction that gambling is an unhealthy behaviour. One study participant, Greg, illustrated this theory. He did not learn gambling as a child because there were very few gambling establishments in Russia while he was growing up. "I didn't gamble [in casinos] at all because in Russia at this time there was no casino. There was no casinos, no prostitution. It was communist regime. In this case there was no problems with gamblers. Gamblers came with capitalism." However, upon coming to Canada, he became friends with an immigrant from Poland, and together they explored Canada's casinos. "I think we went to the Niagara Falls, and he was like, 'Let's go to the casinos here and we will have good luck,' and he showed me how to play. Showing me the tables and everything else." Regardless of the fact that Greg understood gambling as a negative behaviour—a problem of capitalism—a combination of easily accessible gambling venues and a friend who was involved in the activity managed to draw Greg into the world of problem gambling.

These examples of parents and friends modelling gambling behaviours, in contrast with our discussion of societies that condemn gambling, demonstrate that value or belief systems were highly influential in driving some participants to gamble. When a society promotes gambling through the media and by providing opportunities to gamble, the citizens who live within that society are put at a higher risk of developing an addiction. The opposite is true for members of those societies that condemn gambling; these kinds of societies contribute to instilling anti-gambling beliefs in their citizens, which in turn promote non-gambling behaviours among these people. Thus the participants in our study have learned their opinions about gambling from friends, family, and the overriding opinions of their society in general; these beliefs are not instincts they are born with, but ones that their individual life experiences have conditioned.

Finally, Hirschi's "rational component in conformity" also influences whether people decide to engage in or refrain from gambling. This phrase describes people's tendency to consider the positive and negative outcomes of participating in a certain activity or behaving in a certain way. A person's fear of breaking the law, for example, would (most often) discourage him or her from doing anything illegal, as he or she would rationalize that by conforming to the rules the law dictates, she or he would be able to avoid punishment. This theory is applicable to gambling because when people think about participating in gambling, they must take into account the risks and negative outcomes that could potentially arise.

So while factors such as quick, easy money and exhilarating entertainment might make people want to gamble, the potential to lose vast sums of money might discourage them from going ahead and doing it. Culture is an important factor we must discuss in relation to this theory, as different cultures propagate different beliefs and opinions regarding gambling. Some societies can discourage gambling either by creating laws that prohibit it, or simply by deeming these activities dangerous and disagreeable. In such a culture, people would be more likely to refrain from gambling because it would be to their personal advantage to do so; they would avoid either legal punishment, or stigmatization, or both by avoiding gambling.

On the other hand, we interviewed a number of people who came from cultures that integrated gambling as part of national activities. This would have the opposite effect, as this kind of promotion of gambling labels the activity as socially acceptable and even desirable, and encourages people to gamble as a result.

Many participants who struggled with gambling problems seemed to only take into consideration what they thought they could gain from gambling, while they ignored what they had at stake. The idea of easy money was a temptation too strong to pass up for some participants; they didn't seem to think about gambling's potential disastrous effects, which would cause people to avoid these activities. These people saw their gambling behaviour as harmless fun, a way to pass the time, or a thrilling source of entertainment.

Other people we spoke with seemed to be deluded as to how much money they were losing to their addiction; many participated in certain types of gambling that do not require a lot of money to be put down at once, such as buying lottery tickets. The low cost may be what led them to downplay the consequences of their gambling behaviours, because they do not keep track of the amount of tickets they buy, and they therefore lose sight of the amount of money they have wasted. These types of people, who only saw positive effects from their gambling or downplayed the negative effects, continued to gamble. The illusion of having less to lose and more to gain may be what pushes these people to continue gambling.

On the other hand, the participants who had managed to overcome their gambling problems were the ones who had recognized how their gambling was becoming out of control and creating problems. Thus for some, the potential benefits of gambling outweigh the negative consequences, while for others, the opposite is true. According to the "rational component in conformity" (Hirschi 1967), this means that some participants gamble compulsively because they feel that they can benefit more from gambling than they could from abstaining from the activity.

To move on from Hirschi's work, consider a 2002 article by Blaszczynski and Nower that describes a conceptual model of gambling with three different subgroups of problem gamblers. It also highlights the different pathways that can lead to problem gambling. Blaszczynski and Nower's model is relevant to our study because it recognizes the diverse experiences and backgrounds that many problem gamblers come from. Rather than claiming that one common paradigm explains all cases of problem gambling, they have combined many models, such as social learning and biology. This approach helps to provide a more "holistic" understanding and representation of problem gambling because it acknowledges differences between individual problem gamblers, and thus recognizes that different people are driven to gamble for different reasons.

Most of the problem gamblers we interviewed fit into the category Blaszczynski and Nower labelled "pathway 2" gamblers, containing emotionally vulnerable problem gamblers. These people typically came from negative family backgrounds and consequently suffered emotionally during their developmental years. Factors such as parentification, neglect, financial instabilities, or emotional or physical abuse contributed to these kinds of negative family settings, and were commonly reported by participants. Because these people had such negative childhoods, they developed poor coping skills or problem solving strategies to deal with their problems, such as avoiding their problems altogether, or trying to "escape" from them.

These strategies are carried into their adult years, and these people try to use them to cope with the anxiety and depression they experience, likely resulting from the trauma they experienced as children. Their unhealthy gambling, for example, can be viewed as a means of emotional escape, allowing them to forget about their stressors and emotional burdens as they are distracted by this exhilarating activity. Similarly, the gamblers who fit within this category are more inclined to have co-occurring problems, such as alcohol or drug dependencies, as this substance use and abuse would serve as a way to cope with their overwhelming emotions.

So even though all of these findings were most common in those people who had problem gambling parents, we do not believe that their own gambling problems were products of genetic transmissions. Rather, it seems evident from the overwhelming number participants who experienced the childhood and adult problems we have discussed here that these social factors were vital in the development of their gambling behaviour. These experiences made them more emotionally vulnerable, and unable to cope with their pain in constructive, positive ways. As a result, these people are driven to gamble in an effort to cope with the problems that put them in this emotionally vulnerable state.

Our model, in combination with the theories of Hirschi, and Blaszczynski and Nower, asserts that life experiences and environmental influences shape the development of gambling problems. Whatever effect genes may have on addiction, we feel that the social factors to which people are exposed are responsible for activating those vulnerabilities. As such, we stand by the theory that problem gamblers are not born, they are made.

– Appendix 2 –

How We Did This Study

In order to test our model of the development process, we used two sources of data. The main source was two hundred in-depth interviews with residents of Toronto, Ontario. The second and supplemental source was a content analysis of ninety-one English-language print and online (auto)biographical accounts on, by, and about problem gamblers. We discuss how we collected and analyzed each of these data sources in turn below.

In-Depth Interviews

Recruitment

After receiving ethics approval from the University of Toronto Research Ethics Board, we recruited residents from the Greater Toronto Area using colourful posters, advertisements in local and university newspapers, and postings on classified advertisement websites. These advertisements gave interested people all of the information they would need in order to decide whether to participate: a request for participants; the title of the research; a piece of data on gambling prevalence; the requirements for participation (age, experiences with or opinions about gambling); a guarantee of confidentiality; details on the interview location, duration, and honorarium; and contact information (both telephone and email).

Screening

Equal numbers of participants were drawn from four relationships of interest: (1) the parent and child both have a gambling problem (transmission group); (2) the parent has a gambling problem but the child does not; (3) the parent does not have a gambling problem but the child does (non-transmission groups); and (4) neither the parent nor the child have a gambling problem (control group).

In order to fill these groups, we screened interested people using a series of questions to determine whether they were eligible to participate and which group they fit into. Participants were asked questions to find out whether they were at least eighteen years of age; if they were problem gamblers, using the South Oaks Gambling Screen (SOGS; Lesieur and Blume 1987); and if they felt they had a parent or child who was a problem gambler.

This screening procedure also informed participants about the ethical guarantees and limitations of the study. If the person was eligible for the study, his or her contact information was obtained and a meeting time was established.

This process was repeated until we had fifty completed questionnaires and interviews for each of our four sub-samples. If participants repeatedly did not show up for their interviews at the appointed times, or were unable to be reached to rebook an interview time, they were replaced by a new participant.

Questionnaire

At the beginning of the interview, each participant was given a consent form that sought his or her free and informed agreement to participate in the study. The form contained the principal investigator's contact information, details on the purpose of the study, a description of the questions to be asked and the study procedures, the risks and benefits of the study, the steps taken to maintain confidentiality, and the incentives to participate. In addition, a list of general and gambling-specific resources was attached to every consent form so that all participants would have access to help if they required it.

The first part of each interview consisted of a closed-ended questionnaire where answers were selected from those provided to a series of written questions. This questionnaire was completed using an online survey website, SurveyMonkey. Each participant was assigned an ID number based on the group they fit into, and they completed the questionnaire under this ID number. This questionnaire portion of the study typically took between forty-five and seventy-five minutes to complete.

To gather information about our key variables, we asked questions that had been used in previous studies. This allowed us to remain consistent with other studies in the field. Using questions with fixed responses, we asked about the following:

Demographics

1. *Demographics about the participant* using questions from Statistics Canada's General Social Surveys 11, 12, Toronto Ethnicity Study (Breton 1990). The questions asked about the participant's gender, age, marital status, household composition, country of birth, language, education, job status, occupation, and personal income.

Childhood

2. *Information about sources of distress in childhood* using the Childhood Experience of Care and Abuse Questionnaire (CECA.Q; Bifulco et al. 2005). The CECA.Q retrospectively assesses lack of parental care (antipathy and neglect), parental physical abuse, and sexual abuse before age seventeen. In addition to the CECA.Q, this section contained questions that were drafted by the research team to measure emotional abuse.

3. *Information about distress in childhood due to parentification* using the Parentification Questionnaire-Adult (PQ-A; Sessions and Jurkovic 1986). The PQ-A retrospectively assesses caretaking responsibilities and the emotional parent–child relationship (Goglia et al. 1992).

4. *Information about childhood roles in the family* using the Brief Children's Role Inventory (CRI-20; Wampler, Downs, and Fischer 2009). The CRI-20 assesses four extreme roles that the child of an addict may be pressured into taking in the family—Hero, Mascot, Lost Child, and Scapegoat—with the Lost Child and Scapegoat being particularly challenging for the child.

Parenting

5. *Demographics about the participant's children* by asking about the number of children the participant has, and their age and gender.

6. *Information about sources of their child(ren)'s distress in childhood* using modified questions from the CECA.Q. Questions were slightly reworded to measure the parental care (antipathy and neglect) the participant gives or gave to his or her child(ren).

7. *Information about their child(ren)'s distress in childhood due to parentification* using a modified version of the PQ-A. Questions

were reworded to measure the caretaking responsibility and emotional parent–child relationship from the parent's point of view. Additional questions were drafted to further measure parentification.

Gambling

8. *Information about childhood and current acceptability of gambling* with drafted questions that asked who in the participant's childhood and current circle of family and friends was or is a gambler. Questions were also drafted to determine whether the participant's friends and family know of and approve of their gambling.

9. *Information about the gambling behaviour and problem gambling status of the participant's parents* using a modified version of the South Oaks Gambling Screen Revised for Adolescents (SOGS-RA; Magoon and Ingersoll 2006). The modified version contains four questions that address parental modelling and peer influences (Magoon and Ingersol 2006). Parental modelling was also measured using additional questions drafted by the research team.

10. *Information about gambling-focused opportunities* using drafted questions that asked whom the participant first gambled with, whom they currently gamble with, and where they currently do so.

11. *Information about the gambling behaviour and problem gambling status of the participant* using the SOGS.

12. *Information on non-parental influences on gambling* using a modified version of the Gambling Expectancy Questionnaire (GEQ; Gillespie, Derevensky, and Gupta 2007), which assesses benefit and risk themes associated with adolescent gambling. One area of the Gambling Activities Questionnaire (GAQ; Gupta and Derevensky 1996) was used to measure beliefs. Additional questions were also drafted to measure gambling beliefs.

Stressors

13. *Information about the participant's current sources of distress* using the Life Events Inventory (LEI; Cochrane and Robertson 1972). The index documents the occurrence of stressful life events over the past year (i.e., divorce), allowing us to assess the severity of social stressors.

Coping with Stressors

14. *Information about coping processes* using the Ways of Coping Questionnaire (WCQ; Folkman and Lazarus 1988). The WCQ is a widely used measure of how people cope with stress.

15. *Information on current sources of social support* using a slightly modified version of the Multidimensional Scale of Perceived Social Support (MSPS; Zimet et al. 1988). The questionnaire assesses three facets of social support: Special Person, Family, and Friends.

16. *Information about the mental health of the participant* using the Center for Epidemiologic Studies Depression Scale (CES-D; Radloff 1977) and the Beck Anxiety Inventory (BAI; Osman et al. 2002). The CES-D measures depressive symptomatology among the general population. The BAI assesses the severity of anxiety.

While completing the questionnaire, participants were able to skip questions, fill in answers if they selected "other," and ask the interviewer for clarification on the questions. Because of this format, we have a completion rate of 100 percent. All responses were automatically coded and entered into a password-protected Excel database by SurveyMonkey.

The Interview

Once the participant was ready to continue after the questionnaire was complete, the interviewer began to record the discussion and led the participant through our list of open-ended questions. The ID number used in the closed-ended questions was also used to identify the participant's open-ended interview recording. These questions were open-ended in that they were broad, semi-structured and allowed the participant to think up their own answers. Because the closed-ended questions from the questionnaire do not offer room for elaboration, we asked similar questions in the open-ended portion of the interview to confirm and gather more detail on the responses given to the closed-ended questions. The topics covered in our open-ended interview include:

1. Childhood learning of gambling-relevant attitudes and practices from parents and peers;

2. Gambling-related opportunities available to the participant during her or his childhood due to parental addiction and other sources;

3. Effects of childhood home life on participant's experience of stress and mental health;
4. Participant's personal, family, and ethno-cultural perspective on gambling;
5. The place gambling plays in the participant's social life;
6. Information about gambling-focused opportunities, acceptability, and social modelling in adulthood;
7. Childhood coping strategies and experiences of parentification; and
8. Current sources of stress and adulthood coping strategies.

Though we covered each of these topics in all of our interviews, interviewers were encouraged to allow the interview to be conversational, often touching on the topics in a different order. This semi-structured format enabled participants to introduce new themes and express their views in personally meaningful ways. This open-ended portion of the study took between 30 and 120 minutes to complete, depending on the length of the participant's answers.

At the end of the interview, each participant was thanked for his or her time, provided with a fifty-dollar gift card in appreciation of his or her involvement, and asked to spread the word about our study to anyone he or she thought would be interested.

Quantitative Analysis

The closed-ended answers obtained from our questionnaire were analyzed using quantitative analysis. The Excel file generated by SurveyMonkey was uploaded to and analyzed using Statistical Analysis System 9.2 (SAS).

In order to test our model of the development process, we included the variables found in both the childhood distress and childhood learning hypotheses in our quantitative analysis. Namely, we examined parental problem gambling, childhood distress in terms of neglect/abuse and parentification, social modelling of gambling, current stressful life events, ways of coping, mental health in terms of anxiety and depression, and participant (child) problem gambling. In order to ensure that any effects we found were not being caused by demographic differences, we also included gender, age, marital status, education, and personal income in our analysis.

We used multivariate techniques of analysis to examine the conditions under which parental problem gambling leads to problem gambling among children. The steps of our analysis were as follows:

1. construct the standard scales for our variables;
2. examine the descriptive statistics and the correlation matrix to see if the variables are related as we predicted and should be included in our analysis;
3. run forced entry logistic regression analysis to examine whether the steps or groups of variables occur as we predicted; and
4. perform sequential binary logistic regression to determine whether the pathways we predicted in our model were accurate.

Qualitative Analysis

In order to allow for qualitative analysis, the open-ended interview recordings were transcribed verbatim. These typed transcripts were searched for themes to understand how the social modelling of gambling in the home and distress that favours poor coping mechanisms contribute to the inheritance of problem gambling. The first round of analysis focused on the presence of each of our key variables and other variables deemed relevant. The second round of analysis centred on the degree or importance of each of the key variables.

The results of this analysis were drafted into a detailed report for each of our four groups. All the names appearing in Part II onward are pseudonyms. These reports outlined the groups' experiences of childhood trauma, their childhood learning about gambling, their troubles and stress in adulthood, their coping skills, and their current gambling practices. Each group report was compared with our model of the development process in order to determine differences in how the model works across groups and the degree to which our model is supported.

It should be noted that our four groups were not of equal size. Though our screening procedure attempted to gather four equal groups, several participants had to be moved between groups based on their answers to our questionnaire and interview questions. Participants' responses to the problem gambling questions in the questionnaire or interview were sometimes not the same as the answers given during screening. In the end, forty-five participants were found in group 1, where both the parent and child have a gambling problem. Group 2, where the parent has a gambling problem but the child does not, ended up containing forty-three people. Most participants removed from groups 1 and 2 were placed in group 3, where the parent does not have a gambling problem but the child does, which in the end held sixty-one people. Finally, 52 participants fit into group 4, where neither the parent nor the child has a gambling problem.

Content Analysis

As mentioned above, our second and complementary source of data for testing our model of the development process was a content analysis of ninety-one English-language print and online (auto)biographical accounts on, by, and of problem gamblers.

Finding and Selecting Biographies

The first step in this content analysis was creating a list of books and online accounts that featured people's gambling stories. Online bookstores, Google, Toronto area libraries, and the University of Toronto Robarts Library Reserves were searched using the following keywords: *personal stories gambling, gambling family, gambling problem, problem gambling, autobiographical story gambling,* and *gambling biographies and memoirs.*

Once the list had been created, each account was obtained and checked for relevance. Particular attention was paid to whether the accounts discussed problem gambling (not just gambling) and included sufficient detail about childhood.

A total of ninety-one cases (forty-four online accounts and forty-seven print accounts) were relevant for our purposes. Of these, twenty-three accounts involved problem gambling inheritance.

Thematic Analysis

The content analysis of these biographical accounts identified pathways to problem gambling, with a focus on parental problem gambling, childhood social learning, childhood distress, and adulthood stress. It sought to determine if the three key variables—childhood stressors, childhood modelling, and adult stressors—on their own and in combination were prevalent in the cases. The goal of this content analysis was to see if the variables identified in written accounts of and by problem gamblers matched the findings from the quantitative and qualitative data gathered in the in-depth interviews of two hundred Toronto residents.

Additional variables that were deemed relevant through the content analysis include childhood distress occurring outside the family, childhood learning of gambling outside of the family, proximity to gambling establishments, and adulthood learning of gambling.

Similar to the analysis of the qualitative interview material, the results of the content analysis were written up separately for those who did and did not inherit their gambling problems and then compared. Particular attention was paid to how many variables were present among each group.

Notes

Chapter 1 An Introduction to Dostoevsky's Life

1. The Petrashevsky Circle was a discussion group made up of progressive thinkers in St. Petersburg, organized by utopian anarchist Mikhail Petrashevsky. Its members included (among others) writers, teachers, and students, all of whom opposed the tsarist autocracy and Russian serfdom.

2. Vissarion Belinsky (1811–48) was a respected literary critic and editor of two major literary magazines. Ideologically, Belinsky supported the central values of Western liberalism and individualism, criticizing Russian autocracy and serfdom—also poverty, prostitution, drunkenness, and cruelty toward women. During his brief life Russia's most influential liberal critic and ideologist, Belinsky encouraged literature that was socially conscious. He praised Dostoevsky's first novel, *Poor Folk*, but Dostoevsky broke with him soon afterward.

3. For more on this, see the book *Redemption and the Merchant God: Dostoevsky's Economy of Salvation and Antisemitism*, by Susan McReynolds (2011).

4. On this, see the paper by Kingma (2010).

5. For more on the role of close relations, and of honest self-abasement in the recovery process, see Lorne Tepperman's book *Betting Their Lives: The Close Relations of Problem Gamblers* (2009).

Chapter 2 Gambling in Nineteenth-Century Russia

1. Reviewing Helfant's book (2002), critic Martina Winkler (2005) notes:

   > Of late, history and literary criticism appear to be growing ever closer. For some years now, historians interested in cultural history have been using fiction as a source. At the same time, in the realm of literary criticism, Slavists in particular work in a more and more historical context. Theories and models of aesthetics and the narrative no longer drive many Ph.D. theses. Instead, literary scholars are reading Russian literature as a source of information on cultural, social, and political problems. (417)

   Acknowledging that gambling is a central topic in the study of nineteenth-century Russian society and culture, Winkler praises the thoroughness of Helfant's approach and his ability to avoid reductionism: that is, to avoid losing the thread of literary analysis while doing history. At the same time, Winkler (2005) says, he casts his net widely:

   > Though fiction provides the main basis for Helfant's work, his focus is much broader. He uses memoirs, contemporary literary criticism, and journalistic, didactic, and moralistic texts as sources. Sociological and anthropological models such as the theory of play or risk theory inform his approach. He proves to be very flexible in using these models while carefully choosing texts that illustrate the cultural importance of gambling in 19th-century Russia. (418)

2. For a detailed description of the game, see http://www.pagat.com/beating/durak.html or http://www.netintellgames.com/durakrules.htm.

Chapter 3 What Do Dostoevsky's Novels Tell Us?

1. This argument is elaborated in the excellent paper by Kingma (2010) on Dostoevsky's gambling problem.

Chapter 4 Explanations of Dostoevsky's Gambling

1. For the sake of completeness, it should be said that other people have read *The Brothers Karamazov* in other ways. Madigan (2011), for example, reads it as a parable about the relations between Lucifer and God, or perhaps man and God—also a topic of interest to Dostoevsky. On this, Madigan (2011) writes,

   > Dostoevsky clearly believes that the father [in *The Brothers Karamazov*] drove his sons to this deed, and that in a sense it is a communal act. Like Lucifer, they have sought to deny or erase their inadequate father. Only Alyosha is insulated by his option for religion from this murder; only he escapes the contaminating poison. The others are sinned against, but carry on in various ways the evil they have inherited, harming all who come close, including one another. Smerdyakov, his revenge sated, does not hesitate to take his own life. (749)

   So, it does not follow that we have to impose a sexual jealousy interpretation on the parricide. Yet, such was Freud's inclination. By the time of this essay's publication (1928), Freud's theories (about infantile sexuality, among other things) were well known throughout Europe and North America, and his reputation well established. The essay is one of many in which he seeks to extend his original theories, derived from clinical case studies, to great artists, religious and cultural problems, and "civilization" more generally.

2. In his book *Dostoevsky: The Seeds of Revolt, 1821–1849* (1979), Frank describes new information gathered on Dr. Dostoevsky's murder. It has been revealed that the story of this murder was likely an untrue rumour that was spread by a neighbour at Darovoe who could have acquired Dr. Dostoevsky's land if the peasants who inhabited it were deported to Siberia on the charge of murder. Regardless of the true cause of Dr. Dostoevsky's death, Fyodor was told that his father had been murdered, which was a traumatic experience.

Chapter 9 Opportunity and Acceptability

1. This argument is similar to that of Welte et al. (2006), who argue that aspects of social context influence only people's decision to gamble, while the risk for problem gambling depends on an individual's proneness to addictive behaviours and his or her disadvantaged status.

2. Gambling is seen as a leisure activity in societies wherein gambling activities are framed as mainstream social recreation, rather than being stigmatized (Cavion, Wong, and Zangeneh 2008).

3. Cultural history and rationales dictate cultural values and beliefs, which are passed on to members directly through parental modelling or indirectly through parental attitudes (Raylu and Oei 2004). Specifically, societal norms, socialization practices, personal goals, and motivations can be conducive to gambling in certain cultures (Walker, Schellink, and Anjoul 2008).

4. For example, the intensity of problem gambling and its related problems doubled among those who live within fifty miles of a casino (LaPlante and Shaffer 2007).

5. Adolescents who gamble with their parents experience more severe gambling and gambling-related problems (Felsher, Derevensky, and Gupta 2003).

6. Parents and children who gamble together typically see it as a pleasurable, enjoyable experience (Vachon et al. 2004). When depicted as a socially accepted hobby, gambling is said to start around the age of nine or ten, which allows children to gamble with their parents, siblings, or relatives in the spirit of fun (Gupta and Derevensky 1997).

7. Adolescents who are most likely to be or become pathological gamblers report the highest level of peer gambling and the greatest susceptibility to peer pressure (Langhinrichsen-Rohling et al. 2004; Jacobs 2000).

Chapter 10 Learning at Home and in the Community

1. Social learning theory states that individuals model, learn, and maintain behaviours that are observed, appealing, and reinforced (Gupta and Derevensky 1997; Raylu and Oei 2002). Social learning increases the chances of risk taking and/or gambling-like behaviour in children as young as four to five years old (Kearney and Drabman 1992).

2. Children learn about the excitement of gambling by watching their parents respond to their own gambling activities enthusiastically (Walker 1992). Children are therefore more likely to imitate and model this behaviour, since it appears to be rewarding (Gupta and Derevensky 1997). In problem gambling families, children may gamble with their parents. This frames gambling as a rewarding activity, since it provides children with the opportunity to interact with their parents (Gupta and Derevensky 1997), and because their parents see gambling as a pleasurable experience (Vachon et al. 2004).

3. Between 40 and 68 percent of adolescents engage in gambling activities with their family (Hardoon and Derevensky 2002). Research finds that 77 to 85 percent of adolescents receive scratch tickets from their parents, while 50 percent receive lottery draw tickets and 23 percent receive sports tickets (Felsher, Derevensky, and Gupta. 2003; Griffiths 2000).

4. Adolescents are more likely to have a gambling problem if their friends approve of and engage in gambling activities (Hurt et al. 2008).

5. Individuals who respond positively to gambling ads, and those who report that they gamble immediately after viewing these ads, are more likely to believe that the chances of winning improve the longer you gamble, and to gamble on a weekly basis (Derevensky et al. 2010). Among problem gamblers, advertisements for preferred games encourage gambling. During periods of intense gambling involvement, advertisements often encouraged problem gamblers to gamble at an even more dangerous rate, primarily by reminding them of the different types of games that are available (Binde 2009).

6. Problem gambling can be reinforced or encouraged when individuals are praised or admired for their gambling. Consequently, they are encouraged to continue gambling because these appraisals increase their self-esteem (Hardoon and Derevensky 2002).

7. A reward for adolescents engaging in gambling activities may be the increase of their "identification with adult life," or the social advantages of appearing to be courageous or "good at sports" (Delfabbro and Thrupp 2003).

References

Adelman, Gary. 2003. "Tsypkin's Way with Dostoyevsky." *New England Review* 24(2):168–81. Accessed December 16, 2011. http://www.jstor.org/stable/40244269.

Adorno, Theodor W., Else Frenkel-Brunswik, Daniel Levinson, and Nevitt Sanford. 1950. *The Authoritarian Personality.* New York: Harper & Brothers.

Althaus, Chatherine E. 2005. "A Disciplinary Perspective on the Epistemological Status of Risk." *Risk Analysis* 25(3):567–82.

Amoia, Alba Della Fazia. 1993. *Feodor Dostoevsky.* New York: Continuum International Publishing Group.

Andreyev, Nikolay. 1962. Introduction to *The Gambler*, by Fyodor Dostoevsky. Translated by C.J. Hogarth. London: Dent/Vintage Russian Library.

Anikin, Andrei V. 1993. "Money and the Russian Classics." *Diogenes* 41(162):99–109.

Apollonio, Carol. 2009. *Dostoevsky's Secrets: Reading against the Grain. Studies in Russian Literature and Thought.* Evanston, IL: Northwestern University Press.

Baranczak, Stanislaw. 1995. Review of *Dostoevsky: The Miraculous Years, 1865–1871*, by Joseph Frank. *The New Republic* 212(20):35.

Barnett, B., and Parker, G. 1998. "The Parentified Child: Early Competence or Childhood Deprivation?" *Child Psychology and Psychiatry Review* 3:146–55.

Baumann, Christian R., Vladimir P.I. Novikov, Marianne Regard, and Adrian M. Siegel. 2005. "Did Fyodor Mikhailovich Dostoevsky Suffer from Mesial Temporal Lobe Epilepsy?" *Seizure* 14(5):324–30.

Beck, A.T., and R.A. Steer. 1993. *Beck Anxiety Inventory Manual.* San Antonio, TX: Harcourt Brace and Company.

Bergler, Edmund. 1957. *The Psychology of Gambling.* New York: Hill & Wang.

Berman, Anna A. 2009. "Siblings in *The Brothers Karamazov.*" *The Russian Review* 68(2):263–82.

Bifulco, A., O. Bernazzani, P.M. Moran, and C. Jacobs. 2005. "The Childhood Experience of Care and Abuse Questionnaire (CECA.Q): Validation in a Community Series." *British Journal of Clinical Psychology* 44:563–81.

Binde, P. 2009. "Exploring the Impact of Gambling Advertising: An Interview Study of Problem Gamblers." *International Journal of Mental Health and Addiction* 7:541–54.

Blaszczynski, A.P., and L. Nower. 2002. "A Pathways Model of Problem and Pathological Gambling." *Addiction* 97(5):487–99.

Blaszczynski, A.P., A. Wilson, and N. McConaghy. 1986a. "Sensation Seeking and Pathological Gambling." *British Journal of Addiction* 81:109–13.

Blaszczynski, A.P., S. Winter, and N. McConaghy. 1986b. "Plasma Endorphin Levels in Pathological Gamblers." *Journal of Gambling Behaviour* 2:3–15.

Blume, Sheila. 1995. "Pathological Gambling: An Addiction to an Altered Psychological State." *British Medical Journal* 311(7004):522.

Bogg, Richard A. 1999. "Dostoevsky's Enigmas: An Analysis of Violent Men." *Aggression and Violent Behavior* 4(4):371–86.

Bolen, Darrell W., and William H. Boyd. 1968. "Gambling and the Gambler: A Review and Preliminary Findings." *Archives of General Psychiatry* 18(5):617–30.

Breger, Louis. 1989. *Dostoevsky: The Author as Psychoanalyst*. New York: New York University Press.

Breton, R. 1990. *Ethnic Identity and Equality: Varieties of Experience in a Canadian City*. Toronto: University of Toronto Press.

Briere, J. 1992. Methodological Issues in the Study of Sexual Abuse Effects. *Journal of Consulting and Clinical Psychology* 60:196–203.

Broszormenyi-Nagy, I., and G.M. Spark. 1973. *Invisible Loyalties: Reciprocity in Intergenerational Family Therapy*. Hagerstown, MD: Harper & Row.

Burry, Alexander. 2010. "Execution, Trauma and Recovery in Dostoevsky's *The Idiot*." *Slavic and East European Journal* 54(2):255–71.

Carlton, P.L., M. Swatzburg, R. Nora, P. Manowitz, H. McBride, and L. Goldstein. 1987. "Attention Deficit Disorder and Pathological Gambling." *Journal of Clinical Psychiatry* 48:487–88.

Carter, E.J. 2006. "Breaking the Bank: Gambling Casinos, Finance Capitalism, and German Unification." *Central European History* 39(2):185–213.

Cavion, L., C. Wong, and M. Zangeneh. 2008. "Gambling." In *In the Pursuit of Winning: Problem Gambling Theory, Research and Treatment*, edited by M. Zangeneh, A. Blaszczynski, and N.E. Turner, 95–119. New York: Springer Science and Business Media.

Clarke, D. 2004. "Impulsiveness, Locus of Control, Motivation and Problem Gambling." *Journal of Gambling Studies* 20(4):319.

Cochrane, R., and A. Robertson. 1972. "The Life Events Inventory: A Measure of the Relative Severity of Psychosocial Stressors." *Journal of Psychosomatic Research* 17:135–39.

Cotte, June. 1997. "Chances, Trances and Lots of Slots: Gambling Motives and Consumption Experiences." *Journal of Leisure Research* 29(4): 380–406.

Coulson, Jessie. 1962. *Dostoevsky: A Self-Portrait*. London: Oxford University Press.

Darbyshire, P., C. Oster, and H. Carrig. 2001. "The Experience of Pervasive Loss: Children and Young People Living in a Family Where Parental Gambling Is a Problem." *Journal of Gambling Studies* 17:23–45.

De Jonge, Alex. 1975. *Dostoevsky and the Age of Intensity*. London: Secker & Warburg.

Delfabbro, P., and L. Thrupp. 2003. "The Social Determinants of Youth Gambling in South Australian Adolescents." *Journal of Adolescence* 26:313–30.

Derevensky, J.L., and R. Gupta, eds. 2004. *Gambling Problems in Youth: Theoretical and Applied Perspectives*. New York: Kluwer.

Derevensky, J., A. Sklar, R. Gupta, and C. Messerlian. 2010. "An Empirical Study Examining the Impact of Gambling Advertisements on Adolescent Gambling Attitudes and Behaviors." *International Journal of Mental Health and Addiction* 8:21–34.

Diment, Gayla. 1997. "Goliadkin as Cinderella, or the Case of the Lost Galosh." *Russian Review* 56(3):440–44. Accessed December 16, 2011. http://www.jstor.org/stable/131753.

Dostoevsky, Anna Grigorevna. 1926. *Dostoevsky Portrayed by His Wife: The Diary and Reminiscences of Mme. Dostoevsky*. Translated and edited by S.S. Koteliansky. New York: E.P. Dutton.

Dostoevsky, Dimitry. 2005. "Dimitry Dostoevsky Discusses the Image of His Great-Grandfather, Fyodor Dostoevsky, on Russian Lottery Tickets (Interview)." *All Things Considered.* National Public Radio.

Dostoevsky, Fyodor. 1914. *Letters of Fyodor Michailovitch Dostoevsky to His Family and Friends.* Translated by Ethel Colburne Mayne. New York: The Macmillan Company.

_____. 1917[1866]. *Crime and Punishment.* Translated by Constance Garnett. New York: P.F. Collier & Son.

_____. 2003[1867]. *The Gambler.* Translated by Constance Garnett. Edited by Gary Saul Morson. New York: Modern Library.

_____. 2009[1877]. *A Writer's Diary.* Abridged edition. Translated and annotated by Kenneth Lantz. Edited and with an Introduction by Gary Saul Morson. Evanston, IL: Northwestern University Press.

_____. 2011[1864]. *Notes from Underground.* Translated by Richard Pevear and Larissa Volokhonsky. New York: Vintage Books.

Dowling, Nicki A., Alun C. Jackson, Shane A. Thomas, and Erica Frydenberg. 2010. "Children at Risk of Developing Problem Gambling." The Problem Gambling Research and Treatment Centre, Australia.

Earley, L., and D.J. Cushway. 2002. "The Parentified Child." *Clinical Child Psychology & Psychiatry* 7(2):163–78.

Edwards, Griffith, and Susan Savva. 2000. Review of *Gambling, Game, and Psyche,* by Bettina L. Knapp. *Addiction* 95(7):1109–14.

Erikson, Erik H. 1950. *Childhood and Society.* New York: Norton.

Eyres, Harry. 2007. "The Wheel of Existentialism." *Financial Times,* October 13.

Feldman, Bronson. 1958. "Dostoevsky and Father Love." *Psychoanalysis and the Psychoanalytic Review* 45(4):84.

Felitti, V.J. 2003. "The Origins of Addiction: Evidence from the Adverse Childhood Experiences Study." *Praxis der Kinderpsychologie und Kinderpsychiatrie* 52:547–59.

Felsher, J., J.L. Derevensky, and R. Gupta. 2003. "Parental Influences and Social Modelling of Youth Lottery Participation." *Journal of Community and Applied Social Psychology* 13:361–77.

_____. 2010. "Young Adults with Gambling Problems: The Impact of Childhood Maltreatment." *International Journal of Mental Health & Addiction* 8:545–56.

Flaherty, Alice W. 2005. "Frontotemporal and Dopaminergic Control of Idea Generation and Creative Drive." *The Journal of Comparitive Neurology* 493:147–53.

Folkman, S., and R.S. Lazarus. 1988. *Manual for the Ways of Coping Questionnaire.* Palo Alto, CA: Consulting Psychologists Press.

Frank, Joseph. 1979. *Dostoevsky: The Seeds of Revolt, 1821–1849.* Vol. 1. Princeton: Princeton University Press.

_____. 1987. *Dostoevsky: The Years of Ordeal, 1850–1859.* Vol. 2. Princeton: Princeton University Press.

_____. 1988. *Dostoevsky: The Stir of Liberation, 1860–1865.* Vol. 3. Princeton: Princeton University Press.

_____. 1993. "The Gambler: A Study in Ethnopsychology." *The Hudson Review* 46(2):301–22.

_____.1995. *Dostoevsky: The Miraculous Years, 1865–1871*. Vol. 4. Princeton: Princeton University Press.

_____. 2002. *Dostoevsky: The Mantle of the Prophet, 1871–1881*. Vol. 5. Princeton: Princeton University Press.

_____. 2010. *Dostoevsky: A Writer in His Time*. Princeton: Princeton University Press.

Freeborn, Richard. 2003. *Dostoevsky*. London: Haus Publishing.

Freud, Sigmund. 1976[1928]. "Dostoevsky and Parricide." In *The Standard Edition of the Complete Psychological Works of Sigmund Freud*, Volume XXI, edited and translated by James Strachey. New York: W.W. Norton & Company.

Fülöp-Miller, René, and Friedrich Eckstein, eds. 1925. *Dostojewski am Roulette*. Munich: R. Piper.

Geertz, C. 1973. "Deep Play: Notes on the Balinese Cockfight." In *The Interpretation of Cultures*, by C. Geertz, 412–53. New York: Basic Books.

Geha, Richard, Jr. 1970. "Dostoevsky and *The Gambler*: A Contribution to the Psychogenesis of Gambling Part II." *Psychoanalytic Review* 57(2):289.

Gillespie, MA.M., J. Derevensky, and R. Gupta. 2007. "Adolescent Problem Gambling: Developing a Gambling Expectancy Instrument." *Journal of Gambling Issues* 19:51–68.

Goffman, Erving. 1963. *Stigma: Notes on the Management of Spoiled Identity*. Englewood Cliffs, NJ: Prentice-Hall.

Goglia, L.R., G.J. Jurkovic, A.M. Burt, and K.G. Burgecallaway. 1992. "Generational Boundary Distortions by Adult Children of Alcoholics: Child-as-Parent and Child-as-Mate." *The American Journal of Family Therapy* 20(4):291–99.

Goldberg, Carl. 2002. "The Secret that Guilty Confessions Fail to Disclose." *American Journal of Psychotherapy* 56(2):178.

Goodheart, Eugene. 2004. Review of *Summer in Baden-Baden*, by Leonid Tsypkin. *Sewanee Review* 112(2):301–3.

Grant, J.E., and S. Won Kim. 2002. "Parental Bonding in Pathological Gambling Disorder." *Psychiatric Quarterly* 73(3):239.

Greene, J.M., and C.L. Ringwalt. 1996. "Youth and Familial Substance Use's Association with Suicide Attempts among Runaway and Homeless Youth." *Substance Use and Misuse* 31:1041–58.

Griffiths, M. 2000. "Scratchcard Gambling Among Adolescent Males." *Journal of Gambling Studies* 16(1):70.

Gupta, R., and J. Derevensky. 1996. "The Relationship between Gambling and Video Game Playing in Children and Adolescents." *Journal of Gambling Studies* 12:375–94.

_____. 1997. "Familial and Social Influences on Juvenile Gambling Behavior." *Journal of Gambling Studies* 13:179–92.

Hardoon, K.K., and J.L. Derevensky. 2002. "Child and Adolescent Gambling Behavior: Current Knowledge." *Clinical Child Psychology and Psychiatry* 7(2):263–81.

Hardoon, K.K., J.L. Derevensky, and R. Gupta. 2002. "An Examination of the Influence of Familial, Emotional, Conduct and Cognitive Problems and Hyperactivity upon Adolescent Gambling Problems: A Report to the Ontario Problem Gambling Research Centre." R and J Child Development Consultants, Inc., Montreal, Quebec. Accessed April 5, 2012. http://www.gamblingresearch.org/download.sz/familial%20dervensky.pdf?docid=1527.

Helfant, Ian M. 1997. "The High Stakes of Identity: Gambling and Myths of Aristocratic (Dis)honor in the Life and Literature of Pushkin's Age." PhD diss., Harvard University.

_____. 1999. "Pushkin's Ironic Performances as a Gambler." Special issue, *Slavic Review* 58(2):371–92.

_____. 2002. *The High Stakes of Identity: Gambling in the Life and Literature of Nineteenth-Century Russia.* Evanston, IL: Northwestern University Press.

_____. 2003. "His to Stake, Hers to Lose: Women and the Male Gambling Culture of 19th Century Russia." *The Russian Review* 62:223–42.

Hewitt, D. 1994. "Spirit of Bingoland: A Study of Problem Gambling among Alberta Native People." Edmonton, AB: Nechi Training and Research & Health Promotions Institute.

Hirschi, Travis. 1967. *Delinquency Research.* New York: The Free Press.

Hodgins, D.C., and D.P. Schopflocher. 2010. "The Association between Childhood Maltreatment and Gambling Problems in a Community Sample of Adult Men and Women." *Psychology of Addictive Behaviors* 24(3):548–54.

Hogan, D.M. 1997. "The Social and Psychological Needs of Children of Drug Users: Report on Exploratory Study." Dublin: The Children's Research Centre, University of Dublin, Trinity College.

Hooper, L. 2007. "Expanding the Discussion Regarding Parentification and Its Varied Outcomes: Implications for Mental Health Research and Practice." *Journal of Mental Health Counseling* 29(4):322–37.

Hughes, John R. 2005. "The Idiosyncratic Aspects of the Epilepsy of Fyodor Dostoevsky." *Epilepsy & Behavior* 7(3):531–88.

Hurt, H., J.M. Giannetta, N.L. Brodsky, D. Shera, and D. Romer. 2008. "Gambling Initiation in Preadolescents." *Journal of Adolescent Health* 43:91–93.

Iniesta, Ivan. 2007. "Dostoevsky's Epilepsy: A Contemporary Paleodiagnosis." *Seizure* 16(3): 283–85.

Jackson, Robert Louis. 1981. *The Art of Dostoevsky: Deliriums and Nocturnes.* Princeton: Princeton University Press.

Jacobs, D.F. 1986. "A General Theory of Addictions: A New Theoretical Model." *Journal of Gambling Behavior* 2(1):15–31.

_____. 2000. "Juvenile Gambling in North America: An Analysis of Long-Term Trends and Future Prospects." *Journal of Gambling Studies* 16:119–52.

Jessor, R., and S.L. Jessor. 1973. "The Perceived Environment in Behavioral Science: Some Conceptual Issues and Some Illustrative Data." *American Behavioral Scientist* 16:801–28.

Johansson, A., J.E. Grand, S. Won Kim, B.L. Odlaug, and K. Gunnar Gotestam. 2009. "Risk Factors for Problematic Gambling: A Critical Literature Review." *Journal of Gambling Studies* 25:67–92.

Jones, Malcolm. 2008. Introduction to *The Gambler,* by Fyodor Dostoevsky. Translated by Jane Kentish. Oxford: Oxford University Press.

Jurkovic, G. 1997. *Lost Childhoods: The Plight of the Parentified Child.* New York: Taylor & Francis.

Kalischuk, R.G., N. Nowatzki, K. Cardwell, K. Klein, and J. Solowoniuk. 2006. "Problem Gambling and Its Impact on Families: A Literature Review." *International Gambling Studies* 6(1):31–60.

Kauffmann, Stanley. 1999. Review of *The Gambler*, by Karoly Makk, and *Grand Illusion*, by Jean Renoir. *The New Republic* 221(8):28.

Kausch, O., L. Rugle, and D.Y. Rowland. 2006. "Lifetime Histories of Trauma among Pathological Gamblers." *American Journal on Addictions* 15(1):35–43.

Kearney, C.A., and R.S. Drabman. 1992. "Risk-Taking/Gambling-Like Behavior in Preschool Children." *Journal of Gambling Studies* 8:287–97.

Kelley, M., A. French, K. Bountress, H. Keefe, V. Schroeder, K. Steer, W. Fals-Stewart, and L. Gumienny. 2007. "Parentification and Family Responsibility in the Family of Origin of Adult Children of Alcoholics." *Addictive Behaviors* 32(4):675–85.

Kidd, S.A. 2004. "The Walls Were Closing In and We Were Trapped: A Qualitative Analysis of Street Youth Suicide." *Youth & Society* 36:30–55.

_____. 2007. "Youth Homelessness and Social Stigma." *Journal of Youth and Adolescence* 36(3):291–99.

Kingma, Sytze F. 2010. "Dostoevsky and Freud: Autonomy and Addition in Gambling." Paper presented at the 8th European Social Science History Conference, Experiences of Chance, Motivation and Risk in Gambling, Ghent, Belgium, April 13–16.

Krakowiak, Maja K. 2008. "When Good Characters Do Bad Things: Examining the Effect of Moral Ambiguity on Enjoyment." PhD diss., Pennsylvania State University.

Lacoursiere, Roy B. 2003. "Proust and Parricide: Literary, Biographical, and Forensic Psychiatric Explorations." *American Imago* 60(2):179–210.

Langbauer, Laurie. 2008. "Ethics and Theory: Suffering Children in Dickens, Dostoevsky, and Le Guin." *ELH* 75(1):89–108.

Langhinrichsen-Rohling, J., P. Rohde, J.R. Seeley, and M.L. Rohling. 2004. "Individual, Family, and Peer Correlates of Adolescent Gambling." *Journal of Gambling Studies* 20(1):23–46.

Lantz, Kenneth. 2004. *The Dostoevsky Encyclopedia*. Westport, CT: Greenwood Press.

LaPlante, D.A., and H.J. Shaffer. 2007. "Understanding the Influence of Gambling Opportunities: Expanding Exposure Models to Include Adaptation." *American Journal of Orthopsychiatry* 77(4):616.

Lazarus, R.S., and S. Folkman. 1984. *Stress, Appraisal and Coping*. New York: Springer.

Leatherbarrow, W.J. 2005. "Pechorin's Demons: Representations of the Demonic in Lermontov's *A Hero of Our Time*." *The Modern Language Review* 99(4):999–1013. Accessed December 16, 2011. http://www.jstor.org/stable/3738510.

Lesieur, H.R., and S.B. Blume. 1987. "South Oaks Gambling Screen (SOGS): A New Instrument for the Identification of Pathological Gamblers." *American Journal of Psychiatry* 144:1184–88.

Link, B., and J. Phelan. 2006. "Stigma and Its Public Health Implications. *The Lancet* 367(9509):528–29.

Lothene, Zvi. 1992. Review of *Dostoevsky: The Author as Psychoanalyst*, by Louis Breger. *PsycCritiques* 37(9):956–57.

Love, Jeff. 2004. "Narrative Hesitation in *The Gambler*." *Canadian Slavonic Papers / Revue Canadienne des Slavistes* 46(3):361–80. Accessed December 16, 2011. http://www.jstor.org/stable/40860047.

MacHale, S. 2002. "Managing Depression in Physical Illness." *Advances in Psychiatric Treatment* 8:297–305.

Madigan, Patrick. 2011. "The Sorrow That Dare Not Say Its Name: The Inadequate Father, The Motor of History." *Heythrop Journal* LII:739–50.

Magoon, M.E., and G.M. Ingersoll. 2006. "Parental Modeling, Attachment, and Supervision as Moderators of Adolescent Gambling." *Journal of Gambling Studies* 22(1):1.

Malaby, Thomas M. 2007. "Beyond Play: A New Approach to Games." *Games and Culture* 2(2):95–113.

Mann, Thomas. 1945. *The Short Novels of Dostoevsky*. Translated by Constance Garnett, with an Introduction by Thomas Mann. New York: Dial Press.

Martin, Marion, Gaynor Sadlo, and Graham Stew. 2006. "The Phenomenon of Boredom." *Qualitative Research in Psychology* 3(3):193–211. Accessed December 15, 2011. http://dx.doi.org/10.1191/1478088706qrp066oa.

McReynolds, Susan. 2011. *Redemption and the Merchant God: Dostoevsky's Economy of Salvation and Antisemitism*. Evanston, IL: Northwestern University Press.

Meyer, Gerhard, and Tobias Hayer. 2009. "Germany." In *Problem Gambling in Europe: Challenges, Preventions and Interventions*, edited by Mark Griffiths, Tobias Hayer, and Gerhard Meyer, 85–102. New York: Springer.

Meyers, Ronald J. 2001. "Literature and Sport as Ritual and Fantasy." *Papers on Language and Literature* 37(4):337–60.

Mills, C. Wright. 1959. *The Sociological Imagination*. Oxford: Oxford University Press.

Minuchin, S., B. Montalvo, B.G. Guerney, T. Rosman, and T. Schumer. 1967. *Families of the Slums*. New York: Basic Books.

Mochulsky, Konstantin. 1967[1947]. *Dostoevsky: His Life and Work*. Translated and with an Introduction by Michael A. Minihan. Princeton: Princeton University Press.

Morrissey, Susan. 2004. "In the Name of Freedom: Suicide, Serfdom, and Autocracy in Russia." *The Slavonic and East European Review* 82(2):268–91. Accessed December 15, 2011. http://www.jstor.org/stable/4213883.

Nemeroff, C.B. 2004. "Neurobiological Consequences of Childhood Trauma." Supplement 1, *Journal of Clinical Psychology* 65:18–28.

O'Grady, Desmond. 1994. "Dostoevsky Lives." *Commonweal* 121(19):6–7.

Offord, Derek. 2003. Review of *The High Stakes of Identity: Gambling in the Life and Literature of Nineteenth-Century Russia*, by Ian M. Helfant. *The Slavonic and East European Reviews* 81(2):307–9.

Oldman, David. 1978."Compulsive Gamblers." *The Sociological Review* 26:349–71.

Osman, A., J. Hoffman, F.X. Barrios, B.A. Kopper, J.L. Breitenstein, and S.K. Hahn. 2002. "Factor Structure, Reliability, and Validity of the Beck Anxiety Inventory in Adolescent Psychiatric Inpatients." *Journal of Clinical Psychology* 58(4):443–56.

Paperno, Irina. 1997. *Suicide as Cultural Institution in Dostoevsky's Russia*. Ithaca: Cornell University Press.

Peace, Richard. 2004. Review of *Dostoevsky*, by Richard Freeborn. *The Slavonic and East European Review* 82(4):945–47.

Perez de Castro, I., A. Ibanez, P. Torres, J. Saiz-Ruiz, and J. Fernandez-Piqueras. 1997. "Genetic Association Study between Pathological Gambling and a Functional DNA Polymorphism at the D4 Receptor Gene." *Pharmacogenetics* 7:345–48.

Petry, N.M., and K.J. Steinberg, 2005. "Childhood Maltreatment in Male and Female Treatment-Seeking Pathological Gamblers." *Psychology of Addictive Behaviors* 19(2):226–29.

Pevear, Richard. 2007. Introduction to *The Double* and *The Gambler*, by Fyodor M Dostoevsky. Translated by Larissa Volokhonsky. New York: Random House/ Everyman's Library.

Pisak, Gyongyi. 1997. "Homologies between Character Structure and the Structure of Economic Activity in Three Nineteenth Century Novels." PhD diss., Kossuth Lajos University of Arts and Sciences, Hungary.

Popoff, Alexandra. 2012. "The Women Behind the Greatest Works of Russian Literature." *Publishers Weekly*. Accessed November 7, 2012. http://www.publishersweekly.com/pw/ by-topic/industry-news/tip-sheet/article/53396-the-women-behind-the-greatest- works-of-russian-literature.html.

Potenza, M.N. 2001. "The Neurobiology of Pathological Gambling." *Seminars in Clinical Neuropsychiatry* 6(3):217–26.

Premo, Diane G. 1997. "The Dostoevsky Archive: Firsthand Accounts of the Novelist from Contemporaries' Memoirs and Rare." *Library Journal* 122(12):83.

Proust, Marcel. 1984. "Dostoievski." In *Marcel Proust: On Art and Literature, 1896–1919*, translated by Sylvia Townsend Warner, 380–81. New York: Carol and Graf.

Rabinowitz, Peter J. 2001. "A Lot Has Built Up: Omission and Rhetorical Realism in Dostoevsky's *The Gambler*." Special issue, *Narrative* 9(2):203–9. Accessed December 16, 2011. http://www.jstor.org/stable/20107248.

Radloff, L.S. 1977. "The CES-D Scale: A Self Report Depression Scale for Research in the General Population." *Applied Psychological Measurement* 1:385–401.

Raylu, N., and T.P.S. Oei. 2002. "Pathological Gambling: A Comprehensive Review." *Clinical Psychology Review* 22:1009–61.

——————. 2004. "Role of Culture in Gambling and Problem Gambling." *Clinical Psychology Review* 23:1087–1114.

Reith, Gerda. 2007. "Gambling and the Contradictions of Consumption: A Genealogy of the Pathological Subject." *American Behavioral Scientist* 51(1):33–35.

Remnick, David. 2005. "The Translation Wars: Onward and Upward with the Arts." *New Yorker* 81(75, November 7).

Reyfman, Irina. 1999. *Ritualized Violence Russian Style: The Duel in Russian Culture and Literature*. Palo Alto: Stanford University Press.

Rodin, G., and K. Voshart. 1986. "Depression in the Medically Ill: An Overview." *American Journal of Psychiatry* 143:696–705.

Romer, T.K., M.B. Callesen, J. Linnet, M.L. Kringelbach, and A. Moller. 2009. "Severity of Gambling Is Associated with Severity of Depressive Symptoms in Pathological Gamblers." *Behavioral Pharmacology* 20(5–6):527–36.

Ronel, Natti. 2011. "Criminal Behavior, Criminal Mind: Being Caught in a Criminal Spin." *International Journal of Offender Therapy and Comparative Criminology* 55(8):1208–33.

Rosecrance, John. 1985. "Compulsive Gambling and the Medicalization of Deviance." *Social Problems* 32:275–84.

Rosenshield, Gary. 1994. "Choosing the Right Card: Madness, Gambling, and the Imagination in Pushkin's *The Queen of Spades*." *PMLA* 109(5):995–1008. Accessed December 15, 2011. http://www.jstor.org/stable/462967.

_____. 2011. "Gambling and Passion: Pushkin's *The Queen of Spades* and Dostoevsky's *The Gambler*." *Slavic and East European Journal* 55(2):205–27.

Rosenthal, Richard J. 1982. "Dostoevsky's Use of Projection: Psychic Mechanism as Literary Form in *The Double*." *Dostoevsky Studies* 3:80–86.

_____. 2005. "Staying in Action: The Pathological Gambler's Equivalent of the Dry Drunk." *Journal of Gambling Issues* 13.

Rosenthal, Richard J., and Loreen J. Rugle. 1994a. "A Psychodynamic Approach to the Treatment of Pathological Gambling: Part I. Achieving Abstinence." *Journal of Gambling Studies* 10:80–86.

_____. 1994b. "Pathological Gambling: Clinical Issues, Part I." *Journal of Gambling Studies* 1:21–42.

Rugle, Loreen J., and Richard J. Rosenthal. 1994. "Transference and Countertransference Reactions in the Psychotherapy of Pathological Gamblers." *Journal of Gambling Studies* 10:21–42.

Sallaz, Jeffery J. 2008. "Deep Plays: A Comparative Ethnography of Gambling Contests in Two Post-Colonies." *University of Arizona* 9(1):533.

Saraskına, Liudmila Ivanovna. 2003. "Magicheskii Realizm Romana F.M. Dostoevskogo 'Igrok' Kak Fenomen 'Opasnogo' Tvorchestva." *Dostoevskii i Mirovaia Kul'tura* 17:389–98.

Sessions, M.W., and G.J. Jurkovic. 1986. "Parentification Questionnaire-Adult (PQ-A)," unpublished document. Available from Gregory J. Jurkovic, Dept of Psychology, Georgia State University, Atlanta.

Shabad, Peter. 2000. "Giving the Devil His Due: Spite and the Struggle for Individual Dignity." *Psychoanalytic Psychology* 17(4):690–705.

Shah, Kamini R., Seth A. Eisen, Xian Hong, and Marc N. Potenza. 2005. "Genetic Studies of Pathological Gambling: A Review of Methodology and Analyses of Data from the Vietnam Era Twin Registry." *Journal of Gambling Studies* 21(2):179–203.

Shaw, M., and D. Dorling. 1998. "Mortality among Street Youth in the UK." *The Lancet* 352:743.

Sher, Kenneth J., Emily R. Grekin, and Natalie A. Williams. 2005. "The Development of Alcohol Use Disorders." *Annual Review of Clinical Psychology* 1:493–523.

Stang, Ragna Thiis. 1977. *Edvard Munch: The Man and His Art*. New York: Abbeville Press.

Ste-Marie, C., R. Gupta, and J.L. Derevensky. 2006. "Anxiety and Social Stress Related to Adolescent Gambling Behavior and Substance Use." *Journal of Child & Adolescent Substance Abuse* 15(4):55–74.

Taber, J.I., R.A. McCormick, and L.F. Ramirez. 1987. "The Prevalence and Impact of Major Life Stressors Among Pathological Gamblers." *International Journal of Addiction* 22:71–79.

Tepperman, L. 2009. *Betting Their Lives: The Close Relations of Problem Gamblers*. Toronto: Oxford University Press.

Thomas, W.I., and Florian Znaniecki. 1958[1918–20]. *The Polish Peasant in Europe and America*. Vols I and II. New York: Dover Publications.

Vachon, J., F. Vitaro, B. Wanner, and R.E. Tremblay. 2004. "Adolescent Gambling: Relationships with Parent Gambling and Parenting Practices." *Psychology of Addictive Behaviors* 18:398–401.

Veblen, Thorstein. 1912. *Theory of the Leisure Class: An Economic Study of Institutions*. New York: The Macmillan Company.

Vinokurov, Val. 2003. "Levinas's Dostoevsky: A Response to 'Dostoevsky's Derrida.'" *Common Knowledge* 9(2):318–40.

Wagner, Jodi L. 2008. "Gambling and Risk in Victorian Literature and Culture." PhD diss., Purdue University.

Wagner, William G. 1994. *Marriage, Property, and Law in Late Imperial Russia*. Oxford: Oxford University Press.

Walker, M.B. 1992. *The Psychology of Gambling*. Oxford: Butterworth-Heinermann.

Walker, M., T. Schellink, and F. Anjoul. 2008. "Explaining Why People Gamble." In *In the Pursuit of Winning: Problem Gambling Theory, Research and Treatment*, edited by M. Zangeneh, A. Blaszczynski, and N.E. Turner, 11–33. New York: Springer Science and Business Media.

Walters, G.D. 2001. "Behavior Genetic Research on Gambling and Problem Gambling: A Preliminary Meta-Analysis of Available Data." *Journal of Gambling Studies* 17(4):255.

Wampler, R.S., A.B. Downs, and J.L. Fischer. 2009. "Development of a Brief Version of the Children's Roles Inventory (CRI-20)." *The American Journal of Family Therapy* 37:287–98.

Ward, Bruce. 1998. "Canadian Reflections on a Russian in Dresden." *Queen's Quarterly* 105(3):406–21.

Wasiolek, Edward. 1972. Introduction to *The Gambler, with Polina Suslova's Diary*, by Fyodor Dostoevsky and Apollinaria Suslova. Translated by Victor Terras and edited by Edward Wasiolek. Chicago, University of Chicago Press.

_____. 1996. Review of *Dostoevsky: The Miraculous Years, 1865–1871*, by Joseph Frank. *Comparative Literature* 48(4):387–89. Accessed December 16, 2011. http://www.jstor.org/stable/1771240.

Welte, J.W., W.F. Wieczorek, G.M. Barnes, and M.C.O. Tidwell. 2006. "Multiple Risk Factors for Frequent and Problem Gambling: Individual, Social and Ecological." *Journal of Applied Social Psychology* 36(6):1548–68.

Wensley, D., and M. King. 2008. "Scientific Responsibility for the Dissemination and Interpretation of Genetic Research: Lessons from the 'Warrior Gene' Controversy." *Journal of Medical Ethics* 34:507–9.

Winkler, Martina. 2005. "The High Stakes of Identity: Gambling in the Life and Literature of Nineteenth-Century Russia." *Explorations in Russian and Eurasian History* 6(2):417–23.

Wolkowitz, O.M., A. Roy, and A.R. Doran. 1985. "Pathological Gambling and Other Risk-Taking Pursuits." *Psychiatric Clinics of North America* 8:311–22.

Young, Sarah. 2009. Review of *Redemption and the Merchant God: Dostoevsky's Economy of Salvation and Antisemitism*, by Susan McReynolds. *The Modern Language Review* 104(1):301.

Zimet, G.D., N.W. Dahlem, S.G. Zimet, and G.K. Farley. 1988. "The Multidimensional Scale of Perceived Social Support." *Journal of Personality Assessment* 52:30–41.

Index

abuse, as childhood stressor, 104, 106,
125–33, 134, 138, 150, 161, 301, 305;
and divorce, 124; emotional, 115,
117, 124, 125, 126, 130–32, 153, 172,
178, 268–69, 287–88, 310, 323; FD's
experience of, 12, 24, 84, 91, 287–88,
294, 301; FD's preoccupation with,
91–92; for non-gamblers, 268–69, 280;
and parentification, 140, 141, 153;
physical, 91–92, 114, 115, 124, 125,
126, 127–29, 130, 154, 178, 179, 269,
287, 292–93, 294, 310, 323; sexual,
115, 117, 125, 126, 129–30, 131,
140, 141, 153–54, 161–62, 287, 294;
spousal, 126–27, 172, 269. *See also*
neglect, as childhood stressor
abuse, substance, 126, 159, 188–92, 197,
287. *See also* alcoholism; drug use
Academy of Engineers (St. Petersburg),
24, 25, 35, 43, 287, 288–89
"action," of gambling/addiction: in
abstinence, 47–48; vs. mundane
existence, 101; as social experience,
95–96
Adorno, Theodor W.: on "authoritarian
personality," 41–42
adult coping strategies, 182–96;
alcohol/drugs, 188–92; avoidance/
internalization, 134, 182–86, 187, 196,
200, 293, 314; denial, 186–88, 204,
298; gambling, 10–11, 192–96, 291–92,
314–15; neutralization, 187–88, 196,
204, 206. *See also* alcoholism; drug use
adult stresses: of FD, 28–38, 107–8, 287,
289–91; of non-problem gambling
families, 271–73; and poor coping
strategies, 182–96; of problem
gamblers, 10–11, 103–7, 157–76,
289–91. *See also* adult stresses, of
problem gamblers

adult stresses, of problem gamblers,
10–11, 103–7, 157–76, 289–91;
caregiving duties, 140, 158, 173–76,
294; and childhood trauma, 303–4,
310; death and/or loss, 173, 192;
divorce, 172–73, 190, 203–4, 289;
employment-related, 158, 161–62,
165–67, 168, 175, 176, 185, 190;
financial difficulties, 198–203, 291;
legal difficulties, 209–10; poor mental
health, 10–11, 158–63, 211–14; poor
physical health, 10–11, 163–65,
210–11; status-related, 168–69,
195; strained relationships, 169–73,
203–8. *See also* financial difficulties;
relationship difficulties
Adverse Childhood Experiences (ACE)
study, 114
Affleck, Ben, 296
alcoholism: of children/youth, 136, 180,
181, 291; as coping strategy, 120, 126,
156, 178, 183, 188–92, 212; in FD's
family, 12–13, 24–25, 36, 80; in FD's
novels, 83–84, 91; of gamblers' parents,
115–16, 119, 129, 131, 133–35, 140,
150, 179, 229; of non-gamblers, 274,
280; of non-gamblers' parents, 270–71;
and post-addiction behaviour, 48. *See
also* alcoholism, and problem gambling
alcoholism, and problem gambling: and
child abuse, 126, 129, 141, 179; and
child neglect, 133–35, 140–41; and
child/youth rebellion, 180, 181, 291;
as co-addictions, 120, 126, 129, 131,
134, 135, 150, 163, 186, 196, 204, 324;
in *Crime and Punishment*, 91; and
death of family member, 119, 120;
FD's family and, 12–13, 80; as freedom
from restraint, 93; as linked, 115–16,
170, 178; and parentification, 140–41